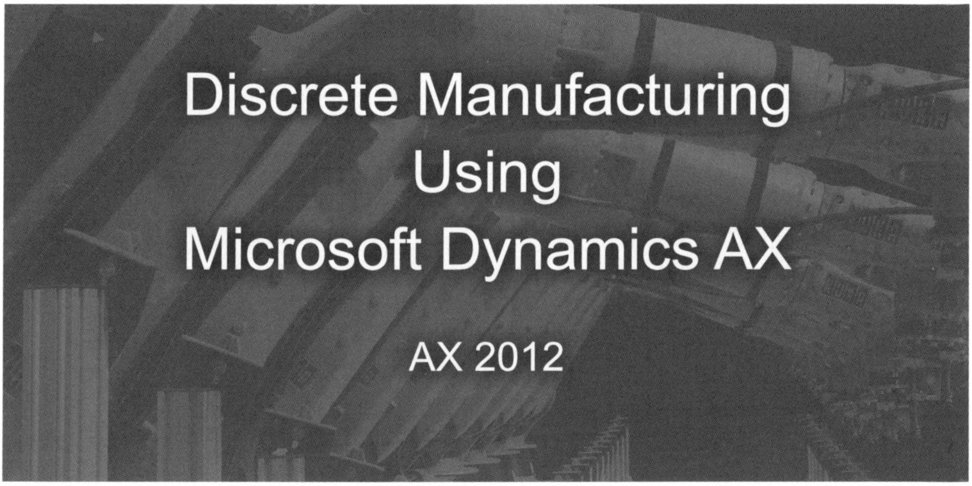
Discrete Manufacturing
Using
Microsoft Dynamics AX
AX 2012

Other books by Scott Hamilton

Food Products Manufacturing Using Microsoft Dynamics AX 2012, Visions Inc. (2012)

Managing Process Manufacturing Using Microsoft Dynamics AX 2009, Visions Inc. (2010)

Managing Wholesale Distribution Using Microsoft Dynamics AX 2009, privately published (2010)

Managing Lean Manufacturing Using Microsoft Dynamics AX 2009, Visions Inc. (2010)

Managing Your Supply Chain Using Microsoft Dynamics AX 2009, Printing Arts (2009)

Managing Your Supply Chain Using Microsoft Dynamics AX 4.0, Printing Arts (2007)

Managing Your Supply Chain Using Microsoft Axapta 3.0, McGraw-Hill (2004)

Managing Your Supply Chain Using Microsoft Navision, McGraw-Hill (2004)

Maximizing Your ERP System, McGraw-Hill (2003)

Managing Information: How Information Systems Impact Organizational Strategy (with Gordon B. Davis), Business One Irwin (1993).

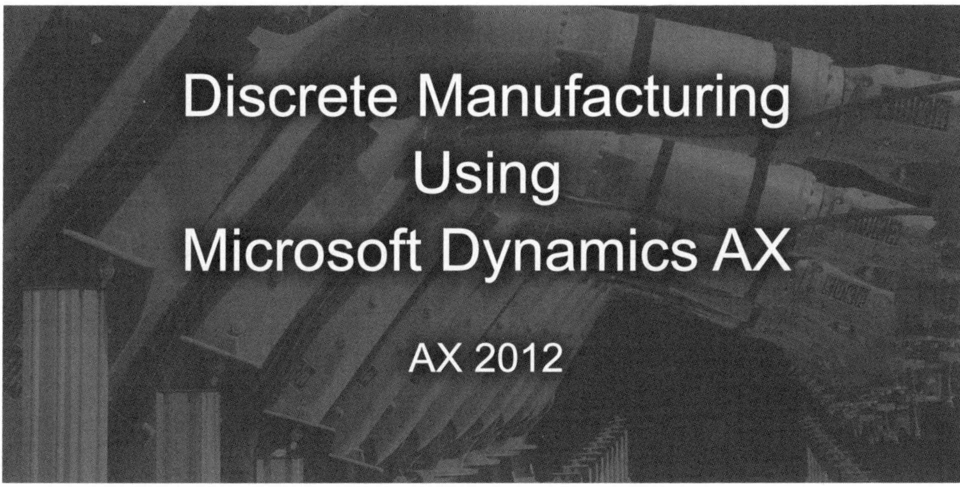

Scott Hamilton, Ph.D.

ISBN 0-9792552-5-2

The front cover photo depicts Kuka robots, and it is used with permission of KUKA Roboter Gmbh. See **www.kuka-roboter.de** for more information.

Contents

Preface

The nature of discrete manufacturing applies to a broad spectrum of industries, ranging from industrial equipment and automotive components to aerospace and electronics. These industries share many similarities in ERP system requirements. The target audience for *Discrete Manufacturing Using Microsoft Dynamics AX 2012* consists of those individuals involved with the operational and supply chain aspects of managing a discrete manufacturing business. In particular, it is focused on those implementing or considering Microsoft Dynamics AX[1] as their ERP system.

As the eighth book in my series about Dynamics AX, it reflects the evolving software functionality and my evolving understanding of how to use the software. It extends three previous books about supply chain management in a broad cross-section of manufacturing and distribution firms. These books covered previous releases of Dynamics AX 3.0, AX 4.0, and AX 2009. In contrast with a broad approach, this book focuses on just one industry—discrete manufacturing—in terms of book topics and case studies. A similar focus characterized my four previous books about process manufacturing, lean manufacturing, wholesale distribution, and food products manufacturing.

As a unique approach, this book includes the typical business processes—using the standards for business process mapping—that represent best practices and dominant business models for using AX 2012 to manage the supply chain. The book provides detailed explanations for each step within these business processes.

Many people helped in completing this book. They include Jan DeGross (in editing and typesetting) and Deb Skoog (in printing the book), and the reviewers of early book drafts. These reviewers included Paul Blott, Nigel Cox, Julia Fitsimones, Brandon George, Kurt Hatlevik, Ladd May, Jennifer Nelson, John Rethman, Don Riggs, Cori Shanks, Deb Vermillion, and Steve Weaver. Pat Moore answered my many requests for technical assistance. It helped to have the support of the management team at Columbus, especially Cody Aufricht, Norm Carmichael, Mark LaBelle, and Thomas Hauge.

---

[1]Dynamics AX is a registered trademark of Microsoft Corporation. This book employs the term "AX" for short.

The book reflects my interpretation of how to use Microsoft Dynamics AX 2012. Errors of omission and commission, and any misunderstandings, are hopefully minimized.[2] Corrections and suggestions are welcome, as well as additional case study examples. Please send to **ScottHamiltonPhD@aol.com**.

Each day of writing was started with the following prayer:

Creator of all things, give me a sharp sense of understanding, a retentive memory, and the ability to grasp things correctly and fundamentally. Grant me the talent of being exact in my explanations, and the ability to express myself with thoroughness and charm. Point out the beginning, direct the progress, and help in the completion.

[2]The book is for information purposes only. The author, publisher, and Microsoft make no warranties, expressed or implied, in the presentation of information.

Chapter 1

Introduction

A primary challenge for many manufacturing firms involves effective implementation and use of an ERP system for managing their operations and supply chain. In some firms, the challenge stems from limitations in the current system such as an old technology platform, multiple nonintegrated applications, or a legacy software package that requires extensive customization or workarounds to satisfy requirements. In firms considering a new ERP package, they are looking for more out-of-the-box functionality to help reduce risk, minimize custom development, and increase predictability of successful implementation and usage. They are also looking for standardized business processes and software functionality to help provide templates for best practices.

This book focuses on how Microsoft Dynamics AX 2012[1] provides an integrated ERP system to support the business practices of discrete manufacturing firms. These firms share many similarities in ERP system requirements, and Dynamics AX provides the foundation for addressing these requirements. The nature of discrete manufacturing applies to a broad spectrum of industries, ranging from industrial equipment and automotive components to aerospace and electronics. Each industry and company often have specialized requirements which can be addressed by specialized solutions built on top of the AX foundation.

The targeted reader includes those individuals implementing or considering Dynamics AX as their ERP system, as well as those providing consulting assistance. The contents of the book provide a complete walk through of functionality related to operations and supply chain management, and numerous case studies highlight system usage related to discrete manufacturing.

[1]Dynamics AX is a registered trademark of Microsoft. This book employs the term "AX" for short.

This chapter starts with suggestions for the targeted reader, describes the prior research and scope of the book, discusses some issues related to mixed mode manufacturing and terminology, and summarizes the case studies within the book.

1.1 Suggestions for the Targeted Reader

The targeted reader includes those individuals implementing or considering Dynamics AX as their ERP system as well as those providing consulting assistance. Firms involved with a system selection process may be considering Dynamics AX as a candidate package, and this book can help evaluate system fit and needed customizations, provide a vision of an integrated system, and reduce selection risks. The book can help businesses involved in implementing and using AX by accelerating the learning process, suggesting prescriptive business processes, reducing implementation time and costs, and reducing user resistance to change. It suggests changes that can improve system usage and revitalize a wayward implementation. For those providing AX consulting services, this book can accelerate the learning process, expand the scope of knowledge, and improve situational fluency. In particular, it can help those with previous AX experience learn the new capabilities within AX 2012. Figure 1.1 summarizes these suggestions for the targeted readers.

The contents of the book have been segmented to support several categories of targeted readers, so that you can focus on just the relevant chapters or sections within a chapter. The suggested chapters for each category are described below.

- *Distribution firms*. The reader can focus on the definition of items, product costing for purchased items, batch and serial tracking considerations, coverage planning data for purchases and transfers, sales and operations planning for distribution scenarios, sales order processing, purchase order processing, transfers in a multisite operation, or quality management for purchased items and inventory/warehouse management. Some distribution scenarios also involve projects or service orders.
- *Manufacturing firms*. The reader can focus on manufacturing-related topics such as bill of material (BOM) information, resources and routings, configuration technologies for defining custom products, product costing for manufactured items, coverage planning data for manu-

<table>
<tr><th colspan="2"></th><th>Discrete Manufacturing or Distribution Firm</th><th>Consultant or Solution Provider</th></tr>
<tr><td colspan="2">Overall Goal</td><td>Improve firm performance through effective supply chain management systems</td><td>Improve customer service through increased knowledge of AX</td></tr>
<tr><td rowspan="3">System Implementation Life Cycle</td><td>System Selection</td><td>Evaluate system fit and needed customizations
Provide vision of an integrated system
Reduce selection risk</td><td rowspan="3">Accelerate learning process
Gain knowledge of new functionality
Reduce new employee ramp-up time
Improve situational fluency
Improve training and consulting efforts
Prescribe business businesses
Support gap/fit analyses
Improve customization efforts</td></tr>
<tr><td>Implementation</td><td>Accelerate learning process of new system
Suggest prescriptive business processes
Take advantage of new business models rather than just replicate previous system
Provide ideas for best practices
Reduce implementation costs , time and risks
Reduce user resistance to change</td></tr>
<tr><td>On-Going Operation</td><td>Suggest changes to improve system usage
Revitalize a wayward implementation</td></tr>
</table>

Figure 1.1 Suggestions for Target Readers

factured items, sales and operations planning for manufacturing scenarios, production orders for internal manufacturing, subcontracted production, quality management for manufactured items, project-oriented manufacturing, and service orders. Some manufacturing scenarios also reflect mixed modes involving formula information (rather than BOMs) and kanban orders (rather than traditional production orders).

❖ *Project implementation team and cross-functional responsibilities for business processes.* Each chapter includes typical business processes that summarize key tasks and the functional roles responsible for these tasks. These diagrams reflect best practices and dominant business models for using AX, and provide an organizing focus for more detailed explanations within the chapter. The typical business processes can help the project team gain an overall understanding of system usage and each team member's roles. Figure 1.2 illustrates some of these business processes.

The initial steps in a typical implementation process involve learning the embedded conceptual models within AX that represent a new business model. Until the project team has a basic understanding of the system capabilities, it is difficult to leverage AX for their business processes except for just asking that the system must do what their cur-

Area	Processes
Design	Define material item Define formula (or BOM) Define production resources Define routing information Define testing requirements
S&OP	Maintain S&OP game plans Perform planning calculations
Sell	Define customer Define sales agreement Process a sales order Process a customer return
Procure	Define vendor Define purchase agreement Process a purchase order Process a return to vendor Process a transfer

Area	Processes
Produce	Process a batch order Process bulk/pack orders Process subcontract mfg Process rework order
Quality	Report test results Report batch disposition
Warehouse	Pick/ship sales order Receive purchase order Ship/receive transfer order Receive customer return
Accounting	Calculate item's cost Maintain standard costs Process/pay vendor invoice Process sales invoice/payment Generate financial reports

Figure 1.2 Examples of Business Processes

rent system does today. The initial steps also involve decisions about what constitutes Phase 1 of the implementation, and the extent to which standard AX functionality (versus customizations) will be used.

- *ERP Selection Committee*. The reader can focus on the typical business processes within each chapter in order to visualize running the business with a new ERP system. The detailed explanations can help evaluate system fit and needed customizations. References to specific screen names or field names (aimed at readers trying to learn the system) can be largely ignored unless they help cement the reader's understanding.
- *Incremental learning of new capabilities within AX 2012*. The knowledgeable AX reader can focus on the new functionality related to AX 2012. For example, the new functionality includes enterprise versus company information for an item, different approaches to item identification, and the definition of resource requirements within a routing operation. The last chapter summarizes the book topics that represent incremental learning for knowledgeable AX readers.

1.2 Prior Research and Scope of Book Topics

The book focuses on supply chain management within discrete manufacturing companies, and this focus guided the prior research and the scope of book topics.

Prior Research Several steps of prior research were undertaken to understand the supply chain management (SCM) requirements of discrete manufacturers and the AX functionality to support those requirements. With respect to AX 2012, these steps included participation in prerelease and post-release training classes, webinars, and conference sessions; reviews of the existing training materials, e-learning lessons, user documentation, and sales demo materials; discussions with users, development personnel, and field consultants; and hands-on testing for thousands of use cases that reflected requirements in discrete manufacturing industries. With few exceptions, only those capabilities personally tested and proven were included in the book. The same approach was also undertaken for my previous books about Dynamics AX. The discussions with experienced field consultants helped identify the dominant business practices at current users. On-going opportunities to consult with current users have supplemented this understanding.

The prior research about SCM requirements included my consulting and teaching experiences with discrete manufacturing firms over the past three decades. These experiences included responses to numerous RFPs (requests for proposal) for an ERP system, face-to-face consulting engagements with several hundred firms, and teaching executive seminars, APICS certification classes, MBA courses, and user group sessions. My understanding is continually being supplemented by staying abreast of the current literature and discussions with the thought leaders for using ERP systems in discrete manufacturing.

One aspect of prior research involved the business processes reflecting best practices and dominant business models in discrete manufacturing firms, as well as the best use of standard functionality within AX. The contents of the book include many prescriptive business processes for using AX 2012 in discrete manufacturing firms.[2] These business processes are described in terms of the end-user experience with standard AX forms. The navigational details of the end-user experience may differ—whether using customized forms, or web-based or hand-held applications—but the business processes must still conform to the embedded conceptual models within AX.

[2] A comprehensive set of prescriptive business processes for discrete manufacturing is available as part of the RapidValue tool from Columbus. See **www.ColumbusGlobal.com** for more information.

Scope of Book Topics The book topics focus on supply chain management, and the selection of book topics was shaped by several factors. First, the selected topics reflect my 80/20 rule about relevance to dominant business practices. Second, several topics were excluded because they could not be personally tested and proven within the budgeted time. Third, some topics were excluded because of book length considerations. For example, the topics related to other integrated applications were generally excluded except for key intersection points, as illustrated below.

- ❖ Human resources. Definition of employee information to support approvals and to identify employee competencies as a resource requirement.
- ❖ Payables. Definition of vendor information for supply chain purposes, and purchase order processing through the vendor invoice.
- ❖ Receivables. Definition of customer information for supply chain purposes, and sales order processing through customer invoicing.
- ❖ General ledger. Definition of product costs and assignment of G/L accounts related to material and resource transactions.

The book length considerations precluded screen shots.[3] Other important topics of system development and usage were also excluded, such as role-centered pages, security, alerts, business intelligence, and the customization capabilities within the AX development environment.

Contributions to the AX Body of Knowledge The body of knowledge related to Microsoft Dynamics AX consists of several levels and components. The foundation level consists of the software, documentation, and training materials provided by Microsoft, augmented by their Technet library and other sources. Additional contributions to the AX body of knowledge build on this foundation. In terms of the book's contributions, I have attempted to summarize the relevant foundation information with an integrative viewpoint of how the whole system fits together to support supply chain management—especially in a discrete manufacturing business. The book explains the embedded conceptual models within AX and provides prescriptive guidance on best practices for business processes.

---

[3]One argument against screen shot examples is that most users tailor the standard screens, and the displayed information is also affected by license key activation. For an excellent explanation with screen shots, see the book *Using Microsoft Dynamics AX 2012* by Andreas Luszczak.

1.3 Mixed Mode Manufacturing Environments

The primary coordination tools for supply chain management in most discrete manufacturing environments consist of production orders and the related BOM and routing information for manufactured items. However, there are many scenarios with requirements for other types of coordination tools. Two major variations include process manufacturing (with batch orders and formula information) and lean manufacturing (with kanban orders). Additional variations include project manufacturing and service order management.

The term *mixed mode manufacturing* is often used to describe scenarios requiring different types of coordination tools. AX provides a single system for supporting mixed mode manufacturing environments. For explanatory purposes, this book focuses on the use of production orders as the primary coordination tool for manufacturing. This approach simplifies the explanation and use of terminology, and provides the baseline for explaining the incremental differences involved in batch orders (with formula information), kanban orders, projects, and service orders. Separate chapters cover these additional coordination tools.

1.4 Terminology Used in the Book

The terminology associated with many aspects of supply chain management can vary widely between companies and ERP systems. It is often difficult to clearly understand the meaning of a term—such as substitution logic, sales or purchase agreements, and reservations—without a lengthy discussion about its significance.

As much as possible, this book consistently uses the same terminology to describe the conceptual models and software functionality for AX 2012. In most cases, the book's terminology reflects the names of forms, tabs, fields, and buttons of the AX software, but it sometimes reflects generally accepted terms or alternative phrasing to clarify understanding.

Some aspects of the AX design create difficulties in terminology. One example involves the AX approach to enterprise- and company-level information about an item. AX employs two different constructs and their identifiers—termed the product number and the item number—to define the enterprise- and company-level information about an item. The product number provides a unique identifier for enterprise-level information about products, and you release a product to a company to create an item number which acts as the identifier for company-level information. As an explanatory approach, the book generally employs the terms *enterprise-level* and *company-level* information about an item, as summarized in Chapter 3 (Section 3.1).

Another terminology issue concerns mixed mode environments. For example, there are several key differences between production orders and batch orders (and the related BOM and formula information), but the majority of software functionality is exactly the same so that terminology becomes the primary difference. It is simpler to focus on the use of production orders and the related BOM information, since these represent the dominant business practices in most discrete manufacturers. This approach provides the baseline for explaining the incremental differences related to formula information and batch orders. This approach also provides the baseline for explaining incremental differences related to kanban orders and production flows.

1.5 Summary of Case Studies

Case studies illustrate how the AX software functionality applies to many different industries that represent discrete manufacturers. These industries are described in the next chapter, along with a baseline model of operations that applies to most scenarios. Each chapter includes case studies applicable to the topic, and a complete list of case studies is provided at the end of the book.

Chapter 2

Common Scenarios in Discrete Manufacturing

Discrete manufacturing firms share many similar requirements, although each environment will also have some industry-specific and company-specific requirements. In order to illustrate how Dynamics AX addresses these requirements, this chapter summarizes the industries representing discrete manufacturers, and describes a baseline model of operations and some common scenarios. A baseline model of operations provides a foundation for simplified explanations about how to use Dynamics AX to manage the business, and about variations to the baseline model. The common scenarios build on this baseline model, as described in the following sections within the chapter:

1. Industries Representing Discrete Manufacturers
2. Baseline Model of Operations
3. Material- Versus Routing-Intensive Production Process
4. Make-to-Stock Versus Make-to-Order Production Strategies
5. Configure-to-Order Custom Product
6. Engineer-to-Order Custom Product
7. New Product Development
8. Multisite and Multicompany Operations
9. Subcontracted Production
10. Lean Manufacturing
11. Polymer Molded Products
12. Equipment Installation and Maintenance
13. Printed Circuit Boards in a CTO Product

The common scenarios include related case studies, and additional case studies throughout the book highlight other common scenarios.

2.1 Industries Representing Discrete Manufacturers

The nature of discrete manufacturing applies to a broad spectrum of industries, ranging from industrial equipment and automotive components to aerospace and electronics. The standard industry classification (SIC) codes provide more detail about illustrative industries within the broad spectrum.

Industrial equipment often comes to mind when considering different industries representing discrete manufacturers, as illustrated by the following categories of products:

- Special and large machinery
- Oil, gas and mining machinery
- High tech machinery
- Commercial and OEM machinery and parts
- Refrigeration and service industry machinery
- Metalworking machinery and equipment

Other industries representing discrete manufacturers include the following:

- Aerospace manufacturing
- Automotive components and aftermarket parts
- Shipping and railroad vehicles
- Transportation equipment
- Audio and video equipment
- Communications equipment
- Computer equipment
- Household appliances
- Optical media
- Measurement and control instruments
- Electrical components

2.2 Baseline Model of Operations

A baseline model of operations represents the common use of Dynamics AX and the dominant business practices within discrete manufacturing and distribution. It provides a foundation for simplified explanations about how to use Dynamics AX to manage the business, and for explaining variations to the baseline model. In summary, the baseline model focuses on a single AX company with one or more AX sites (and their related AX warehouses) with standard products identified by an item number. Inventory is tracked by site, warehouse, and bin location, with inventory replenishment logic at the site/warehouse level. Sales prices and purchase prices are typically company-wide, although they can optionally reflect site-specific prices. Each manufactured item requires bill of material information, with optional definition of routing data. Further explanation of the baseline model of operations is provided below.

- *Single company and AX instance.* The baseline model consists of a single company using a single AX instance. The variations involving multiple companies are explained in Chapter 17.
- *Multiple inventory locations identified by an AX site and warehouse.* Each physical location is identified by an AX site and an associated value for a "site" financial dimension. The site-specific financial dimension supports financial reports by site. In addition, each AX site has at least one AX warehouse, although additional AX warehouses may be necessary to support in-transit inventory (on transfer orders), quarantine inventory, or some other purpose. Each AX warehouse has one or more bin locations, although use of bin locations is not mandatory. Chapter 19 provides further explanation about inventory and warehouse management.
- *Multiple business units within one company identified by an AX financial dimension.* In many cases, different items represent different lines of business that require financial reports by business unit. The business units are identified as different values for the "business unit" financial dimension. The appropriate value of this financial dimension is assigned to the relevant items, thereby supporting financial reports by business unit.
- *Material items identified by item number.* Material items are identified by an item number. In some cases, an item may be identified by an item number and one or more additional fields termed variant codes. Chapter 3 provides further explanation of item identification, and Chapter 7 describes the use of configuration IDs for identification of a custom product configuration.
- *Bill of material for a manufactured item.* A bill of material (BOM) defines the product structure for a manufactured item. Chapter 4 explains BOM information, and Chapter 5 describes special cases requiring a formula approach to defining product structure.

- *Routing information for a manufactured item.* Routing information can be optionally defined for a manufactured item, where routings also require the definition of resources and master operations. Chapter 6 describes resources and routing information, and several alternatives for not using routing data.
- *Standard or actual costing for items.* Each material item must be assigned an inventory valuation method reflecting a standard costing or actual costing method. With standard costing, a costing version must be defined for standard costs, and each material item must have an item cost record for each site with inventory. Chapter 8 provides further explanation of the costing approaches.
- *Inventory replenishment logic applies to the AX site and warehouse.* Replenishment logic is defined by an item's coverage planning data by site/warehouse. Chapter 10 provides further explanation of coverage planning data, and Chapter 11 explains planning calculations.
- *Batch or serial tracking of material items.* The inventory of a given item can be tracked by batch number or serial number, or both. With batch tracking of purchased material, you can also record the vendor's batch number and country of origin information. Chapter 9 provides further explanation of batch and serial tracking considerations.
- *Standard roles within Dynamics AX.* The baseline model employs the standard roles within Dynamics AX to support role-centered pages and role-based security. You assign users to these standard roles, and the predefined privileges for each role may be adjusted. For example, the privileges for the purchasing agent role include maintenance of purchase orders and vendor information. The standard roles are also reflected in business process diagrams throughout the book and illustrate typical business processes.

2.3 Material- Versus Routing-Intensive Production Process

A basic variation in discrete manufacturing involves a material-intensive versus routing-intensive production process. A routing-intensive production process is characterized by a multi-step routing for a manufactured item, and the value-added costs comprise a high percentage of the product costs. Typical examples include the production processes for castings, steel bar, or

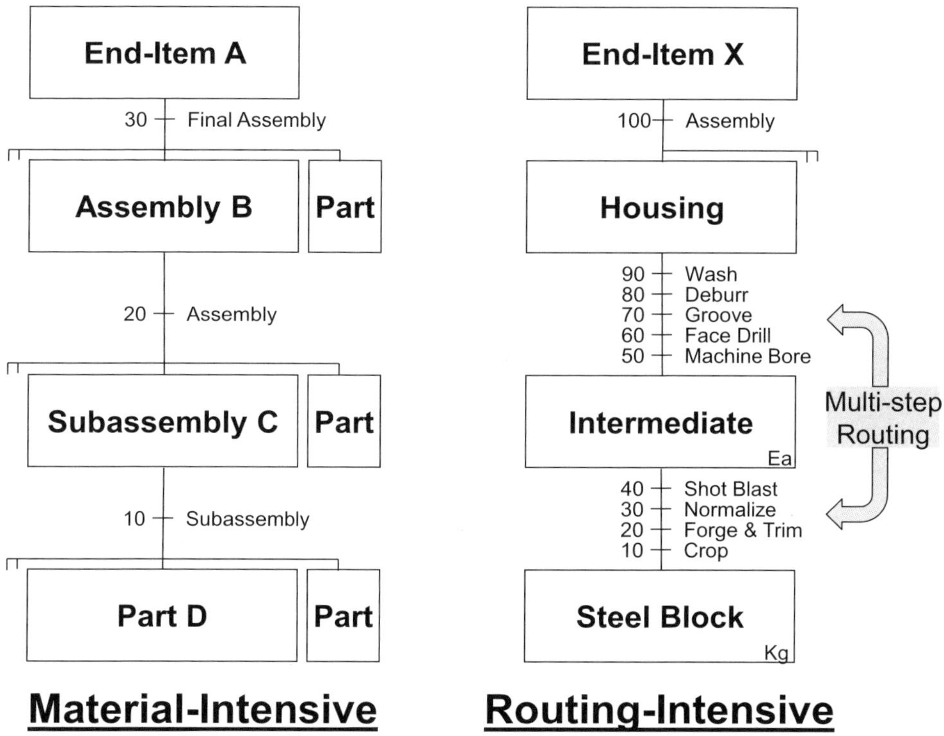

Figure 2.1 Material- Versus Routing-Intensive Production

steel block. A material-intensive production process is commonly characterized by a single routing step for a manufactured item, and the material costs comprise a high percentage of the product costs. Typical examples include assembled products. The routing data may not even be defined in cases with an extremely simple production process. Figure 2.1 illustrates two different product structures and associated routing data for a material-intensive versus routing-intensive production process.[1]

Dynamics AX supports both of these basic variations. There are slight differences in defining and using multistep routings. For example, the multistep routing may reflect a linear progression of operations (as illustrated in Figure 2.1) or a network, and an operation can require a hard link with the

[1]The example for a routing-intensive production process actually represents an automotive part and its associated operations, but the specifics are unimportant. The example is simply intended to illustrate a multistep routing.

previous operation. Another example involves the slight differences in kanban orders for a multistep routing. Other examples apply to an outside operation in a multistep routing, since it requires coordination of the supplied material and the finished item, especially when multiple outside operations require coordination with multiple subcontractors.

2.4 Make-to-Stock Versus Make-to-Order Production Strategies

Another basic variation in discrete manufacturing involves the choice of production strategies as part of the S&OP game plans for an item. The two classic production strategies are termed make-to-stock (MTS) and make-to-order (MTO) with linked orders. You can establish linked orders within AX by first creating a production order from a sales order line for the end-item, and then scheduling this production order to automatically create the linked supply orders for components (termed reference orders). The reference orders reflect BOM information about components, where a BOM line type of *pegged supply* indicates a make-to-order component and a BOM line type of *vendor* indicates a buy-to-order component. Figure 2.2 illustrates how to create linkage between a sales order line item and a production order, and the impact of BOM line type on creating linked production orders and linked purchase orders for components.

Both of these production strategies apply to lean manufacturing scenarios, with fixed kanbans for MTS products and sales event kanbans for MTO products. It is worth noting that sales event kanbans can be automatically created from the sales order line (without requiring a separate step), and line event kanbans for MTO components are also automatically created (much like reference orders). You designate line event kanbans as part of the kanban rules for components rather than using the BOM line type for components. A subsequent section illustrates a common scenario for lean manufacturing.

Other production strategies include make-to-order without any link to orders, and configure-to-order and engineer-to-order with linked orders. Chapter 11 provides further explanation of these production strategies in the context of S&OP game plans.

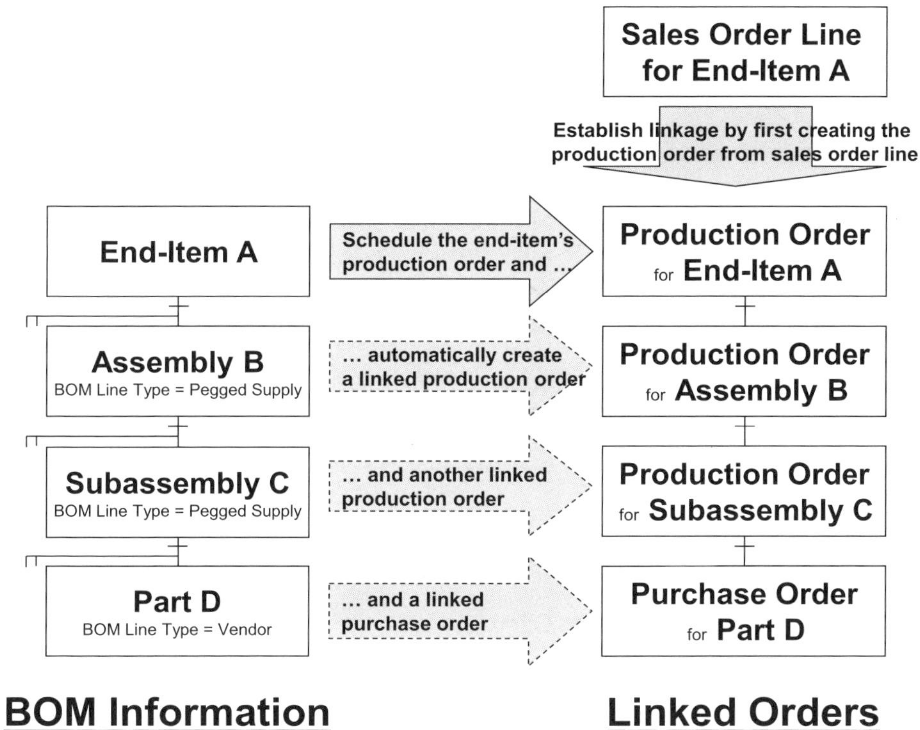

Figure 2.2 Make-to-Order Product with Linked Orders

2.5 Configure-to-Order Custom Product

Many custom product manufacturing scenarios can be modeled as a configure-to-order (CTO) product. When entering a sales order or quote for a CTO product, for example, a configuration technology provides prompts and responses that can be translated into the necessary components and operations for a unique configuration ID. Standard AX functionality supports several different configuration technologies. A common scenario for a CTO product using the constraint-based configuration technology is summarized in Case 1, and Chapter 7 provides further explanation of the approach.

Case 1: Constraint-Based Configuration Technology for CTO Products

An equipment manufacturer had several product lines representing multi-level configure-to-order custom products. Figure 2.3 illustrates the product structure for one product line consisting of a configurable end-item and configurable components. It also indicates the names of options (termed attribute types) for required, optional and common options, and the items representing each option's alternatives (termed attributes).

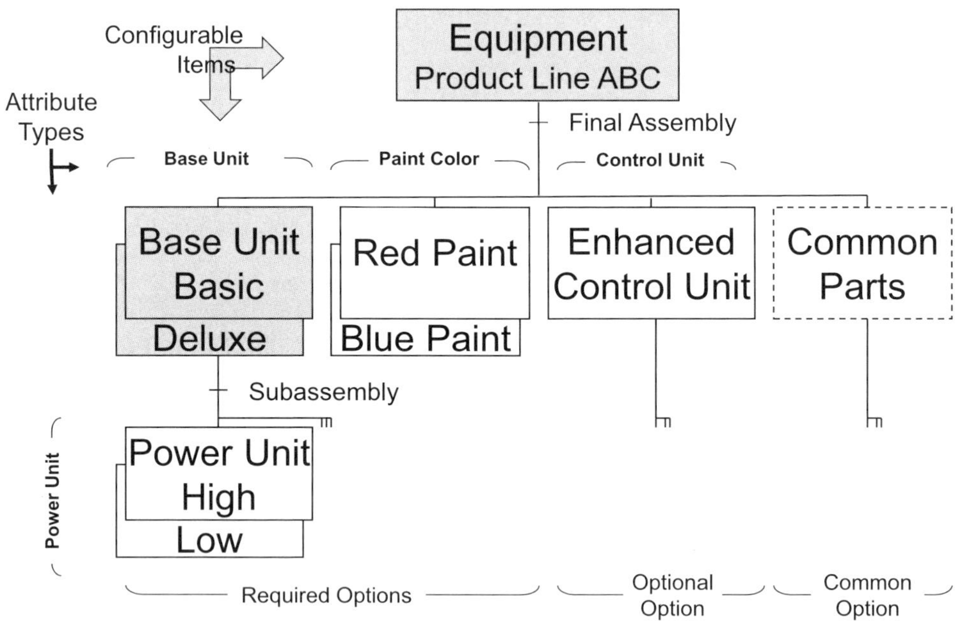

Figure 2.3 Product Structure for Configurable Equipment

In this simple example, the configurable items consist of the end-item "Equipment Product Line ABC" and the two variations of the base unit (labeled Basic and Deluxe). Product configuration models representing each configurable item must be defined, and then assigned to the relevant item with validity dates. As requirements evolve over time, a different model would be defined and then assigned to the configurable item with different validity dates, so that a given configurable item would have several versions of a product configuration model with non-overlapping validity dates.

A product configuration model defines the user interface (UI) prompts and responses needed to configure the product, and maps them to the needed components and operations. It also identifies any configurable components and their product configuration models. After using the model, such as when configuring a sales order line, it automatically creates a unique configuration ID—and the associated BOM and route versions—for each configurable item in the product structure. It also assigns this configuration ID and the BOM/route versions to the sales order line. The BOM and routing information can now be manually maintained, so that the product configurator model does not have to result in 100% of the detailed information.

2.6 Engineer-to-Order Custom Product

An engineer-to-order product typically requires significant engineering time to design the product, and to define the product structure and new items. These engineering activities can be budgeted and tracked against a project, and ultimately charged to the customer based on a time-and-material or fixed-price basis. The finalized design typically evolves over time, so that the definition of item and BOM information also evolves over time. While the design evolves, it is critical to define and order items representing long lead time materials. These items can be identified within a skeleton BOM to help coordinate supply chain activities.

The top levels of the product structure for an ETO product can be modeled as configurable items or as regular items with BOM versions defining the components. They can also be modeled as subprojects, where the item requirements for the subproject specify the components. Case 2 illustrates the use of subprojects for modeling the top levels of the product structure and for managing the engineering time.

Case 2: External T&M Project to Design and Build an ETO Product

A manufacturing company produced engineer-to-order machines requiring significant engineering design time prior to building a machine, and installation services after delivery of the machine. For a typical ETO machine, the engineering manager defines an external time-and-materials (T&M) project consisting of three subprojects reflecting engineering design, final assembly of the machine, and installation services. Figure 2.4 illustrates the typical project and subprojects.

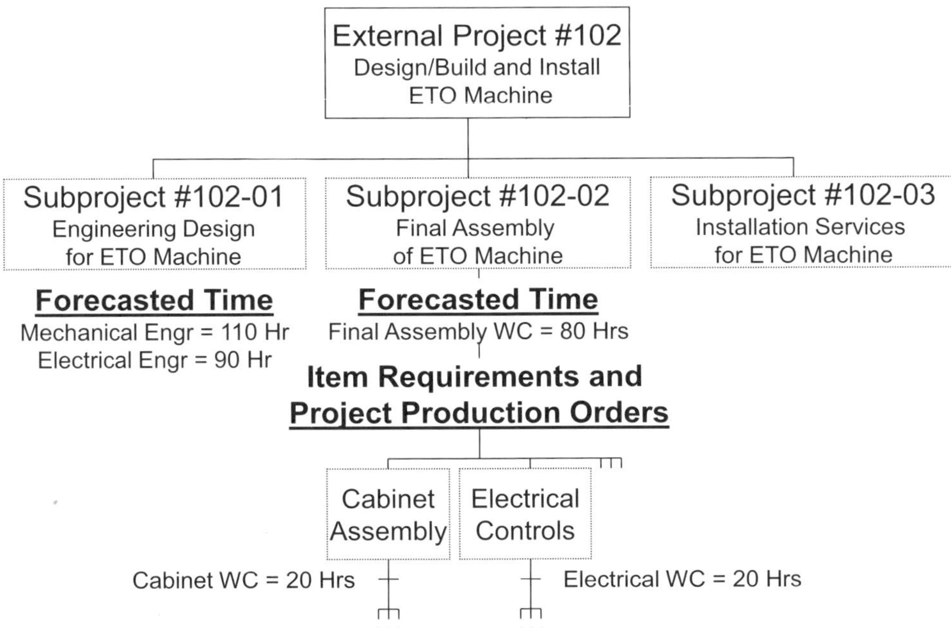

Figure 2.4 External Project to Design/Build an ETO Machine

In this example, a subproject is used to model the top level of the product structure, with forecasted time requirements for a production resource (representing the final assembly work center) to perform final assembly of components. An item requirement is defined for each first level component—such as the cabinet assembly and electrical controls—and a project production order is generated for each item requirement. This approach provides direct linkage between a project's item requirement and the corresponding project production order.[2]

[2]This example represents one approach for managing production of the top levels an ETO product structure. Another approach employs configurable items for the top levels, as described in Case 107.

In this example, the subproject for engineering design has a simple work breakdown structure consisting of several activities (not shown in the figure), and the forecasted time requirements for mechanical engineers and electrical engineers are defined for each activity.

In many cases, a detailed project quotation must be prepared and then accepted by the customer prior to designing and building the ETO machine. The detailed quotation reflects a work breakdown structure of activities, and each activity has forecasted requirements for items and resource hours. After customer acceptance and confirmation of the project quote, the details about item forecasts are transferred to the actual project as item requirements, and the hour forecasts are also transferred.

2.7 New Product Development

New product development is oftentimes undertaken for internal purposes and results in a prototype. Alternatively, the development efforts may be undertaken for a specific customer with requirements for invoicing the customer much like an ETO product. Case 3 summarizes the use of an internal project for new product development.

Case 3: Internal Project for New Product Development

New product development at a discrete manufacturer often entails producing a prototype of the manufactured item, and additional costs associated with engineering time and related expenses. Figure 2.5 illustrates an internal project for developing a prototype. The project's item requirement is specified for just the end-item, which has a multilevel bill of material and routing information. This information is used to calculate the cost of the end-item and its manufactured components, and to coordinate supply chain activities.

The project's forecasted time requirements include engineering time by three major groups of engineers: design engineers, lab technicians, and test engineers. The project also has forecasted expenses (such as travel and consulting fees) that will be incurred during prototype development.

Several project categories provide segmentation of costs related to expenses and resource time. As illustrated in Figure 2.5, the expenses were segmented into three project categories (travel, consulting fees, and other) and the hours were segmented into three categories (design, lab, and test).

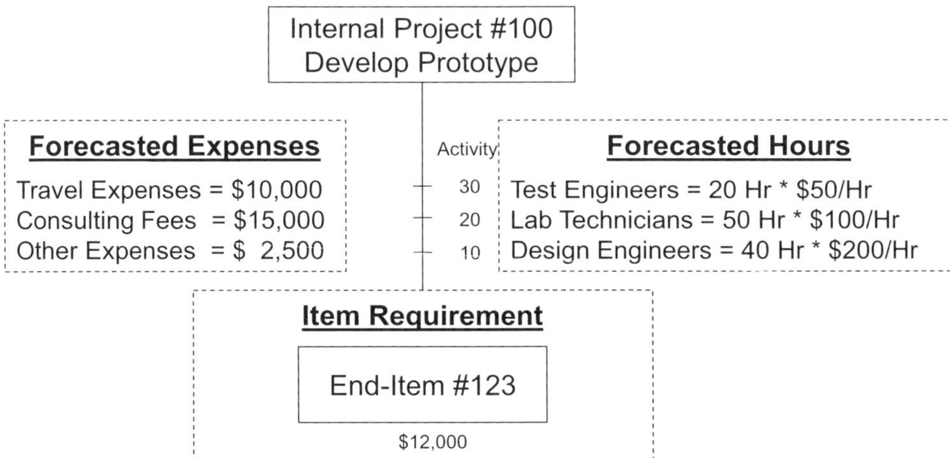

Total Budget for Project #100

Material Items	= $12,000
Time (Hours)	= $14,000
Expenses	= $17,500

Figure 2.5 Internal Project for New Product Development

These project categories help segment budgeted and actual costs for analysis and reporting purposes. Figure 2.5 also illustrates the use of activities for the forecasted hours, where the activities are simply labeled 10, 20, and 30 in this example.

2.8 Multisite and Multicompany Operations

Many businesses involved in discrete manufacturing and distribution have inventory at multiple physical sites and transfers between sites. Transfers between sites can be managed using transfers orders or intercompany orders, depending on the grouping of physical sites into companies. These two approaches are summarized below and in Case 4.

- *Transfer Orders*. Transfer orders represent a two-step approach to transfer material between two sites/warehouses in the same company. The two-step approach means that one transaction records the shipment and a second transaction records the receipt, with tracking of in-transit inventory in a transit warehouse. A one-step approach can also be used, typically when a short transportation time does not require tracking of in-transit inventory. The one-step approach means that one transaction records the shipment, with automatic receipt of the shipped quantity. As an alternative to transfers orders, you can use a transfer journal to record movements between locations.

- *Intercompany Orders*. Intercompany orders can be used when both companies exist within the same Dynamics AX instance, so that placing a purchase order with an intercompany vendor will automatically create a corresponding sales order in the sister company, and vice versa. Intercompany orders require setup information about items and also about the vendors and customers representing the sister companies. For example, a product must be released to both companies in order to support intercompany trading, and the item's company-level information must be defined in both companies.

  Master scheduling across a multicompany supply chain involves sequencing considerations. Planning calculations within AX apply to a single company, which means the master scheduling task should first be performed for the top-tier company. This generates planned intercompany demand that communicates requirements to the second-tier company, which represents an up-stream company within the supply chain.[3] The process must be repeated for additional up-stream companies. To simplify this process, you define a sequence of companies that will be considered by an intercompany master scheduling task.

Case 4: Coordination across a Multisite and Multicompany Supply Chain

A global manufacturer consisted of multiple companies, and transfers between companies. As shown in Figure 2.6, a simplified example consists of two different companies representing a manufacturing company and a distribution company. In the manufacturing company, an intermediate item produced at one manufacturing site was transferred to another site (via transfer

[3]The term *upstream* provides a relative reference within a supply chain indicating a source of raw material, whereas the term *downstream* indicates the direction of the end-customer.

orders) for producing the end item. The manufacturing company sold the end-item to domestic customers. The end-item was also transferred to a different company's distribution center for sales to foreign customers. The primary coordination tools across the multicompany supply chain consisted of planned intercompany demand as well as intercompany purchase orders and sales orders.

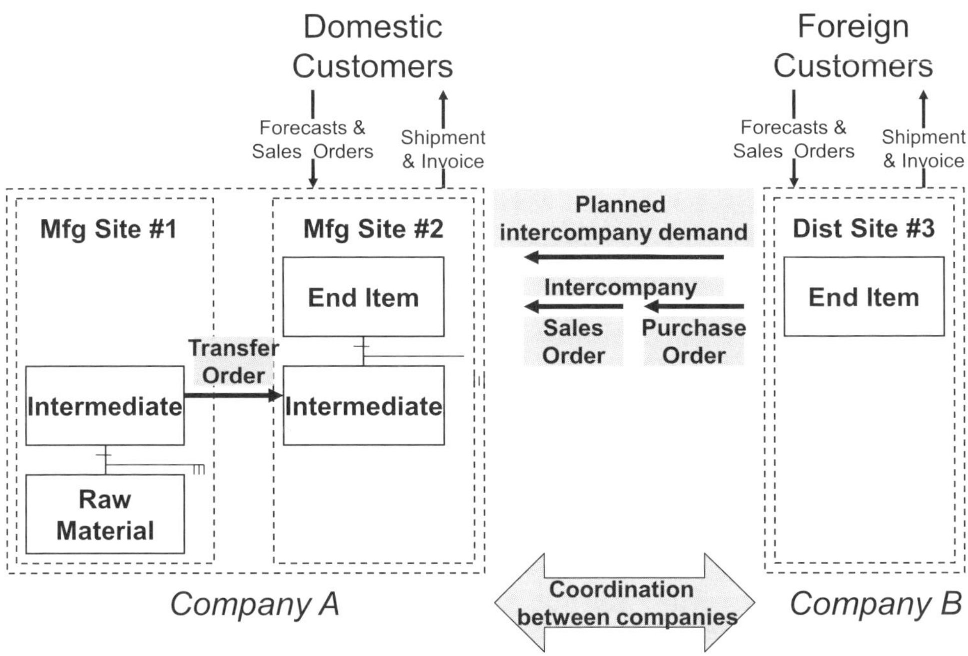

Figure 2.6 Coordination across a Multicompany Supply Chain

2.9 Subcontracted Production

Subcontracted production has many variations that reflect the degree of supplied components, the options for handling supplied material and finished items, and several other factors. For example, the three variations for the degree of supplied components include completely supplied, none supplied (aka turnkey) and partially supplied (aka hybrid). Other factors include the identification of AX sites and warehouses involved in subcontracted production, and the significance of a single order for subcontracted production.

A key issue for subcontracted production includes the inventory visibility of supplied material and the finished items at subcontractor locations. A common scenario with inventory visibility is summarized in Case 5. This scenario employs a single-level BOM to identify the partially supplied components, and the routing consists of a single outside operation. The supplied components are stocked at the subcontractor. A production order provides coordination for the subcontracted production. The finished quantity is reported at the subcontractor site (which triggers backflushing of supplied components), and then transferred to a different site such as a distribution center or manufacturing plant. This approach provides improved visibility and coordination of subcontracted production. Chapter 16 provides further explanation of subcontracted production.

Case 5: Subcontracted Production with Supplied Components

A discrete manufacturer produced several finished goods at subcontractors, and stocked the supplied components at the subcontractor via transfer orders or direct deliveries from suppliers. A given product could be produced at more than one subcontractor so that site-specific BOMs were defined. As illustrated in Figure 2.7, the site-specific BOM for finished good "Product-A" identified two supplied components—labeled "Component #1" and "Component #2"—with a warehouse source representing the subcontractor warehouse. The site-specific BOM also included a component representing the "Subcontracted Service for Product-A," which reflects the AX approach to modeling subcontracted production. This item defines the value-added costs for the subcontracted service, and provides the basis for approved vendors and purchase price agreements. In addition, the purchase order for this subcontracted service is generated by and directly linked to the production order for the parent item. Hence, subcontracted production involves the dual constructs of a production order and its associated purchase order for coordinating the supply chain, as shown in the left side of Figure 2.7.

In this example, the finished quantity for the production order is reported at the subcontractor site (which triggers backflushing of supplied component inventory), and then transferred to a manufacturing plant or distribution center. Given the dual constructs, a separate transaction is also required about the completed quantity of the purchase order for the subcontracted service. This completed quantity may differ from the finished quantity for the production order, since it represents what will actually be paid for.

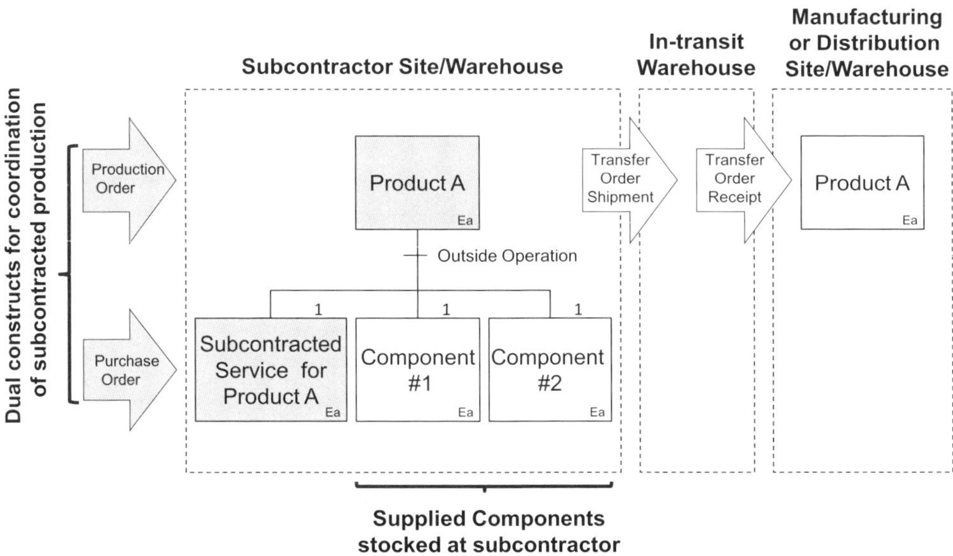

Figure 2.7 Subcontracted Production with Supplied Components

Other variations apply to the finished quantity. It can be stocked at the subcontractor, or transferred to other sites representing a manufacturing plant, a different subcontractor, or a third-party leased (3PL) distribution site to support sales order fulfillment.

2.10 Lean Manufacturing

Lean manufacturing approaches often involve several types of changes, such as changes in factory layout and conceptual viewpoints. One example of a change in conceptual viewpoints involves a production flow, which defines the sequence of activities to produce an item (and replaces the routing information). Another example involves kanban rules, which define how to generate kanban orders for items within the product structure. These conceptual viewpoints are illustrated in Case 6 about using kanban orders for a make-to-order product built from stocked components.

Case 6: Kanban Orders for a Make-to-Order Product

As part of a lean manufacturing operation, a family of make-to-order products were produced from stocked components. The production flow consisted of two work cells and the related activities for subassembly and final assembly, an activity to withdraw material from the stockroom, and warehouses representing the stockroom, the lineside supermarkets at the two cells, and the shipping area. The top part of Figure 2.8 illustrates this production flow viewpoint. The bottom part of Figure 2.8 illustrates the kanban rule viewpoint. Kanban rules determine how to generate kanban orders for items within the product structure—displayed sideways for showing the correlation between the BOM and the production flow.

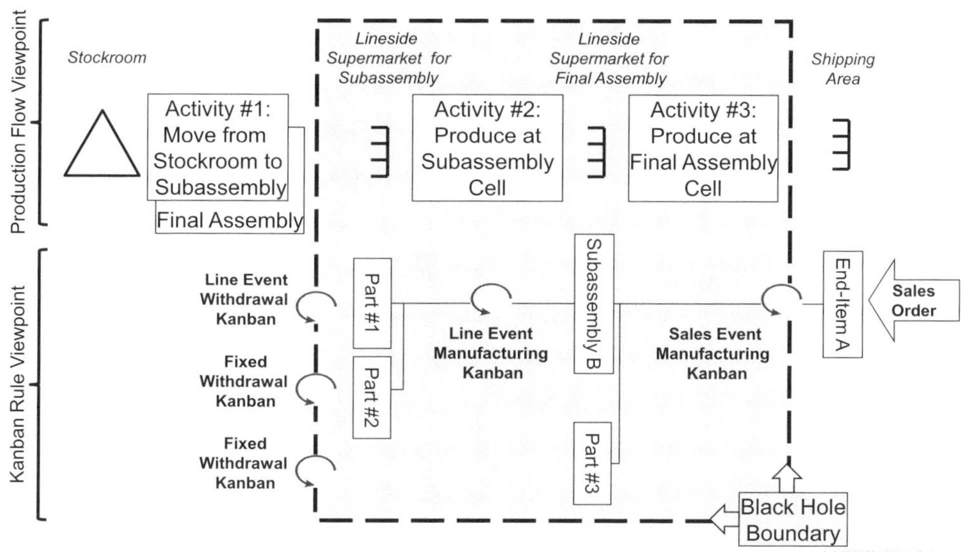

Figure 2.8 Kanban Orders for a Make-to-Order Product

The purchased parts representing the stocked components were received into the stockroom. These deliveries (not shown in the figure) can be coordinated by purchase orders and purchasing kanbans. The lineside supermarkets were replenished using line event withdrawal kanbans (for Part #1) and fixed withdrawal kanbans (for Part #2 and Part #3). After withdrawal, the component inventory was no longer tracked because it was transferred across the black hole boundary, and its value was charged to work-in-process for the value chain. The figure displays the black hole boundary (with a heavy dashed line) and the work-in-process (in light grey shading).

A sales order for the end-item triggered automatic creation of a sales event manufacturing kanban for the end-item (with delivery to the shipping area), which also triggered a line event manufacturing kanban for its key component of the subassembly (with delivery to the lineside supermarket for the final assembly cell). This triggered the line event withdrawal kanban for Part #1. These kanban orders simply provided coordination with no inventory impact until receipt of the end-item within the shipping area. The kanban receipt updated the end-item inventory (after being transferred across the black hole boundary), and the end-item's standard cost was deducted from work-in-process for the value chain.

2.11 Polymer Molded Products

Many discrete manufacturers produce polymer molded items as components for other products. One of the unique aspects of polymer molding involves the nature of a mold, since the mold is often designed with multiple cavities in order to produce multiple parts. Another unique aspect involves the reclaim from the molding process, since the scrapped material can be melted down for reuse in the molding process. The generation of multiple parts and reclaim from a single production process must be modeled using the formula approach to product structure, since they represent co-products. Case 7 illustrates the formula information and co-products for polymer molded products.

Case 7: Polymer Molded Products

A discrete manufacturing firm produced several types of polymer molded products which represented key components of their end items. A simple example consists of a single mold to produce two different parts— a right-hand and a left-hand part—and the two parts require secondary processing for assembly. The formula and routing for this simple example are shown in the Figure 2.9 and explained below.

The product structure in Figure 2.9 indicates several item numbers in the formula information, such as Resin #1, Right-Hand Part, and Assembled Part. A key concept is the planning item "Formula ABC with Mold X," since this

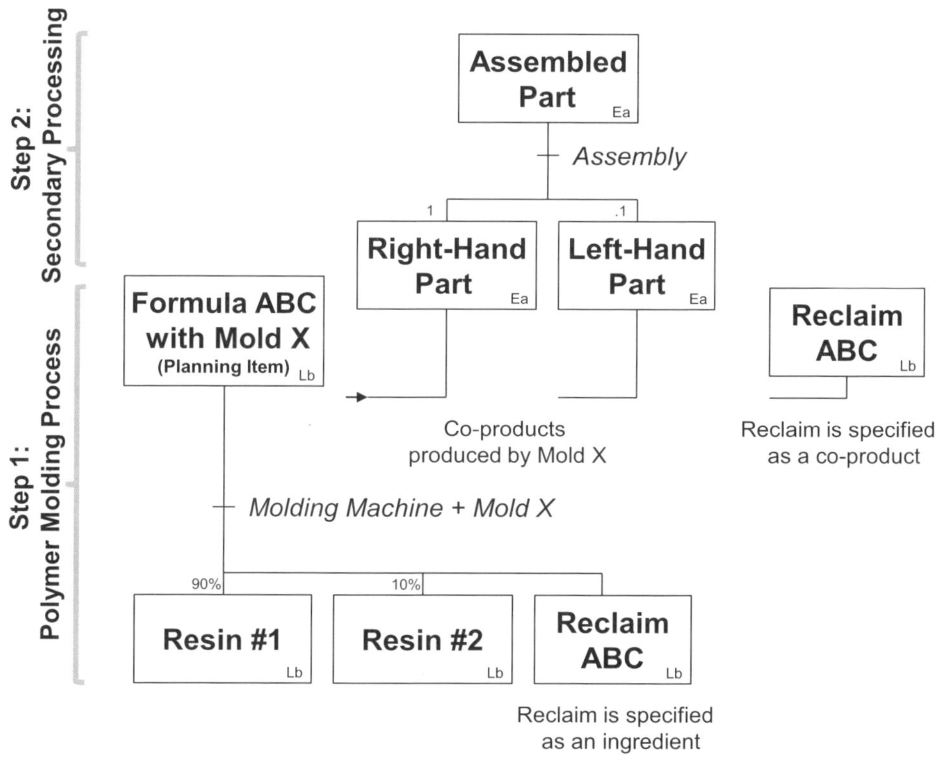

Figure 2.9 Example Formula for a Polymer Molded Product

item provides the basis for defining ingredients, resource requirements, and co-products of a molding process. It is used for planning purposes but is not actually produced.

The first step involves an injection molding machine and the relevant mold (labeled Mold X in the figure). The ingredients for Formula ABC consist of different pelletized resins that must be melted and combined. In this example, the mold consists of two cavities for producing a right-hand and left-hand part, which are identified as co-products within the formula. In addition, the formula indicates that reclaim is a reusable co-product of the molding process, and the reclaim can be used as an ingredient. The second step involves an assembly operation to assemble the right-hand and left-hand parts.

The routing operation for producing the molded parts typically defines the machine cycles that are needed to produce the expected items from a mold. For example, a machine that employs a mold may require 2 cycles to produce a quantity of 10 items. In this case, you define the resource's *batch capacity* as 10. In the operation, you define a *factor* of 2 for the required cycles per batch.

2.12 Equipment Installation and Maintenance

Many manufacturers and distributors provide value-added services such as installation, repair, and periodic maintenance, where services are performed by field service personnel or internal service facilities. The most common examples reflect firms that sell and service equipment, such as computer products, home appliances, and industrial equipment. A service order provides the basic tool for defining requirements and reporting actual consumption of materials and technician time. Common synonyms include a service work order or service call.

Different examples of service orders reflect the differences between field service and internal service facilities. Field service examples include equipment installation, upgrades, and preventive maintenance, which typically reflect scheduled activities with predefined requirements for material and labor. These scheduled activities (and their requirements for material and labor) can be defined within a service agreement, which provides the basis for periodic generation of service orders. Ad hoc activities such as equipment repairs or other emergency situations cannot be scheduled in advance, and the material and labor requirements can be difficult to anticipate. Examples for internal service facilities—such as a repair department—include equipment repairs on a customer return or service work on a customer-supplied piece of equipment.

Service orders build on the foundation of project information, where you typically create and assign a unique project to each service order. Case 8 describes a typical example for a service order for equipment installation, and its related external time-and-material project.

Case 8: Service Order for Equipment Installation

An equipment manufacturer employed service orders to install equipment at the customer site. The service order was typically created as part of sales order processing, since the sales line identified the equipment to be installed.

The key information for an example service order is summarized in Figure 2.10 and described below.

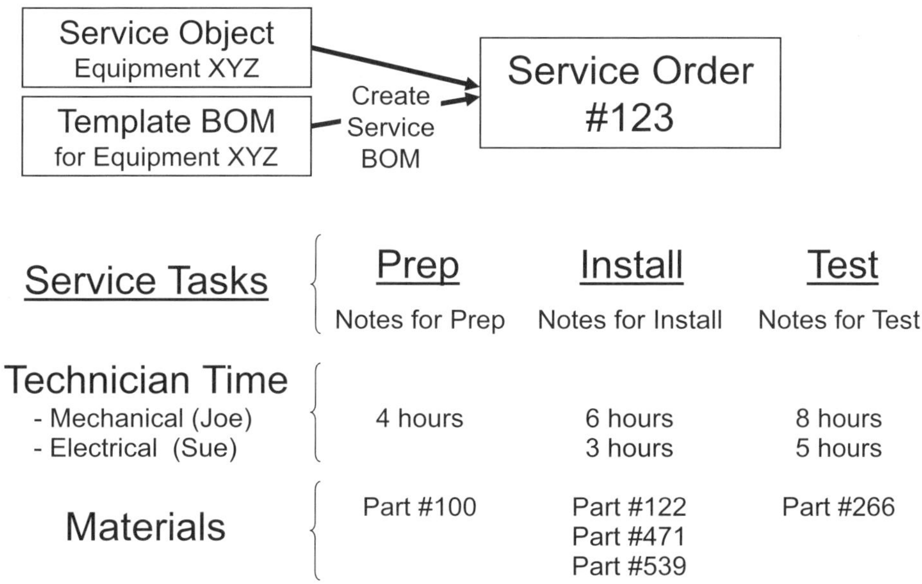

Figure 2.10 Example Service Order for Equipment Installation

In this example, the service manager assigned a service object (identified as Equipment XYZ in the figure) to the service order, and attached a template BOM (reflecting the bill of material for Equipment XYZ) to create a Service BOM. The Service BOM enables a technician to easily review product structure information should the installation require replacement parts. The service manager also assigned three service tasks (labeled Prep, Install, and Test) to the service order, and prepared detailed notes about each task. Finally, the service manager created service order line items that identified the anticipated requirements for materials and the technician's time, and the line items were assigned to the relevant service task. The installation required two types of technicians (mechanical and electrical), and the line items for technician time were assigned to employees (shown as Joe and Sue in the figure). The technicians reported actual consumption of materials and time against the service order line items, and also signed off on the completion of each line item. The signed-off completions provide the basis for generating an invoice proposal for billing the customer.

2.13 Printed Circuit Boards in CTO Products

Printed circuit boards often represent key components for discrete manufacturers of equipment and machines. They may also represent the primary end-items for some manufacturers. The production process for printed circuit boards can be modeled by bill of material and routing information, and coordinated by production orders, as illustrated by the following case study (Case 9). It can also be coordinated by kanban orders and modeled by a production flow and its activities, as described in a subsequent case study (Case 81).

As illustrated in Figure 2.11, a PCB assembly was produced from a raw board and various electronic components such as capacitors and resistors. The figure shows two PCB assemblies for the configuration. The production process for a PCB assembly involved a surface mount technology (SMT) line for populating the board, a hand solder operation, and then testing. There were four SMT lines, and a given PCB assembly could be produced on any of the lines. Prior to a production run on a selected SMT line, the reels of batch-controlled components were moved from the stockroom for mounting on the SMT line, and the raw boards were moved to the start of the line. After the production run, the reels of unused components were moved back to the stockroom.

Case 9: Printed Circuit Boards in CTO Products

A manufacturer of electronic control units produced configure-to-order products consisting of several printed circuit board (PCB) assemblies placed in a frame and enclosure. Each sales order defined a configuration of different PCB assemblies and options (such as labels and power cord), and the delivery date reflected capable-to-promise logic. Many of the PCB assemblies had high-volume demand and some had infrequent demand. A sales quotation was typically required, which was then converted to a sales order.

Some components were added to the board during the hand solder operation, as illustrated by Resistor-3 in the figure.

The completed PCB assemblies were placed in a frame as part of a final assembly operation for the configured product, and other selected options were added (such as the labels and power cord). The completed CTO product was then shipped to the customer.

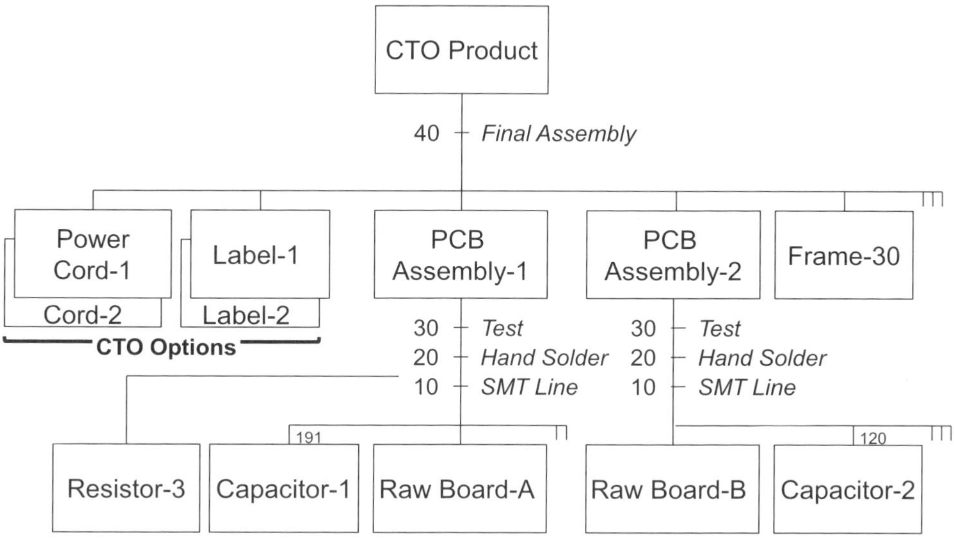

Figure 2.11 Printed Circuit Boards for CTO Product

The manufacturer currently used production orders (and the associated BOM and routing information) to coordinate production, but they were transitioning toward the use of kanban orders (and the associated production flow information) as part of their lean manufacturing initiatives. Case 81 summarizes the use of kanban orders for this scenario.

Chapter 3

Item Definition

Information about material items provides the foundation for managing supply chain activities in distribution and manufacturing environments. A comprehensive common database about item information must satisfy requirements stemming from multiple stakeholders to avoid the problems associated with multiple nonintegrated files. The stakeholders include sales, purchasing, warehouse management, quality, and accounting, as well as product design/engineering and production for manufactured items. Other stakeholder considerations include customers, vendors, industry standards, intercompany coordination, international operations, and web-based applications. The multiple stakeholders often have differing requirements concerning item identification and item attributes.

Item identification, units of measure, and descriptive information represent some of the basic issues for many firms implementing an ERP system for supply chain management. Other issues stem from managing items stocked at multiple sites/warehouses within a company or multiple companies. These basic issues are reflected in the following sections within this chapter:

1. Enterprise Versus Company Information for an Item
2. Typical Business Process for Defining a Material Item
3. Different Approaches to Item Identification
4. Using Templates for Partially Populating Item Information
5. Descriptive Information about an Item
6. Unit of Measure Considerations for an Item
7. Significance of the Production Type for a Material Item
8. Define Information for a Purchased Item
9. Define Information for a Manufactured Item
10. Company Versus Site/Warehouse Information for an Item
11. Inventory Costing and Financial Reporting for Items

12. Significance of the Item Group
13. Alternative Item Identifiers
14. Item Identification Using an Item Number and Variant Code
15. Item Identification of Non-Stock Material
16. Item Identification of a Service

3.1 Enterprise Versus Company-Level Information for an Item

Item definition requires an understanding of enterprise-level versus company-level information, whether you employ AX to manage one or multiple companies within an AX instance. The following explanation focuses on material items identified by an item number. Subsequent sections explain the different approaches to item identification (Section 3.3), and item identification using variant codes (Section 3.14).

In summary, the concept of enterprise- versus company-level information has been implemented within AX 2012 using two different constructs and their identifiers—termed the *product number* and the *item number*.[1] The product number provides a unique identifier for enterprise-level information about products, whereas the item number provides the unique identifier for company-level information about items. The enterprise-level information consists of just a few key policies and some descriptive information, whereas all other item information is defined at the company level.

The conceptual model of enterprise- versus company-level information requires an understanding of several critical fields (and additional fields). It also requires an understanding of a single versus multicompany approach for defining items, as described in the next subsections.

Single Versus Multicompany Approach to Item Definition The conceptual model of enterprise- versus company-level information gives rise to two different approaches for defining items, termed the single-company approach and the multicompany approach.

[1] It is my impression that several factors contributed to the current design of enterprise-level information within AX 2012. First, the new design for product management is a work in process. Second, the construct of the item numbers could not be replaced in this release because it would require changes to the inventory subsystem. Hence, the new product management functionality was designed to the point where it interfaces with inventory, and additional functionality will likely be taken up in the next release. In addition, the previous form "Items" was replaced with the form "Released Products" to reflect the new design and the changes in its functionality.

- *Multicompany approach to defining items.* You employ a two-step process to initially define a product and then release the product to a selected company. Releasing the product creates an item number that matches the product number, and you maintain the company-level information for the item number. After creating the item number, you can apply a template to partially populate the item information. You typically employ the multicompany approach to support a centralized engineering function, especially when the same item number is used in two or more companies.
- *Single-company approach to defining items.* You employ a one-step process to simultaneously create product and item information, which automatically releases the product to the company. The one-step process allows you to specify a template (to partially populate the item information) when initially defining the item, or to apply a template later. This one-step approach can also be used in a multicompany environment to initially create a product and auto-release it to one company.

The identifiers for a product number and item number are typically assigned the same value. For example, releasing a product to a selected company automatically creates an item number that matches the product number. The one-step process also supports the assignment of the same identifier. If needed, you can optionally override the item number for a company.[2] Deleting an item number from a company simply removes its authorization for the company; it does not delete the product number.

Two key forms are employed to maintain product and item information: the Products form (for product information) and the Released Products form (for item information). Figure 3.1 summarizes these two key forms for the single-company and multicompany approaches to item definition, where the multicompany approach employs an additional step (using the Release Products dialogue) to release selected products to selected companies.

When using the single-company approach to create a new product, you access a "Create Item" dialogue from the Released Products form. Using this dialogue, you specify the product number (and item number) and product name, as well as the desired template for populating item information and all of the essential item data.

When you attempt to release a product that has already been released to the selected company, the system prevents release and provides a message

[2]You can override a different value for the item number (after it has been released to a company) using the rename capability, or when creating an item number and product number in a one-step process.

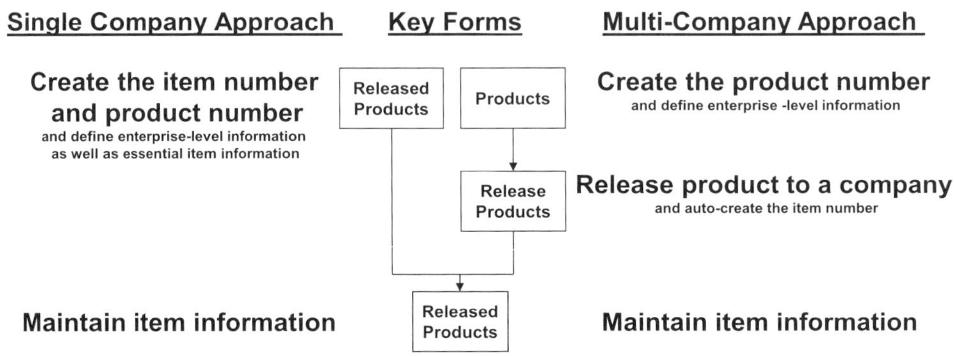

Figure 3.1 Key Forms for Defining Item Information

about the problem. The message can be viewed on the Open Product Release form, or optionally displayed as an infolog, so that you can correct the problem. The message must be manually deleted from the Open Product Release form.

Critical Fields for Enterprise- and Company-Level Information about an Item The critical fields for an item's enterprise- and company-level information are summarized in Figure 3.2 and described below. The figure also displays the AX terminology for the type of information, and highlights the essential item data that enables usage within AX. One other critical field (not shown in the figure) only applies to a catch weight item, which is not typically applicable to discrete manufacturing scenarios.

- *Item Identifier.* You define the product number and its product name at the enterprise level. You create the item number by releasing the product number to selected companies, or by using the single-company approach to item definition. The item number inherits the same value as the product number, although it can be optionally overridden.
- *Item Name.* You define and maintain the product name at the enterprise level, along with optional language-specific translations. The product name applies to the product number as well as related item numbers.
- *Batch or Serial Tracking Policy.* The policy concerning batch or serial tracking is typically specified at the enterprise level, so that tracking will be mandated at all companies authorized for the product. Alternatively,

Type of Item Information		Level of Information		AX Terminology
		Enterprise	Company	
Item Identifier		Specify Product Number	Inherit Item Number*	Product Number & Item Number
Item Name		Specify Product Name	N/A	Product Name
Essential Item Data for a Company	Batch Tracking Policy	Specify Global Policy or Leave Blank	Inherit as a Global Policy or Specify Company Policy	Tracking Dimension Group
	Inventory Storage Policies			Storage Dimension Group
	Inventory Valuation Policy	N/A	Specify	Item Model Group and the Inventory Model field
	Applicable G/L Accounts			Item Group

Release the product to a company

Legend:

* = The item number can be optionally overridden so that it does not match the product number.

Figure 3.2 Enterprise Versus Company-Level Information for Items

you can define a blank value for a product so that each company can specify their own policy. In either case, each company can have a different basis for assignment of batch numbers (to a batch-controlled item) or serial numbers (for a serial-controlled item). The batch/serial tracking policy is embedded in the Tracking Dimension Group assigned to an item. Chapter 9 provides further explanation of batch and serial tracking considerations.

❖ *Inventory Storage Policy.* The inventory storage policies reflect multiple considerations related to the applicability of the site, warehouse, and bin location for an item. Pallet information may also be applicable in some cases. In a similar approach to the batch/serial tracking policy for an item, the inventory storage policies can be specified at the enterprise level (so that it is mandated for applicable companies) or left blank (so that each company can have slightly different policies). The inventory storage policies are embedded in the Storage Dimension Group assigned to an item.

Most scenarios will track an item's inventory by site, warehouse and bin location, while other scenarios simply require site and warehouse. In this regard, the inventory storage policies can reflect the following considerations:

- Specify mandatory entry of the site and warehouse (and bin location) for inventory transactions, and prevent entry of a blank value.
- Indicate the need for physical tracking of inventory by site and warehouse (and bin location).
- Indicate the need for financial tracking of the item's inventory by site and warehouse, or simply by site.
- Indicate whether the item's coverage planning policies apply to the site or the site/warehouse.
- Indicate whether an item's purchase prices will represent company-wide or site/warehouse-specific values.
- Indicate whether an item's sales prices will represent company-wide or site/warehouse-specific values
- Indicate whether you want to lock the specified warehouse when reserving the item's inventory, or allow overrides to the warehouse. This policy is termed the primary stocking policy.

❖ *Inventory Valuation Method.* The inventory valuation method is defined as company-level information for an item. It determines whether actual costing or standard costing applies to an item, and represents one aspect of the Item Model Group assigned to the item. Chapter 8 provides further explanation of product costing for supporting standard costs or actual costs.

❖ *Applicable G/L Accounts.* The applicable G/L accounts are embedded in the Item Group assigned to the item. The item group is defined as company-level information for an item. Additional G/L accounts related to standard cost items must be specified as part of a posting profile, where the account number assignment may reflect an item group or cost group or both.

Significance of the Essential Item Data The fundamental design of AX requires four item-related policies in order to use the item within a company. For explanatory purposes, these policies are termed *essential item data.* The four policies were highlighted in Figure 3.2 and previously described. Two of these policies—about batch/serial tracking and inventory storage—can be inherited from the enterprise-level information for a product, and the other two policies can only be specified at the company-level. You can optionally perform a "validation" to determine whether these policies have been specified for an item, and an infolog displays whether any essential item data is missing.

Additional Enterprise-Level Information about an Item Several additional types of enterprise-level information can be defined for an item, as summarized below. The information can be maintained from the Products form or the Released Products form.

- *Unit of Measure Conversions*. The unit conversions for an item are specified at the enterprise level, although the item's inventory UM can only be specified at the company level. A subsequent section (Section 3.6) provides further explanation about unit of measure considerations.
- *Assignment to a Product Category*. A multi-level category hierarchy can be defined within AX, so that you can assign a product to one product category. The product category provides one basis for discount percentages that are defined within a sales agreement or purchase agreement (as explained in Sections 12.5 and 13.5). Case 10 provides an example of product categories for sales purposes.
- *Search Name*. The value within the search name field can be defined independently for a product number and its related item numbers. The field has no special significance other than supporting a filter on displayed information. Creative uses of the field include the identifier previously used in a legacy system.
- *Product Image*.
- *Related Products*. The user-defined types of related products must be defined within AX, so that you can assign one or more related products to a product. This only provides reference information, and does not affect any logic within standard AX functionality.

Case 10: Product Categories for Sales Purposes

An equipment manufacturer defined a three-level category hierarchy to support sales-related trade promotions. The lowest level of the category hierarchy—termed the product category—was assigned to each saleable product. The category hierarchy represents enterprise-level information. Figure 3.3 summarizes an example of the category hierarchy for sales. As noted in the figure's comments, one level in category hierarchy (the brand level) is also mirrored in the business unit financial dimension assigned to an item number, which represents company-level information and supports financial reports by brand.

Level	Description	Examples	Comments
0	Sales Hierarchy	N/A	
1	Brand	SuperTech	Brand also defined as a Business Unit Financial Dimension, with a value assigned to an Item Number
2	Family	Appliances	
3	Product Category	Blenders	
N/A	Product	12345	Product Category assigned to a Product Number

Figure 3.3 Example of a Category Hierarchy for Sales Trade Promotions

3.2 *Typical Business Process for Defining a Material Item*

This business process focuses on material items identified by an item number. It consists of several steps that require an understanding of enterprise-level versus company-level information about an item, and the single versus multicompany approaches to defining an item, as described in the previous section. The business process starts with a request for a new item, where a product designer role typically has the responsibility for initially defining the product and item information. The steps within the business process are summarized in Figure 3.4 and described below.

Overview The product designer is responsible for initially creating an item— using either a single-company approach or a multicompany approach —and defining the enterprise-level data as well as the essential company-level information. The product designer may employ a template as a short-cut approach to partially populate item information, either when creating a new item or by applying it afterward. In particular, the product designer defines the essential information, the descriptive information, and the units of

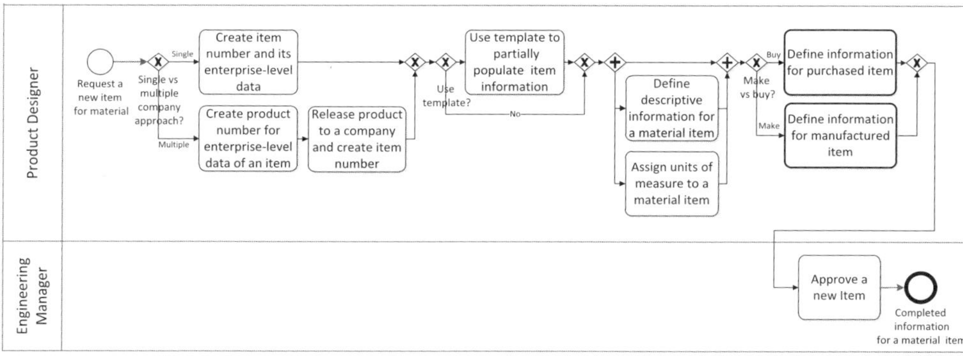

Figure 3.4 Typical Business Process to Define Item Information for a Material Item

measure for an item. Additional roles define the information for a purchased item or for a manufactured item. Upon completion of the item information, the engineering manager can approve the definition of a new item.

Create Item Number and Define its Enterprise-Level Data The product designer employs a single-company approach to create a new item number and define its enterprise-level data. The enterprise-level data includes the product number, product name, and extended description, and the enterprise-level policies for batch/serial tracking and inventory storage. A template may be specified when creating an item in order to partially populate item information. Subsequent maintenance of enterprise-level data employs the product number, otherwise the product designer maintains all other aspects of item information for the item number (aka a released product).

Create Product Number and Define Enterprise-Level Data for an Item The product designer employs a multicompany approach to initially create a product number and define its enterprise-level data. The enterprise-level data includes the product name and extended description, and the enterprise-level policies for batch/serial tracking and inventory storage. Specifying these policies at the enterprise-level means they are mandated for all authorized companies.

Release Product to a Company and Create Item Number In a multicompany approach, the product designer releases selected product numbers to one or more companies, which automatically creates the item number within each company. After the release step, the product designer also assigns several essential fields that must be populated prior to using the item.

Use Template to Partially Populate Item Information The product designer employs a template as a short-cut approach to partially populate item information, either when creating a new item or by applying it afterward. The product designer creates a template from an existing item number, and designates it as a personal or shared template.

Define Descriptive Information for an Item The product designer defines the item's description (and an extended description) as part of its enterprise-level information. Language-specific translations can also be defined. The descriptive information may also include documents, such as notes, Word files, or other file formats.

Assign Units of Measure to an Item The product designer assigns the inventory unit of measure (UM) to an item. The item's inventory UM is used to display inventory balances, define costs, and calculate replenishment. An item may have additional units of measure for purchasing or sales purposes, which may require item-specific UM conversion factors with the item's inventory UM.

Define Information for a Purchased Item The definition of information for a purchased item involves several activities performed by different roles. The purchasing agent defines an item's approved vendors, purchase prices, and planning data. The accounting manager defines the item's accounting information and inventory valuation method (standard versus actual cost), and the cost accountant defines an item's standard cost. If applicable, the quality control manager defines the item's batch tracking policies, shelf life policies, and testing requirements.

Define Information for a Manufactured Item The definition of information for a manufactured item involves several activities performed by different roles. The product designer defines an item's bill of material. The process engineer defines the routing for an item. The production planner defines the item's planning data. The accounting manager defines the item's accounting information and inventory valuation method (standard versus actual cost), and the cost accountant calculates the cost of a manufactured item. If applicable, the quality control manager defines the item's batch tracking policies, shelf life policies, and testing requirements.

Approve a New Item The engineering manager can optionally define restrictions about item usage prior to item approval, and then remove the restrictions upon approval. The restrictions consist of three policies to prevent purchase orders, prevent sales orders, and prevent inventory transactions for an item (or for a specific site for the item).

3.3 Different Approaches to Item Identification

An item number is generally employed as the basis for item identification of tangible material. An alternative basis for item identification—consisting of the combined fields of an item number and one or more variant codes—can also be used. For example, the item number and revision level may be used for item identification.

Item identification may also be required for an intangible service, where the identifier typically consists of an item number. For example, the item number may represent a service that is purchased or sold, or it may represent a subcontracted service in a subcontract manufacturing scenario.

These two factors—the basis for item identification and the tangible/intangible nature of the item—can be used to categorize the different approaches to item identification within AX. Figure 3.5 summarizes the different approaches and the related AX functionality, and highlights the dominant business model of using an item number for identifying tangible material.

The different approaches to item identification involve several AX fields when initially creating an item. When creating a new item number for a tangible item, for example, you would designate the product type of *Item* (rather than Service) and product subtype of *Product* (rather than Product Master). The Products form displays the enterprise-level information for these items.

Item Identification Using an Item Number and Variant Code The creation of a new item number with a variant code involves additional AX fields. When creating the product number, you designate a product subtype of *Product Master* and a configuration technology of *Predefined Variant*. You must also predefine and then select the relevant *Product Dimension*

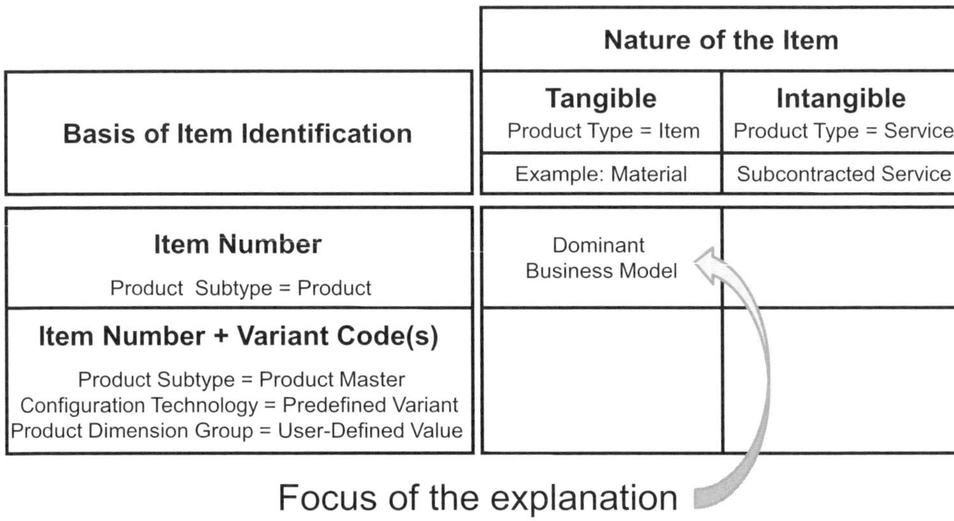

Figure 3.5 Different Approaches to Item Identification

Group identifying the desired variant code, such as a dimension group reflecting color or size. A subsequent section (Section 3.14) provides further explanation of item identification using variant codes. The Product Masters form displays the enterprise-level information for these items.

Item Identification for a Service The creation of a new item number that represents a service is indicated by a product type of Service. A subsequent section (Section 3.16) provides further explanation of item identification for services, especially subcontracted services for supporting subcontract manufacturing scenarios. Chapter 16 explains subcontracted production.

Item Identification of a Configurable Item The AX approaches for item identification of a configurable item are covered in Chapter 7, and not displayed in Figure 3.5 because they only apply to custom product environments. The definition of a configurable item shares many similarities with a normal material item. The key differences include the designation as a product master (rather than a product), the use of a configuration ID (within the product dimension group), and a selected configuration technology. AX supports three major variations of a configuration technology. The use of a configuration technology—such as configuring a sales order or sales quote line item—results in the creation of a configuration ID, and the combination of item number and configuration ID provides a unique identifier.

Guidelines for Item Identification of Material As the dominant business practice, an item number acts as the unique internal identifier for each material item. The item number is manually assigned in most scenarios. If needed, you can employ automatic assignment based on a number sequence mask. The following guidelines are recommended for assignment of a unique item number:

- Define an item number for any stage in the manufacturing process that can be stocked, sold, or purchased complete. While routing operations are often used to reflect various steps in the manufacturing process, the stocking level consideration may mandate a separate item for a given step.
- Define an item number for any manufactured item representing a phantom. You designate a manufactured component as a phantom when defining it within a BOM line.
- Define an item number for each item representing a packaging variation of a product.

3.4 Using Templates for Partially Populating Item Information

A template can be used to automatically populate many aspects of the company-level information for an item, thereby simplifying the item definition process.[3] The following guidelines describe the creation and use of an item template.

- *Create template based on a released product.* A template can only be created for a selected item on the Released Products form (in edit mode). The desired template information should be populated for the item prior

[3]Dynamics AX provide two basic approaches to templates which differ in their creation and use. The item template represents the unique approach in terms of how you create it, and how it can be applied after creating an item. All other templates employ a different approach to creation, and they can only be used when you initially create a record (such as a new customer or a new delivery mode). They cannot be applied after you create a record.

to creating the template, and the template name should reflect the nature of the information. Most firms will employ several templates that reflect their dominant business models for items. Some simplistic examples would be a template for an ingredient with batch tracking, and a template for packaging material identified by revision level.

When creating a template, you designate whether it represents a personal template or shared template. Personal templates are only available to the user who created the template, whereas a shared template can be accessed by any user.

- *Applying a template to an already-released product.* Applying a selected template will update the item information for the selected item. The initial step involves selecting the relevant item on the Released Products form, and then applying the template. This approach allows you to release products and then mass update the newly created item numbers.
- *Applying a template when creating items via the single-company approach to item definition.* You select the desired template as part of the Create Product dialogue.

Some aspects of item information cannot be updated from a template, since they reflect additional tables that must be populated. For example, this includes lead times and order modifiers (defined on the Default Order Settings form), and item costs for a specified costing version (defined on the Item Price form). Figure 3.6 provides additional examples of item information that can and cannot be populated by item templates.

3.4 Descriptive Information about an Item

Several types of descriptive information can be defined for a product and an item. This includes the enterprise-level information such as the Product Name and Extended Description, as well as company-level information such as physical dimensions.

Product Name and Extended Description This enterprise-level information must be maintained for a product number, and it automatically applies to the released product (the item number). The Product Name field is a fixed length field, where the number of characters can be easily expanded, whereas the Extended Description consists of unlimited descriptive text. Language-specific translations can also be defined for both fields.

Category of Information	Populate via Template	Cannot Populate via Template
Engineering	Flushing Principle Production Type	
Inventory Management	Inventory UM Weight	Item-specific UM conversions
Planning	Coverage planning policy	Site-specific coverage planning policies Safety stock quantity for a site/warehouse
Manufacturing		Order quantity modifiers for production Production lead time (with no routing data)
Procurement	Company-wide preferred vendor Buyer responsibility Default purchasing UM	Approved vendors for item Vendor item number Purchasing lead time Order quantity modifiers for purchases
Sales	Default sales UM	Customer item number Order quantity modifiers for sales
Accounting	G/L account numbers for item Financial dimensions Standard vs actual costing policy	Standard cost for an item
Quality Management	Batch numbering policy	Product testing requirements for an item Batch attributes for an item

Figure 3.6 Examples of Item Information Populated by Templates

Document Handling Capabilities (aka Attachments) The document handling capabilities apply to products and items, and allow entry of extended text using a document type of note. Other document types include Word files, Excel spreadsheets, images, and various file formats. One or more documents can be attached to a product or an item. These document handling capabilities apply to more than just items; they apply to almost every construct within AX, ranging from master files and setup information to orders and invoices.

A document type of note has several additional characteristics. You can designate whether the note document relates to internal or external purposes. For example, an external note document assigned to a sales line or purchase line can be optionally printed on order documents, as defined by the form setup policies for each type of document (such as a sales order confirmation). The ability to assign user-defined names to different types of note documents can be creatively used for classification purposes, such as notes related to material handling or quality. These classifications can then be used to selectively print the type of note document.

The document handling capabilities are also used to support MSDS documents for regulated products, and to support printing of these documents with a sales order packing list or invoice. Chapter 18 provides further explanation about regulated products and MSDS documents.

Physical Dimensions As company-level information, an item's net weight and volume are used to calculate total weight and volume on sales orders and purchase orders. In addition, the total net weight for a manufactured item can be calculated based on the component weights.[4]

3.6 Unit of Measure Considerations for an Item

The unit of measure codes, termed UM or UOM for short, are defined as enterprise-level information. Unit of measure codes must be predefined—such as each, carton, pound, and kilogram—in order to support several types of UM requirements, as described below.

Definition of Unit of Measure Codes The unit of measure codes represent enterprise-level information that is language specific. The codes for two different systems of units—metric units and U.S. standard units—are automatically loaded into AX, along with the unit conversion factors (such as grams per kilogram). Additional units of measure must be defined (such as box and case), and the UM conversion factors are often item specific (such as the number of boxes per case).

Inventory UM for an Item Each item requires one UM for costing and inventory purposes. This is termed the inventory UM or base UM. An item's inventory UM is reflected in its inventory balances, replenishment calculations, product costs, and many of the inventory transactions such as transfer orders, picking lists, and inventory adjustments. It is also reflected in the definition of BOM information and routing information for a manufactured item. The inventory UM for an item cannot be changed after you report inventory transactions, so the assignment of an inventory UM requires careful consideration.

[4]The cost calculations for a manufactured item can also calculate its net weight when performing the calculation for a costing version. A subsequent chapter describes how to initiate cost calculations for a costing version (Section 8.7).

Authorized UM for an Item The item's inventory UM represents an authorized UM for the item. Any other UM must be authorized before it can be used for the item. An authorized UM means it has a UM conversion factor that ties it back to the item's base UM. Standard UM conversions apply to UM codes representing metric or U.S. standard units, such as conversions between kilograms, grams, and milligrams. Additional UM codes such as box and case may need to be defined, along with their UM conversion factors. The item-specific UM conversion factors can be defined as enterprise-level information for a product. When entering transactions for an item, you can view an item's authorized UM in the drop-down list for the UM field.

Default UM for Sales and Purchases of an Item You can optionally specify an item's default UM for sales orders and purchase orders. These represent company-wide defaults with the following impacts.

- ❖ *Default UM for Sales Orders.* An item's default sales UM applies to the definition of its order quantity modifiers (for a minimum, multiple, maximum, and standard order quantity) for sales orders. The item's default sales UM and order quantity modifiers are normally reflected in a manually entered sales order line. However, when you specify a sales agreement for the sales order, the item's sales UM will default to the sales agreement.
- ❖ *Default UM for Purchase Orders.* An item's default purchase UM applies to the definition of its order quantity modifiers (for a minimum, multiple, maximum, and standard order quantity) for purchase orders. The item's default purchase UM and order quantity modifiers are normally reflected in a manually entered purchase order line. However, when you specify a purchase agreement for the purchase order, the item's purchase UM will default to the purchase agreement.

Many items only require a single unit of measure. In these cases, you can simplify system usage by assigning the same UM to the item's base UM and to the item's default UM for purchase orders and sales orders.

Business Processes Involving a Different UM for an Item Some business processes require more than one UM for an item, such as selling or buying an item in different units of measure. The following areas support a different UM, and each UM must be authorized for the item:

- *Sales Order Processing.* A sales line can specify any authorized UM for the item, where the sales quantity and price reflect the specified UM. The use of different sales UM can be specified for an item's sales price trade agreements and for sales agreements. Shipment quantities (and related packing slips and invoices) are reported in the specified UM for the sales line, although related picking lists employ the inventory UM for an item.
- *Purchase Order Processing.* A purchase order line can specify any authorized UM for the item, where the purchase quantity and price reflect the specified UM. The use of a different purchase UM can be specified for an item's purchase price trade agreements and purchase agreements. Receipt quantities (and related arrival journals, packing lists and invoices) are reported in the specified UM for the purchase line.
- *Component Quantity in a BOM line.* The component's required quantity can be specified in terms of any authorized UM for the item. This applies to a BOM line and to the order-dependent BOM. The picking list for a production order displays the component's inventory UM.
- *Forecasts.* An item's demand forecast (or supply forecast) can specify any of its authorized UM.
- *Display of Inventory Balances***.** An item's inventory balances are stored in terms of its inventory UM; the system does not retain identification of a different receiving UM once material goes into inventory. You can optionally view an item's inventory balance in terms of its default sales UM or default purchasing UM, or in terms of a specified UM authorized for the item.

3.7 Significance of the Production Type for a Material Item

The assignment of a *production type* to a material item represents company-level information, and impacts how the item can be used. The production type indicates whether an item is manufactured or purchased, and whether a manufactured item employs the BOM or formula approach to product structure information. Most discrete manufacturing scenarios will only use a BOM approach to product structure, and the following two values for a production type.

- *None.* A production type of *None* indicates the item represents purchased material. You cannot define BOM or routing information for the item, or create production orders for the item. This production type also applies to items representing a service.
- *BOM.* A production type of *BOM* indicates a manufactured item, and you can define bill of material and routing information for the item. The item is termed a *BOM item* for short. The item can also be purchased, and the item's planned orders for a given site/warehouse can reflect planned production, purchases or transfers. Chapter 4 explains bill of material information.

The other possible values apply to process manufacturing scenarios, so further explanation is postponed until Chapter 5 (Section 5.2). The production type of an item can be changed from none to BOM. Changing it from BOM to none has an additional impact because the item can no longer have BOM information, so that the Master BOMs assigned to the item (if any) will be automatically removed.

While the production type indicates whether an item is manufactured or purchased, the actual make/buy indicator is embedded in the planned order type for the item. For example, the planned order type indicates whether planning calculations should generate planned production orders or purchase orders. The planned order type also indicates whether cost calculations should consider an item's BOM/routing information.

3.8 Define Information for a Purchased Item

A purchased item is typically indicated by its primary source of supply of planned purchase orders (as part of the item's coverage planning data). However, purchase orders can be created for any material item.

The definition of information for a purchased item involves several activities performed by different roles, such as the purchasing agent, cost accountant, and quality manager. Various aspects of defining a purchased item are summarized in this section, along with references to more detailed explanations provided throughout the book.

- Define and enforce approved vendors for an item (Section 13.3)
- Define purchase prices and discounts for an item using trade agreements (Section 13.5) or blanket purchase agreements (Section 13.6)

- Define planning data for a purchased item (Section 10.1)
- Assign a cost group to a purchased item (Section 8.3)
- Define standard costs for a purchased item (Section 8.4)
- Define serial or batch tracking policies for an item (Sections 9.1 and 9.2)
- Define batch attributes for an item (Section 9.4)
- Define testing requirements for an item (Section 18.4)

3.9 Define Information for a Manufactured Item

A manufactured item is typically indicated by its primary source of supply of planned production orders (as part of the item's coverage planning data). However, production orders can be created for any material item with an approved BOM.

The definition of information for a manufactured item involves several activities performed by different roles, such as the product designer, process engineer, production planner, cost accountant, and quality manager. Various aspects of defining a manufactured item are summarized in this section, along with references to more detailed explanations provided throughout the book.

- Define the bill of material for a manufactured item (Chapter 4)
- Define the routing for a manufactured item (Chapter 6)
- Define the BOM and routing for a subcontract manufactured item (Chapter 16)
- Calculate standard costs for a manufactured item (Section 8.7)
- Calculate planned costs for a manufactured item (Section 8.10)
- Define planning data for manufactured item (Section 10.3)
- Define serial or batch tracking policies for an item (Sections 9.1 and 9.2)
- Define batch attributes for an item (Section 9.4)
- Define testing requirements for an item (Section 18.4)

With the current AX design, a product must be released to a company before you can define its BOM information as part of the company-level information for the manufactured item.

3.10 Company Versus Site/Warehouse Information for an Item

The concept of company versus site/warehouse-specific information applies to several aspects of item information. The concept is introduced now, and subsequent chapters provide more detailed explanations. Figure 3.7 summarizes some of the major examples of company versus site/warehouse information.[5]

The company-wide item information includes the item identifier and inventory UM. Other aspects of an item can reflect company-wide information, or site- and warehouse-specific information. For example, an item's company-wide information includes the costing method for standard versus

		Level of Information		
	Type of Information	**Companywide**	**Site-Specific**	**Warehouse-Specific**
Basic	Item Identifier	Yes	N/A	
	Inventory UM			
Costing	Costing Method (Standard vs Actual)			
	Standard Cost for Item	N/A	Yes	
	Actual Cost for Item		Yes	
Planning	Approved Vendor	Yes	N/A	
	Primary Source of Supply	Specify (Act as default)	Override the default	
	Coverage Group (Set of Policies)			
	Preferred Vendor			
	Purchasing Lead Time			
Price	Purchase Price Trade Agreement	Yes		
	Sales Price Trade Agreement			
Mfg	BOM for a Manufactured Item	Yes	Yes	N/A
	Routing for a Manufactured Item	N/A	Yes	

Figure 3.7 Company-Wide Versus Site/Warehouse Information for an Item

[5] The figure does not include the enterprise-level information about the basis for item identification (item number) and the nature of the item (tangible material), as previously illustrated in Figure 3.2.

actual. An item's standard costs can only be maintained as site-specific information, whereas an item's actual costs can be tracked by site or warehouse.

The company-wide information for a purchased item includes its approved vendors. It also includes the default values for the item's coverage planning policies—such as the preferred vendor—which can be overridden as site/warehouse-specific policies. In addition, the applicability of sales and purchase trade agreement information can be company-wide or site/warehouse-specific, as defined by the policies embedded in the Storage Dimension Group assigned to an item.

A manufactured item produced in more than one site can have a company-wide BOM that applies to all sites, or it can be site-specific. In contrast, the routing for a manufactured item must be site-specific, and resources must be site-specific.

3.11 Inventory Costing and Financial Reporting for Items

Several item-related policies impact inventory costing and financial reporting for items. These policies include the inventory valuation method, the item group, and financial dimension assigned to an item, as described below.

Inventory Valuation Method Item costs provide the basis for valuing inventory transactions. An item's costs can be based on a standard costing or actual costing method (such as FIFO, LIFO, and weighted average cost), as defined by the costing method policy embedded in the Item Model Group assigned to the item. Chapter 8 provides further explanation about maintaining standard costs and actual costs.

G/L Accounts and the Item Group The Item Group assigned to an item defines the G/L account numbers impacted by the item's inventory transactions. For example, some of the key G/L accounts include inventory, revenue, cost of goods sold (COGS), and purchase price variances. The item groups and their G/L account numbers do not need to reflect product lines when using a financial dimension for items. For example, the value for the item's financial dimension supports revenue, COGS and inventory by product line.

The item groups assigned to purchased items typically have a parallel with the cost groups assigned to these same items. Cost groups serve a slightly different purpose, since they provide cost group segmentation in the calculated costs of manufactured items. The cost groups also provide an alternative approach for assigning G/L account numbers related to standard cost variances, as illustrated in Case 11. A subsequent chapter about product costing provides further explanation about the significance of cost groups (Section 8.3).

The item group can serve several other purposes in addition to the assignment of G/L account numbers, as summarized in the next section. These other purposes often result in multiple item groups with the same G/L account numbers.

Case 11: Purchase Price Variances Based on Cost Group

A manufacturer of printed circuit boards defined one item group representing electronic components that was assigned to the relevant purchased items. In addition, the company defined several cost groups for different types of electronic components such as integrated circuit chips and capacitors in order to support cost group segmentation of a manufactured item's calculated costs. These cost groups (rather than the item group) were also used to assign the G/L accounts for purchase price variances.

Financial Dimension Assigned to Items The combination of a financial dimension value and G/L account number provide the basis for financial reporting. With a product line dimension, for example, you define the possible values for different product lines. The applicable value for a product line can then be assigned to an item, which will be inherited by any item-related transaction. On a sales line, for example, the financial dimensions could reflect the customer type and product line, where the product line value gets inherited from the item and the customer type gets inherited from the customer.

The assignment of a financial dimension for a business unit has special significance when assigned to an item, since it supports financial reporting by business unit.

Financial dimensions can also be assigned to other entities such as customers, vendors, and sites to support multidimensional reporting. For example, the financial dimension assigned to sites (with a different value for each site) supports financial reporting site by site.

3.12 Significance of the Item Group

The primary rationale for assigning different item groups to items is to support the assignment of G/L account numbers, as described in the previous section. However, the item group can be used in multiple contexts that may be parallel with (or different from) the assignment of G/L account numbers. The multiple contexts often justify the definition of multiple item groups with the same G/L account numbers. The following examples summarize the major contexts.

Item Groups for Similar Salable Items The item group has multiple purposes related to similar salable items, as illustrated below.

- *Forecasting a Group of Items (aka Planning Bill).* A forecast can be defined for an item group rather than an individual item. This method employs a user-defined template (termed an *item allocation key*) that spreads out a total quantity across several items based on a mix percentage per item. All items must be assigned the same item group.
- *Sales Analysis by Item Group.* As one example, a pivot table inquiry provides multidimensional sales analysis based on sales by item group and customer group.

Item Groups for Similar Manufactured Items The Item Group may represent similarities in the items' production process. As the primary example, you can define the applicability of a master operation to a subset of manufactured items with the same Item Group.

The Item Group provides one basis for the applicability rules related to overhead formulas (as described in Section 8.6). For example, the overhead formulas for material-related overheads can differ for different groups of manufactured items.

As additional examples, you can filter planned production orders based on Item Group and maintain coverage planning policies for a group of items with the same Item Group. In addition, you can assign an Item Group to a Master BOM in order to filter a displayed list of BOMs, but this only acts as reference information.

3.13 Alternative Item Identifiers

Several approaches can support an alternative identifier for an internal item number. These approaches include an external item number for a customer or vendor, and an alternative item number to support bar coding or electronic transactions.

Customer or Vendor Item Numbers (aka External Item Number) An internal item number can be associated with other item identifiers for sales and purchasing purposes. These are termed external item numbers. Each external item number can be mapped to one internal item number and have a separate description.

- *Customer Item Number.* The external item number is specified for a single customer to reflect a customer item number. In some cases, it can be specified for a group of customers (or all customers) to reflect a catalog item number or an industry standard.
- *Vendor Item Number.* The external item number is specified for a single vendor to reflect a vendor item number.

UPC Number for an Item (aka External Code) Different types of external codes can be defined to represent an industry standard such as the UPC (Universal Product Code) number or EAN (European Article Number) identifier. You can then define the mapping between an internal item number and the associated UPC number.

Alternative Item Identifier for Electronic Transactions Electronic exchange of documents with customers and vendors is supported by various methods such as Microsoft Biztalk. These documents include sales orders and purchase orders. As part of the setup for each type of document, the item identification can be based on the internal item number, the external item number (described above), or the external code (described above).

Alternative Item Identifier for Bar Coding Purposes The bar code for an item requires an explicit mapping between the internal item number and the bar code digits, even when the bar code digits are exactly the same. The mapping also defines the bar code size and type (such as EAN13 or EAN128/UCC128). If required, the system supports two different bar code identifiers for the same item: one for scanning and one for printing purposes

3.14 Item Identification Using an Item Number and Variant Code

Some scenarios can benefit from item identification based on the combined identifiers of an item number and one or more additional fields, where each additional field is termed a variant code. For example, packaging material often requires changes, where each change can be represented by a revision level. The combination of item number and revision level provides a unique identifier, and each revision level may have a different standard cost, preferred vendor, vendor item number, purchase price agreement, coverage planning data and so forth. The example of revision level will be used throughout this section to illustrate a variant code.

Standard AX includes three possible variant codes named size, color and configuration. A variant code can be easily renamed, such as changing the name from *size* to *revision.* If needed, you can also create and name additional variant codes. You define the possible values of a variant code for a given item, such the values for an item's revision levels (e.g., A, B, C). The use of multiple variant codes for a given item also requires definition of the valid combinations of these values.

The use of a variant code (and its possible values) represents enterprise-level information of an item. Hence, you define the information for a product number and then release the product and its variants to a selected company in order to create an item number with variants. A prerequisite for using a combined identifier involves the definition of a Product Dimension Group, which identifies the desired variant code (such as color or size) and provides the ability to rename a variant code (e.g., to revision level). You indicate the relevant Product Dimension Group when creating a new product.

With AX terminology, the use of a combined identifier means that the product must be designated as a Product Master with a Configuration Technology of Predefined Variant. A previous section (Section 3.3) introduced this terminology as one of the approaches to item identification. In addition, AX supports three other options for a configuration technology which use the variant code for a configuration, as described in a subsequent chapter (Section 7.1). The configuration process generates a configuration ID, and the combination of the item number and configuration id provides a unique identifier.

A product designer role is typically responsible for initially creating a new product number with a variant code, using either a single-company or a multicompany approach. The steps are similar for both approaches. The product designer designates the use of a variant code when initially creating a product number, and then defines the possible values and the valid combinations (e.g., of a product number and revision levels). With the multi-company approach, the product designer performs an additional step to release the product number and valid values of the variant code to the selected company. For example, only the revision level must be released when adding a new revision level to an existing product number.

Maintain Information for an Item Number and its Variants
Several aspects of item information can only be defined for an item number, so that they apply to all of its variants. These item-related fields include the following;

- Inventory UM, and the defaults for Sales UM and Purchase UM
- Item Group and the associated G/L accounts
- Approved Vendor
- Assignment to a Product Category
- Batch tracking and the policies for assigning a batch number
- Batch attributes
- MSDS document

Other aspects of item information can be defined for each variant, as illustrated below.

- Vendor item number
- Customer item number
- UPC code
- Sales prices, based on a policy within the Product Dimension Group
- Purchase prices, based on a policy within the Product Dimension Group
- Standard costs, based on an item-specific policy (termed the "use combination cost price" policy) that enables variants to have a different cost
- Item Coverage policies, such as planned order type, preferred vendor and lead time
- Attachments
- Routing information for a manufactured item
- BOM information for a manufactured item
- Supplies and demands identified by variant

Advantages of Using a Variant Code for Item Identification A combined identifier provides several benefits, as described below.

- *Data Maintenance.* The user-specified values for each variant code can simplify data maintenance in comparison to using different item numbers. The simplified data maintenance is especially relevant when using multiple variant codes.
- *Viewing Inventory Balances.* You can view inventory balances for just the item number, or for the item number and its variants. Each variant code can represent one segment of a meaningful identifier.
- *Costing of a Variant.* You can choose whether the variants have the same cost or a different cost, as defined by an item-specific policy (termed the "use combination cost price" policy).
- *Transfers of a Variant.* The transfer journal transaction enables you to transfer one variant of an item to another variant, much like you would transfer inventory from one warehouse to another warehouse. For example, with an item number that represents an animal or plant, and a variant code that represents the item's age, you can transfer a one-year-old variant to a two-year-old variant.

Limitations of Using a Variant Code for Item Identification A combined identifier has several limitations, as described below.

- Limitations on defining item-related information. Some aspects of item information cannot be defined by variant, as previously summarized.
- Limitations about using variants in Bulk/Pack scenarios. AX only supports a bulk/pack scenario when using item numbers without variants.
- Limitation for a manufactured Item with variants. A manufactured item and variant can have a BOM, but a component with the same item number and a different variant will result in circularity.

Case 12: Variant Codes for Hardware

A hardware manufacturer of screws, bolts,and nuts was considering the use of variant codes to replace their current item numbering scheme. The current scheme used significant digits in the item number to represent a product, its characteristics, and its pack sizes. For example, the characteristics of a bolt included length, diameter, finish, and head type, and the pack sizes included

10, 100, and 500 counts. The existing item master had thousands of item numbers reflecting different combinations of these attribute values. The number of new items was growing to meet customer-specific demand for additional variations. The proposed scheme consisted of an item number to represent the product (such as a type of bolt) and several variant codes to represent the product characteristics and pack sizes. The proposed scheme would simply data maintenance about item identification, such as simply adding new values for relevant variant codes and automatically creating new combinations of the values.

3.15 Item Identification of Non-Stock Material

The book focuses on items representing material and trade goods in distribution and manufacturing environments. However, item numbers can also identify non-stock items, typically representing indirect material used for maintenance, repair, and operations (MRO) purposes.

An item-specific policy termed *stocked product* (embedded in the Item Model Group assigned to the item) indicates whether inventory should or should not be tracked. In the context of indirect material, for example, you would define an Item Model Group labeled Indirect Material with a "not stocked product" policy and an actual cost valuation method. You would additionally define a separate Item Group for indirect material and assign it to items representing indirect material.

Indirect materials do not typically have a unique item number, such as different types of production supplies or expense items. As a simple approach, you can create and use generic item numbers that represent a category of these indirect materials. These are sometimes called category items. When entering a purchase order for the category item, you enter the vendor's item number and an extended description to define what is being purchased, the G/L account number associated with purchasing the indirect material, and the desired ship-to site/warehouse.

The designation of a "not stocked product" for an item has several implications. One impact is that the item cannot be specified as a component in a BOM. The item can only be purchased or sold, and trade agreements can be defined. In addition, you cannot track transaction history or serial/batch-related information, or report test results via quality orders, for the item. An inventory valuation policy of FIFO must be used.

3.16 Item Identification of a Service

The book focuses on items representing material, but some distribution and manufacturing environments also buy or sell services. A project-oriented approach may be used to sell (or buy) services in some contexts, whereas other contexts simply employ an item number to represent the service. You designate a product type of *Service* when creating a new item number representing a service. As described in the previous section, you also assign an Item Model Group with a "not stocked product" policy and an actual cost valuation method, and a separate Item Group that represents the services.

Some scenarios involve subcontract manufacturing. The AX approach to subcontract manufacturing employs a separate item number to represent the subcontracted service, where you also define the item as a component within the parent item's BOM. Since AX prevents use of a "not stocked product" as a component, the item number representing the subcontracted service must be designated as a stocked product. A subsequent chapter provides further explanation about the definition of items representing subcontracted services (Section 16.3).

Additional Case Studies

Case 13: Customer Supplied Material An item representing customer supplied material was used as a component in a manufactured product. The item was treated just like any other purchased material, except that its site-specific standard costs were assigned a zero value. This approach supported BOM information about the component, and also provided visibility of requirements, coordination via purchase orders, and tracking of receipts, inventory and material usage.

Executive Summary

Item identification, units of measure, and descriptive information represent some of the basic issues for implementing an ERP system in distribution and manufacturing firms. Item definition involves enterprise- and company-level information, and considerations about company-wide versus site/warehouse-specific information. This chapter included a typical business process for defining material items, and summarized the key aspects of purchased items and manufactured items. It also reviewed other item identification issues such as the use of variant codes, non-stock material and service items.

Chapter 4

Bill of Material Information

A key aspect of manufactured items consists of product structure information. The product structure is typically modeled by a bill of material (BOM) in discrete manufacturers. The BOM information defines the product design and provides the basis for product costing, material planning, material usage reporting, batch and serial tracking, and tracking progress through stages of manufacturing.

Standard products have predefined BOM information, whereas custom products typically involve creation of a unique BOM for a configurable item. This chapter focuses on BOM information for standard products, and Chapter 7 describes the use of configuration technologies to create BOM information for configurations of a custom product. The top level(s) of the product structure for engineer-to-order custom products can also be modeled as subprojects, as described in Chapter 20.

Dynamics AX provides a second approach for modeling product structure information for supporting process manufacturing scenarios. This is termed a formula approach rather than a BOM approach. The formula approach supports several special cases in discrete manufacturing, such as scenarios involving co-products, substitute components, or batch-oriented production processes. The next chapter covers the formula approach for handling these special cases.

This chapter begins with a typical business process for defining an item's bill of material. Subsequent sections explain key aspects of the business process, such as the definition of BOM versions and BOM lines, and the maintenance of BOM information. The chapter includes the following sections:

1. Typical Business Process for Defining an Item's Bill of Material
2. Master BOMs and BOM Versions

3. BOM Version Policies for an Item
4. BOM Lines for Components
5. Order-Dependent BOM for a Production Order
6. Maintain BOM Information

4.1 Typical Business Process for Defining an Item's Bill of Material

The typical business process for defining an item's bill of material consists of several steps performed by a product designer role. These steps are illustrated in Figure 4.1 and summarized below. As a starting point, the product designer selects the desired item and accesses a separate form in order to create a new BOM version for the item. The new BOM version may involve creation of a new Master BOM or the assignment of an existing Master BOM. The BOM version policies include the effectivity dates. Each BOM line identifies a component and the required quantity. Upon completion of all information, the product designer approves and activates the item's BOM version.

Create a New Master BOM for the Item The creation of a Master BOM typically occurs in the context of creating a new BOM version for a selected item, where the Master BOM is automatically assigned to the item. Each assignment is termed a BOM Version, and an item may have multiple BOM versions, such as different versions that represent site-specific BOMs or planned changes.

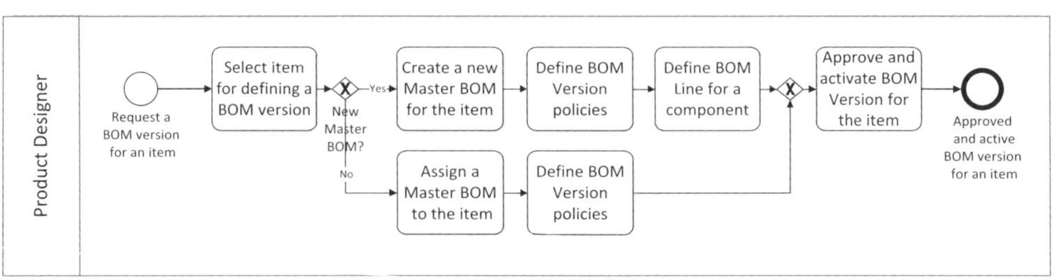

Figure 4.1 Typical Business Process for Defining an Item's Bill of Material

Assign an Existing Master BOM to the Item An existing Master BOM can be assigned to an item, typically reflecting scenarios when the Master BOM has been independently defined beforehand.

Define BOM Version Policies The product designer employs the BOM version policies to specify the effectivity dates and to indicate whether the BOM version represents a company-wide or site-specific BOM for the item.

Define BOM Line for a Component The product designer uses a BOM line to identify a component and its required quantity. Other considerations include the designated warehouse source of the component, the applicable operation number, and a scrap percentage.

Approve and Activate the BOM Version for the Item The product designer must approve a BOM version before it can be specified for a production order, and an approved version is typically activated for use in planning and costing calculations. Electronic signatures can be optionally employed as part of the approval process.

4.2 Master BOMs and BOM Versions

A master BOM has a unique identifier (termed the *BOM Number*) which can be manually or automatically defined. Manual definition should be used when the identifier needs to be meaningful. The creation of a master BOM typically occurs in the context of creating an item's BOM version, where it is automatically assigned to the item. A master BOM can also be created independently and then assigned to an item. Each assignment of a master BOM to an item is termed a *BOM Version*. A BOM version has several policies indicating the effectivity dates and whether it represents a site-specific or company-wide bill of material for the item. Multiple BOM versions can be defined for an item, typically to support the following situations.

- Variations between sites producing the same manufactured item
- Planned changes with effectivity dates
- Revision levels of a manufactured item
- Variations that reflect larger production quantities
- Alternate bills of material
- Prototype or production ramp-up

In summary, a manufactured item can have multiple active BOM versions that reflect different sites, non-overlapping validity periods, and/or different quantity breakpoints. An item can also have approved-but-not-active BOM versions.

An item's BOM version is initially treated as unapproved, which still allows you to calculate the item's costs. It must be approved in order to specify it when creating a production order. Only an approved BOM version can be marked as active. The active BOM version for an item will normally be used in planning and cost calculations.

Electronic signatures can be optionally employed as part of the approval process. For example, you can be prompted for an electronic signature when approving a BOM version, or when designating a BOM version as active. Related situations may also require an electronic signature, such as releasing a production order or reporting the finished quantity for a production order.

Case 14: Revision Levels for a Manufactured Item

A manufacturer employed the BOM versions to represent the revision levels for a manufactured item, such as revision A, B,and C. For reference purposes, the identifier assigned to each Master BOM represented a combination of the item number and revision level. The item's BOM version policies identified the effectivity dates for phasing out (and phasing in) these BOM versions. In order to support the identification of the item's inventory by revision level, the company embedded the revision level in the batch number assigned to a product. However, the inventory resulting from production of different revision levels was treated as interchangeable by planning calculations. A complete change in a product was identified by a different item number, since it represented the maxim about changing form/fit/function.

4.3 BOM Version Policies for an Item

The BOM version policies serve several different purposes. For example, the policies enable a manufactured item to have multiple active BOM versions that reflect different sites and non-overlapping validity periods. The following explanation covers the key fields in the BOM version for an item.

Site-Specific Versus Company-Wide BOM Versions Specifying a blank site for an item's BOM version indicates a company-wide bill of material, whereas a specified site indicates a site-specific bill. The primary difference is that planning calculations will use a site-specific BOM version (if it exists) that matches the site of the item's requirements. If a site-specific BOM version does not exist, the planning calculations will use the company-wide BOM version for the manufactured item. The planning calculations will generate an error message if an appropriate BOM version does not exist.

A secondary difference concerns the options for defining the warehouse source of a component. The warehouse source can be manually specified for a site-specific BOM version, but not for a company-wide BOM version. The next section provides further explanation about designating the warehouse source of component inventory as part of the BOM line information.

Effectivity Dates for an Item's BOM Version The effectivity dates for an item's BOM version can represent planned changes in the item's product structure. For example, a manufactured item may have two BOM versions—one valid to date X and the other valid from date X+1—to indicate planned changes. A blank value for the starting and/or ending date indicates no limitation. An item can have multiple active BOM versions with non-overlapping dates.

Quantity Breakpoints for an Item's BOM Version In discrete manufacturing, the concept of quantity breakpoints does not generally apply to an item's BOM versions although it may apply to an item's route versions. With different route versions for different quantity breakpoints, for example, you can indicate different equipment for producing a larger production order quantity. A planned production order will be assigned the relevant route version based on the required quantity.

4.4 BOM Lines for Components

A BOM line is used to define each component of a manufactured item. Key aspects of a BOM line include the item identifier of the component, the required quantity, the associated operation number, and the warehouse source of the component. This section summarizes these key aspects of defining a component, starting with the different approaches to defining component requirements.

Define Component Requirements as a Quantity The component's required quantity reflects the variable amount needed to produce the parent item. The required quantity also reflects the specified UM for the component. This quantity can be entered as a fraction or decimal. A component's required quantity is normally expressed per a quantity of one parent item, but it can be expressed for a different quantity of the parent item (using the per series field).

Some basic variations to the required quantity include a fixed quantity, the rounding up policy, and planned scrap (expressed as a percentage or a fixed amount or both). Another variation includes a negative component quantity.

Define Component Requirements as a Step Function A special case of a component's required quantity reflects a nonlinear or step-function relationship. You can define this step-function relationship in terms of multiple values for the required quantity and its associated quantity breakpoint. These requirements are treated as a constant, which impacts cost roll-up calculations and planning calculations.

Define the Component's Required Quantity Based on Measurement Calculations A special case of a component's required quantity involves a calculation formula and measurement information, such as height, width, depth, and density. This approach often applies to cut-to-size components, such as a cut-to-length component where the component quantity depends on the length measurement of its parent item. In this way, a single master BOM can be assigned to multiple manufactured items and each parent item will have a different measurement for length.

The component's rounding-up policy and multiple take on special significance in this approach. In the just cited example, let's assume the cut-to-length component has an 8-foot length that will be taken from 10-foot steel rod, so that the multiple is 10 and requirements are rounded to increments of 10.

Impact of the Operation Number Assigned to a Component When routing data exists, the operation number assigned to a component provides the key link between the BOM information and the associated operation within the routing. There are several impacts of assigning an operation number to a component. For example, the operation's scrap percentage affects component requirements, and the resource assigned to the operation can determine the relevant warehouse source for picking the component for a production order. These impacts are summarized below.

- Align the due date of a component with the start of its associated operation. Components with a blank operation number are required at the start of the production order.
- Align the due date of a component with the end of its associated operation, which typically applies to component representing a subcontracted service.
- Calculate component requirements to reflect the scrap percentage of the operation, and its cumulative scrap percentage in a multi-step routing.
- Populate the picking list based on the started quantity for a specified operation number (or a range of operation numbers).
- Segment the picking list by operation number. A picking list can be generated for all components with the same operation number.
- Determine the resource that requires the component in order to support resource consumption logic about the warehouse source of component inventory.

The operation number assigned to a component should correspond to the operation number in the associated route version for the manufactured item. However, the operation number in the routing may not exist in some cases. For example, you can specify a different route version when manually creating a production order, or override the operations in the order-dependent routing.

Warehouse Source of a Component A component's warehouse source indicates where to pick the item for a production order. There are three basic options for defining the component's warehouse source, as summarized in Figure 4.2 and explained below. The third option—termed *resource consumption logic*—provides the most flexibility.

- ❖ *Specify the component warehouse in the BOM version.* The first option only applies to a site-specific BOM version, and the specified warehouse must belong to the site. After creating a production order for the manufactured item, the component in the order-dependent BOM inherits the component's specified warehouse.
- ❖ *Use the component item's default inventory warehouse.* The second option does not specify a component warehouse on the BOM line, and requires additional information about the item's default inventory warehouse for each site (as defined in the item's site-specific order settings). After creating a production order, the component in the order-dependent BOM inherits the component's default inventory warehouse for the required site.

	Option #1	Option #2	Option #3
	Specified Warehouse In Master BOM	Use Item's Default Inventory Warehouse	Assign Warehouse Using Resource Consumption Logic
Master BOM Information	Only for Site-Specific BOM	Applies to Site-Specific or Companywide BOM	
Key Fields: Component Warehouse	Specify Warehouse	None	None
Key Fields: Component's Resource Consumption Policy	No	No	Yes
Key Fields: Operation Number for the Component	N/A	N/A	Specify Operation Number
Additional Information Required	N/A	Item's default inventory warehouse for the required site	Route version for the manufactured item, with a resource for the specified operation number Resource assigned to a production unit Picking warehouse assigned to the production unit
Impact on the component's warehouse in the order-dependent BOM	Inherit the component's specified warehouse	Inherit the item's default inventory warehouse	Inherit the picking warehouse associated with the resource

Figure 4.2 Options for a Component's Warehouse Source

- *Auto-assign the component's warehouse based on the resource for the operation (using resource consumption logic).* The third option does not specify a component warehouse on the BOM line, but it does specify a resource consumption policy and an operation number for the component. This operation number provides a link to the routing operation and the associated resource. In turn, the resource is linked to a production unit that defines the associated picking warehouse.[1] After creating a production order, the component in the order-dependent BOM inherits the picking warehouse associated with a resource requiring the component.

The first two options represent the most straightforward approach and do not require routing data. The third option provides the greatest flexibility for indicating the warehouse source for a component, but also requires routing

[1] A production unit may apply to one or more resources, as described in Chapter 8.

data and involves more complexity. If no information has been entered for the three options, then the component's warehouse on the order-dependent BOM will be blank.

Case 15: Warehouse Source of Components

A manufacturer produced items at different sites and employed site-specific BOM versions to define the components. The warehouse for each component's inventory could be specified as part of the BOM line information. The company felt this approach was the most straight-forward to understand and simplest to maintain. After creating a production order for the manufactured item, the component in the order-dependent BOM inherited the component's specified warehouse.

Impact of the BOM Line Type The BOM line type represents a key policy impacting supply chain management. In most cases, it simply designates whether a manufactured component will be treated as a normal item or a phantom item, as described below. However, it can also designate a make-to-order component or a buy-to-order component (or service), as described in the next subsection.

- *Item (or Normal).* Planning calculations employ netting logic to suggest a planned order to satisfy requirements. These orders are not directly linked to the production order for the parent item.
- *Phantom.* A phantom only applies to a manufactured item. The requirements for a phantom component are passed (or blow-through) to its components and routing operations. The impact of blow-through logic becomes obvious in the order-dependent BOM and routing for a production order. The netting logic within planning calculations ignores the phantom's on-hand inventory and scheduled receipts (if applicable), and suggests planned orders for the phantom's components to satisfy requirements.

BOM Line Type for Make-to-Order and Buy-to-Order Components The BOM line types of *Pegged Supply* and *Vendor* support make-to-order and buy-to-order components, as described below.

- *Make-to-order component.* A line type of *pegged supply* applies to a manufactured item, and represents a make-to-order production strategy with direct linkage between production orders. That is, a production order for the parent automatically generates a linked order (termed a *sub-production* or *reference order*) for each manufactured component with a line type of pegged supply.[2] The system indicates linkage via the reference fields in each production order, and linked orders can be scheduled separately or synchronized.

  The netting logic within planning calculations ignores the component's on-hand inventory and scheduled receipts, since the system assumes the component is being produced just for the parent item's production order. The planning calculations can generate planned production orders to provide visibility of requirements, but these planned orders cannot be firmed.

  A make-to-order component was previously illustrated in a common scenario for a make-to-order production strategy (Section 2.4). Other sections describe its impact on coverage planning data for a manufactured item (Section 10.4) and common S&OP approaches (Section 11.1).
- *Buy-to-order component or service.* A line type of *vendor* applies to a purchased item or service, and it represents a buy-to-order component. That is, a production order for the parent automatically generates a linked purchase order (also termed a reference order) for each purchased component with a line type of vendor.[3] Similar to make-to-order components, the system assumes the component is being purchased just for the parent item's production order, and planning calculations ignore the component's on-hand inventory and scheduled receipts. The planning calculations can generate planned purchase orders to provide visibility of requirements, but these planned orders cannot be firmed.

  A buy-to-order component has one other unique feature, since a preferred vendor can be defined for the component as an override to the preferred vendor for the item. When automatically generating a linked purchase order, the system assigns the component's preferred vendor (if defined) or the item's preferred vendor to the purchase order. This line type is commonly used to support purchases of a component that repre-

[2] The production order for a make-to-order component is automatically generated when the status of the parent item's production order has been changed from created to estimated, or to a higher status such as scheduled.

[3] The purchase order for a buy-to-order component is automatically generated when the status of the parent item's production order has been changed from created to estimated, or to a higher status such as scheduled.

sents a subcontracted service, and Chapter 16 provides further explanation of subcontracted production.

A line type of vendor can also be assigned to a manufactured component, and it works just like the line type of pegged supply. As a minor difference, this type of production order is labeled as *vendor* rather than *standard.* For example, a production order type of vendor could indicate that a subcontractor will produce the manufactured component.

A buy-to-order component was previously illustrated in a common scenario for a make-to-order production strategy (Section 2.4). Other sections describe its impact on coverage planning data for a purchased item (Section 10.2) and purchase order processing (Section 13.8).

Case 16: Subcontracted Service

A manufacturer used subcontractors to produce several items from supplied components. Using the AX approach to subcontracted production, an item number representing the subcontracted service was identified as a BOM component with a line type of vendor. The purchase order for this buy-to-order service was automatically generated by each production order for the parent item.

Considerations about Planned Scrap The planned scrap for a component can be expressed as a percentage or a fixed quantity or both. When using routing data, the planned scrap percentage for an operation can also affect the requirements of components associated with the operation. An accumulated scrap percentage may also apply in a multistep routing because of scrap percentages for previous operations. Each order-dependent BOM and routing (for a production order) inherit the scrap factors from the item's BOM version and route version, and these can be overridden. These scrap factors are included in planning and cost roll-up calculations.

Effectivity Dates of an Component The effectivity dates provide one approach for managing planned changes to BOM information.

Position Information for a Component A component's position information provides reference data that can serve different purposes. For example, it can represent a sequential counter of components, often tied to the find number on drawings. It can identify a grouping of components, such as the material needed for an operation (when routing data does not exist), the delivery area for a group of picked components, or a group representing related parts in the production process. The position field also provides one approach for handling reference designators.

4.5 Order-Dependent BOM for a Production Order

An order-dependent BOM (aka Production BOM) refers to the BOM lines attached to a production order. It initially contains the BOM lines inherited from the BOM version used to create the production order. Changes to the order-dependent BOM do not affect the master BOM. Creation and maintenance of the order-dependent BOM reflect several rules.

- Creation of a production order for a manufactured item also creates an order-dependent BOM.
- The order-dependent BOM initially reflects the item's BOM version that was used to create the production order. In most cases, this will be inherited from the active BOM version for the delivery date and site on the production order. However, you can manually specify a different BOM version for the item when creating the production order, where the BOM version can be approved-but-not-active.
- The order-dependent BOM contains components of a phantom.
- You can modify the components in an order-dependent BOM at any time prior to reporting the production order as ended. For example, you can manually maintain the information, or copy BOM lines from another production order or Master BOM.
- A material item can be issued to a started production order even when the component does not exist on the order-dependent BOM. The issued component will be automatically added to the order-dependent BOM with a zero required quantity.

4.6 Maintain BOM Information

The maintenance of BOM information serves different purposes, and several different approaches can be used. For example, you can directly maintain components in a BOM, update the BOM components using the copy function or the mass change function, or employ a graphical design tool. This section covers the maintenance and analyses of BOM information, such as multi-level and where-used inquiries.

Managing Planned Changes Using Effectivity Dates Planned changes to an item's BOM are normally managed by (1) the date effectivities for a component or (2) by date effectivities for a BOM version. Figure 4.3 illustrates these two approaches to planned changes, where the product has two BOM versions labeled Rev A and Rev B.

The first approach employs date effectivities for a component. Using the example shown in the left side of Figure 4.3, where a Master BOM has been assigned to Product #1, the new component Raw Material #2 becomes effective on the specified date of 12/12/201X.

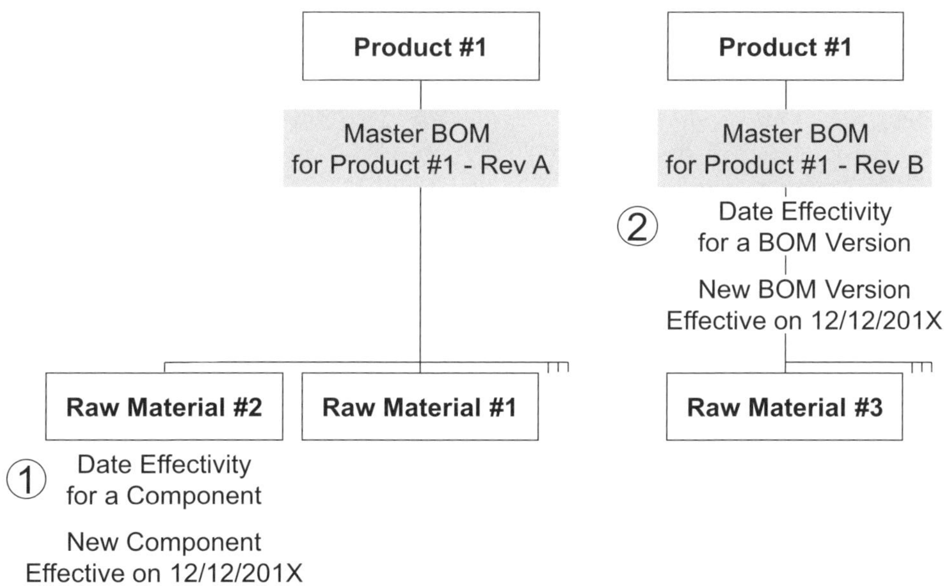

Figure 4.3 Managing Planned Changes to BOM Information

The second approach employs date effectivities for a BOM version. Using the example shown in the right side of Figure 4.3, a different Master BOM can be assigned to Product #1 that represents a different revision level (labeled Rev B versus the original Rev A). You would phase out the assignment of the original Master BOM on the day prior to 12/12/201X, and phase in the assignment of the revised Master BOM on 12/12/201X. The approval status and active status for a BOM version provide an additional consideration for planned changes. Removing the approval status or the active status on a BOM version, or phasing out the effectivity, provides a selective approach to discontinued use.

A third approach to managing planned changes represents a special case, and generally applies to make-to-order custom products. It employs a specified BOM version for a manufactured component, where the item's BOM version is approved but not necessarily active. This third approach can build on the use of component date effectivities to phase in and phase out specified BOM versions for a manufactured component.

Copying Components to a BOM A copy function can be used to add components to master BOMs and to the order-dependent BOM for a production order. For a master BOM, components can be copied from another master BOM as of a specified date. Alternatively, the components can be copied from the order-dependent BOM associated with a specified production order. You determine whether the components will add to or replace the existing components. Hence, the copy function can be used multiple times to generate incremental additions.

The copy function also works for an order-dependent BOM. The copy-to information identifies the specified production order number, and the copy-from can be another production order or a master BOM.

Mass Changes to Components Based on Where-Used Information Where-used information provides the basis for a mass replace and a mass add function for maintaining components. You perform a mass change of BOM information using the periodic task *Change BOM Item* You can select an item to be phased out or replaced, view the affected BOMs, selectively eliminate them from the update or change the required quantity, and then indicate when the new item should be phased in.

Graphical Tools for Maintaining BOM Information The BOM Designer provides a graphical tool for maintaining information about the

BOM versions (and route versions) for an item. The form displays a multi-level product structure with an indented graphical format. You can edit or delete existing components, or add components via drag-and-drop from the displayed list of item master data. This graphical tool is employed in other contexts, such as displaying the BOM information during sales order entry.

Analyzing BOM Information Analysis tools for BOM information include multi-level BOM reports, and a multi-level costed BOM with routing information (based on cost roll-up calculations). The analysis tools also include where-used inquiries about a component item and a master BOM.

There are two other types of where-used inquiries that reflect information about existing production orders and batch tracking. The first type includes single- and multi-level pegging to the sources of demand and supply. The second type includes forward and backward batch tracking throughout the product structure.

Additional Case Studies

Case 17: CAD/PLM Integration The product designers at a manufacturing company required integration between their computer-aided design (CAD) package and information about items and bills of material. For standard products, this involved importing information from the CAD package into the master BOM and viewing the CAD drawings via the document handling capabilities. The CAD package was used to generate 3D models (for viewing) and 2D layout drawings, and cut lists for assisting production personnel in completing the work. This integration helped reduce the man-hours to define drawings and bills, and the cost of errors such as production rework, field installation services and customer confidence.

Case 18: Kit Items A manufacturing company sold kits of material, where a separate item (and associated master BOM) defined each kit's components. Several types of kits could be sold. One type of kit was priced and sold as a single item, and posting the sales invoice resulted in backflushing of the item's components. Another type of kit was priced and sold as separate component items. Each sales order line for a kit item was exploded into its components, thereby creating multiple line items with separate prices that were shipped and invoiced separately. Other scenarios involved the selection of kit components from a predefined list, pricing based on the sum of sales prices for kit components, returns of an entire kit or selected components, and selective printing of kit information on sales-related documents.[4]

Case 19: Light Assembly A manufacturing company performed light assembly for both make-to-stock and make-to-order products, such as packaging purchased materials and painting/finishing items to customer specification. With stocked items, they used an order-less approach to reporting completed units that auto-deducted components. With make-to-order items, a production order was created from (and directly linked to) the sales order line item. Customer specifications were identified on the order-dependent BOM and routing.

Case 20: ECOs and Revision Levels A manufacturing company used Engineering Change Orders (ECOs) to manage changes to their product structure.[5] They required workflow capabilities for an ECO approval process, revision levels for purchased items (reflecting documentation changes) and revision levels for manufactured items (reflecting bill, routing, or documentation changes). The new revision level for a manufactured item, for example, could reflect a nonsignificant change (such as a new BOM version) or a significant change that required a new identifier for the item. The new identifier consisted of the item number and an additional field to identify a revision level.

Case 21: Engineering Versus Production BOMs The engineering department wanted to define a separate engineering BOM and then convert it into a BOM for production purposes. They defined a separate BOM version for a manufactured item that represented the engineering BOM. At the appropriate time, it was copied into a different BOM version for production purposes, and it was subsequently approved and activated for production. The starting effectivity date for the BOM version considered current inventories and other factors.

Case 22: Cut-To-Size Materials A fabricated products company needed to express BOM requirements in terms of the number of pieces of cut-to-size materials, such as steel rod and sheet metal, but did not want to

[4]See **www.AXtension.com** for additional information about their kitting add-on module for Dynamics AX.

[5]See **www.columbusglobal.com** for further information about the ECO capabilities within their Product Engineering module.

create item numbers for each unique size. They solved the problem using the calculation formula and measurements for a component's required quantity. One example involved sheet metal purchased in pounds, costed and stocked in 5 × 10 sheets, and with component requirements expressed in square feet. Each parent item produced from the sheet metal required different height and width measurements, but only one master BOM to calculate the required square footage in sheet-size increments (50 square feet). This approach also identified purchasing and stockroom picking requirements for the raw materials, and provided cut-to-size instructions for production.

Case 23: Phantoms for Intermediate Levels of Packaging A toy company produced and sold cases of toys to retailers, where each case included boxes of the individual toy. Each box represented the consumer unit and an intermediate level of packaging. Each case and box of the toy had separate item numbers, with different UPC codes, weights and measurements. The box with an individual toy was treated as a phantom in the product structure because the packaging line could insert the toy into a box and pack them immediately into cases. It was never stocked or sold separately. Figure 4.4 illustrates the phantom component in the product structure.

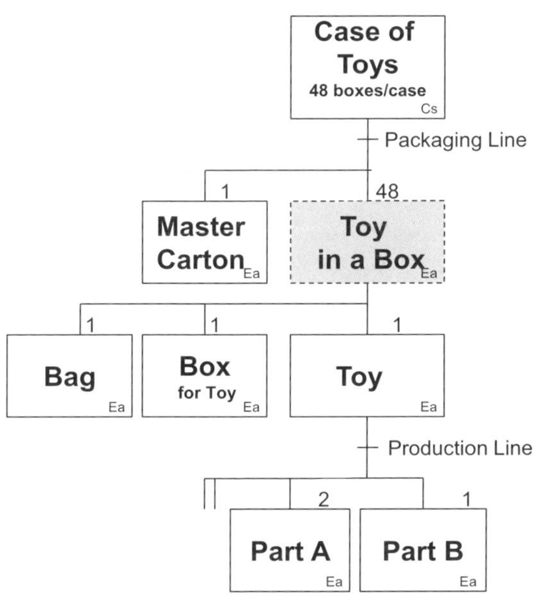

Figure 4.4 Phantoms for Intermediate Packaging Levels

Executive Summary

Discrete manufacturers typically employ bills of material to model their product structure. This chapter summarized a typical business process for defining an item's bill of material, and described the key information about BOM version policies and BOM lines. It explained the different approaches to maintaining and analyzing BOM information. Several case studies illustrated the use of BOM information, such as integration with a CAD package, engineering change control and kit items.

Chapter 5

Formula Information for Mixed Mode Scenarios

Some manufacturing operations involve a combination of discrete and process manufacturing scenarios, which is commonly termed mixed mode manufacturing. Examples of process manufacturing scenarios include the production of chemicals and polymer molded products. The mixed mode scenarios may exist in a single manufacturing site, or a multisite operation may have sites that reflect either a discrete or process manufacturing operation.

The terminology for product structure information often differs between discrete and process manufacturing scenarios. It is typically termed a bill of material (BOM) and a formula respectively. These terminology differences have a special significance within Dynamics AX because the software functionality differs. Dynamics AX employs an additional field—termed the Production Type—to designate whether a manufactured item employs a BOM versus formula approach to product structure information. The designation also impacts coordination of the item's manufacturing activities via production orders versus batch orders. The two approaches can be used together within the same product structure, such as a formula item that represents a component of a BOM item, and vice versa.

The two approaches reflect the design history of Dynamics AX, which initially employed the BOM approach (and production orders) and subsequently added the formula approach (and batch orders).[1] The formula approach provides additional functionality for supporting the requirements of process manufacturing, and for supporting several special cases in discrete manufacturing.

[1]The formula approach and its associated batch order were first incorporated into standard software functionality for AX 2009.

This book focuses on using Dynamics AX in discrete manufacturing.[2] For book length considerations, the explanation of mixed mode scenarios will focus on special cases in discrete manufacturing, and only provide a summary of the formula approach. The following sections reflect this focus:

1. Special Cases in Discrete Manufacturing
2. Significance of the Production Type for a Material Item
3. Typical Business Process for Defining an Item's Formula
4. Summary of the Formula Approach
5. Comparison of the BOM Versus Formula Approach

5.1 Special Cases in Discrete Manufacturing

Some discrete manufacturers have scenarios requiring a formula approach to product structure, and the corresponding use of batch orders to coordinate production activities. This section summarizes some common scenarios, and case studies at the end of the chapter provide further illustrations.

- *Polymer molded products.* One of the unique aspects of polymer molding involves the nature of a mold, since the mold is often designed with multiple cavities in order to produce multiple parts. The generation of multiple parts from a single production process must be modeled using the formula approach to product structure, since they represent co-products. Case 7 previously illustrated the use of formula information for polymer molded products.
- *Slitting rolled goods.* A slitting process often results in multiple slit widths. Using the formula approach, these can be modeled as multiple co-products of a single batch order, or as separate batch orders grouped together into a consolidated order. Cases 27 and 28 illustrate these two approaches to modeling a slitting process.
- *Strip down operation for used products.* The disassembly of a used product can result in multiple reusable parts, which represent co-products within the formula a the planning item. Case 29 illustrates a strip down operation for used devices.

[2]Previous books covering process manufacturing include *Managing Process Manufacturing Using Microsoft Dynamics AX 2009* and *Food Products Manufacturing Using Microsoft Dynamics AX 2012*. These books are available on Amazon.com.

- *Repair and overhaul.* A repair and overhaul business typically starts with a used item, and then goes through three phases (of strip down, repair and rebuild) to refurbish the item. Case 30 illustrates a repair and overhaul scenario.

The formula approach represents one aspect of using the process industry capabilities within AX 2012. Discrete manufacturers can benefit from several other process industry capabilities, including batch attributes (described in Section 9.4), vendor batch numbers (Section 9.3) and the enforcement of approved vendors for purchased material (Section 13.3).

5.2 Significance of the Production Type for a Material Item

The Production Type for a material item was previously introduced in the context of discrete manufacturing (see Section 3.7), and it represents company-level information impacting how the item can be used. The Production Type basically indicates whether an item is purchased or manufactured, and whether a manufactured item employs the BOM or formula approach to product structure information. However, it also has other significance about how an item can be used. The possible values and significance of the Production Type are summarized below, starting with the most common values.

- *None.* A production type of None indicates the item represents purchased material. You cannot define formula/BOM or routing information for the item, or create production/batch orders for the item. This production type also applies to items representing a service.
- *BOM.* A production type of BOM indicates a manufactured item, and you can define bill of material and routing information for the item. The item is termed a BOM item for short. The item can also be purchased, and the item's planned orders for a given site/warehouse can reflect planned production, purchases or transfers. Chapter 4 explained bill of material information.
- *Formula.* A production type of Formula indicates a manufactured item, and you can define formula and routing information for the item. The item is termed a formula item for short. The item can also be purchased,

and the item's planned orders for a given site/warehouse can reflect planned production, purchases or transfers. This chapter summarizes the formula information.

These first three values represent the most commonly used production types. The additional values support manufacturing scenarios involving co/by-products or planning items, as described below.

- *Co-Product or By-Product.* This production type must be assigned to an item representing a co-product or by-product, so that the item can be specified as such within the formula information. The item can also be purchased. For a co-product, the item's planned replenishment for a given site/warehouse can reflect planned purchases or transfers, or planned production of a specified parent item.
- *Planning Item.* A production type of Planning Item indicates a special case of a manufactured item, where the production process only results in co-products or by-products or both. The item is termed a Planning Item for short. You can define formula and routing information for the item, and this information can be used to calculate the costs of its co-products.

The Production Type of an item can be changed, such as changing a formula item to a BOM item. In this example, the change will delete the formula versions for the item (aka remove the assignment of the Master Formulas for the item), and you will need to create BOM information for the item. Changing the Production Type from a BOM item to a formula item has a similar impact.

Differences in the product structure information for a BOM item and formula item also mean that a bill of material cannot be copied to a formula, and vice versa. In a similar fashion, the order-dependent BOM for a production order cannot be copied to the order-dependent formula for a batch order, and vice versa.

5.3 Typical Business Process for Defining an Item's Formula

The typical business process for defining an item's formula shares many similarities to the definition of an item's bill of material. The primary dif-

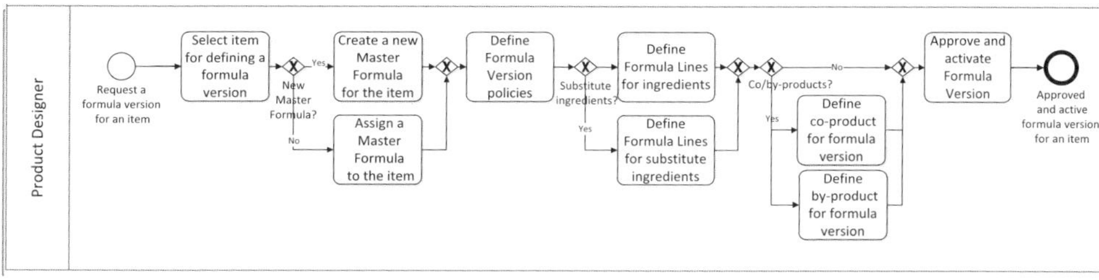

Figure 5.1 Typical Business Process for Defining an Item's Formula

ferences involve the additional options for defining substitute ingredients and co/by-products within the formula information. These additional steps are illustrated in Figure 5.1 and summarized below.

Overview As a starting point, the product designer selects the desired item and accesses a separate form in order to create a new formula version for the item, either by creating a new master formula or by assigning an existing master formula. The formula version policies include the formula size and effectivity dates. Each formula line identifies an ingredient and the required quantity. When applicable, a formula line can define an allowable substitute for an ingredient. Additional information can also be specified about the expected co/by-products of the production process, if any. Upon completion of all information, the product designer approves and activates the item's formula version.

Select the Item for Defining a Formula Version The product designer selects the desired item, which must be designated as a Formula Item or Planning Item (as defined by the Production Type assigned to the item) in order to access and define its formula information.

Create a New Master Formula for the Item The creation of a Master Formula typically occurs in the context of creating a new Formula Version for a selected item, where the Master Formula is automatically assigned to the item. Each assignment is termed a Formula Version, and an item may have multiple Formula versions, such as different versions that represent site-specific BOMs, planned changes or a different formula size and yield percentage.

Assign an Existing Master Formula to the Item An existing Master Formula can be assigned to an item, typically reflecting scenarios when the Master Formula has been defined beforehand for another item. Information about ingredients will be displayed. Information about co/by-products will not be displayed, since this information will need to be updated to reflect the formula version policies about formula size.

Define Formula Version Policies The product designer employs the formula version policies to specify the effectivity dates and to indicate whether the formula version represents a company-wide or site-specific formula. Other policies include the formula size and an expected yield percentage.

Define Formula Lines for Ingredients The product designer uses a formula line to identify an ingredient and the required quantity to produce the formula size. The required quantity can be expressed in different ways such as a quantity or percentage. Other considerations include the designated warehouse source of the ingredient and the applicable operation number.

Define Formula Lines for Substitute Ingredients The product designer uses a formula line to indicate an allowable substitute for a preferred ingredient. Multiple lines can be used to indicate multiple substitutes and their priority. Planning calculations will suggest a substitute ingredient for a planned order when there is insufficient inventory of the preferred ingredient.

Define a Co-Product for a Formula Version When applicable, the product designer employs an additional form to define the expected co-products for an item's Formula Version. These items must be designated with a Production Type of co-product or by-product. The expected output quantity for a co-product reflects the formula size. As an option, additional information can be specified to calculate the costs of a co-product.

Define a By-Product for a Formula Version When applicable, the product designer employs an additional form to define the expected by-products for an item's Formula Version. These items must be designated with a Production Type of co-product or by-product. The expected output quantity for a by-product reflects the formula size. As an option, additional information can be specified to allocate the costs associated with a by-product.

Approve and activate the Formula Version for the Item The Product Designer must approve a Formula Version before it can be specified for a batch order, and an approved version is typically activated for use in planning and costing calculations. Electronic signatures can be optionally employed as part of the approval process.

5.4 Summary of the Formula Approach

The formula approach to defining product structure has many similarities to the BOM approach described in the previous chapter. For example, the concepts of a Master BOM, BOM versions and BOM lines have a parallel within the formula approach. This section summarizes the formula approach, and the next section provides a more detailed comparison between the BOM and formula approaches.

Master Formulas and Formula Versions A master formula has a unique identifier (termed the *Formula Number*) which can be manually or automatically defined. The creation of a master formula typically occurs in the context of creating a formula for a manufactured item, where it is automatically assigned to the item. Each assignment of a master formula to an item is termed a *Formula Version.* A formula version has several policies, including a specified formula size. This policy is important because a formula line within the formula version defines an ingredient's required quantity in terms of the specified formula size.

Formula Version Policies for an Item The formula version polices serve several different purposes. Just like the BOM version policies, the formula version policies indicate (1) a site-specific versus company-wide formula version, (2) the effectivity dates for an item's formula version, and (3) the quantity breakpoints if applicable. The additional formula version policies include (4) the formula size and multiple and (5) a yield percentage. For supporting special cases, they also include (6) the designated bulk item for supporting consolidated orders, and (7) the ability to report unexpected co/by-products for a batch order.

Formula Lines for Ingredients A formula line is used to define each ingredient of a manufactured item. Just like a BOM line, the key aspects of a formula line include the item identifier of the ingredient, the required quantity, the associated operation number, and the warehouse source of the ingredient. However, an ingredient's required quantity reflects the formula size, and the requirement can be expressed as a quantity or percentage. A formula line can also indicate a substitute ingredient, as described in Case 26.

Co-Products and By-Products for a Formula Version A production process may generate co-products or by-products or both. A co-product represents a desirable or reusable output from a manufacturing process for a parent item, whereas a by-product typically represents waste. The differences between a co-product and by-product are reflected in different approaches to costing and master scheduling. For example, a co-product's costs can be calculated, and its requirements can result in the generation of planned batch orders for a designated parent item. In contrast, you can manually specify the costs for a by-product, and the cost calculations will add these costs to the parent item's costs. A by-product's requirements are ignored by master scheduling logic.

Each co/by-product must be identified by an item number, and explicitly designated as a co-product or by-product using the Production Type field. The item number can then be specified as a co-product (or by-product) when defining the formula version for a parent item, or when reporting the finished quantities of co/by-products for a batch order.

Planning Items and Formulas Some scenarios involve a production process that involves disassembly or grading that only results in co/by-products. The formula's parent item is simply used for planning purposes and is never received, therefore it is termed a planning item. The planning item must be identified by an item number, and explicitly designated on the item master with a *Production Type* of Planning Item. The formula version for the planning item defines the ingredient(s) and the expected co/by-products.

Bulk Items and Consolidated Orders Some process manufacturing scenarios involve batch orders for producing a bulk item, and additional batch orders for packaging the bulk into container variations that have unique item numbers. This is termed a bulk/pack production process or containerized packaging. Coordination of the related orders can be simplified by creating a Consolidated Order, and then assigning the related orders to the Consolidated Order. The concept of a consolidated order applies to other scenarios, as illustrated by Case 28 for slitting rolled goods. However, it is easiest to describe the functionality by referring to the bulk/pack scenario.

As part of the setup information, you specify the bulk item as an ingredient of each packed item, and also designate the bulk item in the formula version policies for each packed item. As a prerequisite step, you also define a ratio between these packed items and the item number for the bulk item. The ratio identifies how much of the bulk product is contained within each of the container variations, and the ratio can only be defined between formula items.

Catch Weight Items The formula approach supports catch weight items, either as an ingredient or as the parent item. A catch weight item is characterized by two units of measure—for pieces and weight—for reporting inventory transactions, although the formula information is always expressed in pieces.

Maintain Formula Information You can maintain formula information just like you maintain BOM information, such as using planned changes, the copy function, mass changes to components, and a graphical design tool. The analyses of formula information include multi-level and where-used viewpoints.

5.5 Comparison of the BOM Versus Formula Approach

The two different approaches to product structure information—termed the BOM approach and the Formula approach—must be considered when supporting special cases in discrete manufacturing. This section summarizes the differences in the two approaches. Both approaches employ a common foundation, so that terminology often represents the only difference. Figure 5.2 summarizes a comparison of the terminology for both approaches.

Common terminology can be used when functionality applies to both approaches, such as the terms *formula/BOM information* and *batch/production order*. The specific terms—such as *formula item* and *batch order*—can be used when the functionality only applies to one approach. The differences between the two approaches can be segmented into several topics, as summarized in the following subsections.

	AX Terminology	
	For the Formula Approach	**For the BOM Approach**
Production Type for the item	Formula Item*	BOM Item
Product Structure	Master Formula Formula Version Formula Line (aka Ingredient) Substitute ingredients Co/By-Products Catch Weight Items	Master BOM BOM Version BOM Line (aka Component) N/A N/A N/A
	For a Batch Order	**For a Production Order**
Production Activity	Batch Order Planned Batch Order Formula Lines for a Batch Order Co/By-Products for a Batch Order Catch Weight Items	Production Order Planned Production Order Production BOM N/A N/A

* = The formula approach also applies to a Production Type of planning item

Figure 5.2 Terminology for the Formula and BOM Approach

Basic Formula Information The basic information about product structure applies to both approaches, and terminology represents the major difference (with a few exceptions). For example, the terminology differences include a Master BOM and BOM versions versus a Master Formula and Formula Versions. The primary exception involves batch size considerations, as described below.

- *Batch size considerations for a formula item.* Batch size considerations are modeled as a specified formula size and multiple for the item's formula version. This means a component's required quantity is expressed per the specified formula size. The formula size has several other impacts. This includes the planned order quantity, the quantity for manually entered orders, and the quantity used in cost-roll-up calculations for amortizing constant costs of a manufacturing item. Order quantity modifiers about a minimum and maximum can also be defined.
- *Batch size considerations for a BOM item.* Batch size considerations are modeled by an item's order quantity modifiers, and component quantities

are typically expressed per one parent item (termed the per series quantity). There are several other impacts of the item's order quantity modifiers and standard order quantity. This includes the planned order quantity, the quantity for manually entered orders, and the quantity used in cost-roll-up calculations for amortizing constant costs of a manufacturing item.

Additional Formula Information The unique aspects include the yield percentage and formula size/multiple in formula version policies. Other unique aspects include the ability to express requirements as a percentage of the formula size, substitute ingredients, co-products and by-products, and the use of catch weight items for components or parent items. A unique aspect includes the designation of the bulk item associated with formula versions for items representing its packaging variations to support coordination of bulk/pack production. One other unique aspect includes a planning item, where the expected output only consists of co/by-products. A common capability to support quantity-sensitive formulations and routings is generally more applicable to process manufacturing environments.

Batch Tracking Considerations Applicable to Both Approaches These considerations include assignment of batch numbers to the finished quantities of batch/production orders. Batch-related information includes batch attributes, batch disposition codes (with restricted usage policies), and shelf life information.

Routing Information Applicable to Both Approaches The same routing information applies to both types of manufactured items and orders. This includes the use of master routings and routing versions, and the definition of resource requirements for an operation.

Differences in Product Costing The same concepts of product costing apply to both types of manufactured items. The only major differences involve the consideration of co/by-product costs and the basis for amortizing constant costs, as previously described for batch size considerations.

Differences in Planning Data The planning data is almost exactly the same for both types of manufactured items, with several exceptions. First, the planned order quantities reflect the differences in the above-described batch size considerations. Second, the yield percentage only applies to formula items. A third exception involves the planning data for a co-product item (when sourced from production rather than a transfer or purchase), since its replenishment will reflect planned batch orders for a designated parent item. A fourth exception involves a planning item, where the expected output only consists of co/by-products.

Differences in Master Scheduling Logic The master scheduling logic is almost exactly the same for both types of manufactured items, with several exceptions. The first four exceptions include the above-mentioned planning data. Additional exceptions include the planned batch orders to optimize bulk item production and its packaging variations, the assignment of substitute ingredients to planned batch orders, and the calculations for catch weight items.

Differences in Sales Order Processing Sales order processing is almost exactly the same for both types of manufactured items. One exception is that calculated sales price agreements based on commodity pricing only apply to formula items.

Differences in Batch/Production Order Processing The same order processing steps and concepts apply to both types of orders, and Figure 5.3 summarizes the common terminology.

There are several major differences in coordinating, reporting and costing the orders, as described below.

- *Coordination via planned orders*. The planned orders reflect differences in master scheduling logic, such as the planned order quantities, the assignment of substitute ingredients to a planned batch order, and planned batch orders for parent items to cover requirements for co-product items.
- *Coordination via consolidated orders*. You can create a consolidated order by consolidating and firming the planned batch orders for a bulk item and its packaging variations. A consolidated order can also be created manually, with manual assignment of existing batch orders. The consolidated order provides a single point for coordinating and reporting actual production for the related batch orders.

<table>
<tr><th></th><th colspan="2">Terminology</th></tr>
<tr><th></th><th>For a Batch Order</th><th>For a Production Order</th></tr>
<tr><td rowspan="2">Order Information</td><td colspan="2">Batch/Production Order
Planned Batch/Production Order
Order-Dependent Formula/BOM</td></tr>
<tr><td>Co/By-Products for a Batch Order</td><td>N/A</td></tr>
<tr><td>Production Activities</td><td colspan="2">Firm the planned order
Schedule the order
Report the order as started
Generate picking list and report material usage
Generate route card and report operation time/units completed
Report the finished quantity
Report the order as ended</td></tr>
<tr><td rowspan="2">Production Costs</td><td colspan="2">Price calculation inquiry
Order variances</td></tr>
<tr><td>Co/By-Product variances</td><td>N/A</td></tr>
</table>

Figure 5.3 Common Terminology for Batch/Production Orders

- *Reporting co/by-product receipts.* There may be changes to cost allocations and also standard cost variances related to finished quantities for co/by-products.
- *Assignment of a yield percentage to a batch order.* The yield percentage initially inherited from the formula version can be overridden.

Quality Management Considerations Applicable to Both Approaches These considerations include receiving inspection via quarantine orders, product testing via quality orders, batch disposition codes, MSDS documents, and coordination of quality-related activities. Chapter 18 explains quality management.

Applicability of Kanban Orders Kanban rules and their associated kanban orders seem to apply to both BOM items and Formula items, but these capabilities have not yet been verified in my testing efforts. Chapter 15 explains kanban orders.

Applicability of Configuration Technologies The variations of configuration technologies always apply to BOM items, and sometimes apply to

Formula items, as summarized below. Chapter 7 explains configuration technologies.

- *Predefined Variants.* This approach applies to BOM items and Formula items.
- *Bill of Options Approach.* This approach only applies to a BOM item.
- *Rules-based Configuration Approach.* This approach employs a product model to map the prompts and their responses into the desired BOM information for a configuration. They cannot be mapped into formula information. Hence, the approach only applies to BOM items.
- *Constraint-Based Configuration Approach.* This approach has the above-mentioned problem in mapping into formula information, so it only applies to BOM items.

Additional Case Studies

Case 24: Cleaning Equipment and its Solvent A manufacturer of cleaning equipment also produced the cleaning solvent used by the equipment. Formula information and batch orders were used to coordinate production of the cleaning solvent, whereas BOM information and production orders were used for coordinating equipment production, especially the customized equipment that was configured to customer specification.

Case 25: Lawn Furniture and its Webbing A manufacturer of lawn furniture also produced a key component—the slit webbing—from rolled goods. Formula information and batch orders were used to coordinate production of the rolled goods and slit webbing, whereas BOM information and production orders applied to the furniture.

Case 26: Substitution Logic for a Component The production planner at a manufacturing firm was trying to decide whether to use the substitute component logic within AX. With this logic, master scheduling automatically considers a substitute component when there is insufficient inventory of the original component, and then assigns the appropriate substitute component to the formula lines for a planned batch order. Hence, the formula lines may include some of the original component and some of the substitute component.[3] This logic requires the definition of the original component and the substitute component as separate formula lines within the formula version for a manufactured item. You also indicate the relationship by assigning a user-defined plan group and a priority to both lines. The substitute component logic only applies to planned batch orders generated by the master scheduling task; the logic does not apply to manually created batch orders.

Case 27: Slitting Rolled Goods A slitter process for a rolled product such as paper or metal results in one or more slit rolls. The simplest example of a slitter process results in the same item number, as illustrated in left side of Figure 5.4 for producing multiple slit rolls of 2 inch width (the item's UM = Linear Yards or LY for short) from a master roll of 60 inch width (the item's UM = Square Yards or SY for short). In this example, an extrusion process produces the master roll from various resins, and the slitter and extruder process can generate a regrind co-product.

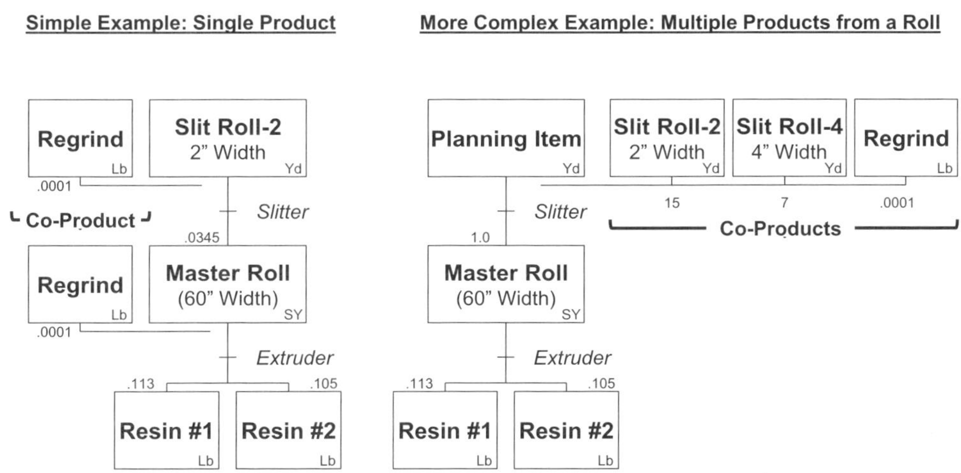

Figure 5.4 Example Formulas for Slitting a Rolled Product

[3]The master scheduling logic will also assign the original component to a planned batch order when there is no available inventory of any substitute.

A slightly more complex example of a slitter process results in multiple item numbers, where the same items are produced every time. The right side of Figure 5.4 illustrates the definition of a planning item, and its co-products of two different slit rolls with 2 inch and 4 inch widths. This concept can be extended to partially model the most complex example, where multiple different items are produced by slitting a master roll. The combination of different items typically reflects trim optimization logic performed by a separate software package. Predefined item numbers can provide an approximation of the unique widths for the slit rolls generated by the slitting process, and the batch number can identify the exact width of a slit roll. With this scenario, there are some cases in which you can predefine the co-products in the formula information, although most cases will report the actual co-products as manually specified lines in the report-as-finished journal for the batch order.

Case 28: Consolidated Orders for Slitting Rolled Goods A manufacturer of rolled goods was considering different approaches to coordinate slitting operations. One approach identified the 60-inch width master roll as a bulk item, with an inventory UM of linear yards. Item numbers representing the various slit widths were defined with an inventory UM of linear yards, and their formula versions identified the bulk item in the header information and as a component. The component's required quantity was also reflected in the definition of bulk item conversion factors. Using this approach, the master scheduling logic suggested planned batch orders for the bulk item and the slit items, which provided some basic optimization for producing master rolls. When viewing the planned orders, the production scheduler consolidated and firmed the batch orders to reflect trim optimization logic. The resulting consolidated order provided a single point for reporting actual production activities about slit products.

Case 29: Strip Down Operation A manufacturing company purchased several types of used consumer electronics devices, and stripped them down to obtain reusable parts that could be sold. Figure 5.5 illustrates the planning item for disassembling one type of used device (Device XYZ), along with its sole component and its multiple co-products of several reusable parts. The expected quantity of each co-product reflected the reusable fraction that could be obtained from used devices. Unusable parts were thrown into a waste container, and the company paid a disposal fee per pound of waste. The item number for this waste was identified as a by-product, with an inventory UM of pounds and a cost reflecting the disposal fee per pound. From an S&OP perspective, the management team defined sales forecasts for the planning items that represented different used devices, and planning calculations identified the expected receipts of reusable parts.

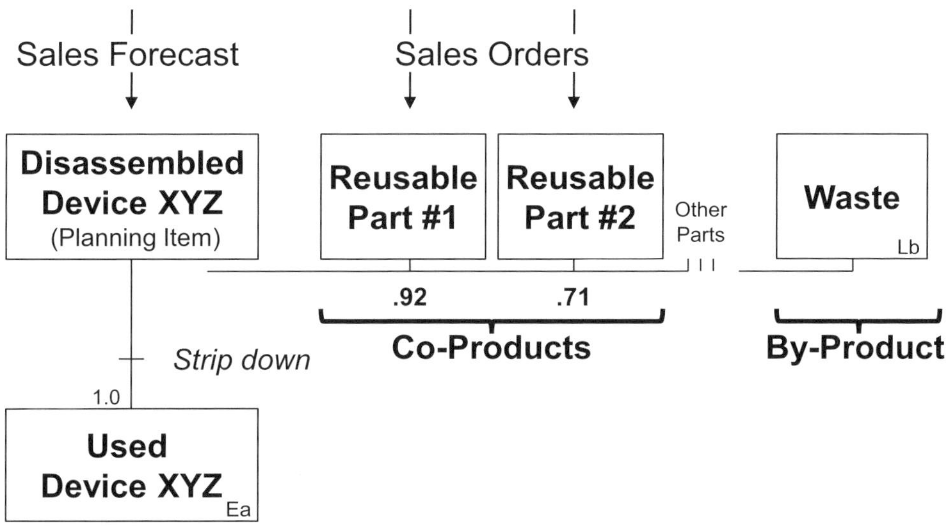

Figure 5.5 Strip Down of Used Consumer Electronics Device

Case 30: Repair and Overhaul of Used Equipment A repair-and-overhaul business typically starts with a used item, and then goes through three phases (strip-down, repair and rebuild) to refurbish the item. Examples of used items may be transportation equipment, engines, auto parts, computers or other types of equipment. The used items may reflect a customer supplied item, a customer return, or purchases of used equipment. Figure 5.6 illustrates the formula for a typical scenario, where a planning item represents the disassembled equipment, and co-products represent the reusable parts (with a decimal quantity reflecting the fraction that can actually be reused).

In this example, the Used Part-1 must be repaired and Used Part-3 can be "used as is." The figure shows a used assembly (Used Assy-2) that requires repair. However, it could be the starting point for further strip-down, which

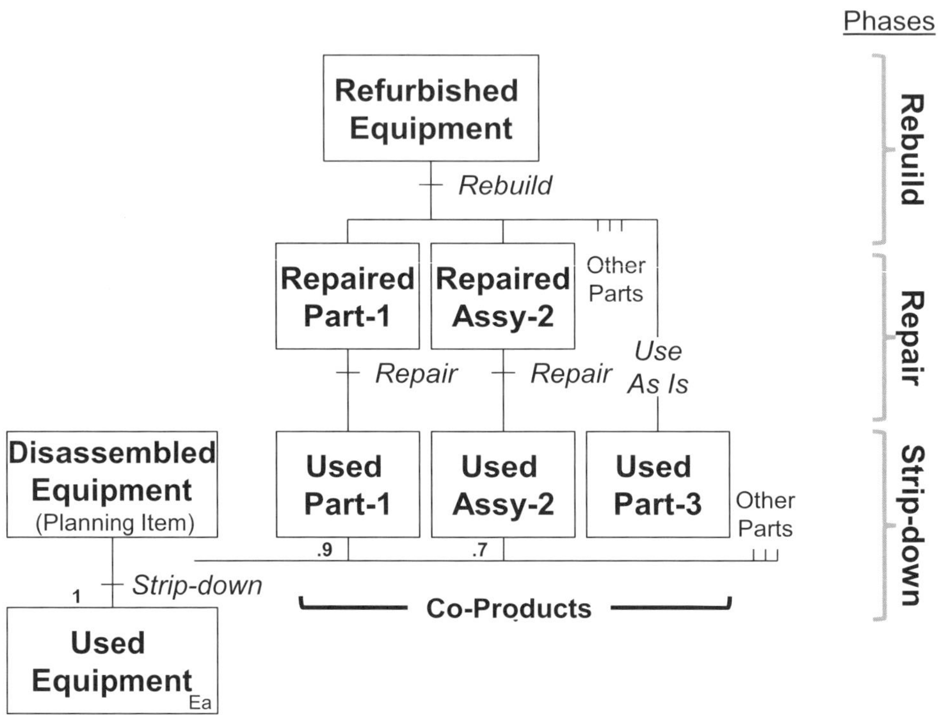

Figure 5.6 Formula for Repair and Overhaul of Used Equipment

means it would be the only component of another planning item with co-products representing the expected parts. In many scenarios, inspection of the used equipment may identify the need for a predefined or ad hoc repair procedure. A predefined repair procedure can be modeled as an item number with predefined BOM and routing information, and a production order is used to report completion of the task. Ad hoc procedures are also modeled as an item number, but the required materials and labor are defined in the order-dependent BOM and routing. This example represents combination of the BOM and Formula approaches, since the formula and batch orders for a planning item model the strip-down steps and production orders can model the repair/rebuild steps.

Executive Summary

Some operations involve a combination of discrete and process manufacturing scenarios. These scenarios may exist in a single manufacturing site, or a multisite operation may have sites that reflect either a discrete or process manufacturing operation. Dynamics AX supports two approaches to product structure—termed the BOM approach and the Formula approach—for supporting these discrete and process environments. The two approaches can be used together in the same product structure.

The chapter focused on special cases in discrete manufacturing requiring a formula approach to product structure, and provided several illustrative case studies such as rolled goods, strip down, and repair/overhaul of used equipment. It described the typical business process for defining an item's formula, summarized the key aspects of the formula approach, and provided a comparison between the formula and BOM approaches.

Chapter 6

Resources and Routings

Routing information provides a model of the processing steps for a manufactured item, expressed as operations within a routing. Each operation identifies its resource requirements. A single version of an item's routing may be sufficient in some scenarios, but many scenarios require multiple route versions in order to model variations in the manufacturing process. For example, the route versions may reflect planned changes to the manufacturing process (such as new equipment or a different factory layout) or variations between sites producing the same item.

This chapter covers information about resources and routings. It starts with a typical business process to define production resources, and provides more detailed explanations about several steps in this business process. It also explains the typical business process to define routing information, which builds on an understanding of master routings and their assignment to items. More detailed explanations cover several steps in this business process, such as the definition of master operations and the feasibility of an item's route version. Additional sections explain the maintenance of routing information, scheduling method considerations, and alternatives to the use of routing information. The chapter includes the following sections:

1. Typical Business Process to Define Production Resources
2. Define Resources and Resource Groups
3. Define Capabilities and Assign to Resources
4. Define Competencies and Assign to Employees
5. Master Routings and Route Versions
6. Typical Business Process to Define Routing Information
7. Define Master Operations

8. Define an Internal Operation in a Routing
9. Review Feasibility of Resource Requirements
10. Scheduling Method: Job Versus Operation Scheduling
11. Order-Dependent Routing for a Production Order
12. Maintain Routing Information
13. Alternatives to the Use of Routing Information

When defining routing information—and the resource requirements for an operation—there are multiple scenarios involving preferred equipment for producing an item. These scenarios include a dedicated machine (specified as the required resource for the operation) and a machine within an interchangeable group of machines (specified as the required resource group for the operation). Other scenarios may involve a preferred machine based on the required capability or minimum capability, or the production quantity (specified as a different route version with a quantity breakpoint). The chapter explains the solution approaches to various scenarios for preferred equipment.

6.1 Typical Business Process to Define Production Resources

A typical business process consists of several basic steps to define each production resource and its resource group. An internal resource often represents a machine, a type of production worker, or a specific employee. It can also represent some other capacity constraint or costing consideration. A resource group represents similar resources in close proximity within the same site. A resource or a resource group can then be specified as the resource requirement for a routing operation.

Additional steps may be involved for modeling resource capabilities or employee competencies. Resource capabilities, for example, can be used to model alternate resource logic based on a prioritized list of preferred resources or a minimum level of capability. Employee competencies apply to scenarios with highly skilled employees as a scheduling constraint, where you define an employee competency (such as skills, certifications or courses) as the resource requirement for an operation, and maintain information about each employee's competencies. Figure 6.1 illustrates these steps and their applicable roles for three variations of production resources—representing

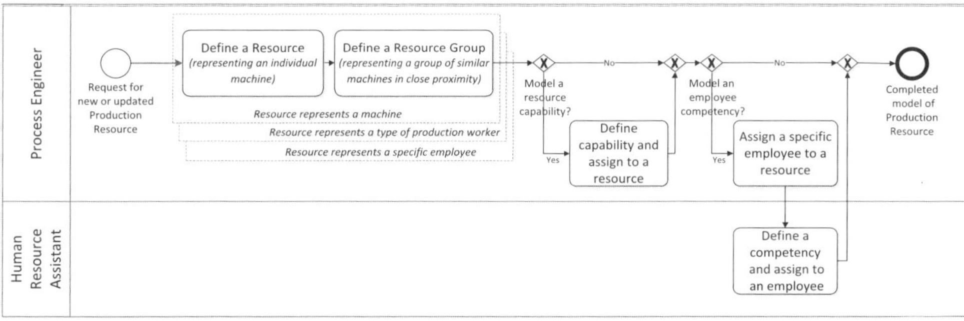

Figure 6.1 Typical Business Process to Define Production Resources

a machine, a type of production worker, and a specific employee—as illustrated by the three boxes within the figure.

Define a Resource Representing a Machine A process engineer role typically has the responsibility for defining a production resource that represents a machine, and assigning it to a resource group that represents similar machines in close proximity within the same site.[1] A machine may subsequently be moved to a different location, which can be modeled in terms of validity dates for the assignment to a resource group. The basic information for a resource includes a calendar of working hours and a designation whether its available capacity should be considered finite or infinite. Since multiple time elements can be specified for performing an operation at the resource—such as run time, transit time and queue times—you may also need to designate the scheduling significance of each time element. The relevant costs (aka machine rate code) may also be assigned to the resource, such as the hourly costs for run time and setup time.

Define a Resource Representing a Production Worker or a Specific Employee A production resource can represent a type of production worker or a specific employee, and you assign it to a resource group that represents similar workers in close proximity within the same site. A

[1]A scenario involving a unique machine often requires a resource group with only one resource that reflects the unique machine.

worker may subsequently be assigned to a different group, as identified by the validity dates of the assignment. The crew size requirements for an operation can be modeled by specifying the required resource group and the number of resources.

Define Capabilities and Assign to Resources The process engineer defines capabilities and assigns capabilities to a resource, where the resource typically represents a machine or production worker. A capability can be assigned to one or more resources, and a resource can have more than one capability assigned to it. The process engineer can then define a capability as the resource requirement of a routing operation. When assigning a capability to multiple resources, the process engineer can specify the priority associated with each resource so that the priorities will be considered by the scheduling logic. In addition, the process engineer can define a capability level for a resource, expressed as a numeric value (such as 50 tons for a press). The process engineer can then define the minimum required capability level as the resource requirement for an operation so that the capability levels will be considered by scheduling logic in determining which resource should perform the operation.

Assign a Specific Employee to a Human Resource The process engineer defines a human resource to represent an individual employee, and assigns the employee number to the resource. After competencies have been defined and assigned to employees, the process engineer can define an employee competency as the resource requirement for an operation.

Define Competencies and Assign to Employees A human resource assistant typically defines employee-related competencies such as certifications, skills, and courses, and maintains the assignment of competencies to employees. As an illustrative example concerning certifications, the human resource assistant defines the possible types of certifications and assigns a certification (and a starting date for the certification) to employees. The process engineer can then specify a required certification as part of the resource requirements for a routing operation. Similar steps apply to the use of skills and courses as the basis for human resource requirements.

6.2 Define Resources and Resource Groups

Resources and resource groups represent two of the primary approaches for specifying the resource requirements for a routing operation.[2] The other primary approaches include resource capabilities and employee competencies, as explained in subsequent sections. A resource may represent a machine, an individual worker, a tool, or some other type of capacity constraint or manufacturing cost. It may also represent a tightly linked group of machines or a manufacturing cell that can be treated as single resource. Each resource must belong to a resource group, where the group typically represents similar resources located in close proximity within the same site. You can specify a resource or a resource group as the resource requirement for a routing operation.

Identification of Resources and Resource Groups A resource has a unique identifier and description, and a resource group also has a unique identifier and description.

Type of Resource The common types consist of a machine or human resource, and sometimes a vendor when the scenario involves subcontract manufacturing. Only the designation of a human resource has any significance, since it acts as a prerequisite for the assignment of an employee number and the use of employee competencies. Some suggested guidelines for identifying resources and resource groups are provided below.

- *Machine.* A machine resource often represents a single machine, but it may also represent a tightly linked group of machines that acts as a single entity for capacity planning and scheduling purposes. The resource capacity for a single machine is typically expressed as one.

  When defining a resource group related to machines (and then assigning machines to the group), the grouping typically represents machines in close physical proximity with similar characteristics in terms of capabilities and operating costs.

  A machine resource is sometimes used to model a miscellaneous area comprised of a mixture of personnel and equipment performing various operations. This provides the basis for defining routing operations, and

[2] The constructs of Resources and Resource Groups within AX 2012 replace the constructs of Work Centers and Work Center Groups that were used in previous versions of Dynamics AX.

an approximation of costing, capacity planning, and scheduling considerations. The resource capacity provides an approximation of how many operations can be concurrently processed within the miscellaneous area.

- *Human Resource.* A human resource typically represents a specific person (with optional assignment of the employee number) or a type of worker. As one example, the type of worker could be "machine operator," so that a workforce of ten operators would be represented by ten different resources that are identified by Operator-1, Operator-2 and so forth.

  When defining a resource group related to human resources, the grouping typically represents a labor pool or a team of people in close physical proximity with similar characteristics in terms of capabilities and labor rates. In this way, you can model crew size requirements in a routing operation by specifying the resource group and the number of required people within the group.
- *Vendor.* A vendor resource typically represents a specific subcontractor (with optional assignment of the vendor number) that performs subcontract manufacturing using supplied material. Chapter 16 provides further explanation of how to model subcontract manufacturing.
- *Tool.* A tool resource is rarely specified unless it represents a critical scheduling constraint. Examples of a tool include a serialized die, mold or reuseable fixture. A tool is typically specified as a secondary resource for performing an operation. A resource group for tooling generally represents several serial numbers of the exact same tool. A tool resource does not support tool inventory management or the tracking of tool cycle usage (e.g., for triggering replacement or rebuild). A serialized tool must be identified as an item to support these purposes.
- *Location.* A location resource is conceptually similar to a tool resource, and is rarely specified unless it represents a critical scheduling constraint. One example would a clean room. The clean room would typically be specified as a secondary resource for performing an operation. A resource group could represent several clean rooms. Modeling a location as a resource simply provides a scheduling constraint. Actual inventory locations must be defined in terms of the site, warehouse and bin location.

Guidelines for Specifying a Resource or Resource Group in a Routing Operation Several factors must be considered in choosing whether to designate a resource or a resource group for performing an operation. The following guidelines focus on machines and human resources.

- *Specify a Resource for the Operation.* This approach assumes the operation can only be performed at the specified machine, where the operation identifies the machine-specific times and costs. A similar assumption applies to a specified human resource, where the resource represents a production worker or a specific employee.
- *Specify a Resource Group for the Operation* This approach assumes the operation can be performed on any machine within the group, and the machines have similar run times and cost structures. As part of defining a routing operation, you specify which machine will provide the default values for cost information, and which machine will provide the default values for time requirements. The same machine can be specified for both sets of default values. This information will be used in cost roll-up calculations and scheduling calculations. The scheduling calculations for planned orders will assign a specific machine (within the group) to an operation in order to meet the due date.

  With human resources, the resource group typically represents a group of individuals with interchangeable skills and similar hourly rates. When defining an operation for the resource group, you can specify the required number of people (aka crew size) for the operation. You can also specify which human resource will provide the default values for cost information. The scheduling calculations will assign specific human resources (within the group) to an operation in order to meet the due date and crew size requirements.

Changing the Assignment of a Resource to a Resource Group In a static environment, you assign a resource to a single resource group. In a dynamic environment with changing assignments, you indicate the expiration date for the current assignment, and also indicate the new assignment. For example, a piece of equipment or a person may be moved to a different site, which would be modeled by assigning the resource to a different resource group. Note that a site is assigned to a resource group, and the site applies to all resources assigned to the group.

Production Unit for a Resource Group A production unit represents multiple resource groups located within a manufacturing site. It provides a grouping of resource groups. After defining a production unit, you assign it to the relevant resource groups. This enables you to view aggregate capacity requirements for all associated resources within the production unit, and also perform filtering of information on forms and printed documents.

A production unit also represents those resources that obtain component material from the same warehouse. In this context, you can assign a picking warehouse to a production unit, and the linkage between a production unit and a resource enables the system to determine the warehouse source of components for operations performed at the resource. This is termed resource consumption logic for the warehouse source of component material, as described in Section 4.4.

Available Capacity for a Resource A resource's available capacity is defined by two basic factors: the calendar defining the hours of operation and the capacity per hour.

- *Hours of Operation*. The calendar assigned to a resource center defines the hours of operation (such as 7:00 a.m. to 4:00 p.m.) for each calendar day. Exceptions to this calendar of daily working hours can be specified for the individual resource, or for all resources using the assigned calendar.
- *Capacity per Hour*. A single resource that can perform one task at a time has a capacity of 1.00 during working hours. However, a resource sometimes represents a number of people or machines, where more than one task can be performed at the same time. The average number of concurrent tasks is termed the *resource capacity*. With a capacity of 5, for example, up to 5 different operations can be scheduled concurrently for each hour of operation.

The system calculates a resource's available capacity based on a periodic task to compose working times. The system also calculates available capacity for a resource group (and for a production unit) based on the sum of available capacities of its related resources.

A third factor—termed the *operations scheduling percentage* for a resource—affects how scheduling logic views the resource's available capacity. A scheduling percentage of 80%, for example, means that the scheduling logic will only consider 80% of the available capacity when assigning loads to the resource. This approach provides flexibility for handling unexpected time requirements at the resource.

Infinite Versus Finite Available Capacity for a Resource A resource's available capacity can be designated as finite or infinite for scheduling purposes. An infinite capacity viewpoint means that scheduling logic ignores existing loads when scheduling a given order, but still considers constraints related to hours of operation and concurrent task capabilities to calculate operation durations. An analysis of resource load versus capacity can be used to identify overloaded periods, so that adjustments can be made to loads or available capacity.

A finite capacity viewpoint means that scheduling logic considers current loads and the concurrent task capability for each resource when scheduling a given order. Finite capacity considerations can be optionally included/excluded when performing the master scheduling task or when scheduling individual orders.

Designating Bottleneck Resources for Finite Capacity Planning Purposes The optional designation of a bottleneck resource can improve performance of planning calculations. Additional master plan policies must be defined for the use of bottleneck scheduling and for three time fence policies related to bottleneck scheduling (the finite capacity time fence, the backward capacity time fence, and the bottleneck capacity time fence).

Efficiency The time requirements expressed in routing operations can be factored up or down based on the efficiency percentage assigned to the resource. The resource's efficiency percentage acts as a default in the resource's assigned calendar. The efficiency for selected working times (such as a lower efficiency for late night hours) can then be manually overridden in the calendar.

Resource Costs The costs associated with a resource are typically expressed in terms of hourly rates for setup and processing time.[3] That is, you define hourly rates for a cost category, and assign the cost category to a resource. Different cost categories must be defined for each labor rate or machine rate, and different categories may be needed to differentiate the rates related to setup or run time. You also assign a cost group to a cost category, which supports cost group segmentation in the calculated costs for a manufactured item. The costs associated with setup and run times are normally included in the cost calculations. You can selectively exclude these costs based on the policies embedded in the Routing Group assigned to a resource. Chapter 8 provides further explanation of product costing, and the definition of costs for resources (Section 8.5).

[3] Costs can also be defined in terms of piece rates for output units. The concept may apply to labor that is paid on a piece rate basis, or to the allocation of overhead costs per unit of output.

Time Reporting and Auto-Deduction Policies The time associated with processing and setup can be manually reported or auto-deducted, as indicated by *Automatic Route Consumption* policies embedded in the Routing Group assigned to a resource.

Block Scheduling via Properties Block scheduling represents one approach to scheduling similar operations together, and involves the use of properties in two ways. First, a property must be assigned to a specified block of working time within the resource's calendar.[4] Second, a property must be assigned to operations. Scheduling logic can then schedule operations with the same property to the designated block of time, thereby helping to minimize setups for similar operations.

Summarized Information for a Resource A resource's statistics summarizes available capacity, actual reported time, and a capacity utilization percentage for the current accounting period, current year to date, and the preceding year. A resource's load inquiry summarizes available capacity, expected load, and a capacity utilization percentage for various time increments, such as months and weeks. It also provides drill down to the orders causing the expected load.

Aggregate Capacity and Loads for a Resource Group The aggregate capacity for a resource group is based on the sum of available capacity for the related resources. The aggregate load for the resource group includes the time requirements for its related resources. An analysis of aggregate load versus capacity can help anticipate overloaded periods.

6.3 Define Capabilities and Assign to Resources

Capabilities provide one approach for modeling the resource requirements of a routing operation, and they apply to any type of resource. They build on the use of resources described in the previous section. You assign a capability to one or more resources, and a resource can have more than one

[4]Block scheduling requires that the resource must be flagged as having a finite property, and that production orders must be scheduled based on a finite property.

capability assigned to it. In addition, you specify the required capability for a performing a routing operation.

Each capability has a user-defined identifier and description, and you specify a list of which resources can provide the capability. Conversely, you can assign a capability to resource. The following subsections provide guidelines concerning the definition and use of resource capabilities.

Specify Date Effectivities of the Resource Capability Each resource assigned to a capability can be assigned a starting and ending effectivity date. A resource can be listed more than once with different effectivity dates, typically to represent a capability that cannot be performed for a period of time. When a requirement date for the capability falls outside of the effective period, the resource will not be scheduled by the planning calculations.

Assign Priorities to Support Alternate Resource Logic Each resource assigned to a capability can be assigned a numeric priority, where a value of 0 (or 1) represents the highest priority. The priority provides the basis for alternate resource logic in planning calculations.[5] That is, the resource with the highest priority will be considered first by the scheduling logic. The resource with the next-highest priority will only be considered when the requirement date cannot be met.

Specify the Level of Capability to Support Alternate Resource Logic The level of capability provides an additional basis for determining whether a resource can satisfy the capability. You specify the capability level as numeric value. In a similar fashion, you specify a value for the minimum level needed as part of the resource requirements in a routing operation. The scheduling logic will only consider resources in the list with an equal or higher value than the minimum level needed.

An example concerning presses illustrates how to use these two values. Let's say we have three machine resources that represent a 20-ton press, a 50-ton press, and a 100-ton press. The first step is to define a capability termed Press, and assign the three resources to the capability. The three resources are assigned a capability level of 20, 50 and 100 respectively. As

[5] A policy— termed *primary resource selection*— determines whether scheduling logic assigns resources based on *duration* or *priority*. Selecting a policy value of *priority* supports alternate resource logic based on priorities. The policy can be company-wide or site-specific, as defined on the Scheduling Parameters or Scheduling Parameters by Site form.

the second step, you assign the minimum level needed to perform a routing operation requiring the Press capability. Let's say the value of the minimum level needed is 40. At this point, the scheduling logic considers the requirement specified for the operation (of 40) in selecting which resource can satisfy the requirement, which means only the 50-ton and 100-ton presses would be considered.

Specify the Capability as the Resource Requirement for a Routing Operation One or more capabilities can be specified as the resource requirements for a routing operation. Since the required capability may be satisfied by different resources, you should specify the approximate costs for performing the operation. These hourly rates can be manually specified using the cost category fields, or the cost categories can be initially populated by specifying a "costing resource" for the operation. A subsequent section provides further explanation about defining an internal operation in a routing.

Case 31: Preferred Equipment for a Capability

The production supervisor wanted to schedule production using the optimal packaging line (out of the three possible packaging lines). When the optimal packaging line was fully booked, the production could be scheduled on another line. To support this logic, the operation's resource requirements (in the route version for each manufactured item) were defined for a "packaging line" capability, and the capability was assigned to the three packaging lines along with a priority sequence. In this way, the scheduling logic assigns the optimal line to meet the production due date. If the due date cannot be met, the scheduling logic assigns a different line based on the prioritized list.

Case 32: Preferred Equipment Based on Minimum Capability

The production supervisor wanted to schedule production using the optimal packaging line (out of the three possible packaging lines). One packaging line could only handle small packages, another line could handle small or medium packages (but not large packages), and the third line could handle any package size. To support this logic, the operation's resource requirements (in the route version for each manufactured item) were defined for a "packaging line" capability and a minimum capability level of 1, 2 or 3 (that represented the three package sizes). The capability and a capability level were also assigned to the three packaging lines. In this way, the scheduling logic would only assign production to a packaging line that could meet the minimum required capability. For example, large packages were only assigned to the packaging line that could handle them.

6.4 Define Competencies and Assign to Employees

Some production environments require scheduling of highly skilled employees with specific competencies, such as a certification, course, or skill level. After defining a competency, you maintain the related information about each employee's competencies as part of the employee master information. You also define the competency as one of the resource requirements for a routing operation. This approach to resource requirements only applies to resources (with a type of human resource) representing individual employees where the employee number has been specified. The following subsections provide guidelines concerning the definition and use of employee competencies.

Employee Skills A skill has a user-defined identifier and description, and also a rating model consisting of a rating and skill level. You assign an actual skill (and a starting date for the skill) to an employee, and an employee can have more than one skill. In addition, you specify the skill as the required resource for a performing a routing operation.

Employee Certifications A certification type has a user-defined identifier and description. You assign a certification type (and a starting date for the certification) to an employee, and an employee can have more than one certification. In addition, you specify the certificate as the required resource for a performing a routing operation.

Employee Course A course has a user-defined identifier and description. You assign a course (and a completion date for the course) to an employee, and an employee can have more than one course. In addition, you specify the course as the required resource for a performing a routing operation.

6.5 Master Routings and Route Versions

The concept of a master routing enables you to define it once, and then assign it to multiple items with the same production process. When you create a master routing, the identifier (termed a *Route Number*) can be automatically or manually assigned, as defined by the number sequence policy for Route Numbers. Manual assignment should be used when the master routing identifier needs to be meaningful, such as the process specification for a common routing or the item number for an item-specific routing.

After creating a master routing identifier, you can define the associated operations and also assign the master routing to relevant items. Each assignment is termed a *Route Version*, and a manufactured item can have multiple route versions. Each route version must be site-specific, and the associated operations must reflect resources within the site. Planning calculations will use an item's site-specific routing version based on the site of the requirement.

Creating and Assigning a Master Routing There are two basic approaches for creating and assigning master routings, as described below. Each assignment is termed a *Route Version*.

- *Create a new routing for an item.* This approach starts from a selected item (on the Released Products form), where you access its routing information in order to create a new master routing and define its operations. The new master routing is automatically assigned to the item. There is a single approval step, which results in approval of the master routing and the route version.

  As an alternative to creating a new master routing for an item, you can assign an existing one to the item. This alternative represents a "new" assignment for an existing master routing; the assignment can also be "deleted." Each assignment requires a separate approval step. The assignment of a master routing to relevant items is also employed in the second approach.
- *Create a master routing and assign to items.* This approach starts from the list of master routings (termed the All Routes form), where you create

a master routing and its operations, and then assign it to the relevant items.[6] There is an approval step for the master routing, and a separate approval step for each assignment (aka the route version). The creation of a master routing can also originate from the first approach, so that it can be subsequently assigned to other items.

Approved and Active Route Versions A master routing and a route version must be approved, as described above. You can optionally employ electronic signatures as part of the approval process, as previously described for approving BOM information (in Section 4.2).

Only an approved route version for a manufactured item can be marked as active. The active route version for a manufactured item will normally be used in planning and cost calculations. There are several scenarios requiring multiple active route versions for an item, and even multiple approved-but-not active route versions, as described in the next topic.

Rationale for Multiple Route Versions for a Manufactured Item A manufactured item can have multiple active route versions that reflect different sites, non-overlapping validity periods, and/or different quantity breakpoints. Other route versions may be approved but not active, typically to model an alternate production process. The reasons for multiple route versions are explained below.

- *Routing Variations between Sites Producing the Same Manufactured Item.* The site-specific route versions reflect variations in the resources and operations for producing the item.
- *Planned Changes with Effectivity Dates.* The multiple route versions can represent planned changes to the production process, where each route version has a different validity period. For example, a manufactured item may have two route versions—one valid to date X and the other valid from date X+1—to indicate planned changes.
- *Variations Due to Order Quantities.* The multiple route versions can represent variations in the preferred production process for larger order quantities, where each route version has a different quantity breakpoint. For example, a route version can reflect use of a faster equipment for producing a large order quantity.

[6]The assignment of master routings to a manufactured item can be assisted by an attribute (the item group) assigned to each master routing. Based on this attribute, the drop-down list of master routings can display the subset with an item group that matches the manufactured item.

- *Alternate Routings.* Additional route versions can represent alternate processes for producing the manufactured item. The alternate would be an approved-but-not-active route version that could be specified for a manually created production order or rework order. It could also be specified for a sales order line item (for a make-to-order product) or for a BOM line about a manufactured component (for a make-to-order component), so that planning calculations employ the specified route version rather than the active route version.
- *Routings for Prototypes or Production Ramp-Up.* A different route version may identify the production process for prototypes or different stages of production ramp-up.

In summary, a manufactured item can have multiple active route versions that reflect different sites, non-overlapping validity periods, and/or different quantity breakpoints. An item can also have approved-but-not-active route versions.

Case 33: Preferred Equipment Based on Production Quantity

The production supervisor at a manufacturing firm wanted to schedule production using the optimal equipment for small and large order quantities. The large order quantities (over 1,000) were produced on larger faster equipment. To support this logic, two different route versions were defined for the relevant manufactured items, where the quantity breakpoint for one route version reflected 1,000 units. This route version contained an operation with resource requirements for handling a large quantity, and the other route version contained an operation with resource requirements for handling the small quantity. In this way, the planning calculations assign the optimal route version to a planned production order based on the required quantity.

6.6 Typical Business Process to Define Routing Information

A typical business process to define routing information builds on an understanding of master routings and route versions. In summary, you define a master routing consisting of one or more operations and assign it to the appli-

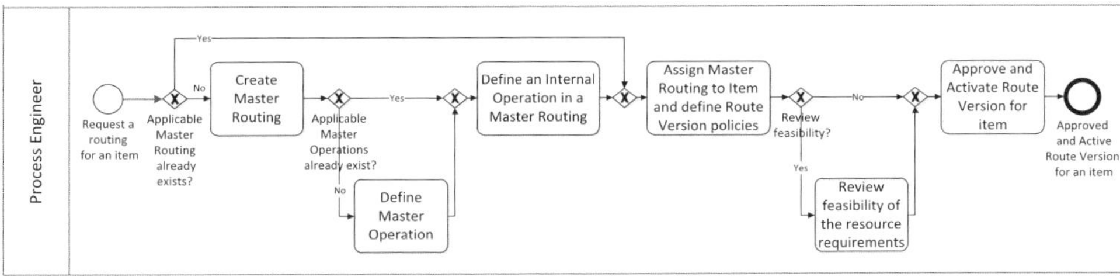

Figure 6.2 Typical Business Process to Define Routing Information for a Manufactured Item

cable manufactured items. Each assignment is termed a route version, and the item's route version policies specify the relevant site and validity dates. In many cases, an item may require multiple route versions to reflect planned changes in the production process or variations between sites producing the same item. As part of defining an operation in a master routing, you identify an operation number, the resource requirement, and a master operation identifier. You define these master operations beforehand, so that an operation automatically inherits the resource requirements from the master operation. You can optionally review the feasibility of the resource requirements after completing the assignment of a master routing to an item. You can then approve and activate the item's route version, or simply approve it. These steps and their applicable roles are illustrated in Figure 6.2 and described below.

Create Master Routing The process engineer typically creates a Master Routing and its operations so that it can be assigned to items going through the same production process. As an alternative starting point, the process engineer can start from an item and create a Master Routing, which is automatically assigned to the item.

Define Master Operation The process engineer employs the Master Operation concept to help minimize data maintenance efforts. By defining the resource requirements and applicability rules of a Master Operation, the process engineer can simply specify the Master Operation identifier in a routing operation, and the operation inherits the resource requirements. A Master Operation may have more than one applicability rule (and its associated resource requirements), such as a different applicability rule for a different group of items. Changing the resource requirements for the Master Operation will automatically update all applicable operations.

Some scenarios do not employ the Master Operation concept. In these scenarios, the process engineer simply defines a Master Operation identifier without the applicability rule and associated resource requirement. An identifier must still be specified for a routing operation, where the process engineer must define the resource requirements for the operation (since nothing is inherited). However, the system will automatically track use of the Master Operation identifier by creating an applicability rule, such as the specific item number and master routing. In this way, the process engineer can still maintain the resource requirements using the Master Operation form.

Assign Master Routing to Item and Define the Route Version Policies The process engineer defines an item's route version policies, which include the Master Routing identifier, the relevant site, the validity dates, and an optional quantity breakpoint for a quantity-sensitive route version.

Review Feasibility of the Resource Requirements for an Item's Route Version The process engineer analyzes route feasibility to determine whether applicable resources exist to satisfy the resource requirements of operations in an item's route version. For example, an operation's resource requirements may be infeasible due to lack of an assigned resource group (for a resource), or the lack of capabilities or employee competencies with valid dates. Attempts to activate an infeasible route version result in a soft warning infolog, and an option to review route feasibility. As a supplemental approach, the process engineer can also analyze availability of applicable resources when defining a master operation or specific operation within a routing.

Approve and Activate Route Version for Item The process engineer approves and activates an item's route version to enable actual usage on production orders and in planning/costing calculations. Attempts to activate an infeasible route version result in a soft warning infolog, and an option to review route feasibility. The process engineer may approve and activate multiple route versions for an item to reflect different sites, validity periods, or quantity breakpoints. In addition, the process designer may simply approve an item's route version but not activate it.

6.7 Define Master Operation

The concept of a master operation is central to the definition of routing operations within AX. A master operation (termed *Operation*) has a unique user-defined identifier and a description, and you define master operations on the Operations form. The identifier typically has some meaning so that its significance is easily understood, such as an abbreviation for an operation or a process specification number. An identifier for a master operation must be specified for each routing operation. The master operation provides default values for the operation's information such as the required resource and associated time. Changing the values for a master operation will automatically update the information on the associated routing operations, subject to applicability rules.

The applicability rules for a master operation represent a key related concept. In defining a master operation, you can specify one or more sets of data that will serve as default values in a given routing operation. Each set has an applicability rule. For example, a set of data could apply to a specified group of items, and an additional set of data could apply to another group of items. The combination of an applicability rule and a set of data is termed an *Operation Relation*.

The applicability rule can reflect a specific item, a group of items (based on the item group) or all items. In addition, the applicability rule can reflect a specific master routing or all master routings. These applicability rules reflect decreasing levels of specificity. When multiple applicability rules have been defined, the most specific level will be used to inherit values from a master operation.

The applicability rule and set of data (aka the Operation Relation) can be specified when you initially define a master operation. The set of data provides default values when the master operation is specified for a routing operation. No default values will be inherited if the applicability rules do not apply.

Manually overriding the values on a routing operation will automatically create an additional applicability rule for the master operation, and the set of data reflects the manually overridden values. The new applicability rule indicates the item and master routing in which you performed the manual override. In this way, subsequent changes to the master operation will only affect the one routing operation.

The use of master operations varies from company to company. Many companies already employ the concept of master operations, and they can replicate their current conceptual model within AX. If the concept of master operations does not apply, you can simply create a master operation without any applicability rules or data. When you specify the master operation in a routing operation, no values will be inherited and you must define them. This will automatically create an Operation Relation for the master operation.

6.8 Define an Internal Operation in a Routing

The critical information for an internal operation consists of an operation number, a master operation identifier, the resource requirement, and the time requirements. Previous sections described the various methods for defining a resource requirement and the concept of a master operation. This section explains the other aspects of defining an internal operation.

Operation Number The operation number provides a unique numeric identifier for each operation within a routing, and the basis for scheduling a serial routing. The system automatically assigns new operation numbers in increments of 10 but this operation number can be overridden. The use of operation numbers has several implications as described below.

- *Sequence the operations in a multistep routing.* The operation number itself does not provide sequencing logic. For sequencing purposes, each operation requires additional information about the next operation number, whether you are modeling a serial or parallel sequence.
- *Identify the last operation within a routing.* You must identify which operation represents the last operation in a routing (with a value of zero "0" in the Next Operation field). This information is helpful when reporting actual production activity for the last operation, so that reporting the units completed at the last operation can automatically update the finished quantity for the production order.
- *Identify the material components required for an operation.* Assigning the operation number to the required material (in the BOM line information) allows the planning calculations to synchronize material due dates with the operation start date. It provides the basis for calculating the impact of operation scrap percentages on the associated material requirements. It also provides the basis for populating the picking list for a production order based on the started quantity for the operation number.

- *Provide an identifier to report actual production activity.* You report actual time and/or unit completions against an order number and operation number.
- *Indicate when tests should be performed during production of an item.* The required tests for an item (via the automatic creation of a quality order) can reflect a specified operation number within the routing.

Primary Versus Secondary Resources (Operation Priority) Each operation requires a primary resource, and most production environments can be modeled using operations with just a primary resource. Some production environments have operations requiring one or more secondary resources, such as the people and tools for running a machine. The operation's primary resource represents the pacing resource that determines operation duration. The same operation number must be assigned to each secondary resource, and the same time requirements apply because it is not the pacing resource. Operations with the same operation number are termed *simultaneous operations.*

The type of linkage between a primary and secondary resource affects scheduling logic, where the link type can be hard or soft. That is, you can indicate that the secondary resources for an operation must start at the same time as the primary resource (a link type of hard). The alternative allows a time gap (a link type of soft or blank).

Case 34: Simultaneous Requirements for a Machine, Operator, and Tool

One production process at an equipment company required a dedicated machine, a skilled operator, and a specialized mold. In order to model these simultaneous resource requirements for the operation, the route version for each manufactured item contained three lines with the same operation number. The first line identified the primary resource requirement of the machine, since this acted as the pacing resource. The next two lines identified the secondary resource requirements for the skilled operator and the mold tool.

Resource Requirement Each operation must include at least one resource requirement. The resource requirement can be expressed for a resource, a resource group, a resource capability or an employee competency, as previously described.

Resource Quantity The resource quantity indicates the number of resources required to perform the operation. It can be illustrated by a resource group for human resources containing resources that represent individual people. For example, a run time requirement of 3 hours and a resource quantity of 2 people would be interpreted as a total load of 6 hours (for the resource group). The detailed scheduling method creates a load of 3 hours for 2 different resources (people).

Time Requirements Time requirements are normally expressed as hours per unit or units per hour. They can also be expressed in minutes or days (which applies to all time elements for the operation), but cost and planning calculations will convert these time requirements back into hours.[7] This approach to defining time requirements is termed a "standard" resource consumption policy, and you assign the policy to an operation. The next subsection describes some alternate approaches to defining time requirements, whereas this section focuses on the standard approach.

The time requirements are typically defined for run time and optional setup time, but some scenarios employ additional time elements to model the production process. The following considerations apply to the definition of time requirements for various time elements.

- *Run Time per Unit* The run time is typically expressed per 1 unit. It can be expressed for a different quantity, such as the run time per 100 units (as defined by the process quantity field). Alternatively, you can define a run rate, such as specifying a time requirement of 1 hour and a process quantity that represents the run rate per hour.
- *Setup Time*. Setup time represents a fixed requirement before starting the run time for production. Short setup times are typically not defined.
- *Changeover Time*. Changeover time represents a fixed requirement after completing the run time for production. It is modeled by the "queue after" time element within AX, as described in the next point.

[7] Time requirements expressed in hours reflects an "hours per time unit" value of 1. This "hours per time unit" field can also be used to define time requirements in minutes (a value of 1/60 or .0167) or days (a value of 24) or some other user-specified interval.

- *Other Time Elements for Scheduling and Capacity Planning Purposes.* Other time elements include the number of hours for queue time before and after the operation, and the transit time to the next operation. Many scenarios employ different names for these time elements, such as a changeover time or cooling time rather than a queue time after the operation. Several policies (embedded in the Route Group assigned to the operation) determine the impact of time requirements for these time elements, since they can optionally consume capacity. The impact of route group policies are described in a following subsection.
- *Overlapping Operations.* An operation can have a specified overlap quantity (also termed the transfer batch quantity) so that the next operation can start before operation completion.

Alternative Approaches to Defining Time Requirements An alternative approach to defining time requirements typically applies to a machine and its machine cycles. The capacity of the machine is expressed as the number of cycles per hour, and the resource requirement identifies the number of required cycles to produce an item. This approach to defining time requirements is termed a "capacity" resource consumption policy, and you assign the policy to an operation. This alternative approach requires the following information.

- *Normal Cycles per Hour for a Machine.* The normal cycles per hour are defined in the resource's *capacity* field. An optional capacity unit provides reference information about the run rate—such as strokes per hour, meters per hour, or pounds per hour—but has no other significance.
- *Required Cycles per Unit for an Operation Performed by the Machine.* An operation's required capacity is expressed in cycles per unit, as defined by the factor field. For example, a factor of 10 means 10 cycles will produce 1 unit, whereas a factor of .5 means that 1 cycle produces 2 units. The operation's run time will be calculated based on the required cycles per unit and the machine's normal cycles per hour.

A second alternative approach builds on the use of machine cycles, and applies to a machine using a mold or die to produce a "batch quantity" of an item. This approach to defining time requirements is termed a "resource batch" resource consumption policy, and you assign the policy to an operation. For example, a machine that employs a mold may require 2 cycles to produce a quantity of 10 items. In this case, you define the resource's *batch capacity* as 10. In the operation, you define a *factor* of 2 for the required cycles per batch. This approach would apply to the use of molds for polymer molded products (Case 7).

Time Requirements and the Impact of Route Group Policies A route group defines a set of policies that determine how an operation's time requirements will be treated. An explanation of these policies can be grouped into the various time elements, as described below. Most scenarios only require one or two route groups with policies reflecting common business practices. The following explanation covers these common practices and the typical exceptions:

- *Run time and setup time.* The costs associated with these time elements are normally included in cost roll-up calculations, and the time elements are normally included in scheduling and capacity planning. In addition, the actual time for run and setup can be manually reported or auto-deducted for a production order.

  The typical exception to these normal business practices occurs when the time requirements should be ignored in cost calculations or planning calculations or both. For example, the time requirements may only apply to capacity planning purposes, so that a separate Route Group should be defined (with policies to ignore setup and run time in cost calculations) with assignment to relevant resources and operations.
- *Queue time.* Two different queue times represent the fixed amount of elapsed time that occurs before setup time and after run time. Costs cannot be defined for these time elements. The amount of elapsed time normally reflects the Gregorian calendar (of a 24-hour day and a 7-day week), and it does not reserve capacity of the relevant resource.

  The typical exception occurs when resource capacity must be scheduled for queue time. A typical example consists of a resource (such as a kettle or tank) used for an extended period to support fermentation or cooling of its contents. In this case, the Route Group policies must indicate that scheduling and capacity reservations apply to the time elements for queue time. In most cases, the amount of elapsed time will reflect the Gregorian calendar, but it can optionally reflect the working hours in the resource calendar.
- *Transit time.* The transit time represents the fixed amount of elapsed time that occurs after performing an operation, where you move material to the next operation. Costs cannot be defined for transit time, and the elapsed time normally reflects the Gregorian calendar without reserving capacity of the relevant resource.

Case 35: Cooling Period after Completing Production

The production process for a manufactured item involved a burn-in period after completing assembly. The number of burn-in hours was specified using the "queue after" time element. This approach requires the definition of a Route Group in which "queue after" time is designated as working time that consumes available capacity, and the assignment of this Route Group to operations performed by the kettle resource.

Yield Percentage for an Operation The planned yield percentage for an operation affects the required runtime and the materials tied to the operation. The system automatically calculates and displays an accumulated yield percentage for each operation in a routing with multiple operations.

Cost Data for an Operation The cost data for an operation includes the cost categories defining the hourly rates. The cost categories would normally default from the required resource, and can be overridden. You can optionally specify which resource should be used for costing purposes (aka the costing resource) in order to populate the cost categories; the costing resource has no other purpose.

The costs associated with an operation can be optionally ignored in cost calculations, as determined by the policies embedded in the Route Group assigned to the operation.

Reporting Operation Time The auto-deduction policies for an operation reflect the Route Group assigned to the operation.

Operation Description The operation description consists of unlimited free-form text, and the optional use of documents such as a Word file or an image.

6.9 Review Feasibility of Resource Requirements

An item's route version may be infeasible due to the lack of applicable resources. When you attempt to activate an infeasible route version for an item, you receive a soft warning infolog to prevent activation. The infolog also provides the option to view information about route feasibility so you can identify which operations do not have applicable resources. This route feasibility information can also be viewed before you attempt to activate a route version.

The Route Feasibility form summarizes the feasibility of the resource requirements for operations within a selected route version for an item. It displays a list of the routing operations, and identifies those operations without an applicable resource as of a specified date. The specified date is relevant because of different validity dates for the assignment of resources to a resource group, the assignment of capabilities to resources, and/or the assignment of employee competencies (for skills, courses and certificates) to human resources representing a specific employee. In some cases, it is helpful to view the feasibility information for a different specified date (within the effectivity dates for the route version) in order to analyze changes in validity dates.

In addition to a specified date on the Route Feasibility form, you must also specify which scheduling method to consider. The feasibility can be different for the two scheduling methods of operation scheduling and job scheduling. For example, the resource requirements for an employee competency (such as skills) only apply to job scheduling. The next section provides further explanation about scheduling method considerations.

The Route Feasibility form provides a starting point for analyzing and correcting those operations without applicable resources. It does not provide sufficient detail to indicate the exact reasons for the problem. The Route Feasibility form can be accessed from the Route form (displaying the Route Versions for an item) or from the Route Details form (for a selected Master Routing). An infolog also provides access when you attempt to active an infeasible route version, as mentioned above.

The availability of applicable resources can also be analyzed for an individual operation, typically in the context of defining a master operation or an operation within a routing. To support this analysis, you can access the Applicable Resource form for a selected master operation or a routing operation.

Case 36: Feasibility of a Routing with New Equipment

A discrete manufacturing firm was implementing a change in equipment that also required skilled operators with the relevant equipment certification. As part of the new route versions for manufactured items produced by the equipment, an operation specified the resource requirements for the new equipment (as a primary resource) and for the employee certification (as a secondary resource). One concern was the match-up between the equipment availability date (defined by the effectivity date for its resource group) and the availability of certified operators (defined by their certification date). This date could be analyzed by reviewing the feasibility of the resource requirements for an item's route version.

6.10 Scheduling Method: Job Versus Operation Scheduling

The scheduling logic within AX is slightly different for the two scheduling methods, which are termed *operation scheduling* and *job scheduling*. The term *job scheduling* may be confusing to those people that think of a job as synonymous with a production order or project, but in this context job refers to the individual time elements within an operation. These time elements include setup, process and queue times. The scheduling significance of these time elements is defined within the Route Group assigned to an operation.

The ability to handle detailed time elements represents a primary difference between the two scheduling methods. A second key difference concerns the detailed information about employee competencies. The job scheduling method can handle these details, whereas the operation scheduling method cannot. The differentiating factors between the scheduling methods are summarized in Figure 6.3 and explained below.

- *Job Scheduling Method.* This method supports (1) scheduling the time elements for an operation, (2) assigning resources based on a requirement for employee competencies, (3) block scheduling based on a property, and (4) use of a Gantt Chart to display production schedule information. Minor differences include the printed shop traveler, the approach for reporting operation time and unit completions, and computer processing time.

		Scheduling Method	
		Operations Scheduling	**Job Scheduling**
Differentiating Factors	Scheduling Focus	Resource Group	Resource
	Capacity Planning	Aggregate (by Group)	Detailed (by Resource) and Aggregate (by Group)
	Scheduling Capabilities		Schedule detailed time elements (aka jobs) Lock a job and synchronize related time elements Assign a resource based on employee competencies Perform block scheduling via properties Use of Gantt Chart to display production schedule
	Time Granularity	Schedule by date	Schedule by date and time
	Printed Shop Traveler	Route Card	Job Card
	Reporting Operation Time and Unit Completions	Use Route Card Journal	Use Job Card Journal or Route Card Journal
	Computer Processing Time	Faster	Slower

Figure 6.3 Comparison of Scheduling Methods

- *Operation Scheduling Method.* This method does not support some scheduling capabilities, as mentioned above.

With planning calculations, the scheduling logic based on routing data only applies within the time horizon defined by a capacity time fence (expressed in days). You define the capacity time fence as one of the policies within the coverage group assigned to an item, or as one of the policies for a master plan. In most cases, the capacity time fence reflects near-term scheduling requirements (such as a 30 day horizon), although a longer horizon (such as 365 days) would be used to calculate long-term capacity requirements.

6.11 Order-Dependent Routing for a Production Order

An order-dependent routing refers to the routing operations attached to a production order. It is also termed the Production Route. Changes to an order-dependent routing do not affect the master routing. Creation and maintenance of the order-dependent routing reflect several rules, which parallel the rules for maintaining an order-dependent BOM.

- Creation of a production order can also create an order-dependent routing.
- The order-dependent routing initially reflects the item's route version that was used to create the production order. In most cases, this will be inherited from the active route version for the delivery date and site on the production order. However, you can manually specify a different route version for the item when creating the production order, where the route version can be approved-but-not-active.
- The order-dependent routing contains the routing operations of a phantom.
- You can modify the operations in an order-dependent routing at any time prior to reporting the production order as ended. For example, you can manually maintain the information, or copy operations from another production order or Master Routing.
- Time can only be reported when the operation sequence number exists in the order-dependent routing.

6.12 Maintain Routing Information

Routing information can be maintained using several approaches. You typically maintain multiple master routings in order to support multiple active route versions for an item, and a copy function provides one approach to data maintenance. Other approaches include the master operation concept to support mass updates to routing operations, and a mass update wizard for updating the assignment of resource requirements within master operations. Another aspect of maintaining routing information includes the review of route feasibility, since a routing may be infeasible due to the lack of applicable resources for one or more operations. These approaches to routing maintenance are summarized below.

Maintain Multiple Active Route Versions for an Item Planned changes can be identified by the validity dates assigned to the route versions for an item, so that multiple route versions can be approved and active. Multiple active route versions may also be necessary to support site-specific or quantity-sensitive versions.

Use the Copy Function to Populate Operations in a Master Routing The copy function involves a destination for the "copy to" master routing, and a source for the "copy from" information. Initiating the copy function for a selected master routing will identify the copy to destination. The copy function is also provided when you create an additional route version for an item.

Mass Updates via the Master Operation Concept In order to support mass updates, the applicability rule for a master operation must reflect a group of items (or all items). In this way, changes to the master operation will automatically update the operations that specified the master operation identifier. If an applicability rule only applies to a single item and its master routing, the changes to the master operation only updates the single occurrence. Section 6.7 previously described the use of master operations.

Mass Update the Assignment of Resource Requirements Within Master Operations A mass update wizard uses information about existing resource requirements within master operations so that you can delete the existing resource requirement, replace it with a different one, or add another resource requirement. The wizard—termed the Maintain Resource Requirements wizard—consists of several steps and their associated screens, as described below.

- *Step 1: Identify an existing resource requirement based on Search Criteria.* Use the first screen (labeled Search Criteria) to specify the search criteria for existing resource requirements, such as a specific resource or capability. More than one search criteria can be specified. The search criteria can optionally include the identifier of a master operation.
- *Step 2: Specify the mass update action.* Use the second screen (labeled Action) to specify whether you want to delete, replace or add to the existing resource requirement. As part of this step, you also indicate the option for where to apply the action. The option would be "routing" information in this scenario, but another option could be the order-dependent routing information (aka production route).[8]

[8]The other options include project-related information about resource requirements (termed hour forecasts) and custom product-related information about resource requirements defined in a Product Configuration Model or a Product Model. Chapter 20 describes project-oriented operations, and Chapter 7 describes the configuration technologies for custom products.

- *Step 3: Specify the new resource requirement.* The third screen (labeled New Resource Requirements) is only displayed when the action involves adding to or replacing an existing resource requirement.
- *Step 4: Review a summary of the proposed mass update.* The final screen (labeled Summary) summarizes the information from the first three steps. You can accept the proposed changes, go back to a previous step and make adjustments, and cancel the proposed mass-update. Accepting the proposed mass update will change the resource requirements within master operations.

Review Feasibility of the Resource Requirements for Operations Within a Routing A key aspect of data maintenance involves reviewing the feasibility of the resource requirements for an item's route version. A routing may be infeasible due to the lack of applicable resources for one or more operations. Section 6.9 previously described how to review the feasibility information.

Analysis Tools for Routing Information Analysis tools for an item's routing information include where-used inquiries about a resource, a master routing and a master operation. They also include a multilevel cost analysis, which shows the cost contributions of resources and related overheads in the calculated cost of a manufactured item.

6.13 Alternatives to the Use of Routing Information

Some production processes are extremely simple and easily coordinated. These scenarios do not necessarily warrant the definition of routing data and the scheduling methods within AX. Some suggested alternatives to the use of routing data include the following:

- *Production schedule of production orders.* Attributes of a manufactured item—such as production group, production pool or property—can represent the required machine. These attributes are inherited by a production order (and can be overridden), and provide the basis for segmenting the production schedule by machine. This approach replaces a production schedule by resource.

- *Capacity planning.* A dummy item number can represent the labor or machine hours for production time, with a unit of measure in hours. You can include this dummy item as a BOM line with a relevant required quantity, so that planning calculations can determine the "capacity" requirements for the item. This approach replaces the use of resources for capacity planning.
- *Value-added costs.* Assigning costs to the dummy item representing labor hours (or machine hours) provides the basis for calculating value-added costs.
- *Fixed lead time.* The fixed lead time assigned to a manufactured item will be used by planning calculations to determine when components must be available. The fixed lead time should also reflect the significance of a single production order. For example, the production order may reflect a week's worth of production and a Friday due date, so that a one week lead time ensures components will be available beforehand. Alternatively, the production orders may reflect daily granularity, so that a one day lead time should be used.

Additional Case Studies

Case 37: Equipment Maintenance The plant manager at a discrete manufacturer wanted to implement an integrated equipment maintenance application, also termed an Enterprise Asset Management (EAM) application.[9] The key issue concerned the lack of coordination between production planning and maintenance scheduling. The plant manager preferred a software module built using the standard AX constructs rather than a separate best-of-breed software package with its own constructs and interface requirements. With standard AX constructs, for example, the spare parts for equipment maintenance could be defined in the item master, procured using requisitions and purchase orders, and tracked via inventory transactions in the same way as other purchased items. Three aspects of integration were especially important. First, the downtime at machines (reflecting planned and ad hoc maintenance) must be identified and coordinated in the production schedules. Second, the triggers for planned maintenance must reflect actual and projected equipment usage. And third, inventory tracking

[9] See **www.ColumbusGlobal.com** for additional information about their Enterprise Asset Management module.

was required for the tools used in maintenance, so that each serialized tool could be easily checked out and checked in.

Case 38: Truck Fleet Maintenance A manufacturing company had numerous trucks that needed scheduled and as-required maintenance. The manufacturer of each truck provided suggested maintenance schedules and replacement parts. A separate group of maintenance personnel were responsible for purchasing and inventorying these replacement parts, and performing maintenance on the trucks in a separate repair facility and in the field. Scheduled maintenance reflected the manufacturer's suggested schedules, which was typically based on utilization metrics for actual and projected usage (such as operating hours or truck miles). The actual time reporting by maintenance employees identified the relevant work order for maintenance, and also provided the basis for handling time-and-attendance and payroll.

Executive Summary

A master routing represents a model of production activities for a manufactured item. Assignment of multiple master routings to an item (termed route versions) can support site-specific variations, planned changes, preferred equipment based on production quantity, and alternate equipment. Each operation within a route version defines the resource requirements and associated time requirements. For example, the resource requirements can be defined for a specific resource, a resource group, a resource capability or an employee competency. The case studies illustrated variations in the use of routing data, such as designating the preferred equipment, integration with equipment maintenance, and simultaneous requirements for a machine, operator and tool.

Chapter 7

Configuration Technologies for Custom Products Manufacturing

The nature of custom product manufacturing scenarios can differ significantly. The scenarios can range from the simple to complex, and from a single-level to a multilevel custom product. They often involve a configure-to-order product built from predefined options. Most of these scenarios can benefit from a configuration technology that simplifies the configuration process and embeds engineering expertise.

Dynamics AX provides several variations of a configuration technology for supporting different custom product scenarios. This chapter summarizes the variations, and provides more detailed explanation of one variation called the constraint-based configuration technology. The chapter also summarizes the use of modular bills of material to support configure-to-order products. The chapter consists of the following sections:

1. Variations of the Configuration Technology
2. Example Product Structure for a Configurable Item
3. Define Item Information for a Configurable Item
4. Define a Product Configuration Model
5. Configuration Process Using a Product Configuration Model
6. Considerations about the Constraint-Based Configuration Technology
7. Modular BOMs to Support Configurable Items

More detailed explanations of the other two configuration technologies—the bill of options approach and the rules-based approach—are not included because of book length considerations. Detailed explanations for the two topics can be obtained by contacting the author.

7.1 Variations of the Configuration Technology

A configurable item provides the starting point for configuring a custom product, typically in the context of a sales order or sales quote. Dynamics AX provides three different configuration technologies to support configurable items. With each approach, the configuration process results in a configuration ID, and the combination of item number and configuration ID provides a unique identifier.

The definition of a configurable item shares many similarities to a normal material item. The key differences include the designation as a product master (rather than a product), the use of a configuration ID (within the product dimension group), and a selected configuration technology. The three major variations of a configuration technology are summarized in Figure 7.1

Configuration Technology	Summarized Description of Approach
Constraint-Based Configuration	Define a Product Configuration Model and assign to the configurable item Use the model to configure an item Automatically create Configuration ID and its BOM/Route Versions
Rules-Based Configuration	Define a Product Model and assign to the configurable item Use the model to configure an item Automatically create Configuration ID and its BOM/Route Versions or Automatically create new Item and its BOM/Route Versions
Dimension-Based Configuration (aka Bill of Options Approach)	Define a BOM Version (aka Bill of Options) for the Configurable Item Define a Route Version for the Configurable Item Use the Bill of Options to configure an item Manually assign a Configuration ID
Predefined Variant	Define applicable variant code(s) and the possible values for a variant code and Define valid combinations of values when using multiple variant codes Specify the item and the variant code value(s) on transactions

Figure 7.1 Variations of the Configuration Technology

and described below. The bottom of the figure displays a fourth configuration technology for modeling custom product scenarios with predefined variant codes rather than using a configurable item.

Constraint-Based Configuration Technology The constraint-based configuration technology represents a new capability for AX 2012, and it requires the definition of a product configuration model. The model provides the dialogue of prompts/responses used in the configuration process, and a mapping of the prompts/responses to the needed components and operations. You can then assign the model to a configurable item along with validity dates.

When using the model, such as configuring a sales order line item, the configuration process results in three key outputs from a supply chain perspective. One output consists of an automatically created configuration ID for the configurable item. The other two outputs consist of the automatically created BOM version and route version for the configuration ID. These three outputs are also created for each configurable component in a multilevel custom product. You can manually maintain these BOM and route versions, which helps when the configuration process results in partially defined information. Additional aspects of the configuration include a calculated ship date and a calculated cost and sales price.

As the model changes, you define a new model and assign it to the configurable item with different validity dates. You typically duplicate the existing model as the starting point for the new model. Hence, a configurable item will ultimately have different assigned models (aka versions) with non-overlapping validity dates. The configuration process automatically uses the relevant model based on the order date.

Rules-Based Configuration Technology The rules-based configuration technology represents a historical capability that will be phased out in future AX versions, since it has been replaced with the above-mentioned Constraint-Based Configuration Technology.[1] This historical capability has several synonyms, such as using a modeling-enabled item, using a product model, and using the Product Builder. With this approach, you define a product model that provides the dialogue of prompts/responses used in the

[1]One of the primary reasons for the new approach is to eliminate the need for a developer license and the related need for a skilled developer with X++ expertise. The new approach also builds on capabilities within the Microsoft Solver Foundation.

configuration process, and a mapping of the prompts/responses to the needed components and operations. You can then assign the model to a configurable item along with validity dates.

When using the model, such as configuring a sales order line item, the configuration process results in several key outputs from a supply chain perspective. There are two variations of the key outputs based on policies within the product model. The first variation is similar to the previously described product configuration model.

- *Create a configuration ID for the configurable item.* One output consists of an automatically created configuration ID for the configurable item. The other two outputs consist of the automatically created BOM version and route version for the configuration ID.
- *Create a new item number.* One output consists of an automatically created item number. The other two outputs consist of the automatically created BOM version and route version for the new item. The new item inherits information from the configurable item, including the enterprise-level information and the partially populated company-level information (much like a template). The other item information must be manually maintained.

You can manually maintain these BOM and route versions, which helps when the configuration process results in partially defined information. Additional aspects of the configuration process for a sales line include a calculated sales price and promised ship date.

As the model changes, you define a new model and assign it to the configurable item with different validity dates. You typically copy the existing model as the starting point for the new model. Hence, a configurable item will ultimately have different assigned models (aka versions) with non-overlapping validity dates. The configuration process automatically uses the relevant model based on the order date.

Dimension-Based Configuration Technology (aka Bill of Options Approach) This configuration technology employs a dramatically different approach to the configuration process in comparison to the above-mentioned configuration technologies. Rather than using a model (that defines the mapping between prompts/responses and needed components), you define a BOM version for the configurable item to support option selection of needed components. You also manually assign the configuration ID resulting from the configuration process. The approach represents a historical capability within AX.[2]

The bill of options approach involves a slight reconceptualization for defining and using BOM lines within the BOM version for a configurable item. For example, a group of BOM lines identity the alternatives for a required option (termed a configuration group), where you select one of the alternatives during the option selection process. When the required options or their alternatives change, you define a new BOM version for the configurable item with different validity dates. You typically copy the current BOM version as the starting point for the new BOM version. The configuration process automatically uses the relevant BOM version based on the order date.

The bill of options approach can be employed in reasonably simplistic situations for configuring a custom product via an option selection process. Using the standard AX functionality, it is typically limited to scenarios involving predefined options for 100% of the configuration, where the component quantity for a selected option cannot be manually overridden during the configuration process. The resulting BOM information for a configuration cannot be manually maintained. The route version for the configurable item (if defined) will be inherited by all configurations, and (unlike BOM information) the route version can be manually maintained for a specific configuration. Some simplistic rules can be defined to automatically select of an option or preventing selection of an option. The options reflect a one-to-one correspondence to items, and the option selection process displays a list of item numbers, so that the user must be comfortable with the internal item numbers.

Predefined Variant Configuration Technology The use of predefined variants supports item identifiers based on the combination of an item number and one or more variant codes, as previously described (Section 3.14). In summary, you identify the applicable codes (such as color and size) as part of the Product Dimension Group assigned to an item. You also define the possible values for each variant code (such as red/green and large/small), and then define the valid combinations of values. Standard AX includes several variant codes named color, size and configuration; they can be easily renamed and additional variant codes can be defined if needed. You specify the item and the valid value for each applicable variant code as the item

[2]The bill of options approach was previously termed the configurable item approach. This book uses the term "configurable item" as a generic term applicable to the three major variations of a configuration technology.

identifier for inventory transactions and for other information such as the BOM for a manufactured item.

The predefined variants approach does not support a configuration process in the same way as the three other variations of a configuration technology. However, some custom product manufacturing scenarios can employ predefined variants as an alternative for a configuration process. The predefined variant approach requires definition of the BOM and routing information for each item identifier (consisting of an item number and a value for the applicable variant codes).

7.2 Example Product Structure for a Configurable Item

A simple example of custom equipment can help illustrate the use of configurable items and the constraint-based configuration technology. As shown in Figure 7.2, the simple example consists of a two-level custom product,

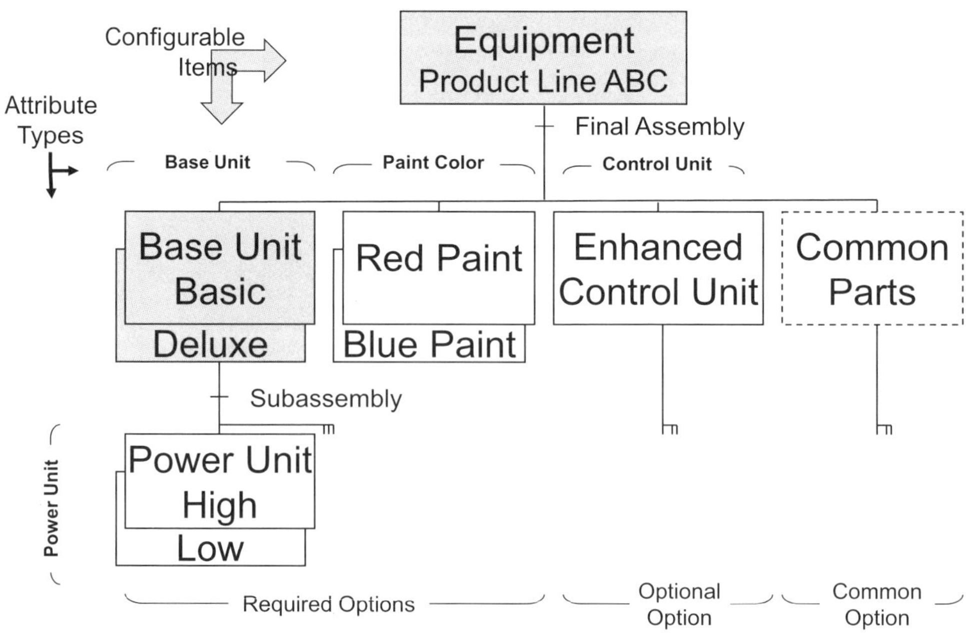

Figure 7.2 Product Structure for Configurable Equipment

where the end-item and two variations of a key component have been identified as configurable items. In summary, the configurable "Equipment for Product Line ABC" consists of a configurable "Base Unit" (either Basic or Deluxe), a paint color (either Red or Blue), an optional enhanced control unit, and a set of common parts. Each configurable "Base Unit" consists of a "Power Unit" (either Low or High) and some other parts. This example product structure will be used in the subsequent explanations.

The figure highlights several key aspects. First, the configurable items are highlighted in grey. Second, the major options are identified as "attribute types" (such as base unit or paint color), and each attribute type has an enumerated list of values (such as red and blue for possible paint colors). This approach reflects modularized BOMs, so that the UI prompts/responses can be easily mapped to the relevant item. Third, the bottom of the figure indicates the required, optional and common options. The required and optional options will require mandatory entry of the related UI prompts and responses.

7.3 Define Item Information for a Configurable Item

The definition of a configurable item has many parallels to one for a regular material item. The primary differences involve the designation of a product master (rather than a product) and the configuration technology. The key steps within the typical business process for defining a configurable item are illustrated in Figure 7.3 and described below.

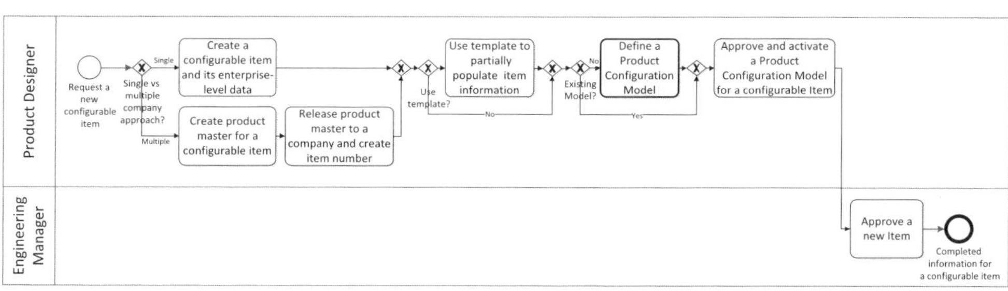

Figure 7.3 Typical Business Process to Define Item Information for a Configurable Item

The figure does not include all of the steps and associated roles for defining a configurable item. For example, it does not include the definition of accounting policies for a manufactured item, the planning data, the testing requirements, and the serial and batch tracking policies.

The product designer is responsible for initially creating a configurable item—using either a single-company approach or a multi-company approach —and defining the enterprise-level data as well as the company-level information. The enterprise-level data includes the designation as a product master and the selected configuration technology, and the use of a configuration ID for uniquely identifying a specific configuration. The product designer may employ a template as a short-cut approach to partially populate item information, either when creating a new item or by applying it afterward. A key aspect of company-level information includes the policy for separate costing for each configuration.

The product designer also defines a product configuration model corresponding to the configurable item, and then approves and activates the model for the item. Upon completion of the item information, the engineering manager can approve the definition of a new item.

In addition, the product designer can maintain the enterprise-level data about the product name for each Configuration ID (after the configuration process results in automatic creation of a Configuration ID), and release a Configuration ID to other companies.

7.4 Define a Product Configuration Model

The typical business process to define a product configuration model consists of several steps illustrated in Figure 7.4. The first step involves the creation of a new model. You can optionally create a new model by duplicating an existing model, typically in the context of creating an updated version of the model. Information within a model defines the UI prompts and responses needed to configure an item, and consists of several sections. The two key sections for supply chain purposes specify the mapping between these prompts/responses and the needed components and operations. The mapping will populate the automatically created BOM version and Route version that result from using the model to configure an item. As you define and complete a model, you can validate the model to identify errors, and also test the model to view the end-user experience. After the entire model has been completed and validated, you can approve and activate it for a configurable item. Additional explanation for several key steps is provided below.

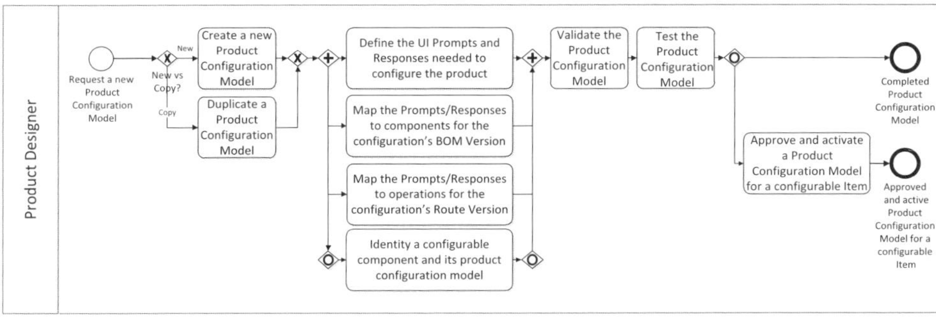

Figure 7.4 Typical Business Process to Define a Product Configuration Model

Create a New Product Configuration Model Each model is uniquely identified by a user-assigned name. The name and description (and their translations) represent properties of the product configuration model, and you can edit these values. The model name frequently reflects the relevant configurable item. For example, the configurable item of "Product XYZ" would have a related model called "Product Configuration Model for Product XYZ.

Duplicate a Product Configuration Model You typically duplicate n existing model in the context of creating a new version, so that you can simply make changes to the newly-created model. You can create a new name and description when duplicating a model, and the system automatically retains the originating source of the model (aka the root component).

Define the UI Prompts and Responses Needed to Configure the Product The "Attributes" section of a product configuration model provides the primary basis for defining User Interface (UI) prompts and responses. In particular, it defines each SolverName and SolverValue that represent key constructs within the model. These key constructs reflect the algebraic modeling language called Optimization Modeling Language (OML) used by the Solver Foundation. One example could be a SolverName of "PaintColor" and the two values of "Red" and "Blue" represent a SolverValue. These two key constructs become critical in defining relevant conditions, such as the condition for including a BOM line or an operation.

Map the Prompts/Responses to Components for the Configuration's BOM Version The "BOM Lines" section of a product configuration model defines the mapping for populating an automatically created BOM version for the item's configuration. The mapping requires a detailed understanding of BOM line information, such as the variations for defining a component's required quantity, the warehouse source of a component, and the BOM line type. You can specify the condition for adding a BOM line. The mapping for each field within a BOM line can reflect a specified value or an attribute, such as an attribute for calculating a component's required quantity. Other sections explain a BOM line for a material item (Section 4.4) and for an item representing a subcontracted service (Sections 16.3 and 16.4).

Map the Prompts/Responses to Operations for the Configuration's Route Version The "Route Operations" section of a product configuration model defines the mapping for populating an automatically created route version for the item's configuration. The mapping requires a detailed understanding of information for an internal operation, such as the variations for defining the required resource and time requirements. You can specify the condition for adding an operation. The mapping for each field within an operation can reflect a specified value or an attribute, such as an attribute for calculating time requirements. Other sections explain an internal operation (Section 6.8) as well as an external operation (Chapter 16).

Identify a Configurable Component and its Product Configuration Model In order to support a multilevel custom product, the "Subcomponents" section of a product configuration model defines the configurable components of a configurable item. Each configurable component requires a product configuration model.

Validate the Product Configuration Model You can validate a model after completion, or at any stage of completion, in order to identity potential errors.

Test the Product Configuration Model You can test a model after completion, or at any stage of completion, in order to view the UI prompts and responses.

Approve and Activate a Product Configuration Model for a Configurable Item You can assign the model to a configurable item along with validity dates, and then approve and activate the assignment. Each assignment is termed a version. As the model changes, you define a new model and assign it to the configurable item with different validity dates. Hence, a configurable item will ultimately have different versions (aka assignments of different models) with non-overlapping validity dates.

7.5 Configuration Process Using a Product Configuration Model

A sales order line item represents a typical starting point for configuring a custom product. The typical business process for this starting point is illustrated in Figure 7.5 and summarized below. In this example, the customer service rep initially enters the sales order line for a configurable item, and then configures the line using the currently-effective Product Configuration Model. As an alternative, the customer service rep can select an existing configuration ID for the item.

The configuration process results in three key outputs from a supply chain perspective. One output consists of an automatically created configuration ID for the configurable item. The other two outputs consist of the automatically created BOM version and route version for the configuration ID. These three outputs are also created for each configurable component in

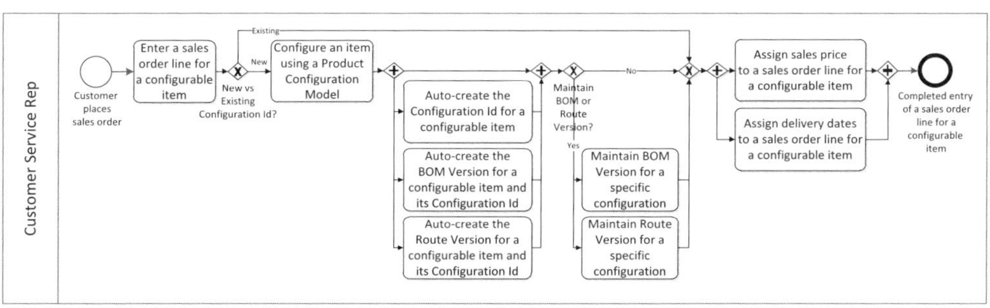

Figure 7.5 Typical Business Process to Enter a Sales Order Line for a Configurable Item

a multilevel custom product.[3] You can manually maintain these BOM and route versions, which is especially helpful when the configuration process results in partially defined information. Additional aspects of the configuration process for a sales line include a suggested sales price and promised ship date for the configuration.

- *Suggested sales price for a configuration.* An order-specific calculation for a configuration's cost and sales price (described in Section 8.11) can be performed within the configuration process, or performed for the sales line after completion of the configuration process.
- *Promised ship date.* The earliest possible promise date for shipment can be calculated based on two different approaches (described in Section 11.6). One approach employs a delivery date control policy of "CTP" for the sales line, so that the automatic calculation of a ship date can be performed within the configuration process. The second approach can be performed after completion of the configuration process, and employs a net change explosion to calculate a future ship date. This future date can then be transferred to the ship date for the sales order line item.

The typical business process varies slightly for other starting points of the configuration process. For example, a promised ship date cannot be calculated for a sales quotation, and a calculated sales price may not apply in some situations such as a manually-created production order.

7.6 Considerations about the Constraint-Based Configuration Technology

Several considerations apply to the constraint-based configuration approach, including the starting points for the configuration process and the use of configuration templates.

Starting Points for the Configuration Process A sales order line item for a configurable item represents one starting point for the configuration process, as described in the previous section. Additional starting points

[3]With the current version of AX, the configuration process results in automatic creation of a configuration ide, and the same configuration ID is used for every configurable item in a multilevel custom product.

include a sales quotation line item (Section 12.10), a replacement order line item for a customer RMA (Section 12.8), and a manually created production order.

Other starting points only apply to project-oriented operations or service orders, such as a project quotation line item (Section 20.10), a project-specific item requirement (Section 20.4), or an item requirement for a service order (Section 21.2).

Configuration Templates as a Short-Cut to Populating Values A configuration template represents a partially or completely finished configuration process for a product configuration model. You can create one or more templates for a model, and then use a selected template (when configuring an item) as a short-cut to populating suggested values. The suggested values can be overridden.

Default Value of the Configuration ID for a Configurable Item A default value for an item's configuration ID may be defined when it represents the dominant business practice, otherwise it can be left blank.

Release an Existing Configuration to Other Companies An existing configuration is typically released to other companies that represent distributors of the product. After the release step, you must define the company-level information for the item and configuration, just like any other purchased item.

7.7 Modular BOMs to Support Configurable Items

Many manufacturers with multiple variations of similar products can benefit from modularizing their bills of material to support configurable items. There are warning signals for needed modularity: an explosive growth in the numbers of items and BOMs, overly complex bills of material, a perceived need for negative component quantities, difficulties in anticipating demands, and longer-than-necessary delivery lead times. BOM modularization makes it easier for using configurable items to define and sell a custom product.

The definition of modular BOMs starts with a detailed understanding of the product structure. One starting point involves deconstructing the product variations to identify common and unique items, and then restructuring the BOM to reflect the new groupings of common and unique options. This typically results in disentangling an overly complex BOM, isolating the unique items for usage late in the production process, and the use of phantoms for groups of common components. Another starting point involves lead time analysis of the multilevel product structure to identify the highest possible stocking level that supports the desired minimum delivery lead time. The stocking level may be stated in the new groupings of common and unique options, typically leading to a reduction in the number of items to forecast.

Modular BOMs typically impact routing operations. Final assembly operations can be assigned to the configurable end item. Operations can also be embedded in the routings for phantom components.

When modular BOMs and configurable items replace a standard products approach, there are many implications for other aspects of the business. It requires changes to item planning parameters, and the approach to sales and operations planning. It also requires changes to manufacturing documentation and drawings, sales literature and product pricing, order entry and delivery promises, paperwork (such as confirmations, packing lists and invoices) and sales analysis.

Additional Case Studies

Case 39: Custom Windows A manufacturer of custom windows employed a product configurator for each product line. With a window product line, for example, the user dialogue captured information about the dimensions, glass type, casing and other key attributes. The configurator defined the rules for generating the BOM and routing to build the window, including the calculation of glass and wood component quantities and routing operation times. The configurator also calculated the sales price.

Case 40: Custom Store Fixtures A manufacturer of store fixtures employed a product configurator to identify the desired options for horizontal racks and vertical supports in a customized store fixture. This involved a two-level custom product, since a customized rack consisted of various subassemblies, and the rack went into a customized store fixture.

Case 41: Custom Surgical Kit One product line at a medical products distributor involved a customer-specified kit of components that represented surgical items. For example, a surgical kit was configured based on the requirements to perform a surgery at a hospital. A product configurator provided an option selection process to identify the desired components in the surgical kit. The sales price for a surgical kit reflected the selected components and a cost-plus-markup approach embedded in an order-specific cost calculation.

Case 42: Skeleton BOM for an ETO Product One product line at an equipment company involved building customized machines to customer specifications. Every customized machine had a unique identifier, and its product structure consisted of the same type of customized subassemblies (such as a power unit, a horizontal table, and a vertical column) with unique item identifiers. Each customized subassembly required several unique components with long purchasing lead times, and subassembly production was initiated prior to receipt of these unique components. Substantial engineering time was required to define the unique item identifiers, initiate purchases of the long lead time components, and ultimately define each machine's product structure (with unique components correctly placed in BOMs). Any delays in these engineering efforts impacted the purchasing and production activities, and the delayed definition of the product structure information made it difficult to coordinate requirements. As a solution approach, the company employed a product configurator to automatically create the unique item numbers and the product structure skeleton, with the unique purchased components correctly placed in the subassembly BOMs. The solution approach resulted in significant reductions in engineering time and the number of delays.

Case 43: Custom Overhead Crane One product line at an equipment company involved a customized overhead crane for moving heavy material around a factory floor. The user dialogue in the product configurator identified usage characteristics, such as maximum load weight, mounting height, and the factory floor dimensions. The product configurator translated the usage characteristics into the required materials and operations to produce the customized overhead crane.

Case 44: Custom Plastic Assembly One product line at a fabricated products company involved customized plastic assemblies that reflected a two-level custom product. Plastic components were produced to custom specifications, and then assembled into a customized plastic product. A product configurator provided the user dialogue to capture the customer specifications, and also provided a mapping to the required materials and operations. The two-level custom product enabled warehouse personnel to find the customized plastic components that were prepared for final assembly.

Executive Summary

The nature of custom products manufacturing can differ significantly, ranging from special one-time items to a configure-to-order product built from predefined components. Dynamics AX provides several options for a configuration technology to support custom products manufacturing. The chapter summarized these variations of a configuration technology, and provided more detail about the variation for a Constraint-Based Configuration Technology. Several case studies illustrated how to handle custom products for windows, store fixtures, surgical kits and overhead cranes.

Chapter 8

Product Costing

Product cost information defines the value of an item's inventory transactions and provides the basis for profitability analysis. The primary variations in product costing involve standard versus actual costs, and purchased versus manufactured items. For a manufactured item, the calculation of product costs reflects the item's formula/BOM and routing information. These calculations can be used to project future costs, simulate the impact of cost changes, analyze cost reduction opportunities, analyze profitability, and calculate an item's suggested sales price.

Product cost information represents one of the most complex and critical aspects of an integrated ERP system. As an explanatory approach, we'll start with the foundation of costing versions and the rationale for different costing versions. A costing version contains cost records about items, labor rates and overheads. The foundation also requires an understanding of the terminology about item cost records and cost calculations, and the significance of cost groups. We'll build on this foundation in order to explain standard costs for purchased items, the costs for resources and overheads, and the standard cost calculations for manufactured items. These topics and others are reflected in the following sections within the chapter:

1. Summary of Costing Versions
2. Terminology for Item Cost Records and Cost Calculations
3. Significance of Cost Groups
4. Standard Costs for Purchased Items
5. Define Resource Costs via Cost Categories
6. Define Overhead Costs via Overhead Formulas
7. Standard Cost Calculations for Manufactured Items
8. Convert Items to a Standard Cost Model
9. Planned Cost Calculations for Manufactured Items
10. Calculation of a Manufactured Item Sales Price

11. Order-Specific Calculations of an Item's Sales Price
12. Summary of Standard Cost Variances
13. Actual Costing

8.1 Summary of Costing Versions

The primary purpose of a costing version is to define the cost records about items, labor rates and overhead formulas. You designate whether a costing version contains standard costs or planned costs. With a version containing standard costs, the cost records about items define their site-specific standard costs, and the cost records about items, labor rates and overhead formulas are used to calculate a manufactured item's standard cost. A costing version containing planned costs can be used in a standard cost or actual cost environment. It is used for simulation purposes in standard cost environments, where you calculate a manufactured item's planned cost. An actual costing environment can use a costing version containing planned costs to define the labor and overhead costs associated with manufacturing, and to support simulation purposes. Whether the costing version contains planned costs or standard costs, the calculation of a manufactured item's cost creates an item cost record within the costing version, which enables you to analyze the calculated costs.

A secondary purpose of a costing version involves the calculation of a suggested sales price for a manufactured item. This section summarizes the various purposes of costing versions, especially the use of item cost records. It starts with the rationale for different costing versions for standard costs.

Rationale for Different Costing Versions for Standard Costs

The significance of a costing version depends on how you conceptualize your approach for maintaining standard costs. Some example approaches are described below.

- *Multiple costing versions represent standard costs for different calendar years (or quarters).* With this approach, you maintain all item cost records within one costing version that represents the current calendar year, and use an additional costing version for maintaining next year's standard costs. You can copy the active cost records from one costing version to create pending cost records in the other cost version, thereby providing a starting point for updating next year's standard costs.

- *Multiple costing versions represent site-specific standard costs for different sites*. This approach typically applies to a multi-site operation with transfers between a production site and a distribution/manufacturing site, where you define a different costing version for each site. Within a given costing version you only maintain the item cost records for applicable items at the site, ranging from raw materials to end-items. In this way, you can calculate costs for a manufactured end-item within one costing version (that represents a production site), and then copy just the end-items' costs to another costing version (that represents the distribution site). Case 34 illustrates this approach to maintaining site-specific standard costs.
- *Multiple costing versions represent incremental changes to standard costs*. A costing version can contain the incremental changes to standard costs, such as pending cost records that represent new items or cost changes. The use of separate costing versions for incremental changes is commonly termed the two-version or n-version approach to maintaining standard cost data. This approach takes advantage of the fallback principle for calculating a manufactured item's cost, as described in a subsequent section (Section 8.7). For example, the fallback principle can identify the use of the active costs contained within other costing versions (the n-version approach), or within a specified costing version (the two-version approach). In contrast, cost calculations for item cost records within a single costing version employ a fallback principle of none.

In summary, the rationale for different costing versions depends on how you want to conceptualize your approach to maintaining standard costs. The conceptual approach should be shaped by AX capabilities such as copying costs to another costing version, site-specific costs, the effective date of pending and active cost records, the fallback principle, the policies affecting standard cost calculations, cost calculations within a single site, and calculating costs for items with missing costs. Subsequent sections provide further explanation of these capabilities.

Item Cost Records for Standard Cost Purposes Standard costing employs one or more costing versions that contain item cost records about each item's standard cost. A costing version typically represents a user-defined time period such as a year or a quarter. For example, three costing versions could represent the three different time periods for years 2010, 2011,

Identifier of Costing Version	Costing Type	Purpose of Costing Version
Std-2010	Standard Cost	Contains item cost records for 2010, plus cost records for labor and overhead formulas
Std-2011	Standard Cost	Contains item cost records for 2011, plus cost records for labor and overhead formulas
Std-2012	Standard Cost	Contains item cost records for 2012, plus cost records for labor and overhead formulas
Simulated-Cost	Planned Cost	Contains selected cost records for simulation purposes and item cost records generated by cost calculations

Figure 8.1 Examples of Costing Versions for Standard Costing Purposes

and 2012. These examples of a costing version are displayed in Figure 8.1 and described below.

The concept of an annual time period is reflected in the first three costing versions displayed in Figure 8.1, all of which have a designated Costing Type of standard cost. In these examples, we'll assume a current date of December 2011 and an implementation cutover date that occurred in the previous year of 2010. Hence, the costing version *Std-2010* contains the initially-loaded item cost records, and the costing version *Std-2011* contains item cost records that were activated on January 1, 2011. The item cost records for the following year will be defined in costing version **Std-2012**, but not activated until January 1, 2012.

A costing version has two blocking policies that constrain the ability to enter and activate cost records. For example, these blocking policies would enforce the frozen standard costs for the *Std-2011* costing version, since all cost records have been entered and activated. The *Std-2012* costing version represents next year's standard costs, so the blocking policies should allow entry of cost records but prevent activation. The blocking policy for activation would be removed at the appropriate time to allow activation. The blocking policies would then be enforced again after activation.

Item Cost Records for Calculation of Planned Costs A costing version can be designated as a set of planned costs, such as the *Simulated-Cost* costing version shown in Figure 8.1. The designation supports several simulation capabilities not applicable to cost calculations based on standard costs, such as indicating a different basis of purchased material costs when performing cost calculations for manufactured items. A subsequent section provides further explanation of cost calculations for a manufactured item's planned cost.

Cost Records Related to Resources and Overheads The hourly costs for a resource (termed *Cost Categories*) and the manufacturing overhead costs are defined as cost records within a costing version. The costing version must reflect standard costs to support standard cost environments, and actual costing environments can employ a costing version for standard or planned costs. Subsequent sections provide further explanation about resource costs and overhead costs.

Applicability of Item Cost Records to Actual Cost Items The concept of item cost records has limited applicability to items with actual costing as an inventory valuation method (such as FIFO). In a typical scenario, you may employ a costing version for planned costs, and perform cost calculations for a manufactured item in order to create (and analyze) the item's cost record. Activating this item cost record simply populates an initial value for the item's actual cost, as displayed in the item master. A subsequent section provides further explanation of actual costing.

Calculation of Manufactured Item's Sales Price You can calculate a suggested sales price for a manufactured item in order to create an item sales price record within a costing version. A subsequent section provides further explanation about calculation of a manufactured item's sales price.

Policies about the Contents of a Costing Version The policies can limit the information contained within a costing version. As noted earlier, you designate whether a costing version contains standard costs or planned costs, and whether it contains cost records for a single site or all sites. In addition, you typically designate that it only contains item cost records so that you do not clutter things up with item sales price records.

8.2 Terminology about Item Cost Records and Cost Calculations

Item cost records within a costing version, and the cost calculations for manufactured items, provide the foundation for standard cost environments. This information is viewed and maintained on several AX forms. However, an explanation using these form names leads to cumbersome English-language sentences.[1] This section summarizes the terminology used in the book and the associated names of AX forms, as shown in Figure 8.2 and described below. The explanation focuses on costing versions containing standard costs, but it also applies to costing versions containing planned costs (which typically do not require activation of item cost records).

View an Item Cost Record An item cost record defines an item's site-specific costs within a costing version. The initial entry of an item cost record has a pending status, and activating the cost record changes the status

Terminology used in Book		Name of AX Form
View an Item Cost Record	For a pending cost For an active cost	Item Price
Manually enter an Item Cost Record	For a pending cost	Item Price
Perform a Cost Calculation	For a single item For an item's BOM version For items within a costing version	Cost Calculation for an Item Cost Calculation for a Costing Version
View Results of a Cost Calculation for an item	View an item cost record View costs segmented by cost group View costs in multi-level format	Item Price Summary Calculation Inquiry Complete Calculation Inquiry
Activate Item Cost Record	For a single item For items within a costing version	Item Price Activate Prices

Figure 8.2 Terminology for Item Cost Records and Cost Calculations

[1]The form name "Item Price" is one example. The name may have originated because several types of information can be viewed on the Item Price form, such as a calculated value for an item's suggested sales price (aka item sales price record). However, the name does not indicate the primary purpose of viewing/maintaining information about an item's costs.

to active. Using the Item Price form, you can view both pending and active item cost records for an item.

Manually Enter an Item Cost Record An item's site-specific costs can be manually entered within a costing version (using the Item Price form) to create an item cost record. The initial entry of an item cost record has a pending status, and activating the cost record changes the status to active. Manual entries typically reflect the site-specific costs for a purchased or transfer item, whereas the item cost record for a manufactured item can be automatically created via a cost calculation.

Perform a Cost Calculation for a Manufactured Item (and Create an Item Cost Record) The cost calculation of a manufactured item's site-specific cost creates an item cost record.[2] You can perform the cost calculation for an individual item or one of its BOM/formula versions. Alternatively, they can be performed for multiple items within a costing version, typically in the context of updating standard costs on a periodic basis. A subsequent section (Section 8.7) provides further explanation about performing standard cost calculations.

View Results of a Cost Calculation for a Manufactured Item The results can be viewed for an item cost record on the Item Price form, which provides access to additional inquiries to view costs in a multilevel format or to view costs segmented by cost group.

Activate Item Cost Record The initial entry of an item cost record has a pending status and pending effectivity date. Activation changes the status to active, and the effectivity date to the actual activation date. You can activate the item cost record for an individual item, or for multiple items within a costing version.

[2]Previous versions of Dynamics AX employed several different terms for *Cost Calculation*, including BOM Calculation and BOM/Formula Calculation. The new term reflects additional functionality related to purchased items (for purchased material overheads), whereas the previous functionality only applied to manufactured items.

8.3 Significance of Cost Groups

Cost groups serve multiple purposes. Cost groups are user-defined, and you assign them to items, cost categories and overhead formulas Their purposes include the segmentation (by cost group) of a manufactured item's calculated costs, the calculation of a suggested sales price for a manufactured item based on cost-plus-markup percentages (by cost group), and the assignment of G/L accounts to standard cost variances (based on the cost group assigned to an item). The definition and purposes of cost groups are described below.

Defining a Cost Group and its Cost Group Type A cost group has a user-defined identifier and a designated cost group type. The cost group type indicates the purpose and constrains the assignment of a cost group. The assignment of a cost group type of *direct material* to a cost group, for example, means that the cost group can only be assigned to material items. Figure 8.3 summarizes the significance of a cost group type, and provides examples of cost groups.

Cost Group Type	Examples of Cost Groups	Significance for Using the Cost Group
Direct Material	Electrical Fabricated Packaging	The cost group can only be assigned to material items (Product Type = Item)
Direct Outsourcing	Subcontract	The cost group can only be assigned to items identified as a service (Product Type = Service)
Direct Manufacturing	Labor Machine	The cost group can only be assigned to cost categories, which define the hourly costs (or piece rate costs) for a resource
Indirect	Overhead	The cost group can only be assigned to an overhead formula
Undefined	Subcontract *	The cost group assignment is not constrained; it can be assigned to an item, service, cost category or overhead formula.

* = This approach supports standard costing for an item representing a subcontracted service (Product Type = Item), whereas actual costing must be employed for services (Product Type = Service)

Figure 8.3 Significance of Cost Group Type

A cost group type of *undefined* does not constrain the assignment of a cost group. For example, an item number that represents a subcontracted service may require standard costing, which involves assignment of a cost group with a type of undefined (and a Product Type = Item).

Assigning a Cost Group You typically assign a cost group to purchased items. It may be assigned to manufactured items with standard costing, since the cost group can optionally support segmentation of production-related variances. You also assign cost groups to cost categories and overhead formulas in manufacturing environments. As summarized in Figure 8.3. the cost group type constrains the ability to assign a cost group, such as constraining the assignment of direct material cost groups to items.

Using Cost Groups for Standard Cost Variances Cost groups represent one factor for the assignment of a G/L account to standard cost variances, such as a purchase price variance or a production-related variance. You define these factors and the relevant G/L accounts on the Posting Profile form. At one extreme, a different G/L account can be assigned to individual item numbers. In most cases, the relevant G/L account will reflect the item group and/or the cost group assigned to an item.[3] Case 11 previously described purchase price variances based on cost groups.

Using Cost Groups for Segmenting the Calculated Costs of a Manufactured Item Cost groups provide the basis for segmenting and analyzing cost contributions in a manufactured item's calculated costs, such as the cost contributions for material, labor and overhead. Synonyms for cost group segmentation include cost breakdown, cost decomposition, and cost classification. Cost group segmentation serves the following purposes.

- Segment costs for different types of material based on the cost group assigned to purchased items. These cost groups represent direct material costs.
- Segment costs for different types of resources based on the cost categories assigned to a resource and its operations. Examples include different types of labor and machines, and differences in setup versus run time. These cost groups represent direct manufacturing costs.

[3] A company-wide policy (defined on the parameters for Inventory and Warehouse Management) determines whether standard cost variances can actually be assigned based on the cost group.

- Segment costs related to subcontracted services. The cost group is assigned to the item number representing the subcontracted service. Chapter 16 provides further explanation of subcontracted production.
- Segment costs for different types of overheads based on the cost groups assigned to overhead formulas. These cost groups represent indirect costs.
- Segment costs by cost group type. The cost group type (such as direct material and direct manufacturing) assigned to each cost group provides supplemental segmentation for reporting purposes.

Information about cost group segmentation for a manufactured item's calculated cost can be viewed on the Summary Calculation Inquiry form, Cost Rollup by Cost Group form, and the Variance Analysis Statement report.

Using Cost Groups for Calculating the Suggested Sales Price of a Manufactured Item Cost calculations can be used to calculate a manufactured item's suggested sales price based on a cost-plus markup approach, where the markup reflects the profit-setting percentages assigned to cost groups. For example, a profit-setting percentage of 50% could be defined for a cost group assigned to purchased material, and a profit-setting percentage of 80% could be defined for a cost group assigned to a cost category for labor operations. A subsequent section (Section 8.11) provides further explanation about calculating this suggested sales price.

8.4 Standard Costs for Purchased Items

The standard costs for a purchased item are defined by item cost records within a costing version. Each item cost record is uniquely identified by five key fields. An understanding of these key fields provides the starting point for explaining how to maintain an item's standard cost across time.

Key Fields in an Item Cost Record The standard cost for a purchased item is defined by an item cost record within a costing version containing standard costs. The key fields and other fields in an item cost record are summarized in Figure 8.4 and explained below.

Field		Significance of the Field
Key Fields in Item Cost Record	Item Identifier	The identifier indicates the item number; it sometimes includes variant codes.
	Costing Version	The costing version can contain standard costs or planned costs; this costing type affects the calculation policies for a manufactured item's calculated cost.
	Site	A standard cost item requires an item cost record for each site that stocks the item. Transfers between sites can result in a variance when standard costs differ.
	Effective Date Status	Initial entry of an item cost record has a pending status and effectivity date. Activation changes the status (to active) and effectivity date (to the activation date). Activating an item's standard cost record revalues existing inventory if costs change. An item's active standard cost record is used for valuing inventory transactions. Pending item cost records are used in Cost Calculations based on effectivity date.
Cost		An item's cost is expressed for its inventory unit of measure. A manufactured item's cost can be calculated or directly entered.
Other Fields		Charges for a manufactured item reflect the calculated amount of amortized constant costs.

Figure 8.4 Key Fields in an Item Cost Record

- *Item Identifier.* The item identifier normally consists of an item number. When the item identifier includes a variant code such as color and size, an item-specific policy (termed *use combination cost price*) determines whether item cost records can be maintained for the various combinations of the item identifier.
- *Costing Version.* A costing version contains cost records for standard costs or planned costs, as indicated by its costing type. The costing type also affects the calculation policies for a manufactured item's calculated cost, since standard costing principles must be enforced for standard cost items.
- *Site.* An item's cost record must be defined for each site that stocks the standard cost item. For example, an item purchased (or manufactured) at one site and transferred to a second site will require two item cost records, one for each site. The item's cost at the transfer site can be different, such as an increased cost because of handling and transportation. Transfers between sites when an item's standard costs differ will generate a variance (termed a *cost change* variance).
- *Effective Date and Status.* The two fields concerning the status and effective date (also termed the activation date or from date) work together in tandem. The initial entry of an item cost record has a pending status

and pending effectivity date. Activation changes the status to active, and the effectivity date to the actual activation date.

A standard cost item can only have one active standard cost record for each site, which will be used for valuing an item's inventory transactions at the site. The concept of one active cost record applies to the item regardless of the associated standard costing version. Activating an item's standard cost record will revalue existing inventory if costs change, and generate a variance (termed a *cost revaluation* variance).

Pending item cost records are used in cost calculations based on their effectivity date, and the future date specified for the cost calculation.

- *Cost.* An item's cost is expressed for its inventory unit of measure. A purchased item's cost must be directly entered, whereas a manufactured item's cost can be calculated or directly entered.
- *Other Fields.* Price charges—or *charges* for short—must be included in an item's cost when the costing version contains standard costs.[4] The primary rationale is that AX employs the charges field to indicate the calculated amount of amortized constant costs for a manufactured item, and the related field (termed price quantity) to indicate the accounting lot size used in the calculations. Ignoring these charges would run counter to standard costing principles.

  In terms of purchased items, it is suggested that you enter a zero value for the charges field. The item's standard cost (including charges) is compared to a purchase order price in order to calculate a purchase price variance. You obtain a false variance if you entered a value in the charges field.

You can enter the item cost records and activate individual pending records (using the Item Price form), or activate all pending records within a costing version (using the Activate Prices form).

Maintaining Standard Costs for a Purchased Item The maintenance of a purchased item's standard cost involves the definition of item cost records within a costing version, as described in the previous subsection. The data maintenance starts with the initial loading of an item's cost prior to system cutover, and subsequent updates reflect a progression through time. For example, you would activate the initially loaded costs, and subsequently

[4]Previous versions of Dynamics employed the term miscellaneous charges. The new term is price charges, although the functionality is the same.

enter and activate a pending cost in a costing version that represents next year. You may enter a pending cost in a costing version that represents a simulated cost in order to perform simulated cost calculations for manufactured items.

Suggestions for Copying Item Cost Records A copy function facilitates preparation of item cost records, such as preparing the next period's standard costs or preparing costs for a new site or a different site. The copy function (embedded in the Copy Costing Version form) focuses on the copy-to costing version, and there are two basic options for the copy-from source. You can copy the item cost records from a specified costing version, or copy the active item cost records regardless of costing version. The item cost records can be selectively copied (such as copying selected item numbers) to populate the copy-to costing version. The item cost records can also be selectively changed as part of the copy process. For example, you can change the costs based on a factor or amount, change the site (thereby creating cost records for another site), or change the effectivity date (thereby creating cost records applicable to a future time period). The newly created item cost records have a pending status and can be manually maintained.[5] Costs for manufactured items need to be recalculated.

Purchase Price Variances An item's standard cost provides the basis for calculating purchase price variances at the time of purchase order receipt (reflecting the difference with the purchase order price) and invoice entry (reflecting the difference between the purchase order price and invoice price).

8.5 Define Resource Costs via Cost Categories

Cost categories define the hourly costs for a resource and its related routing operations. Common synonyms include labor rate codes and machine rate codes. If applicable, a cost category can also define the piece rate for a resource. The cost categories assigned to a resource will act as default values for its operations. The preparation of cost category information includes the

[5]Several restrictions apply to the copy process. First, the copy process cannot create duplicate item cost records in the copy-to costing version. Second, planned costs can only be copied to another costing version that contains planned costs; they cannot be copied to a costing version that contains standard costs. Third, the copy process does not apply to cost records for cost categories and overhead formulas.

assignment of a cost group. Different cost categories will be needed to support different purposes, as illustrated below.

- Assign different hourly costs by resource, such as different costs for various types of labor skills, machines, or manufacturing cells.
- Assign different hourly costs for an operation's setup and run time.
- If applicable, assign piece rates by resource by assigning a cost category to the output units associated with an operation.
- Segment different types of direct manufacturing costs in cost calculations, such as segmentation of labor and machine costs, based on the cost group assigned to cost categories.
- Provide the basis for routing-related overhead calculations, such as an hourly overhead amount for a resource.

Definition of a Cost Category The definition of a cost category requires two steps: one step to define a *shared cost category* and a second step to define the *cost category* for production purposes. The second step requires additional information when the cost category also applies to project-related time estimates and reporting. This additional information includes the assignment of a project category group (that supports a transaction type of hours), a line property (that indicates how reported hours will be charged to a project), and the hourly costs and sales prices associated with a project.

Define Standard Costs for a Cost Category Each cost category has its associated cost records within a costing version containing standard costs. The cost records can reflect site-specific costs or company-wide costs. Cost calculations for a manufactured item employ the current active cost records for a cost category, and also consider pending cost records (based on effectivity date) when using a future calculation date. Figure 8.5 summarizes the key fields in the cost record for a cost category.

The key fields for a cost category are similar to those of an item cost record, but there are several differences. These differences can be highlighted using an example of a labor rate code. The labor rate can be site-specific or company-wide, the labor rate can be different for run time and setup time elements (or piece rate). There is also a slight change in handling the cost record status, where activation of a pending cost record changes its status to current active, and also changes the status of an existing record (if any) from current active to previous active.

<table>
<tr><th colspan="2">Field</th><th>Significance of the Field</th></tr>
<tr><td rowspan="5">Key Fields in Cost Record</td><td>Identifier</td><td>The identifier indicates the cost category (e.g., labor rate code)</td></tr>
<tr><td>Costing Version</td><td>The costing version type can be standard cost or planned cost.</td></tr>
<tr><td>Site</td><td>The cost record for a cost category can be site-specific or company-wide.</td></tr>
<tr><td>Effective Date</td><td rowspan="2">Initial entry of the cost record has a pending status and effectivity date.
Activation of the cost record changes the status (to current active) and effectivity date (to the actual activation date). If an existing record has a current active status, activation changes its status to previous active.
The current active cost record (regardless of costing version) will be used for valuing the estimated and actual time on a production order.
Pending cost records are used in cost calculations based on effectivity date.</td></tr>
<tr><td>Status</td></tr>
<tr><td colspan="2">Cost</td><td>The cost represents a resource's hourly cost (for setup and run time), or its piece rate cost (for output quantity), expressed in the local currency.</td></tr>
<tr><td colspan="2">Other Fields</td><td>The cost group assigned to each cost category provides the basis for segmentation of direct manufacturing costs in cost calculations.</td></tr>
</table>

Figure 8.5 Key Fields in the Cost Record for a Cost Category

Define Planned Costs for a Cost Category Planned costs can be assigned to a cost category for simulation purposes. In addition, an actual costing environment typically defines planned costs (rather than standard costs) for a cost category, so that actual costs on a production order can be calculated.

8.6 Define Overhead Costs via Overhead Formulas

The definition of an overhead formula supports the calculation of a manufactured item's overheads (termed *indirect costs*). An overhead formula can calculate different types of overheads for a manufactured item, such as material- or routing-related overheads, or overheads based on the item's weight or volume. Each overhead formula has a unique identifier, and it must be defined as part of the Costing Sheet Setup form. After defining the identifier, you can maintain the cost records associated with the overhead formula.

Define an Overhead Formula Within a Costing Sheet Setting up the costing sheet involves defining a format for displaying information about the cost of goods manufactured (COGM) for a manufactured item or a production order. The format (termed a *costing sheet*) segments material, labor and overhead costs based on the cost groups assigned to items, cost categories, and overhead formulas. The definition of a costing sheet format is required to support overhead formulas. An overhead formula can define different types of overheads, as described below.

- *Surcharge Percentage for Material-Related Overhead.* An overhead formula for a material-related overhead employs a surcharge percentage. For example, the percentage can be applied to the value of an item's first level components that have a specified cost group. Each overhead formula has an assigned cost group.
- *Rate Amount for Routing-Related Overhead.* An overhead formula for a routing-related overhead employs a rate amount. The rate amount will be added to the hourly cost for run time (or setup time) when the operation's cost category has a specified cost group. Each overhead formula has an assigned cost group.
- *Per-Unit Amount Based on the Manufactured Item's Weight, Volume, or Quantity.* The overhead formula (termed an *output unit based* formula) defines a per unit amount that reflects the specified weight or volume for the manufactured item. It can also simply reflect a per unit amount for a quantity of one. The overhead formula does not employ an assigned cost group.
- *Per-Unit Amount Based on the Component's Weight, Volume, or Quantity.* The overhead formula (termed an *input unit based* formula) defines a per unit amount that reflects the weight or volume for the components of a manufactured item. Each overhead formula indicates the applicable cost group of the components.

With each of these approaches, you can optionally define applicability rules within the cost records for the overhead formula, so that an overhead formula only applies to a specific manufactured item or group of items.

Key Fields in a Cost Record for an Overhead Formula You can maintain the cost records for each overhead formula, such as indicating the overheads for different sites, years, and manufactured items. Figure 8.6 summarizes the key fields in the cost record for an overhead formula.

Field			Significance of the Field
Key Fields in Cost Record		Identifier	The user-defined identifier assigned to a node within the costing sheet
		Costing Version	The costing version can reflect a cost type of standard cost or planned cost.
		Site	The cost record for an overhead formula can be site-specific or company-wide.
		Effective Date Status	Initial entry of the cost record has a pending status and effectivity date. Activation of the cost record changes the status (to current active) and effectivity date (to the actual activation date). If an existing record has a current active status, activation changes its status to previous active. The current active cost record (regardless of costing version) will be used for calculating estimated and actual overheads on a production order. Pending cost records are used in cost calculations based on effectivity date.
		Applicability Rule	The overhead formula can apply to a specific manufactured item, a subset of items (based on item group), or all manufactured items.
	Overhead	Surcharge Percentage	The surcharge percentage is used to calculate material-related overheads.
		Rate Amount	The rate amount is used to calculate routing-related overheads.
		Output Unit Based Amount	The per-unit amount applies to the manufactured item's weight or volume, or to a quantity of one.
		Input Unit Based Amount	The per-unit amount applies to the components' weight or volume.

Figure 8.6 Key Fields in the Cost Record for an Overhead Formula

The key fields for an overhead formula's cost record share some similarities to those of an item cost record, but there are several differences. These differences can be highlighted using an example of a surcharge percentage for a material-related overhead. For example, the surcharge percentage can be site-specific or company-wide, and vary by manufactured item based on applicability rules. There is also a slight change in handling the cost record status, where activation of a pending cost record changes its status to current active, and also changes the status of an existing record (if any) from current active to previous active.

Alternative Approaches to Routing-Related Overheads Several approaches can be used to model routing-related overheads. One approach involves the just-described overhead formula to calculate an incremental overhead cost for an operation's run time or setup time, or its piece rate. A second approach employs a secondary resource for a routing operation, where the secondary resource represents a resource overhead. A third approach applies to cases where overheads can be tied to output units (rather than time), where the cost category assigned to an operation's output quantity can indicate the overhead amount per unit.

Overhead Costs for Purchased Material The overhead costs for purchased material often reflect internal handling costs or the costs associated with acquisition, such as duties, freight and other landed costs. These overhead costs (termed *purchase indirect costs*) can be calculated as a surcharge percentage of the item's value, or as a per-unit amount based on the item's weight or volume. They are defined within a separate section of the Costing Sheet labeled "Costs of Purchase," much like defining overhead formulas within the Cost of Goods Manufactured section.

8.7 Standard Cost Calculations for Manufactured Items

The cost calculations for a manufactured item will create an associated item cost record within a costing version. The cost calculations require some preparation information about purchased items and manufactured items. The dialogue for initiating the cost calculations varies slightly based on how you initiate them, such as initiating them for a costing version versus a single item. Several policies affect the cost calculations for standard costs, and constant costs will be amortized over an accounting lot size. These topics are included in the following subsections.

- Prepare item information for cost calculations
- Initiate a cost calculation
- Policies affecting standard cost calculations
- Amortizing constant costs for a manufactured item
- Calculating costs for items with missing costs
- Cost calculations using the fallback principle

Prepare Item Information for Cost Calculations Cost calculations use item master information about purchased components and manufacturing items, as described below.

❖ *Information about Purchased Components.* Each purchased component should have an item cost record containing its standard cost. Each component should also be assigned a calculation group and a cost group. The calculation group assigned to a purchased item defines applicable warning conditions in cost calculations (such as zero cost or a zero component quantity for the item). The cost group assigned to a purchased item provides segmentation in the calculated costs of its parent item.

- *Information about Manufactured Items.* Each manufactured item should be assigned a calculation group. The calculation group defines applicable warning conditions in cost calculations, such as the lack of an active BOM/formula version. When a manufactured item has constant costs, you should also assign the accounting lost size for amortizing these constant costs. The approach for defining the accounting lot size differs for BOM items and formula items, as described in a subsequent subsection about amortizing constant costs.
- *Ignoring a Component's Costs in the Cost Calculations.* As part of the BOM/formula information, you can optionally flag a component so that its costs are not included in the cost calculation of its parent item.
- *Ignoring a Routing Operation's Costs in the Cost Calculations.* You optionally flag a routing operation so that its costs (associated with run time, setup time or piece rate) are not included in the cost calculation of its parent item. These policies are embedded in the Route Group assigned to the operation.
- *Treating a Manufactured Item as a Purchased Item.* An item-specific policy will prevent calculation of the item's costs. The policy (termed the Stop Explosion checkbox) is embedded in the Calculation Group assigned to the item.

Initiate a Cost Calculation Initiating a cost calculation involves a dialogue, and the nature of the dialogue varies slightly depending on where you initiate it. The cost calculations can be initiated for a single manufactured item or its BOM/formula version, or for multiple items within a costing version, as summarized in Figure 8.7 and described below.

- *Cost Calculation for an Item.* Initiating the cost calculation for a single manufactured item will display a dialogue so that you can enter relevant information. As shown in the middle column of Figure 8.7, this form inherits the item number, and you specify the relevant costing version. Other information can be inherited from the costing version policies (such as the site and calculation date), and from the item's active formula/BOM and route versions for the site. Figure 8.7 displays the inherited information and the ability to override the information. For example, you can override the item's active formula/BOM version with another approved version. As another example, the costing version may

Dialogue Information		Initiating a Cost Calculation	
		For an Item	For a Costing Version
Key Fields in Item Cost Record	Item Identifier	Inherited	All items or selected items or where-used items
	Costing Version	User specified	Inherited
	Site	Inherited from costing version policy; Or manually enter the site and calculation date (if not mandated)	
	Calculation Date		
Formula/BOM Version		Inherit active version for the item and site; Override with an approved version	Inherit active version for the item and site
Route Version			
Calculation Quantity		Inherit the item's accounting lot size*; Override the quantity	Inherit the item's accounting lot size*

Calculated Cost	Generate an item cost record for the single item	Generate an item cost record for each selected item

* = The default value for an item's accounting size differs between a BOM item and a Formula item

Figure 8.7 Dialogue for Initiating a Cost Calculation

represent next year's standard costs with a mandated calculation date of January 1st which cannot be overridden. You can initiate the dialogue from the Item Price form.

❖ *Cost Calculation for an Item's BOM/Formula Version.* You can initiate the dialogue for an item's BOM/Formula version from several places, which affects the inherited values in the dialogue.

❖ *Cost Calculation for a Costing Version.* Initiating the cost calculation for a costing version will display a dialogue form so that you can enter relevant information. As shown in the right hand column of Figure 8.7, the dialogue inherits the costing version, and you can optionally select items and employ the where-used concept.[6] Other information can be inherited from the costing version policies (such as the site and calculation date), and from the item's active formula/BOM and route versions for a site. Figure 8.7 displays the inherited information and the ability to override

[6]The concept of where-used updates is motivated by the single-level cost calculation for standard costs, since an item's recalculated cost can impact higher levels within the product structure. This impact on higher levels can also be calculated by performing the cost calculations for all manufactured items.

the information. As an example, the costing version may contain costs for a specified site so that the inherited site cannot be overridden.

Policies Affecting Cost Calculations The nature of cost calculations varies slightly depending on whether the calculations involve a costing version for standard costs or planned costs, and the policies that can be inherited from the specified costing version. These policies are explained below.

- *Cost Calculation Policies for Standard Costs.* Cost calculations with standard costs must be restricted by costing version policies because the restrictions ensure standard costing principles will produce accurate consistent results. For example, these mandated restrictions mean that cost roll-up calculations are limited to a single level (termed a single level *explosion mode*), the source of a purchased item's cost data must be from the item cost records within a costing version, and charges must be included in the unit cost of an item. Charges for a manufactured item reflect the calculated amortization of constant costs.
- *Cost Calculation Policies for Planned Costs.* Cost calculations with planned costs do not have to follow standard costing principles. This means you can optionally mandate a restrictive policy in the costing version, perform multilevel cost roll-up calculations, and the source of a purchased item's cost data can be from item cost records or from another source such as purchase price trade agreements (as specified by an item's calculation group).
- *Other Cost Calculation Policies.* Cost calculations generate an infolog containing warning messages[7] and other types of messages. Several policies determine whether these other messages will be included in the infolog. For example, the infolog message should display the fallback information (when using the fallback principle), and indicate items which did not get updated with cost calculations (when updating calculated costs for items with missing cost records).

Amortizing Constant Costs for a Manufactured Item A manufactured item's constant costs reflect operation setup times, the components

[7]The warning messages reflect the applicable warning conditions defined within the Calculation Group assigned to items, and you can override these warning conditions in the dialogue for initiating a cost calculation. For example, a warning message can indicate a zero quantity component or the lack of an active formula/BOM version for a manufactured item.

with a constant quantity (or constant scrap amount), or a component quantity expressed as a step function. The concept of an accounting lot size is used to amortize these constant costs in cost calculations. The definition of an item's accounting lot size differs between BOM items and formula items, as described below.

- *Accounting lot size for a BOM item.* The item's site-specific standard order quantity (for inventory) acts as the default value for the accounting lot size; the quantity may be greater to reflect a multiple.
- *Accounting lot size for a formula item.* The formula size for the item's active formula version acts as the default value for the accounting lot size. With a catch weight item, this formula size reflects a calculated value for the specified CW Size (multiplied by the item's nominal weight).

The default value for an accounting lot size is displayed as the calculation quantity when performing a cost calculation for a single item, and it can be overridden. The specified calculation quantity only applies to the parent item. An alternative approach only applies to planned cost calculations, where you specify a make-to-order explosion mode so that the specified quantity acts as the accounting lot size for the parent item and all manufactured components.

The calculated amount of a manufactured item's amortized constant costs is termed *price charges* (or *charges* for short). After calculating a manufactured item's cost, these charges are displayed as two fields identifying the total amount and the accounting lot size (termed the *price quantity* field). These two fields are displayed on the Item Price form. Activating a manufactured item's cost record updates this information on the item master. These charges are always included in the item's standard cost and used for valuing inventory transactions.

Calculating Costs for Items with Missing Costs The concept of a *missing cost* refers to a manufactured item without a pending cost record (for the relevant key fields). For example, when you prepare item cost records within a costing version for a new period (prior to activation), a pending cost may not yet exist for an item. A missing cost typically reflects a new manufactured item, or an item that requires recalculation because the pending cost record was intentionally deleted. Cost calculations can be performed for just the items with a missing cost record, thereby supporting a net change approach to cost calculations.

When attempting to update costs for items with missing costs, it may be useful to be notified (via the infolog messages) that an item already has a pending cost record thereby preventing the desired outcome of updating the missing costs.

Cost Calculations Using the Fallback Principle The fallback principle indicates an alternative source of cost data (for a cost calculation) when an item's cost data does not exist within the specified costing version. Cost calculations for item cost records within a single costing version employ a fallback principle of none. However, several situations can benefit from cost calculations employing a fallback principle of using another costing version or the active cost records. The following situations illustrate use of the fallback principle with standard costs.

- *Two-Version Approach to Maintaining Standard Costs*. A costing version can contain the incremental changes to standard costs, such as pending cost records that represent new items or cost changes. The use of separate costing versions for incremental changes is commonly termed the two-version or n-version approach to maintaining standard cost data. In this situation, the fallback principle can identify the use of the active costs contained within other costing versions (the n-version approach), or within a specified fallback costing version (the two-version approach).
- *Simulating the Impact of Cost Changes on Standard Costs.* A costing version that represents next year's standard costs can contain pending cost records about selected cost categories, overhead formulas, and/or purchased material. For example, the entry of pending cost records can reflect the anticipated cost changes for critical purchased components and labor rates. In this situation, the fallback principle can identify the use of the current year's costing version, and the cost calculation can create pending cost records for all manufactured items.

  Simulations about the impact of cost changes are generally performed using cost calculations with planned costs, where the fallback principle reflects the active standard costs. The cost calculations can be multilevel (rather than single level), and the costs for purchased components can be based on different sources, such as purchase price trade agreements (rather than item cost records).

9.8 Convert Items to a Standard Cost Method

A standard cost conversion refers to changing an item's inventory valuation method from an actual costing approach to a standard costing approach. The conversion process involves performing a prerequisite inventory close, performing several steps during a transition period (defined by a transition start date and a planned conversion date), and then performing the conversion and an associated inventory close at the end of the conversion period.

After successful completion of the conversion process, each item will have a standard cost inventory model and the item's standard costs will be activated. Subsequent inventory transactions will be valued at the item's standard cost. In addition, the system converts the item's physical inventory transactions during the transition period (for receipts and issues) to standard cost as per the conversion date. The system also converts the item's financial on-hand inventory to standard costs, and posts the value difference as an inventory revaluation variance.

You can analyze revaluation variances using the variance analysis report. You can also analyze inventory value before and after the conversion date using the inventory value by inventory dimension report.

8.9 Planned Cost Calculations for Manufactured Items

Cost calculations can be used to calculate a manufactured item's planned cost, where the costing version reflects a costing type of planned cost. One advantage of using planned costs is that cost calculations can be multilevel rather than single level. A second advantage is the ability to designate the source of component cost data. You can also creatively use the fallback principle in planned cost calculations, which minimizes data maintenance for simulation purposes.

Source of Component Cost Data for Planned Cost Calculations

There are two basic options on the source of component cost data. You indicate the choice (termed the Cost Price Model) when performing a planned cost calculation.

- *Costing Version* (termed Version Cost Price). Component costs are based on item cost records within a costing version. An additional option (termed the purchase price model) provides an alternative approach for using purchase price trade agreement information in planned cost calculations, as described in the next subsection.

- *Calculation Group*. Component costs are based on the source of cost data designated by the component item's calculation group. In this case, the source of information can be (1) the item's inventory cost, such as the item's actual cost or active standard cost (2) the item master information about the item's standard purchase price, which can be updated automatically by the last purchase invoice, (3) the item master information about the item's inventory cost, or (4) the purchase price trade agreement information with the item's preferred vendor. The designated calculation group can reflect a company-wide policy, which requires the assignment of a blank value for each component item.[8]

A planned cost calculation employs the active cost records for cost categories and overhead formulas. The cost calculations generate an item cost record (for manufactured items) within the specified costing version. This item cost record provides the starting point for viewing the cost calculation details, such as viewing the costs in a multilevel format. This item cost record provides reference information, and is typically never activated. Activating this cost record will only update the item master information about the item's inventory price.

Using Planned Cost Calculations to Create Item Cost Records for Purchased Items Based on Purchase Price Trade Agreements

Planned cost calculations can use item cost records within a costing version as the source of component costs. In addition, the planned cost calculations can automatically create these item cost records (for purchased items) based on purchase price trade agreements. The cost calculation approach is labeled the Purchase Price Model with the option for Trade Agreements. The approach involves the following steps.

- *Identify purchased items*. A purchased item is designated by the planned order type of "purchase order", which can be specified as a company-wide or site-specific policy for the item.
- *Create item cost records for purchased items*. Planned cost calculations will automatically generate the item cost records for purchased items, but

[8]The company-wide policy for a calculation group is defined as part of the parameters for Inventory and Warehouse Management.

only when you designate the relevant policy (termed the "items procured using purchase order" checkbox) for performing the cost calculation. The associated cost will reflect the item's purchase price trade agreements with its preferred vendor. The associated cost will also reflect a quantity of 1, regardless of quantity breakpoints in the trade agreement. The newly created item cost records can then be used in planned cost calculations for manufactured items.

The Purchase Price Model has one other option. The option is labeled Item Purchase Price, but a longer phrase would be more informative such as "item purchase price records within the costing version." This approach means that an item cost record will be automatically created based on previously entered information about item purchase price records within the costing version. The approach only works when the costing version allows entry of the item purchase price records.

8.10 Calculation of a Manufactured Item's Sales Price

The alternative approaches to defining an item's sales price are described in a subsequent chapter (Section 12.3). One of these approaches employs cost calculations to calculate a manufactured item's suggested sales price based on a cost-plus markup approach or a rolled price approach, as described below.

- *Cost-Plus Markup Approach.* The markup reflects the profit-setting percentages assigned to cost groups, where a cost group can be assigned to each purchased item, cost category, and overhead formula. Each cost group can be assigned up to four sets of profit-setting percentages, labeled Standard, Profit 1, Profit 2, and Profit 3. Within the Profit 1 set, for example, a profit-setting percentage of 50% could be defined for a cost group assigned to purchased material, and a profit-setting percentage of 80% could be defined for a cost group assigned to a cost category for labor operations.
- *Rolled Price Approach* The rolled price approach only applies to a component. The cost calculation uses the component's standard sales price (rather than its cost) to calculate the manufactured item's sales price.

A policy within the calculation group assigned to a purchased item (termed the *sales price model*) determines whether the component's sales price or cost-plus-markup will be used in the calculation of a sales price.

A cost calculation generates an item sales price record (rather than an item cost record) within a specified costing version.[9] The item sales price record provides the starting point for viewing the calculation details, such as viewing costs and sales prices in a multilevel format. An item's sales price record primarily acts as reference information. However, activating an item's sales price record will update the item's standard sales price on the item master, which represents one option for an item's sales price.

8.11 Order-Specific Calculations for an Item's Cost and Sales Price

An order-specific cost calculation typically applies to make-to-order products in the context of line item on a sales order or quote, and results in a calculated cost and sales price for the line item. It shares many similarities to a cost calculation with planned costs, but it reflects a different purpose and different capabilities. The major differences are summarized in Figure 8.8 and described below.

Primary Purpose An order-specific cost calculation is performed in the context of a sales order, sales quotation, or service order line item, typically to calculate an estimated sales price based on a cost-plus-markup approach. An order-specific calculation has the exact same logic as a cost calculation with planned costs using the items' calculation group to indicate the source of component costs, an explosion mode of "according to BOM line type", and the current active costs as the fallback principle (for labor rates and overhead formulas).

Key Outputs An order-specific calculation generates a *Calculation Record* containing the calculated cost and sales price. It may be performed multiple times for a single order, such as simulating the calculated sales price using different sets of profit percentages, thereby generating multiple calculation records. The Calculation Results form displays an item's calculation

[9]The costing version must be able to contain item sales price records.

	Cost Calculation with Planned Costs	Order-Specific Calculation
Primary Purpose	Calculate the planned cost of a manufactured item	Calculate the estimated cost and sales price of a make-to-order product for sales purposes
Key Outputs	Generate an item cost record within a costing version	Generate a calculation record containing the calculated cost and sales price; Transfer the calculated sales price to the order
Key Inputs	Information specified for cost calculation Source of component's cost data within a a costing version Source of labor rates and overhead formula within a costing version	Inherit information from originating sales order Source of component's cost data based on calculation code assigned to items Current active costs for labor and overheads
Secondary Purposes	Calculate an item's suggested sales price and generate an item sales price record within a costing version Simulate an item's calculated cost using a set of item cost records, or using a source of component's cost data (when calculating planned costs)	Simulate an order's calculated sales price using a different set of profit percentages, a different manufacturing site, a different quantity, or a different date.

Figure 8.8 Order-Specific Calculations of Cost and Sales Price

records. The sales price for a selected calculation record can be transferred to the originating line item.

An order-specific calculation only applies to a sales context. It does not generate an item cost record or an item sales price record within a costing version.

Key Inputs The key inputs for an order-specific calculation initially reflect the values from the originating line item. These initial values include the ship-from site, ship date, order quantity, and the sub-BOM and sub-route (if specified). The initial values can be overridden. In particular, the site can be overridden to reflect a different manufacturing site, which may involve a different formula/BOM version, route version, and costs for material, labor and overhead.

You can specify the desired set of profit-setting percentages, and an explosion mode (of multilevel or make-to-order). The explosion mode impacts the assumption of an accounting lot size for amortization of constant costs.

Secondary Purposes An order-specific calculation has a few secondary purposes, such as simulations of an order's calculated sales price using different sets of profit percentages, a different manufacturing site, and a different quantity or date (which would affect usage of purchase price agreement information). The retention of previous calculations (viewed on the Calculation Results form) also supports comparisons of price.

8.12 Summary of Standard Cost Variances

Several types of standard cost variances can be generated, and each variance will be posted to a relevant G/L account. This section summarizes the variances and definition of G/L accounts.

Purchase Price Variance An item's site-specific standard cost provides the basis for calculating purchase price variances at the time of purchase order receipt (reflecting the difference with the purchase order price) and invoice entry (reflecting the difference between the purchase order price and invoice price).

Cost Change Variance Transfers between sites will generate a cost change variance when there are differences between an item's site-specific standard costs. The variance is generated at the time of receipt for a transfer order. An item's standard cost at two different sites can be different for several reasons. For example, the item's costs may be higher because of the associated transfer costs to another site, or because of different manufacturing or purchasing costs.

Inventory Revaluation Variance Activating an item's standard cost record will revalue existing inventory if costs change, and generate a cost revaluation variance. This variance can also be created when converting to a standard cost model, since conversion of an item's financial on-hand inventory to standard costs will generate a variance for the value difference.

Production-Related Variances Production-related variances are automatically calculated after ending a production order for a standard cost item. The variances reflect a comparison between the reported production activities and the item's standard cost calculation (not to the order's estimated costs). Four types of variances are calculated: lot size variance, production quantity variance, production price variance, and production substitution variance. Similar variances are also calculated for co/by-products. A subsequent chapter about production orders (Section 14.14) provides further explanation of production-related variances.

G/L Accounts for Standard Cost Variances Item groups and cost groups represent two factors for the assignment of a G/L account to standard cost variances, such as a purchase price variance or a production-related variance. You define these factors and the relevant G/L accounts on the Posting Profile form.

8.13 Actual Costing

Actual costing provides different approaches for valuing an item's on-hand inventory. Several actual costing inventory models are supported by Dynamics AX, as summarized in Figure 8.9. Each item must be assigned an inventory model group, which defines the inventory model and related policies. For example, the policy to prevent negative physical inventory should be enforced to avoid calculation problems in actual costing. With the exception of moving average, these inventory models impact an inventory close process, as described in the next two subsections.

Inventory Model	Impact of Inventory Model on the Inventory Closing Process
Weighted Average	Issues will be settled against a summarized weighted average for the month
Weighted Average Date	Issues will be settled against a summarized weighted average for each day
FIFO	Issues will be settled against the oldest receipts within monthly period
LIFO	Issues will be settled against the newest receipts within monthly period
LIFO Date	Issues will be settled against the newest receipts closest to the issue date
Basic Rules for the above Inventory Models	An item's issues will be valued at a running average cost (as of the transaction date). The running average cost reflects the average of the financially updated transactions; it can optionally include physically updated transactions. The user can optionally link (aka mark) a specific receipt to a specific issue transaction.
Moving Average	None. Inventory close only closes the accounting period..

Figure 8.9 Actual Costing Methods

Impact on the Inventory Closing Process Most of the inventory models for actual costing are based on periodic calculations termed *inventory closing and adjustment.*[10] Several basic rules apply to these inventory models, as described below.

- An item's issue transaction (such as a sales order shipment) will be valued at a running average cost as of the transaction date. The running average cost reflects the average of the financially updated transactions; it can optionally include physically updated transactions.
- The month end closing process will settle (aka match) the relevant receipt transactions to the issue transaction based on the item's inventory model, and adjust the item's issue transaction to the correct cost as of the closing date. The receipt transactions must be financially updated, such as an invoiced purchase receipt or the ended status for a production order.
- You can optionally link (aka mark) a specific receipt to a specific issue transaction, which will be used in month-end settlements regardless of the item's inventory model. Marking can occur before or after an issue transaction has been posted.

An inventory closing is normally performed at month end. Each inventory model for actual costing has a slightly different impact on the inventory closing process, as shown in right side of Figure 8.9. The inventory close process will settle issue transactions to receipt transactions based on the inventory model assigned to an item, and create adjustments to the value of on-hand inventory quantities based on financially updated receipts. These adjustments reflect corrections to the running average cost that was originally used to value an inventory transaction. An inventory close prevents users from posting inventory transactions to a prior period, and you can reverse a completed inventory close.

Prior to the inventory closing, you should identify open quantities (via the Open Quantities report) that reflect financial issue transactions that cannot be matched to a financial receipt. A related step identifies excessively high financial receipts that exceed an item's cost and user-specified deviation percentage (via the Investigation of Cost Price for Receipts report). You can then take action on the open quantities and deviations.

[10]The concept of continuously updating actual costs can eliminate the need for month end closing and adjustment. As an example, see **www.InventoryII.com** for more information about their add-on module for Dynamics AX.

Moving Average Cost This approach does not involve the inventory closing process, and primarily applies to purchased material. With moving average, a purchased item's cost is determined at the time of receipt based on its purchase price. If the price differs on the vendor invoice, the difference is proportionally adjusted to current inventory, and any remaining amount is expensed. The approach can apply to a manufactured item, where a production order receipt is valued at the estimated cost for the order, and no adjustments occur after ending the order (even if actual costs differ).

Additional Case Studies

Case 45: Cost Segmentation of Manufacturing Costs A discrete manufacturer calculated the total cost for each of their salable products, and employed cost group segmentation to understand their cost structure. The material costs were segmented into different cost groups (such as electrical parts and fabricated parts) and the manufacturing costs were segmented into different cost groups (such as fabrication, subassembly and final assembly).

Case 46: Simulate Impact of Cost Changes The cost accountant at a discrete manufacturer wanted to simulate the impact of potential cost changes on the calculated costs of manufactured items. The company had already been maintaining the active standard costs for all items within multiple costing versions, and the active cost records for labor rates and overhead formulas, so that active cost records could be used as the fallback principle in cost calculations. The cost accountant employed a separate costing version containing planned costs to define pending cost records (for selected items, labor rates and overhead formulas) that represented the potential cost changes, and then performed a cost calculation for this costing version to simulate the impact. The resulting item cost records were analyzed using the Complete Calculation inquiry.

Case 47: Allocate Overheads Based on Material The cost accountant at a discrete manufacturer wanted to allocate overheads based on material, especially since routing information was not defined. An overhead calculation formula was employed to apply a surcharge percentage to the value of components in order to allocate overheads to the manufactured items.

Case 48: Maintain Standard Costs in Multisite Operations A discrete manufacturing company had multiple manufacturing sites producing different end-items that were transferred to a distribution site. In order to maintain standard costs, the cost accountant defined multiple costing versions representing the different sites. These costing versions also represented each site's standard costs for the current year, so that the cost accountant defined additional costing versions to represent each site's standard costs for next year. The cost accountant used these costing versions in a three-step approach to maintaining next year's standard costs, as summarized below.

- *Step 1: Prepare next year's standard costs at the manufacturing sites.* For each manufacturing site, the cost accountant copied the active cost records from one costing version (representing the current year's standard costs) to create pending cost records within another costing version (representing next year's standard costs) with a pending date of January 1st. The cost accountant updated the pending costs for purchased items to reflect expected cost changes and calculated the costs for manufactured end-items, thereby preparing next year's standard costs as pending cost records.
- *Step 2: Prepare next year's standard costs at the distribution site.* The cost accountant copied the pending cost records (for end-items) from the costing versions for each manufacturing site to the costing version for the distribution site. As part of the copying process, the item cost records were marked up by 5% to reflect the freight/handling costs associated with transfers to the distribution site.
- *Step 3: Activate next year's standard costs.* On January 1, the cost accountant activated the pending cost records within the costing versions representing next year's standard costs.

Case 49: Calculate Sales Prices Based on Cost The sales manager at a discrete manufacturer wanted to calculate a suggested sales price for manufactured items based on a cost-plus-markup approach. The company had already been maintaining a costing version containing the standard costs for all items, labor rates and overhead formulas. The sales manager defined the profit-setting percentages for the various cost groups associated with material, labor and overhead. The sales manager also defined a separate costing version that only contained item sales price records. The sales manager then performed a cost calculation for this costing version to calculate the suggested sales price using a specified set of profit-setting percentages.

Case 50: Calculate Sales Prices for a Sales Quotation The sales manager at a discrete manufacturer wanted to calculate an item's suggested sales price for sales quotations, which could then be used to support price negotiation efforts. The sales manager wanted the calculated price to reflect a cost-plus-markup approach and the purchase price trade agreements as the source of cost data for purchased components. As part of entering a sales quotation, an order-specific cost calculation was performed to calculate the suggested sales price, and the suggested price could then be transferred to the sales quotation line item.

Case 51: Costing for Precious Metal Components A fabricated products company used several types of precious metal components with purchase prices that could vary widely on a week-to-week basis. They wanted to immediately reflect new purchase prices of the precious metals in each end-item's cost and sales price. Using a standard cost approach, the standard cost of each precious metal was updated after a change in purchase price, and the end-items' costs (and suggested sales prices) were recalculated using cost calculations. The cost changes revalued the existing inventory of components and products, but the company generally carried a minimum level of inventory.

Executive Summary

Product cost information supports valuation of an item's inventory transactions using a standard cost or actual cost method. Standard costs for items are maintained in a set of standard cost data termed a costing version. Manufacturers can also maintain labor rates and overhead formulas in a set of cost data, and use cost calculations to maintain the standard costs for manufactured items. In addition, the cost calculations can be used for simulating the impact of cost changes, or to calculate a suggested sales price. These simulations can optionally employ a set of planned cost data, which supports additional options in cost calculations. As an example option, the source of cost data for purchased items can reflect purchase price trade agreements rather than the item cost records within a costing version.

With actual costing methods, an item's actual cost is not maintained in a costing version. An item's actual cost reflects financially-updated receipt transactions such as invoiced purchase orders. For manufactured items, the actual production costs for a production order reflect the active labor rates for routing operations and the overhead formulas, where labor rates and overhead formulas are defined in a costing version. Planned costs for manufactured items can also be calculated and maintained in a set of cost data. The cost calculations can be used for simulating projected costs or the impact of cost changes, or to calculate a suggested sales price. With planned cost calculations, the source of cost data for purchased items can reflect their actual cost or purchase price trade agreement, or item cost records within a costing version.

An order-specific cost calculation can be used in the context of a sales order, sales quotation or service order line item in order to calculate the estimated cost and sales price of a manufactured item, and optionally transfer the calculated sales price to the originating line item.

Several case studies illustrated product costing functionality, such as cost segmentation for a manufactured item, simulating the impact of cost changes, and allocating overheads based on material.

Chapter 9

Serial and Batch Tracking

Some manufacturing scenarios require tracking of serial numbers or batch numbers for a material item, or both. The term batch number is used because Dynamics AX employs the term *lot number* as a system-assigned internal identifier for inventory transactions. A serial number or batch number is typically assigned upon receipt, such as the receipt of a purchase order or the finished quantity of a production order. Subsequent transactions identifying these numbers automatically create tracking history. Several additional capabilities apply to batch tracking for an item, including vendor batch information, batch attributes, and batch disposition codes to indicate restricted usage. The following sections of the chapter reflect these topics:

1. Serial Tracking
2. Batch Tracking
3. Vendor Batch Information
4. Batch Attributes
5. Batch Disposition Codes and Restricted Usage

Many of these topics also involve quality management considerations, such as product testing and quality orders. For example, the test results associated with a quality order can apply to a serial number or batch number. Many of the quality management considerations apply to items with and without tracking requirements. Chapter 18 provides further explanation of quality management.

9.1 Serial Tracking

Serial number tracking traditionally refers to a unique serial number for each unit of inventory. AX also supports a single serial number for multiple units of an item (conceptually similar to lot tracking), but this section focuses on serial numbers for individual units. The explanation starts with the assignment of a serial tracking policy to an item, and then covers the creation of serial numbers.

Serial Tracking Policy Serial tracking is designated by the Tracking Dimension Group assigned to an item, which must include the serial number. An additional policy—termed *serial number control*—ensures that individual units will be assigned a serial number. The Tracking Dimension Group has several other policies not typically used, such as sales pricing or coverage planning for specific serial numbers.

Serial Numbering Policies Dynamics AX supports several different approaches for assigning a serial number to each unit of an item's inventory. Three approaches are described below, and the third approach requires an additional set of policies (termed the serial number group) for a serialized item.

- *Manual assignment of a serial number.* You can manually assign a serial number to inventory receipt transactions with a quantity of one, so that receipts for a larger quantity must first be split into quantities of one. Manual assignment allows you to enter the existing serial number on received material.
- *Automatic assignment using an ad hoc serial number mask.* The existing serial numbers for received material often reflect a pattern. For example, the pattern might consist of the same 10 characters and three unique digits in a numerical sequence, where the three unique digits differentiate the serial numbers. In this scenario, you can use the "Create Serial Numbers" dialogue with AX to specify an ad hoc serial number mask that reflects the pattern. If the pattern has more than one variation, you can split the quantity and use different ad hoc masks.

  You can use the "Create Serial Numbers" dialogue as part of registering arrivals for a purchase order, or you can access it beforehand. The dialogue can also be accessed when reporting the finished quantity on production orders, or at any time after order creation. In some cases, the serial numbers for the finished item must be assigned beforehand in order to track testing results against serial numbers.

❖ *Automatic assignment using the item's serial number mask.* A mask can help enforce internal guidelines about assignment of serial numbers to an item, where you place your internal serial number on the received material. It represents one policy within the serial number group assigned to the item. The mask may simply reflect a prefix and counter, or include the date, order number, and/or system-assigned lot ID. A second policy determines when to assign the serial number; it is typically assigned when recording inventory transactions.

The set of policies associated with a serial number group can be defined (aka activated) for one or more types of transactions. The types include purchase orders, production orders, kanban orders, sales order returns, and inventory journals, and you indicate the applicable types as part the batch number group's policies.

Information about a Serial Number Information about each serial number for an item consists of descriptive text and a manufacturing date. This information can be viewed and maintained on the Serial Numbers form.

Serial Tracking History The history is automatically maintained based on receipt and issue transactions. Using the Serial Numbers form, you can view historical information about a selected item or serial number, such as forward or backward tracking information using a multilevel indented format. Each entry in the indented format indicates a receipt or issue. An entry can also reflect a transfer. A transfer may also reflect the assignment of a different serial number to an existing serial number via the Transfer Journal.

Serial Tracking on Intercompany Orders When using intercompany orders in a multi-company operation, the serial numbers assigned to the shipped material (on the intercompany sales order) can automatically apply to the received material (on the intercompany purchase order).

Printing Serial Numbers on Documents The serial numbers can be printed on sales and purchase documents based on the form setup policies. For example, the serial numbers can be printed on the sales order packing slip and invoice.

Case 52: RMAs for Serialized Items

A manufacturing company required RMA processing on customer returns of their serialized electronic items. Each serialized number had a 12 month warranty period (from date of sale) for free replacement. The customer identified an item's serial number when requesting an RMA, which was used to verify the applicability of its warranty period. The customer shipped the returned item after receiving an electronic copy of the printed RMA. Items were shipped to a repair facility, which verified the serial number and sent a free replacement (when it was within warranty) or charged for the replacement (when it was not within warranty). The repair facility assigned a disposition to each returned item during an inspection process, which determined whether the item was usable, scrapped, or repairable. A scrapped item could also be stripped down for reusing the high value components.

9.2 Batch Tracking

Batch tracking provides the foundation for handling batch-related information such as batch attributes and batch disposition codes. Batch tracking involves two sets of policies for an item. The first set of policies indicates that an item requires batch tracking, and the second set of policies indicates how and when the internal batch numbers are assigned. Batch numbers frequently have significance, which requires careful consideration of batch number creation and assignment.

Several additional aspects of batch tracking—such as shelf life information— do not generally apply to discrete manufacturing scenarios, and are not covered within this book.

Batch Tracking Policies Batch tracking is defined by the Tracking Dimension Group assigned to an item, which must include the batch number. The batch number dimension has several policies that enforce batch tracking for issues and receipts, and optionally support unique requirements such as batch-specific costing and pricing.

Batch Numbering Policies A second set of policies (termed the batch number group) determines how batch numbers are created and when they are assigned to inventory transactions for received material. A batch number can be created manually or automatically, with two basic timing variations for automatic assignment to received material. An additional consideration includes the quantity associated with an automatically assigned batch number.

- *Manual versus automatic creation.* Automatic creation allows specification of a batch number mask, such as a prefix and counter. The mask can also include the date, order number, and/or system-assigned lot ID. Other approaches to a batch number mask may need to be customized to meet requirements for a meaningful batch number.

  Manual creation means that you define an item's batch number prior to using it on an inventory transaction, and the batch numbering mask does not apply. For example, an item's batch number may be created during transaction entry and then assigned to a receipt.
- *Automatically assigning different batch numbers to multiple receipts for an order.* An item's batch numbers can be automatically created upon receipt of an order, such as a purchase order line or a production/batch order. When reporting multiple partial receipts against the same order, or splitting a receipt quantity, a batch numbering policy determines whether to assign the same batch number or a different batch number to each partial receipt.[1]

  As an example, the order quantity for a production order may represent several production runs, and you would report the finished quantity for each production run so that a different batch number will be assigned. Alternatively, you could report the entire order quantity as finished, and use the split function to identify the different quantities representing different batch numbers. However, some scenarios may want the same batch number when reporting multiple finished quantities.
- *Fixed increments associated with an automatically assigned batch number.* Some scenarios require a unique batch number for fixed increments of a receipt quantity, such as assigning unique batch numbers for every 100 units received when receiving a quantity of 1000. This requirement may reflect the item's packaging characteristics, production characteristics or a quality management consideration. You can optionally specify this "per quantity" increment as a batch numbering policy.

---

[1] The same batch number will be assigned to partial receipts when the numbering policy is simply "assignment on inventory transaction." Different batch numbers will be assigned by specifying the additional policy "assignment upon physical update."

- *Applicability of the Batch Number Group policies.* The set of policies associated with a batch number group can be applied (aka activated) to one or more types of transactions. The types include purchase orders, production orders, sales order returns, and inventory journals, and you indicate the applicable types as part the batch number group's policies.

Another approach can be used regardless of the policies, where you manually assign a batch number to a purchase order line or a batch production order, and the batch number will apply to all transactions for the line item.

Information about each internal batch number can include descriptive text, a vendor batch number and related information (for purchased material), shelf life dates, batch attributes, and a batch disposition code. Subsequent sections explain these aspects of batch-related information.

Viewing the Internal Batch Numbers The key form for batch information—termed the Batch Details form or Batch form for short—provides a list of all internal batch numbers and the related items. It also displays the batch-related information such as shelf life dates and batch attributes.

Combining or Changing Batch Numbers of On-Hand Inventory You can change or combine the batch number for an inventory quantity by using the Transfer Journal, much like you would change or combine inventory in a bin location. You transfer the inventory quantity from one batch number to another (when combining batches), or to a newly created batch number (when changing batch numbers). As part of reporting a Transfer Journal, you can chose to copy the batch attributes to the to-batch. You can also change a batch number (such as correcting an error in the identifier) by using the rename capability.

Batch Tracking on Intercompany Orders When using intercompany orders in a multi-company operation, the batch numbers assigned to the shipped material (on the intercompany sales order) can automatically apply to the received material (on the intercompany purchase order).

Printing Batch Numbers on Documents The batch numbers can be printed on sales and purchase documents based on the form setup policies. For example, the batch numbers can be printed on the sales order packing slip and invoice.

Historical Information about Batch Number Tracking The batch-trace history is automatically maintained based on receipt and issue transactions. Using the Batch form, you can view historical information about a specified item or batch number, and the on-line inquiry avoids the need for extensive printed reports. In a manufacturing environment, you can view forward or backward trace information using a multilevel indented format that reflects the product structure. Each entry in the indented format indicates a receipt or issue. For example, the batch number for a sales order shipment can be traced backward through the production orders to purchase order receipts. A receipt can also be traced forward.

Batch Tracking and Serial Tracking for an Item Some scenarios require batch and serial tracking for an item. The two tracking numbers represent separate constructs, and a hierarchical relationship does not exist between a batch number and serial numbers for an item.

9.3 Vendor Batch Information

The vendor batch information normally applies to a purchased item, but it can also be used for other items. The information includes a vendor batch number, a field for the vendor-specified manufacturing date, and two fields for capturing country of origin information. The information is typically assigned at the time of receipt, but you can also update the information on the Batch Details form (by accessing the Reset Vendor Batch Details form).

9.4 Batch Attributes

One or more batch attributes can be assigned to a batch-controlled item, and actual values recorded against an item's batches. The use of batch attributes requires some setup information.

Setup Information for Batch Attributes The setup information consists of the following steps.

❖ *Define batch attributes.* The identifier and description of a batch attribute are user-definable, and the attribute can be designated as an integer, fraction, date, string, or enumerated list (which requires definition of possible values in the list). When designated as an integer or fraction, the batch attribute must also be assigned values for a minimum, maximum, and increment as well as a tolerance policy. The tolerance policy has two options—provide warning or prevent entry—concerning the actual values for the batch attribute.

- *Define a group of batch attributes.* This approach provides a shortcut for assigning multiple batch attributes to an item, and represents an optional step. The identifier and description of a batch attribute group are user-definable, and one or more batch attributes can be assigned to the group. When an assigned attribute consists of an integer or fraction, the values for the minimum, maximum, increment, and tolerance policy are inherited but can be overridden. For example, the attribute's minimum and maximum values can be overridden each time it is assigned to an attribute group.
- *Assign batch attributes to an item.* One or more batch attributes or groups can be assigned to a batch-controlled item using the Batch Attributes by Item form. Those attributes consisting of an integer or fraction will inherit values (such as the minimum and maximum) from the definition of the batch attribute, and these can be overridden to indicate item-specific values.

An additional setup step is needed when using the test results from quality orders to update a batch attribute value, since the test must be mapped to the batch attribute. Section 18.4 provides further explanation of quality orders and their test results.

Recording Actual Values for Batch Attributes The actual value for an item's batch attribute can be recorded after creation of a batch, and subsequently viewed for the batch. When the batch attribute reflects an integer or fraction, the system provides a warning or prevents entry (based on the tolerance policy) when the actual value exceeds the minimum or maximum.

Additional Capabilities Regarding Batch Attributes Several capabilities related to batch attributes do not typically apply to discrete manufacturing scenarios. For example, you can search for an appropriate batch based on actual values of the item's batch attributes. This is termed a batch attribute search. In addition, a customer may have specific requirements for the values of batch attributes, so that a batch attribute search can be based on the customer requirements.

9.5 Batch Disposition Codes and Restricted Usage

Disposition codes represent an optional approach for managing the inventory of batch-controlled material, since the policies associated with a disposition code can enforce restricted usage.[2] This section describes the setup information for disposition codes, the assignment (and reassignment) of a disposition code to an item's batch, and the impact on planning calculations. Those scenarios that do not require enforcement of restricted usage can define and use a single disposition code that reflects available material without restricted usage.

Setup Information for Disposition Codes The user-defined disposition codes must be set up on the Disposition Master form. One disposition code should reflect available material, where the disposition status is designated as available. The number of additional codes will depend on the desired variations in restricted usage, where the disposition status is designated as unavailable. The typical requirements for two additional disposition codes include (1) quarantined material treated as non-nettable and with all usage restrictions, and (2) quality hold material treated as nettable and with some usage restrictions.

The following policies can be assigned to a disposition code with an unavailable disposition status, where the policies indicate aspects of restricted usage:

- *Nettable*. This policy determines whether inventory will be considered available by planning calculations.
- *Restricted usage for sales orders*. You can designate one or more of the following policies on restricted usage:
  - Block reservations. This policy prevents reservation of the batch inventory.
  - Block picking. This policy prevents picking of the batch inventory.
  - Block shipping. This policy prevents shipment (aka packing slip update) of the batch inventory.

---

[2]Batch disposition codes represent a different construct than the disposition codes for handling return orders from customers, which are described in Section 12.8.

- *Restricted usage for transfers.* You can designate one or more of the following policies on restricted usage. However, you should not block transfers if you intend to return a purchased batch to the vendor, or move the batch to a different location.
  - Block reservations. This policy prevents reservation of the batch inventory.
  - Block picking. This policy prevents picking of the batch inventory.
  - Block shipping. This policy prevents shipment (aka packing slip update) of the batch inventory.
- *Restricted usage for production orders.* You can designate one or more of the following policies on restricted usage:
  - Block reservations. This policy prevents reservation of the batch inventory.
  - Block picking. This policy prevents picking of the batch inventory.

Assignment of a Disposition Code to an Item's Batch Number

The initial value of the disposition code is automatically assigned to a batch number based on two different approaches, as described below.

- Default value specified for the item, as defined in the Item Model Group assigned to the item.
- Default value related to the use of quality orders (if applicable). This approach builds on the use of test groups and quality orders described in Chapter 17. When defining a test group, the default value for a disposition code can be defined for an open quality order, and for the outcome of a failed or passed quality order.

Once an internal batch number has been created, you can manually override the disposition code (by accessing the Reset Disposition Code form). A history of changes to a batch's disposition code is automatically maintained by the system, and viewable on the History of Disposition Inventory form.

Impact on Master Scheduling and Capable-to-Promise Logic

Master scheduling and capable-to-promise logic will ignore non-nettable inventory, as identified by the disposition code assigned to a batch. The physical non-nettable quantity of an item's inventory can still be viewed on the On Hand form.

Additional Case Studies

Case 53: Vendor Batch Numbers A manufacturer used several purchased components that were batch-controlled items. At the time of product receipt, the warehouse workers recorded an internal batch number and the vendor's batch number. A bar-coded label with the internal batch number was affixed to the product receipt, and subsequent transactions referred to the internal batch number.

Case 54: Country of Origin for Purchased Material A manufacturer used several purchased components that were batch-controlled items. They recorded the country of origin as part of the vendor batch dctails for each batch of these purchased items. Most cases involved a single country of origin, although a few required two different countries. This information was used to support government reporting requirements about country of origin.

Executive Summary

Some manufacturing scenarios require tracking of serial numbers or batch numbers for a material item, or both. Each batch may also require batch-related information, such as batch attributes or batch disposition codes to indicate restricted usage. This chapter summarized how to setup and use serial numbers and batch numbers for an item, and included several case studies about system usage.

Chapter 10

Coverage Planning Data for Item Replenishment

Planned orders communicate the need to replenish an item's inventory, and are generated by planning calculations based on an item's coverage planning data. This chapter explains coverage planning data, whereas the next chapter explains planning calculations. The term *coverage planning data* (or planning data for short) has several synonyms, such as reordering or replenishment policies. Most of an item's planning data can be specified as company-wide policies that act as default values for site/warehouse-specific policies that can be overridden. For example, you can specify a company-wide policy about a purchased item's preferred vendor and override the preferred vendor for a given site/warehouse.

The planning data defines an item's preferred source of supply, so that planning calculations generate a planned order to purchase, manufacture or transfer the item. These variations of planned orders provide an organizing focus for explaining coverage planning data, as reflected in the following sections.

1. Planning Data for Purchased Items
2. Special Cases for Purchased Items
3. Planning Data for Manufactured Items
4. Special Cases for Manufactured Items
5. Planning Data for Transfer Items
6. Significance of Planning Data for Negative Days and Positive Days

Subsequent chapters explain usage of these planned orders for purchasing, manufacturing, subcontracted production, and transfers.

10.1 Planning Data for Purchased Items

Planning calculations suggest planned purchase orders based on an item's planning data. Figure 10.1 summarizes the planning data for purchased items, and highlights the company-wide versus site/warehouse policies. The bottom of the figure also highlights the four key forms for maintaining an item's planning data. Further explanation covers each aspect of planning data within the figure.

Relevant Inventory Dimensions for Coverage Planning Policies

An item's replenishment logic typically applies to the combination of site and warehouse, as defined by the relevant inventory dimensions for coverage planning. You indicate the relevant inventory dimensions as part of the Storage Dimension Group assigned to the item. In some cases, the relevant inventory dimensions for coverage planning may include a bin location or just the site. Coverage planning does not apply to the inventory dimensions for batch, serial, or pallet. The book's baseline model assumes that sites, warehouse, and bin locations are used for inventory tracking, and that coverage planning applies to the combination of site and warehouse.

<table>
<tr><th></th><th></th><th>Companywide Policies</th><th>Site-Specific Policies</th><th>Site/Warehouse Policies</th></tr>
<tr><td rowspan="10">Planning Data for Purchased Items</td><td>Relevant Inventory Dimensions
For Coverage Planning Policies</td><td>Specify</td><td rowspan="6">N/A</td><td>N/A</td></tr>
<tr><td>Primary Source of Supply
(Planned Order Type = Purchase Order)</td><td rowspan="7">Specify
Act as Defaults</td><td rowspan="6">Override</td></tr>
<tr><td>Preferred Vendor</td></tr>
<tr><td>Coverage Code (Reordering Policy)</td></tr>
<tr><td>Action Message Policies</td></tr>
<tr><td>Coverage Group (Set of Policies)</td></tr>
<tr><td>Purchase Lead Time</td><td rowspan="2">Override</td></tr>
<tr><td>Order Quantity Modifiers for Purchasing</td><td>N/A</td></tr>
<tr><td>Minimum Quantity (Safety Stock)</td><td>N/A</td><td rowspan="2">N/A</td><td>Specify</td></tr>
<tr><td>Buyer Responsibility</td><td>Specify</td><td>N/A</td></tr>
<tr><td></td><td></td><td>Use Released Products form or Default Order Settings</td><td>Use Site-Specific Order Settings form</td><td>Use Item Coverage form</td></tr>
</table>

Figure 10.1 Planning Data for Purchased Items

Primary Source of Supply A planned order type of *Purchase Order* indicates the primary source of supply for an item, so that planning calculations generate planned purchase orders. An item's planned order type (aka default order type) can be specified as a company-wide policy, and optionally overridden for a given site/warehouse. For example, a purchased item may be replenished via purchase orders at one warehouse, but replenished via transfer orders at a different warehouse.

Preferred Vendor An item's preferred vendor can be specified as a company-wide policy, and optionally overridden for a given site/warehouse. It must reflect one of the item's approved vendors when enforcing this policy. The planning calculations assign the preferred vendor to planned purchase orders for the item.

The approach to defining an item's preferred vendor differs slightly for buy-to-order components, or when sourcing to the vendor with the lowest price or delivery lead time. The next section provides further explanation of these special cases for purchased items.

Coverage Code (aka Reordering Policy) The coverage code represents a key part of the buyer's decision-making logic about generating planned purchase orders. It is embedded within the coverage group assigned to an item, but its importance merits a separate explanation. The four reordering policies include min-max (time-phased order point logic), period (period lot-sizing logic), requirement (order-driven logic), and manual. Each method can be characterized by its primary planning parameters, order quantity modifiers, and inventory plan, as shown in Figure 10.2 and summarized below. The left-hand columns characterize each policy in terms of its underlying logic, such as order point or period lot-sizing logic.

- *Min-Max (also known as Order Up To).* When an item's projected inventory falls below its *minimum quantity*, the planning calculations suggest an order quantity that achieves the item's *maximum quantity*, subject to an order quantity modifier for a multiple. The projected inventory reflects future demands and scheduled receipts for the item. The values for minimum and maximum quantity can be specified using a fixed or variable approach. A variable approach, for example, can specify a different quantity for each month to reflect seasonality or trends.
- *Period (also known as Period Lot Size).* When an item's projected inventory reaches zero (or its minimum quantity), the planning calcula-

Logic Basis	Coverage Code and its significance	Planning Data: Primary Parameters	Planning Data: Order Qty Modifiers**	Planning Data: Safety Stock
Order Point	**Min-Max** Suggested order quantity achieves maximum inventory quantity subject to order quantity multiple	Minimum Quantity* Maximum Quantity	Multiple	N/A
MRP	**Period** Suggested order quantity covers multiple demands within the period subject to order quantity modifiers	Period Size (in days)	Minimum Multiple Maximum	Minimum Quantity*
Order Driven	**Requirement** Suggested order quantity covers one demand subject to order quantity modifiers		Minimum Multiple Maximum	Minimum Quantity*
Manual Planning	**Manual** No suggested orders	N/A	N/A	N/A

* = The minimum quantity represents a site/warehouse-specific safety stock quantity, and differs from the order quantity modifiers for a minimum.

** = Three different sets of order quantity modifiers can be defined for an item: for sales orders, purchase orders and for production/batch orders. Planned transfer orders use the order quantity modifiers related to production/batch orders.

Figure 10.2 Significance of Coverage Codes

tions suggest an order quantity that covers demands over the *period size,* subject to order quantity modifiers. The period size reflects the frequency of replenishment or reorder cycle, such as daily, weekly or monthly.

The site/warehouse-specific minimum quantity represents an explicit inventory plan or safety stock for an item. An implied inventory plan reflects the extent to which the period size and order modifiers (for minimum and multiple) inflate the suggested order quantity so that it exceeds the requirements.

❖ *Requirement (also known as Order-Driven or Lot-for-Lot).* The planning calculations suggest an order quantity that covers each individual demand, subject to order quantity modifiers. As noted above, the minimum quantity and order modifiers represent explicit and implied inventory plans respectively.

❖ *Manual.* The planning calculations do not suggest planned orders, but they do calculate net requirements to support manual planning efforts.

	Message	Significance	Message Filters		
			Tolerance	Suppress	Horizon
Actions	Advance	Expedite the order to an earlier date	Advance Tolerance (in days)	Yes/No	Actions Look-Ahead Horizon (in days)
	Postpone	De-expedite the order to a later date	Postpone Tolerance (in days)	Yes/No	
	Increase	Increase order to a suggested quantity	N/A	Yes/No	
	Decrease	Decrease order to a suggested quantity		Yes/No*	
	Cancel	Cancel order because the requirement has been changed or cancelled		N/A*	
Futures	Delay	Projected completion date does not meet requirement date	N/A	Yes/No	Futures Look-Ahead Horizon (in days)

* = Suppressing the decrease message will also suppress the cancel message.

Figure 10.3 Significance of Suggested Action Messages

Action Message Policies Action messages represent a key tool for coordinating an item's supply chain activities. Action message policies are embedded within the coverage group assigned to an item, but their importance merits a separate explanation. Planning calculations can generate two types of action messages termed actions and futures, as shown in Figure 10.3 and explained below.

- *Actions Message.* An actions message indicates a suggestion to advance/postpone an order's delivery date, to increase/decrease an order quantity, or to cancel an order. Suggested advancement of an existing order reflects the item's rescheduling assumption, so that the system suggests expediting rather than a new planned order to cover a requirement within the item's lead time. A subsequent section provides further explanation of the rescheduling assumption (Section 10.6). When applicable, actions messages are displayed for planned orders, and also summarized on the Actions form.
- *Futures Message.* A futures message indicates that the projected completion date for supply chain activities will cause a delay in meeting a

requirement date such as a sales order shipment. When applicable, futures messages are displayed for planned orders, and also summarized on the Futures form.

Message filters can eliminate unnecessary suggestions about actions and futures, as shown in the right side of Figure 10.3. Message filters about actions, for example, include the ability to suppress a message, a look-ahead horizon to limit the number of messages, and tolerances that eliminate unnecessary messages to advance or postpone a scheduled receipt.

As a general observation, most companies struggle with effective use of action messages because the volume can easily overwhelm the planner so that the messages become meaningless. The problem typically stems from poor sales and operations planning efforts that ignore the suggested guidelines which results in a high volume of messages regardless of filters. There are other potential sources causing ineffective use of action messages, such as an unrealistic model of the planner's decision making as defined by the item planning data, BOM information, and routing information. To really be effective, you should consider ways to reduce the number of messages so that you achieve a target "hit rate" of 90+% for taking action on messages.

Coverage Group (Set of Policies) The coverage group assigned to an item contains the coverage code, action message policies, and other policies that represent a model of the buyer's decision making logic about planned purchase orders and existing orders. The previous subsections explained the coverage code and action messages; this section covers the other policies. The company-wide policy for an item's coverage group acts as a default value for a given site/warehouse, and it can be overridden.

- *Planning Horizon and Related Time Fence Policies.* The planning horizon for requirements calculations generally extends several months (e.g., 6 to 12 months) beyond the cumulative lead time to obtain the product. This planning horizon should be reflected in several time fence policies, including the forecast plan and coverage time fences.
- *Policies for Automatic Firming.* The planning calculations can automatically create purchase orders from planned orders within a specified time horizon termed the *firm time fence*. With automatic firming, planned purchase orders with suggested vendors can be grouped into multi-line purchase orders based on grouping preferences, such as a multi-line purchase order reflecting the same vendor and weekly time period.

- *Use of a Frozen Period.* The frozen period (termed a *freeze time fence*) for a purchased item represents the shortest possible turnaround time to obtain material with a new purchase order. When the required date falls within the freeze time fence, planning calculations will place the new planned order at the end of the frozen period.
- *Safety Margin.* A safety margin represents a safety lead time, so that material will be delivered prior to the requirement date. Although it can be expressed as three different values, the planning calculations only use the sum as the safety margin. As an example, a safety lead time may be assigned to a purchased item that experiences delays in delivery.
- *Calendar.* Most environments will use the shop calendar assigned to each warehouse for planning calculation purposes. Some environments require a calendar assigned to items, such as a 24/7 operation for selected products that can be received and shipped at any time.

Purchase Lead Time An item's purchase lead time can be specified as a company-wide policy, and optionally overridden as part of the item's site-specific order settings or as part of the item's coverage policies for a site/warehouse. Each delivery lead time is defined in terms of calendar days unless explicitly flagged as working days.

The item's purchase lead time can also be specified in purchase price trade agreements, but planning calculations typically ignore this information.[1] However, the information is considered when manually creating a purchase order, so that the delivery date reflects the lead time within the applicable trade agreement record. If an applicable trade agreement record does not exist, then the item's purchase lead time (described above) will be reflected in the delivery date.

Order Quantity Modifiers for Purchasing Planning calculations suggest a planned purchased order quantity subject to order quantity modifiers for a minimum, maximum and multiple. The modifiers only apply when using Period or Requirement as the item's coverage code. In addition, a soft warning will be displayed during purchase order entry when you enter a quantity that does not meet these criteria.

---

[1] As a company-wide policy (defined in the Master Planning parameters), the planning calculations can optionally consider lead times in the purchase price trade agreements as part of suggesting a vendor for planned orders based on the shortest lead time.

- *Minimum.* The minimum represents the smallest suggested order quantity.
- *Multiple.* The suggested order quantity will always reflect the multiple, even if it exceeds the maximum.
- *Maximum.* The maximum represents the largest order quantity, so that planning calculations suggest multiple planned orders to cover requirements exceeding the maximum.

Some situations require a fixed order quantity, perhaps reflecting considerations about batch tracking, transportation, production or some other factor. Using the same values for maximum and multiple means that planning calculations will generate multiple planned orders for the fixed quantity.

Standard Order Quantity for Purchasing The item's standard purchase order quantity is used as a default when manually entering a purchase order line item. The company-wide value can be overridden for a given site/warehouse.

Inventory UM and Default Purchase UM The planning calculations and planned purchase orders for an item reflect its inventory UM, whereas firming up a planned purchase order results in a purchase order for the item's default purchase UM.

Minimum Quantity The minimum quantity represents an item's inventory plan or safety stock for a given site/warehouse. It typically reflects average demand over lead time when using the Min/Max coverage code. Alternatively, it reflects the desired safety stock to cover demand variations when using sales forecasts and a coverage code of Period or Requirement. Considerations about the minimum quantity include the interpretation of its requirement date, automatic calculation based on historical data, and use of a variable minimum quantity by time period.

- *Requirement Date for Minimum Quantity.* The requirement date for the minimum quantity typically reflects a future date that accounts for the item's lead time. The system supports other bases of the requirement date, such as today's date. The basis is defined in the warehouse-specific coverage data for an item.
- *Automatically Calculating the Minimum Quantity.* The minimum quantity can be automatically calculated based on historical data, using either

average issues during lead time or a desired service level reflecting the standard deviation. The calculation requires at least three months of historical data.[2] Using the calculation capability (termed the *item coverage* or *safety stock journal*) involves four steps: identifying the items and historical date range, calculating the proposed minimum inventory, reviewing and possibly overriding the proposed minimum, and finally updating the minimum quantity. The projected impact on inventory value can be viewed prior to updating the minimum quantity. The calculations can help identify items that have less than the minimum inventory level; correcting this situation can reduce potential stock outs.

- *Using a Variable Quantity for Minimum or Maximum Quantity.* The variable quantity approach reflects different quantities by time period such as months. The variable quantity for each period is expressed as a multiplier (such as 1.5 or .75) of the minimum quantity. Each pattern of time periods and multipliers is termed a *Minimum/Maximum Key,* and must be user-defined. A separate key can be assigned to the item's minimum quantity and to the item's maximum quantity as part of the warehouse-specific planning data. Each pattern typically has a specified starting date (such as January 1, 20XX) to model seasonality or trends in demands across the calendar year. The variable quantity approach provides flexibility in modeling changing demand patterns in comparison to a fixed quantity approach.

Buyer Responsibility The concept of buyer responsibility provides an organizing focus for communicating the need to synchronize supplies with demands. The concept of buyer responsibility is typically based on the buyer group field; an alternative basis could be the item group field. A user-defined buyer group can be assigned to an item to indicate responsibility for maintaining planning data, whereas the buyer group assigned to a vendor indicates responsibility for coordinating purchases. Planning calculations generate planned orders identified with the buyer group associated with the vendor. A purchase order header contains a buyer group that applies to all purchase order line items.

Maintaining an Item's Coverage Planning Data An item's planning data must be specified for each relevant site/warehouse which requires

[2] Although the calculation requires a minimum of three months of historical usage, a longer period is typically required to accurately model average usage.

replenishment. An item stocked in three warehouses, for example, would require three records for its item coverage data. An item's coverage data can be maintained by accessing it from the Released Products form or from the Item Coverage Setup form. In either case, you can directly maintain the records, or use a wizard to create new records for selected sites/warehouses (which can then be directly maintained). Use of the Item Coverage Setup form provides several advantages.

- View items without any item coverage records, thereby making initial data maintenance easier.
- View a subset of items by filtering on the item group or buyer group, or the currently assigned coverage group or storage dimension group.
- Use the default settings (of a selected record of one item's coverage data) as the copy basis for initially creating a new record for selected items without data.
- Delete the item coverage data records for selected items, so that you have a fresh start at maintaining the data.

Replenishment Limitations for a Purchased Item Replenishment limitations can stop purchases of an item (using a purchasing stop flag), or limit purchases to the single site (and warehouse) that actually buys the item. The stop flag means that existing orders cannot be received, and prevents creation of new orders. However, these limitations do not impact planning calculations so that planned purchase orders can still be generated.

10.2 Special Cases for Purchased Items

The previous section focused on the planning data for purchased items, and several special cases require additional considerations. These special cases include buy-to-order components, the suggested vendor based on lowest price or delivery lead time, and purchased items requiring internal production.

Buy-to-Order Component for Material A purchased item can be designated as a but-to-order component in the BOM information of its parent item, where you specify a BOM line type of Vendor. The preferred vendor for a buy-to-order component can be optionally overridden as part of the component information, otherwise it reflects the company-wide or site-specific preferred vendor for the item.

Planning calculations will calculate requirements for a buy-to-order component, and even generate planned orders based on the item's planning data.[3] The planning calculations ignore on-hand inventory for meeting the buy-to-order requirements. However, the planned orders simply provide visibility about these requirements, and these planned orders cannot be firmed (for creating a purchase order). Instead, you automatically create a linked purchase order for a buy-to-order component when you update the status of the parent item's production order, such as updating the status to *estimated* or *scheduled.* The quantity for the linked purchase order reflects the production order quantity and the BOM information about the component quantity. Deleting the parent item's production order will delete the linked purchased order.

Buy-to-Order Component for a Subcontracted Service The AX approach to subcontracted production employs a buy-to-order component to represent the subcontracted service. The above explanation also applies to these buy-to-order components. Chapter 16 provides further explanation of subcontracted services to support subcontract manufacturing.

Suggested Vendor Based on Lowest Price or Delivery Lead Time Some scenarios will source a purchased item based on price or delivery considerations rather than a preferred vendor. In this case, the preferred vendor field should be left blank in order to support automatic vendor assignment on planned purchase orders based on trade agreement information for lowest price or delivery lead time.[4] Chapter 13 provides further explanation of purchase price trade agreement information.

Purchased Items Requiring Internal Production Some scenarios involve internal production of a purchased item, either on an intermittent basis or as part of a planned change. In this case, the item must have BOM information to support the use of production orders. When you primarily purchase the item, you assign a planned order type of Purchase Order. You may also need to assign a standard cost reflecting the item's purchase price

[3] You typically assign a coverage code of *requirement or period lot size* to a purchased item that has buy-to-order requirements.

[4] A company-wide policy (defined in the master planning parameters) determines whether the planning calculations will use the purchase price trade agreement information to suggest a vendor for purchased items (when a preferred vendor has not been specified). A related policy specifies whether price or delivery lead time serves as the basis for suggesting a vendor.

rather than calculating the item's manufacturing cost. The cost calculations for higher level items should also employ the item's purchase cost, which requires a *stop explosion* policy in the calculation group assigned to the item.

10.3 Planning Data for Manufactured Items

Planning calculations suggest planned production orders based on the planning data for a manufactured item. Much of the planning data reflect an item's company-wide policies, which can be overridden to reflect the site- and warehouse-specific policies for the item. Figure 10.4 summarizes the planning data for a manufactured item, and highlights the company-wide versus site/warehouse policies. The bottom of the figure also highlights the four key forms for maintaining an item's planning data. Further explanation covers each aspect of planning data within the figure.

Relevant Inventory Dimensions for Coverage Planning Policies

An item's replenishment logic typically applies to the combination of site and warehouse, as defined by the relevant inventory dimensions for coverage

Planning Data for Manufactured Items	Companywide Policies	Site-Specific Policies	Site/Warehouse Policies
Relevant Inventory Dimensions For Coverage Planning Policies	Specify		
BOM Version	Specify BOM as Company-Wide	Specify BOM as Site-Specific	N/A
Route Version	N/A	Specify Routing as Site-Specific	
Primary Source of Supply (Planned Order Type = Production)			
Coverage Code (Reordering Policy)		N/A	Override
Coverage Group (Set of Policies)	Specify Act as Defaults		
Production Lead Time (when routing data does not apply)		Override	
Order Quantity Modifiers for Production Orders			N/A
Minimum Quantity (Safety Stock)	N/A	N/A	Specify
Planner Responsibility	Specify		N/A
	Use Released Products form or Default Order Settings	Use Site-Specific Order Settings form	Use Item Coverage form

Figure 10.4 Planning Data for Manufactured Items

planning. You indicate the relevant inventory dimensions as part of the Storage Dimension Group assigned to the item. In some cases, the relevant inventory dimensions for coverage planning may include a bin location or just the site. Coverage planning does not apply to the inventory dimensions for batch, serial, or pallet. The book's baseline model assumes that sites, warehouse, and bin locations are used for inventory tracking, and that coverage planning applies to the combination of site and warehouse.

BOM Version The BOM versions for a manufactured item can be site-specific or company-wide. Planning calculations will use an item's site-specific BOM version (if it exists) based on the site of the item's requirements. If a site-specific BOM version does not exist, the planning calculations will use the company-wide BOM version (if it exists).

Route Version Planning calculations will use an item's site-specific route version (if it exists) based on the site of the item's requirements. The routing data can be used by planning calculations to determine the variable lead time for a production order.

Primary Source of Supply A planned order type of *Production* indicates the primary source of supply for a manufactured item, so that planning calculations generate planned production orders. An item's planned order type (aka default order type) can be specified as a company-wide policy, and optionally overridden for a given site/warehouse. For example, a manufactured item may be replenished via production orders at one warehouse, but replenished via transfer orders at a different warehouse.

Coverage Code (aka Reordering Policy) The coverage code represents a key part of the planner's decision making logic about creating planned production orders. The four reordering policies—min-max (time-phased order point logic), period (period lot-sizing logic), requirement (order-driven logic), and manual—were previously described and summarized in Figure 10.2. The same policies also apply to planned production orders.

Coverage Group (Set of Policies) The coverage group assigned to a manufactured item contains the coverage code, action message policies, and other policies that represent a model of the planner's decision making logic about planned and existing orders. The previous section explained these policies for a purchased item, and the same policies apply to a manufactured item. However, there are several policies for manufactured items that merit additional explanation.

- *Planning horizon and related time fence policies.* The planning horizon for a manufactured item must extend beyond its cumulative manufacturing lead time in order to provide visibility on the requirements for purchased items, and to anticipate potential capacity constraints. This planning horizon should be reflected in the time fences for coverage, explosion, and forecast.
- *Capacity time fence and the use of routing data* The capacity time fence determines when routing data should be ignored by the planning calculations. For example, routing data may be used for near-term scheduling purposes within the next 30 days, and then ignored after the 30 day time fence so that a fixed lead time applies to the manufactured item.
- *Assignment of order status after firming a planned production order.* Firming a planned production order can result in a status of scheduled, released or started. Several factors influence the choice of an assigned status. As a typical approach, the "scheduled" status should be assigned so that planning calculations recognize material and capacity requirements for the production order, and the planner can subsequently start the order at the appropriate time. An item-specific policy (embedded in the coverage group assigned to the item) defines the choice of an assigned status.
- *Policies for automatic firming.* Automatic firming (based on the firm time fence) can be employed when planned production orders do not require review and changes.
- *Use of a frozen period.* The frozen period (termed a *freeze time fence*) for a manufactured item represents a management policy about making changes to the near-term schedule. Changing the schedule within the frozen period typically creates inefficiencies, especially when setups and sequencing have been established.

Production Lead Time A manufactured item's lead time can reflect a variable or fixed elapsed time. The variable time can be calculated based on routing information and order quantity. An item's fixed production lead time (expressed in days) can be specified as a company-wide value, and overridden for a site/warehouse.[5] The fixed lead time is only used when routing

[5]You can override the company-wide production lead time as part of the item's site-specific order settings, or as part of the item's coverage policies.

data does not exist, or when planning calculations ignore the routing data beyond the capacity time fence. The fixed lead time will always be used with a capacity time fence of zero.

Order Quantity Modifiers for the Planned Order Quantity Planning calculations suggest a planned order quantity subject to the item's order quantity modifiers (if specified). A maximum quantity that matches the minimum quantity will result in a fixed quantity for planned orders.

Minimum Quantity The minimum quantity represents an item's inventory plan or safety stock for a given warehouse. The previous section explained the considerations about a minimum quantity, such as automatic calculation based on historical data, and the use of a variable minimum quantity by time period.

Planner Responsibility The concept of planner responsibility provides an organizing focus for communicating the need to synchronize supplies with demands. The concept of planner responsibility is often based on the production pool or the buyer group assigned to a manufactured item. For example, planning calculations generate planned production orders identified with the buyer group, so that a planner can selectively view and mark planned orders for which they have responsibility. In addition, production orders inherit the item's production pool thereby enabling the planner to selectively view orders for which they have responsibility. Changes to the order status of production orders can be based on the production pool, and a planner can selectively view action messages by production pool.

Maintaining an Item's Coverage Planning Data The approaches for maintaining an item's planning data were described in the previous section for purchased items, and the same approaches apply to manufactured items.

Replenishment Limitations for a Manufactured Item Replenishment limitations can stop production of an item (using a inventory stop flag), or limit production to the single site (or site/warehouse) that actually produces the item. The stop flag means that existing orders cannot be received, and prevents creation of new orders. However, these limitations do not impact planning calculations so that planned purchase orders can still be generated.

10.4 Special Cases for Manufactured Items

The previous section focused on the planning data for manufactured items, and several special cases require additional considerations. These special cases include phantoms, make-to-order components, and assigning a sub-BOM to a manufactured component.

Phantoms A manufactured item can be designated as a phantom component in the BOM information of its parent item, where you specify a line type of Phantom. Planning calculations will calculate requirements for the phantom and ignore its on-hand inventory. Planning calculations will also generate a planned order for the phantom, but the planned order cannot be firmed.

Make-to-Order Components A manufactured item can be designated as a make-to-order component in the BOM information of its parent item, where you specify a BOM line type of Pegged Supply (or Vendor).

Planning calculations will calculate requirements for a make-to-order component, and even generate planned orders based on the item's planning data.[6] The planning calculations ignore on-hand inventory for meeting the make-to-order requirements. However, the planned orders simply provide visibility about these requirements, and these planned orders cannot be firmed (for creating a production order). Instead, you automatically create a linked production order for a make-to-order component when you update the status of the parent item's production order, such as updating the status to *estimated* or *scheduled.* The quantity for the linked production order reflects the parent item's production order quantity and the BOM information about the component quantity. Deleting the parent item's production order will delete the linked production order.

Assign a Sub-BOM to a Manufactured Component The assignment of a sub-BOM to a manufactured component will override the normal use of the active BOM version for the item. The use of sub-BOMs for a manufactured component generally applies to custom product manufacturing scenarios.

---

[6]You typically assign a coverage code of *requirement or period lot size* to a manufactured item that has make-to-order requirements.

10.5 Planning Data for Transfer Items

Planning calculations suggest planned transfer orders based on the item's site/warehouse-specific planning data. Figure 10.5 summarizes the planning data for transfer items, and highlights the company-wide versus site/warehouse policies. The bottom of the figure also highlights the four key forms for maintaining an item's planning data. Further explanation covers each aspect of planning data within the figure.

Relevant Inventory Dimensions for Coverage Planning Policies

An item's replenishment logic typically applies to the combination of site and warehouse, as defined by the relevant inventory dimensions for coverage planning. You indicate the relevant inventory dimensions as part of the Storage Dimension Group assigned to the item. In some cases, the relevant inventory dimensions for coverage planning may include a bin location or just the site. Coverage planning does not apply to the inventory dimensions for batch, serial, or pallet.

<table>
<tr><th></th><th></th><th>Companywide Policies</th><th>Site-Specific Policies</th><th>Site/Warehouse Policies</th></tr>
<tr><td rowspan="9">Planning Data for Transfer Items</td><td>Relevant Inventory Dimensions
For Coverage Planning Policies</td><td>Specify</td><td colspan="2">N/A</td></tr>
<tr><td>Primary Source of Supply
(Planned Order Type = Transfer)</td><td rowspan="2">N/A</td><td rowspan="4">N/A</td><td rowspan="2">Specify</td></tr>
<tr><td>Preferred Refilling Warehouse</td></tr>
<tr><td>Coverage Code (Reordering Policy)</td><td rowspan="4">Specify
Act as Defaults</td><td rowspan="3">Override</td></tr>
<tr><td>Coverage Group (Set of Policies)</td></tr>
<tr><td>Transfer Lead Time*</td><td rowspan="2">Override</td></tr>
<tr><td>Order Quantity Modifiers for Transfers</td><td>N/A</td></tr>
<tr><td>Minimum Quantity</td><td>N/A</td><td rowspan="2">N/A</td><td>Specify</td></tr>
<tr><td>Planner Responsibility</td><td>Specify</td><td>N/A</td></tr>
<tr><td></td><td></td><td>Use Released Products form or Default Order Settings</td><td>Use Site-Specific Order Settings form</td><td>Use Item Coverage form</td></tr>
</table>

* = Normally defined as transport lead time (expressed in days) between a pair of warehouses

Figure 10.5 Planning Data for Transfer Items

Primary Source of Supply (Transfer) Replenishment based on transfers must be designated in the item's site/warehouse-specific coverage data, where you indicate a planned order type of *transfer* so that planning calculations generate planned transfer orders. A related field defines the preferred refilling warehouse.

Preferred Refilling Warehouse The preferred refilling warehouse can be defined for transferring individual items to a warehouse (as part of each item's site/warehouse-specific coverage planning policies). Alternatively, it can be defined for an entire warehouse, which indicates all warehouse inventory will be replenished from one refilling warehouse unless specifically overridden. With the warehouse-level policy, you can override an item's preferred refilling warehouse and/or primary source of supply (as part of the item's site/warehouse-specific coverage planning policies).

Coverage Code (aka Reordering Policy) The coverage code (also termed a reordering policy) represents a key part of the planner's decision-making logic about creating planned transfer orders. The four reordering policies—min-max (time-phased order point logic), period (period lot-sizing logic), requirement (order-driven logic), and manual—were previously described and summarized in Figure 10.2. The same policies also apply to planned transfer orders.

Coverage Group (Set of Policies) The coverage group assigned to a transfer item contains the coverage code, action message policies, and other policies that represent a model of the planner's decision making logic about planned transfer orders and existing orders. The previous section explained these policies for a purchased item, and the same policies apply to a transfer item.

Transfer Lead Time The transfer lead time (aka transportation time) is expressed in days. It can reflect a warehouse viewpoint or an item viewpoint. The warehouse viewpoint defines the typical transportation time between a pair of warehouses, as defined on the Transport form. The item viewpoint defines the transfer time as part of the item's site/warehouse-specific coverage planning policies.

Order Quantity Modifiers for Transfer Orders Planning calculations suggest a planned transfer order quantity subject to order quantity modifiers for a minimum, maximum and multiple (for inventory). The system also provides a soft warning during manual creation of a transfer order when you enter a quantity that does not meet these criteria.

Minimum Quantity The minimum quantity represents an item's inventory plan or safety stock for a given warehouse, as described in the previous sections about planning data for purchased and manufactured items.

Planner Responsibility The concept of planner responsibility for transfer orders is often based on the ship-from or ship-to warehouse, or the buyer group assigned to the item. For example, planning calculations generate planned transfer orders identified with the buyer group and the ship-from/ship-to warehouses, so that a planner can selectively view planned orders for which they have responsibility.

Special Case for Suggested Transfers between Warehouses at an AX Site Warehouses within a given AX site often reflect close proximity, so that actual transfers between warehouses are generally handled through a transfer journal rather than a transfer order. In this case, planned transfer orders can be used to communicate requirements, but firming the planned orders should generate a transfer journal which can be subsequently posted after physically moving the material. This approach requires a site-specific policy termed "Use transfer journals for movements within site," otherwise firming a planned order results in a transfer order.

10.6 Significance of Planning Data for Negative Days and Positive Days

One of the more confusing aspects of planning data within Dynamics AX involves the significance of the policies for negative days and positive days. The names of these two policies reflect the mathematics within the planning calculations, but the names do not readily convey their significance. Understanding and correctly applying these policies directly impacts the generation of planned orders for an item, and the overall effectiveness of using AX to model your business decisions.

It is easier to view these policies as two fundamental assumptions related to the generation of planned orders. The two assumptions can be labeled the *rescheduling assumption* and the *fast-moving inventory assumption.* Each assumption has two options, where one option represents dominant business practices and the second option represents a special case.

Rescheduling Assumption (Negative Days Policy) The rescheduling assumption represents a key aspect of planning calculations in every ERP system. In summary, it is typically easier to expedite an item's existing supply order (to meet demand within the item's lead time) rather than generating a new order. A supply order can be a purchase order, transfer order or production order. Stated another way, the planning calculations should generate an action message to expedite or "advance" an item's existing supply order to meet demand within the item's lead time, or generate a new planned order if that is not possible. There are two basic options for the rescheduling assumption, as described below.

- **Dominant Business Practice: Rescheduling Assumption Based on Item Lead Time**. Most firms employ a company-wide policy to indicate rescheduling assumptions should be based on each item's lead time. The policy is labeled *Use Dynamic Negative Days* checkbox and defined on the Master Planning Parameters form. This company-wide policy was introduced within AX 2009 as an alternative for the historic approach, which involved a separate construct that forced you to define an item's lead time twice in order to support the rescheduling assumption. The separate construct is labeled the *negative days* field, and embedded in the coverage group assigned to an item. When using the company-wide policy and correctly maintaining item lead times, most firms simply define a zero for the separate construct. A value greater than zero will be added to an item's lead time for rescheduling assumption purposes.

  Several considerations apply to the rescheduling assumption. First, the rescheduling assumption only applies when the item's replenishment reflects a coverage code of Period or Requirement; it does not apply to Min/Max or Manual. Second, the "advance" action message communicates the need to expedite an existing supply order. The message can be generated for a planned order as if it is an existing supply order. This confusion can be minimized by deleting the planned orders within the set of master plan data prior to performing the master scheduling task. The combined message of "Advance and Increase" can also be generated, along with other variations of action messages.
- **Special Case: Limited Ability to Reschedule Existing Supply Orders.** Some scenarios require a different basis for the rescheduling assumption (rather than the item's lead time), such as a purchased item or transfer item with delivery via an ocean vessel. Let's say it is impossible to expedite an item's existing supply orders in this scenario, so that a new planned order should always be generated. In this scenario, you should

use the historical approach of a separate construct rather than the company-wide policy. This approach enables you to specify zero (for the negative days) as the basis for the rescheduling assumption, yet still have a lead time for the item.

Fast-Moving Inventory Assumption about Current Inventory (Positive Days) This assumption involves an exception to normal netting logic about an item's current inventory. With normal netting logic, an item's requirements can be met with current inventory and scheduled receipts, even when the requirement date is in the distant future. The classic exception involves fast-moving inventory with daily replenishment, especially perishable inventory such as fresh fruits or fish. In this scenario, current inventory should only be sold for today's sales orders, and sales orders for future shipment dates should be fulfilled by planned supply orders rather than current inventory. This assumption can be called the *fast-moving inventory assumption*, or the *shelf life assumption about current inventory.* I prefer the term *fast-moving inventory assumption* to differentiate it from the shelf life capabilities with Dynamics AX. There are two basic options for this assumption, as described below.

- **Special Case: Fast-Moving Inventory Assumption Is Applicable.** The assumption about current inventory is expressed as a time horizon termed positive days. In the classic example of a perishable fruit with daily replenishment (mentioned above), the time horizon would be expressed as 1 day. Other scenarios may involve a slightly longer time horizon, depending on the rate of sales, the frequency of replenishment and the inventory plan for an item.

  Stated another way, the current inventory can be viewed as unusable after the specified time horizon, so that demands for future dates must be satisfied with planned supply orders. This viewpoint helps explain the generation of planned supply orders to cover future demand even when there is sufficient inventory, and builds on AX functionality for managing shelf life expiration dates.
- **Dominant Business Practice: Fast-Moving Inventory Assumption Is Not Applicable.** The assumption does not apply in most cases, so that the time horizon of positive days should be specified as some large number that exceeds the item's cumulative lead time. An arbitrary large number such as "100" or "365" is often used. The large number ensures that normal netting logic applies to replenishment. There does not appear

to be any benefit to shades of different values, since you are trying to indicate that the assumption does not apply.

In summary, the planning data associated with negative days and positive days represents two fundamental assumptions impacting the generation of planned orders for an item.

Additional Case Studies

Case 55: Suggested Vendor Based on Lowest Price A machine manufacturer purchased several components from the vendor offering the lowest price, whereas other purchased components were always sourced from a single preferred vendor. Each vendor provided price quotes for selected items (with date effectivities), and the quotes were used to update purchase price trade agreement information. Using this information, master scheduling logic generated planned purchase orders for the selected items, where the suggested vendor reflected the one with the lowest price.

Case 56: Buy-to-Order Component A manufacturer produced configure-to-order products which included a specialized purchase component requiring delivery that was closely synchronized with the parent item's production order. Due to its size and specialized nature, it was critical for the purchased component to be delivered when actually required. By designating the item as a buy-to-order component for the parent item, a linked purchase order was automatically created after scheduling the parent item's production order, and also synchronized automatically as the schedule changed.

Executive Summary

Planned orders communicate the need to replenish an item's inventory, and are generated by planning calculations based on an item's coverage planning data. An item's preferred source of supply—defined on a company-wide or site/warehouse-specific basis—determines whether it reflects a purchase, transfer or production order. This chapter summarized the coverage planning data related to generation of planned orders, and also covered special cases such as buy-to-order components and suggested vendors for planned purchase orders based on lowest price.

Chapter 11

Sales and Operations Planning

A firm's sales and operations planning (S&OP) process typically starts with the definition of all demands for the firm's salable items. It formulates *game plans* that drive supply chain activities to meet those demands. The approach for each product's game plan depends on the scenario. For example, the S&OP approach focuses on a stocked end-item in distribution and make-to-stock scenarios, whereas the S&OP approach for a configurable item focuses on the sales orders for specified configurations and also any stocked components. A given company typically has several major scenarios where each scenario employs a different S&OP approach. The chapter starts with a brief overview of different scenarios and their S&OP approaches.

A typical business process for maintaining an item's S&OP game plan provides an organizing focus for further explanation. Since the business process must reflect the S&OP approach, we'll focus on two common scenarios—for a make-to-stock item and a configure-to-order item—to illustrate key aspects of the typical business process. For the first scenario, the typical business process involves demand forecasts, inventory plans, and sales order promises based on available-to-promise logic. A related business process explains how to perform the planning calculations and analyze results, and provides the context for explaining the Forecast Scheduling task and Master Scheduling task within AX. For the second scenario, the typical business process involves supply forecasts for stocked components and sales order promises based on capable-to-promise logic. These topics are reflected in the following sections within this chapter.

1. Common S&OP Approaches
2. S&OP Game Plans for a Make-to-Stock Item
3. Using Demand Forecasts for Salable Items

4. Using Supply Forecasts for Stocked Components
5. Using Safety Stock Requirements
6. Assign Delivery Promises to a Sales Order
7. Run Planning Calculations and Analyze Results
8. Understanding Planning Calculations
9. S&OP Game Plans for a Configurable Item Built from Stocked Components
10. Using Simulations for S&OP Purposes
11. Guidelines Concerning S&OP Game Plans

11.1 Common S&OP Approaches

The nature of an S&OP game plan depends on several factors, such as the need to anticipate demand for the item, the item's primary source of supply, and the need for linkage between a sales order and the supply order. It also depends on the production strategy for manufactured items, such as make-to-stock, make-to-order or configure-to-more. Consideration of these factors can be illustrated with several common S&OP approaches for manufactured items.

The common S&OP approaches can be segmented into two groups reflecting the need for linkage between a sales order and the production order for the end-item. The S&OP approaches within the first group (summarized in Figure 11.1) do not require linkage, and planning calculations can account for the end-item's inventory and scheduled receipts. The second group of S&OP approaches (summarized in Figure 11.2) requires linkage by generating the production order from the sales order, which means that the production order quantity ignores the item's existing inventory and scheduled receipts. The concept of linkage also applies to make-to-order components (identified by a BOM line type of pegged supply) with reference orders linked to the parent item's production order. The reference order quantity also ignores existing inventory.

Different types of operations have slightly different S&OP approaches. Other sections of the book describe the S&OP approaches for lean manufacturing (Section 15.5), project-oriented operations (Section 20.7) and a service-oriented operation (Section 21.6).

The figure displays several S&OP approaches for stocked end-items. A stocked end-item may reflect a specific configuration id and item number, where the configuration id was generated by using a configuration technology (described in Chapter 7).

	Scenario	S&OP Approach	Comments	Basis of Delivery Promises
No Link to Sales Order	Stocked End-Item	Min-Max	Calculation of minimum quantity	ATP
		Demand Forecast	Forecast consumption policies Using an inventory plan (safety stock)	
		Manual Master Schedule		
	Completely Make-to-Order End-Item	Sales Order		CTP or CTP via Net Change Explosion
	Make-to-Order End-Item with Stocked Components	Sales Order for End-Item Supply Forecast for stocked components	Forecast consumption policies	

Figure 11.1 Common S&OP Approaches

Stocked End-Item Based on Min-Max The simplest S&OP approach employs min-max logic to carry inventory in anticipation of actual demand, where an item's coverage planning policies define the minimum and maximum quantities. With min-max logic, when an item's projected inventory falls below its minimum quantity, the planning calculations suggest a planned order that achieves the item's maximum quantity (subject to an order quantity multiple). The values for an item's minimum and maximum quantities can be fixed, or specified as a pattern (termed the minimum key and maximum key). The minimum quantity can be automatically calculated based on historical usage.[1] Sales order delivery promises can be based on available-to-promise (ATP) logic.

Stocked End-Item Based on Demand Forecast A demand forecast and inventory plan for a manufactured item can be used to generate planned production orders reflecting the item's planning data, such as a coverage code of period lot size or requirement. An inventory plan—expressed as safety stock requirements—can be used to anticipate higher-than-expected

[1]The calculation of a minimum quantity can be based on the desired service level percentage or the average usage over the item's lead time. The calculations require at least 3 months (preferably 12 months) of usage history. You calculate the minimum quantity for specified items using the Item Coverage Journal.

customer demand, and meet customer service objectives regarding stock outs, partial shipments and delivery lead times. The planned orders are typically firmed up in the near term to reflect the desired production schedule and to account for material and capacity constraints. The combination of planned orders and actual production orders represents the item's master schedule, and provides the basis for making delivery promises using ATP logic. Sales orders can consume the demand forecast based on forecast consumption policies. Subsequent sections provide further explanation for using demand forecasts and safety stock requirements.

Stocked End-Item Based on a Manual Master Schedule The master schedule for the manufactured item consists of manually-created production orders with a scheduled status. The item's coverage code is manual, and demand forecasts are not typically entered. This approach avoids the complexities associated with forecast consumption logic, and provides the basis for making delivery promises using ATP logic.

Completely Make-to-Order End-Item The S&OP game plan consists of actual sales orders for a completely make-to-order end-item, where CTP logic provides the basis for delivery promises. The planning calculations generate planned production orders to meet the sales order demand, where the planned orders reflect the item's planning data and the active BOM and route versions. This scenario generally implies that the customer will accept the delivery lead time. It may also reflect a pipeline of sales orders that exceeds the item's cumulative lead time.

Make-to-Order End-Item with Stocked Components The use of stocked components can shorten the delivery lead time for a make-to-order item, where CTP logic provides the basis for delivery promises. The S&OP game plan consists of supply forecasts for stocked components in order to generate planned orders for replenishment. It also consists of sales orders in order to generate planned production orders for final assembly of the end-item. These planned orders reflect each item's planning data, such as a coverage code of period lot size or requirement.

Summary of S&OP Approaches with Link to Sales Order The second group of S&OP approaches (summarized in Figure 11.2) requires linkage by creating the production order from the sales order. This means that the production order quantity ignores the item's existing inventory, and the production order can inherit the specified BOM and route versions on the sales order line. The concept of linkage also applies to make-to-order components with reference orders linked to the parent item's production order.

Completely Make-to-Order End-Item with Link to Sales Order The S&OP game plan consists of actual sales orders and their linked production orders, where CTP logic provides the basis for sales order delivery promises. When creating the linked order, the production order will inherit the specified BOM and route versions for the sales order line (if specified), otherwise it will inherit the active BOM and route versions for the item. The BOM line type of a component determines whether it will be coordinated through planned orders or reference orders; these variations are not displayed in Figure 11.2.

Make-to-Order End-Item with Link to Sales Order, and Built from Stocked Components The use of stocked components can shorten the delivery lead time for a make-to-order item, where CTP logic provides the

<table>
<tr><th colspan="2">Scenario</th><th>S&OP Approach</th><th>Comments</th><th>Basis of Delivery Promises</th></tr>
<tr><td rowspan="4">Link to Sales Order</td><td>Completely Make-to-Order End-Item</td><td>Sales Order
with link to Production Order</td><td>Active BOM & route versions for item
versus
Specified BOM & route versions for SO</td><td rowspan="4">CTP
or
CTP via Net Change Explosion</td></tr>
<tr><td>Make-to-Order End-Item
with
Stocked Components
or
Make-to-Order Components</td><td>Sales Order
with link to Production Order

Supply Forecast
for stocked components

Reference Order
for make-to-order components</td><td>Active BOM & route versions for item
versus
Specified BOM & route versions for SO

Forecast consumption policies

Automatically create reference order linked to production order</td></tr>
<tr><td>Configure-to-Order End-Item</td><td>Sales Order
with link to Production Order</td><td>Define configuration and its BOM & route versions</td></tr>
<tr><td>Engineer-to-Order End-Item</td><td>Sales Order
with link to Production Order</td><td>Define configuration and its skeleton BOM & route versions</td></tr>
</table>

Figure 11.2 Common S&OP Approaches with Link to Sales Order

basis for delivery promises. The S&OP game plan consists of supply forecasts for stocked components in order to generate planned orders for replenishment. It also consists of sales orders and their linked production orders. When creating the linked order, the production order will inherit the specified BOM and route versions for the sales order line (if specified), otherwise it will inherit the active BOM and route versions for the item. The S&OP game plan also consists of automatically created reference orders for each make-to-order component (aka BOM line type of pegged supply).

Configure-to-Order End-Item with Link to Sales Order The S&OP game plan consists of sales orders for the configurable item. The item's configuration technology determines how you define the configuration and its associated BOM version and route version. This information enables CTP logic to provide a delivery promise. When using stocked components to shorten delivery lead time, the S&OP game plan also includes supply forecasts in order to generate planned orders for replenishment. The S&OP game plan may also consist of automatically created reference orders for each make-to-order component.

Engineer-to-Order End-Item with Link to Sales Order Many engineer-to-order products can be modeled with a skeleton BOM identifying the major components in the product structure and with the typical routing operations. As engineering design progresses, additional details about purchased material (especially those items with a long lead time), subassemblies and routing operations can then be added to the skeleton BOM. The skeleton BOM approach simplifies supply chain coordination because it handles an evolving product structure which can be used by planning calculations.

The S&OP game plan consists of sales orders for a configurable item, where the associated configuration defines the skeleton BOM and creates item numbers for the major components. As a general rule, you do not immediately create a linked production order because planned orders will recognize the evolving product structure for the end-item. The skeleton BOM can provide the basis for a delivery promise using CTP logic, typically via a net change explosion. The S&OP game plan may also consist of automatically created reference orders for make-to-order components.

Other S&OP Approaches Other scenarios requiring slightly different S&OP approaches include the following:

- *Pipeline of Sales Quotations*. Some scenarios have a pipeline of sales quotations that can be used to anticipate actual demand. With this approach, a win probability is assigned to each sales quote (actually to the opportunity associated with the sales quote), and sales quotes exceeding a specified win percentage (say 90%) will be considered as demand by planning calculations. This represents additional demand when also using demand forecasts.
- *Special Orders and Direct Orders*. Creating a purchase order from the sales order can result in a special order or direct order, typically in the context of a distribution environment. Alternatively, you can first create a purchase order for the item, and then link it to a sales order. The chapter about sales order processing provides further explanation of special orders and direct orders (Section 21.7), which represent S&OP approaches with a link to the sales order.

11.2 S&OP Game Plans for a Make-to-Stock Item

Several different S&OP approaches can be used for a make-to-stock item, such as using min-max, demand forecasts or a manually maintained master schedule. For illustrative purposes, this section focuses on a typical business process for maintaining the S&OP game plan using demand forecasts to drive planned production orders representing the master schedule. The game plans are typically reviewed and updated on a periodic basis. The typical process consists of multiple steps performed by different roles, as summarized in Figure 11.3 and described below.

The business process starts with an analysis of historical and projected demands so that the sales manager can prepare a sales plan and inventory plan for each product. The production planner uses this information to enter the item's demand forecast and safety stock requirements. After planning calculations have been performed, the production planner analyzes the results to determine the need for adjustments, and to firm the master schedule—expressed as production orders for the item. The S&OP game plan can be used by the customer service rep when creating a sales order, resulting in realistic promised delivery dates based on available-to-promise logic. Actual sales orders consume the item's demand forecast within user-defined forecast periods.

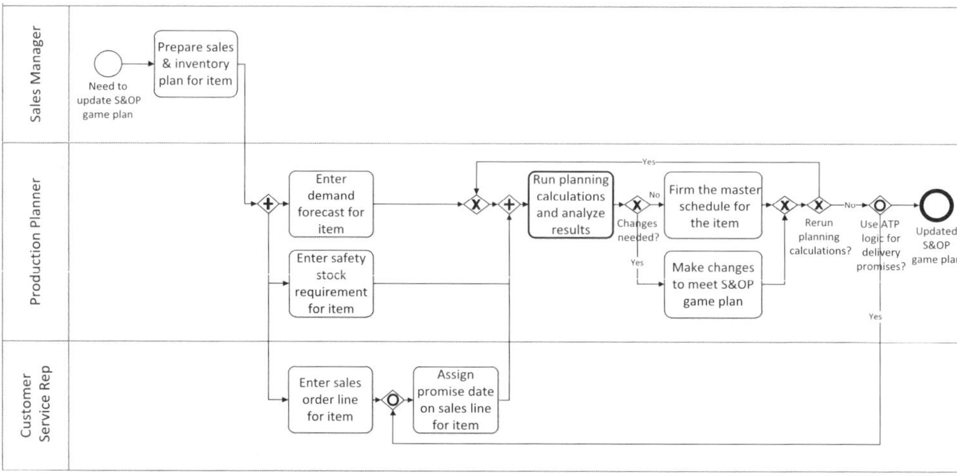

Figure 11.3 Typical Business Process to Maintain S&OP Plans for a Make-to-Stock Item

Prepare a Sales Plan and Inventory Plan for the Item The sales manager analyzes historical and projected demands for the item in order to prepare a sales plan by ship-from location, typically expressed in monthly increments. The analysis also results in an inventory plan for the item (by ship-from location) to meet the desired customer service levels when actual demands exceed forecast. The analyses may reflect a statistical forecasting technique or some other method.

Enter Demand Forecast for the Item The production planner uses the item's sales plan as the basis for entering a demand forecast by ship-from location, typically expressed in weekly increments (or even daily increments) in the near-term time frame. Actual sales orders for an item will automatically consume the item's demand forecast within the user-defined forecast periods.

Enter Safety Stock Requirement for the Item The production planner uses the item's inventory plan as the basis for entering safety stock requirements by ship-from location. The safety stock requirements can be entered as a single value or as different values for future time periods.

Run Planning Calculations and Analyze Results The production planner ensures that planning calculations are performed on a regular basis. The planning calculations consist of a forecast scheduling task to calculate gross requirements and a master scheduling task to calculate net requirements. The production planner analyzes the results for manufactured items within their responsibility, whereas the purchasing agent does the same for purchased items and transfer items. In the context of the S&OP planning process, the production planner responsible for the end-items must consider constraints and multiple objectives in maintaining realistic S&OP game plans.

Firm the Master Schedule for the Item The production planner manages the production orders for the end-item, where the orders represent the master schedule in the context of S&OP game plans. The production planner may simply use planned orders to represent the master schedule, and ultimately firm them just prior to starting production. Firming a planned order creates a production order with a scheduled status, and you can optionally lock the order to prevent rescheduling.

Alternatively, the production planner may firm the planned orders to represent the near-term production schedule in order to account for material constraints, capacity constraints or some other consideration. For example, the production planner may firm the planned orders to account for projected delays due to problems with material or capacity availability. The impact of projected delays can be identified by futures messages, such as delays in meeting due dates for sales orders or forecasts.

Make Changes to Meet the S&OP Game Plan The production planner coordinates several types of changes to meet the master schedule. These changes may involve adjusting capacity at bottleneck resources, using alternate routings, or revising production schedules. The changes may involve working with the purchasing agent to expedite purchase orders for components, or they may involve working with the production supervisors to adjust capacity or schedules. When the master schedule cannot be met, the production planner may need to work with customer service representatives to delay the promised delivery date on sales orders.

Enter Sales Order Line for Item The customer service rep enters sales orders for the item, or the incoming sales orders may reflect EDI transactions. Each sales line indicates a quantity, ship-from location and requested delivery date. Actual sales orders for an item will automatically consume the item's demand forecast within the forecast period.

Assign Promise Date on Sales Line for the Item When the customer service rep creates a sales order line for the item, the earliest promised delivery date is automatically assigned based on available-to-promise (ATP) logic. The ATP logic reflects the S&OP game plan, which helps align actual sales orders to the game plan. The customer service rep can view available to promise information to answer questions about availability, but must disable the delivery date control logic to assign an unrealistic promise date.

The impact of projected production or material delays on the promised delivery date can be identified by futures messages (generated by the planning calculations). The futures messages provide a continuous check on realistic delivery promises.

11.3 Using Demand Forecasts for Salable Items

A demand forecast for a salable item represents the desired inventory quantity on the specified date in order to support sales orders. Each forecast entry consists of an item identifier, quantity, date, ship-from site/warehouse, and a forecast identifier (aka forecast model). A forecast model has a user-defined identifier. In most cases, one forecast model is used to represent the current demand forecast continuously updated as part of the S&OP game plan. Additional forecast models may be defined, such as one identifier for the original annual forecast and other identifiers for supporting simulations.

Time Horizon for Entering and Using Demand Forecasts Demand forecasts are entered for future periods. As time progresses, the demand forecasts for today's date or earlier (aka past-due forecast) will be ignored by planning calculations. Several factors affect usage of the demand forecasts for future periods, as summarized below.

- *Time horizon for the Forecast Scheduling task.* The time horizon typically reflects one of two different objectives. A long-term horizon is typically used for aggregate planning purposes, and a short-term horizon (such as weeks) is typically used for managing current operations. You define the desired time horizon—expressed as three time fences for coverage, explosion and capacity—as part of the policies for a forecast plan.

- *Time horizon for the Master Scheduling task.* The time horizon considerations mentioned above (for the Forecast Scheduling task) also apply to the Master Scheduling task. You typically define the desired time horizon as part of the policies for a Master Plan. An alternative approach defines these time horizon policies for each item (as part of the coverage planning policies assigned to the item), but this alternative approach is not typically used.

Demand Forecasts by Customer Some scenarios involve just a few major customers, so that a demand forecast can be entered for a specific customer in addition to (or in place of) a general demand forecast. This provides reference information for pegging to the source of demand, since the customer-specific forecasts are consumed by sales orders from any customer.

Two-Level Forecast Model Some companies use the concept of a two-level forecast model. With a two-level forecast model, for example, the forecast identifier representing the company-wide forecast can be associated with several forecast identifiers representing regional forecasts. Each forecast entry has a forecast model corresponding to a regional forecast, so that the forecast scheduling task automatically rolls up the company-wide forecast from the regional forecasts.

Translating a Weekly Demand Forecast into Daily Increments Some scenarios employ daily increments in the near-term demand forecast so that planning calculations can generate daily planned orders. As one approach, you can enter a weekly demand forecast (for the date corresponding to the first working day of the week) along with a *Period Allocation Key* that will automatically result in daily increments. For example, you would predefine the period allocation key indicating five daily increments and a percentage for each daily increment such as 20%.[2] This example means that a weekly forecast of 100 would result in daily increments of 20. The assigned percentage may vary for each day to reflect typical demand patterns within a week, such as higher sales on a Friday.

[2]Several period allocation keys may be predefined to reflect different situations, such as spreading a weekly forecast across a 5-day week, a 4-day week and a 3-day week. The percentages assigned to each daily increment could be 20%, 25% and 33%. The names for these period allocation keys could be 5DayWeek, 4DayWeek and 3DayWeek.

Demand Forecasts for a Group of Items Some scenarios employ demand forecasts for an item group rather than an individual item. This approach employs a user-defined template (termed an *item allocation key*) that spreads out a total quantity across several items based on a mix percentage per item. The synonyms for an item allocation key include a planning bill. With this approach, a forecast entry for the item group would specify the item allocation key and the ship-from site/warehouse. The items within the period allocation key must be assigned the same item group.

Each template entry can optionally define the ship-from site/warehouse. For example, the template entries could define the mix percentages for shipping the same item from different sites/warehouses. With this approach, a forecast entry for the item group would simply specify the item allocation key.

Handling the Combination of Actual and Forecasted Sales Demand The combination of sales orders and forecasts must be considered to avoid doubled-up requirements. Several different approaches can be employed, where the primary policy differentiating the approaches is termed the *reduction principle.* Synonyms include forecast consumption logic. You specify the desired reduction principle as part of the policies for a forecast plan and a master plan, since it affects the planning calculations. The three major variations of the reduction principle are summarized below along with their related policies.

- *Manually adjust the demand forecast to reflect forecast consumption (Reduction Principle = None).* With this approach, the demands from sales orders and demand forecasts will be added together by planning calculations, so that demand forecasts must be manually adjusted to reflect forecast consumption. This approach does not involve additional policies (such as forecast periods) and represents the simplest approach.
- *Sales orders consume demand forecasts within specified forecast periods (Reduction Principle = Transactions with Reduction Key).* This approach involves two related policies that are defined within the coverage group assigned to items. One policy indicates the applicable forecast periods (termed a reduction key), and the second policy indicates that demand forecasts should only be consumed by sales orders.[3] A third policy only applies to multi-company scenarios, since it determines whether intercompany sales orders will consume the demand forecast.

[3] In rare scenarios, the demand forecast should be consumed by all types of issue transactions such as inventory adjustments, as indicated by the "reduce forecast by" policy within the coverage group assigned to an item.

Any sales orders within a forecast period will consume demand forecasts within the same period.

A reduction key provides a template of user-specified forecast periods. Examples of a reduction key include monthly periods for the next 12 months, or a combination of weekly periods (for the next 4 weeks) and monthly periods thereafter. The two basic approaches for defining a reduction key consist of a fixed starting date and floating start date. The first approach represents the simplest to understand, but it typically only applies to monthly or weekly time periods within the reduction key. For example, the fixed starting date can be specified as January 1 of the current year, and the reduction key defines 12 monthly periods. As time progresses, this approach requires additions to the monthly periods within the reduction key or a change in the fixed starting date. The second approach employs the current date as the floating start date, and provides greater flexibility and granularity in modeling forecast consumption logic. For example, the reduction key may consist of daily periods across a 2 week horizon, weekly period for the next 6 weeks, and monthly period thereafter.

It should be noted that a reduction key can be used for one other approach to forecast consumption, identified as a Reduction Principle of Percent Reduction Key. This approach employs a reduction percentage (for each time period in the reduction key) to arbitrarily reduce forecasted demand, so it does not involve forecast consumption by actual sales orders.[4] The approach is rarely used.

- *Sales orders consume demand forecasts within implied forecast periods (Reduction Principle = Transactions with Dynamic Period).* This approach employs implied forecast periods defined by the dates of forecast entries, and does not employ the reduction key. The dynamic period ends with the next forecast date for the item. As a related policy within the coverage group assigned to items, you indicate that demand forecasts should only be consumed by sales orders.

The recommended approach for a reduction principle, and the definition of specified (or implied) forecast periods, depend on the scenario.

[4]This approach automatically reduces forecasts based on a user-defined template (aka reduction key) of a reduction percentage by forecast period. It reflects the concept of a demand fence where planning calculations ignore forecasted demands within a specified time horizon from today's date, and the time horizon represents the sold-out backlog for an item. Let's say an item always has a sold-out backlog of one month and a partially sold-out backlog in the second month, so that 100% of an item's demand forecast can be ignored for the first month and 50% for the second month relative to today's date.

11.5 Using Supply Forecasts for Stocked Components

An inventory of stocked components can serve multiple purposes. As one purpose, the stocked components can support shorter delivery lead times with make-to-order production strategies. An item with long lead time represents a classic example of a stocked component. A supply forecast provides one approach to drive replenishment of stocked components.

A supply forecast defines an estimated demand for a stocked component, expressed as a quantity, date, ship-to site/warehouse, and forecast identifier. It is different from a demand forecast, since actual supply orders (rather than sales orders) consume the supply forecast. For example, the creation of a purchase order consumes the supply forecast for a purchased item. Many of the considerations about demand forecast consumption also apply to supply forecast consumption. For example, the reduction principle is defined by a master plan policy, and the forecast periods are defined by the reduction key assigned to an item.

Two caveats apply to the use of supply forecasts. First, the demands stemming from a supply forecast are not easily visible within current AX functionality, whereas the demands stemming from demand forecasts are visible. For example, the inquiry about net requirements does not display the supply forecast, and it is not displayed in pegging information about the source of demand. However, the system does display a checkbox (labeled supply forecast) to indicate whether a planned order or actual supply order stems from a supply forecast. The second caveat applies to the action messages for an item with supply forecasts. The action message for decrease should be suppressed so that planning calculations do not generate a message to cancel the item's supply orders for satisfying the supply forecast.

As an alternative to using supply forecasts for a stocked component, you can define safety stock requirements for the item. The next section describes how to define safety stock requirements. Another alternative consists of demand forecasts for end-items to drive replenishment of long lead time materials, and manual maintenance of the demand forecast to account for forecast consumption, as described in Case 57.

Case 57: Manual Forecast Consumption for MTO Products with Stocked Components

A manufacturing company produced several standard products on a contract manufacturing basis for large customers. They only produced end-items to actual customer demand. The limited forward visibility of these sales orders meant that long lead time materials must be ordered and stocked prior to obtaining actual sales orders. Demand forecasts for the salable items were used to drive replenishment of these long lead time materials. The master scheduler avoided any confusion in forecast consumption logic by using a manually maintained demand forecast. He developed demand forecasts in a spreadsheet based on close coordination with the customers, and periodically imported the data as a "drop in forecast.

11.5 Using Safety Stock Requirements

Many firms carry additional inventory of an item to anticipate variations in customer demand, and meet customer service objectives regarding stock outs, partial shipments, and delivery lead times. The additional inventory is commonly called an inventory plan or safety stock. An inventory plan is typically expressed at the highest possible stocking level—such as a saleable end-item or a stocked component—and for the relevant sites/warehouses that stock the item.

An item's inventory plan can be explicitly expressed as a safety stock quantity when using demand forecasts and a coverage code of Period or Requirement. The safety stock quantity is termed the minimum quantity in AX. It reflects the desired inventory to cover demand variations, and should not reflect the average demand over lead time (which would be applicable to a Min-Max coverage code). It is typically specified as a single quantity with a future requirement date reflecting the item's lead time. Alternatively, it can be specified as multiple quantities—one for each future period—by using a minimum quantity key. An inventory plan can also be implicitly expressed by a large quantity for an order quantity minimum or multiple.

Another way to explain safety stock is that it represents a percentage of forecast accuracy for a given item. It does not represent a desired inventory position.

11.6 Assign Delivery Promises to a Sales Order

Realistic promise dates for sales order shipments and deliveries can help improve customer satisfaction and supply chain coordination. The initial assignment of a realistic delivery promise should align with the item's S&OP game plan, and a sales line with an unrealistic promise date should be highlighted as an exception requiring follow up. After initial assignment, the dates should be changed to reflect changes in the situation, such as changing dates to reflect projected delays. Sales orders with unrealistic or past due dates will negatively impact the usefulness of an item's S&OP game plan and the suggestions for supply chain coordination.

The initial assignment of realistic delivery promises can be supported using several different approaches that reflect a delivery date control policy. The three major options for a delivery date control policy include sales lead time, ATP and CTP, and the relevant policy depends on the scenario and S&OP approach. All three options enforce basic rules to help ensure realistic promise dates. A fourth option (labeled none) disables the enforcement of the basic rules, thereby allowing assignment of unrealistic dates. This fourth option is also referred to as disabling delivery date control.

This section starts with a brief background about the sales order dates for shipment and delivery, and the basic rules for delivery date control, and then summarizes the options for the delivery date control policy. Separate subsections provide suggestions for using each option. The explanation focuses on sales order lines for simplicity's sake, although it also applies to the delivery schedule for a sales line. A similar set of policies applies to promise dates on a transfer order, as described in a subsequent chapter (Section 17.3).

Sales Order Dates for Shipment and Delivery A sales order header has a requested ship date and a requested delivery date, where the difference represents the transportation time (termed *transport days*) between the ship-from warehouse and the delivery address. It also has a confirmed ship date and confirmed receipt date. These dates within the sales order header will be initially inherited by the sales lines, and changes in the header dates can optionally update information for the sales lines. The confirmed ship date for a sales line (if specified) will drive planning calculations, otherwise planning calculations use the requested ship date.

Several basic rules can be enforced for the shipment and delivery dates on a sales order header and for each line item, but only when the header and line items have been assigned any one of the three major options for delivery date control. The next subsection describes these basic rules, and subsequent subsections describe the additional rules associated with the ATP and CTP options.

Basic Rules for Delivery Date Control The sales order dates for shipment and delivery should reflect the following basic rules in order to be realistic. These rules apply to the automatic assignment of dates when initially entering a sales order header or line item, and when manually entering a date.

- *Calendar for the ship-from warehouse.* The calendar assigned to the ship-from warehouse determines the working days when items can be shipped.
- *Calendar for the customer receiving point.* The calendar assigned to the customer (or the applicable customer address) determines the working days when items can be received.
- *Transportation time to customer.* The number of days for transportation time are specified for the different combinations of the ship-from warehouse, delivery address characteristics (such as the country, state, county, or ZIP code), and mode of delivery (such as air or truck).[5]
- *Calendar for mode of delivery.* A calendar can be assigned to various modes of delivery for the ship-from warehouse, where the calendar determines the working days when items can be transported. For example, a truck route may only occur on Thursdays.
- *Order entry deadlines for taking sales orders.* The concept of an order entry deadline means that orders received after a specified time are treated as if they were received the next day. You define a set of deadlines for each day within a week (termed an order entry deadline group), and then assign the deadline group to each customer and site.
- *Sales lead time for preparing items for shipment.* A sales lead time typically represents the number of days to prepare items for shipment, such as a value of 0 or 1 day. It will be automatically reflected in the shipment date when using any of the three major options; it is not just for the Sales Lead Time option. The value for sales lead time is specified as

[5]The transportation time is based on the ship-from warehouse. In cases where a sales line does not specify a ship-from warehouse, there is insufficient information to calculate the transportation time. In these cases, the transportation time will be calculated assuming use of the site's fallback warehouse.

a company-wide value, and you can optionally define item-specific overrides. In addition, the value of a sales lead time can be defined within sales trade agreements, so that an applicable sales line (for the customer and item) inherits the sales lead time as well as the sales price or discount.

As an alternative viewpoint, the sales lead time can represent a quoted lead time for an item. For example, a quoted lead time of 7 days can result in automatic assignment of a shipment date 7 days from today's date. This viewpoint generally applies to sales lead times defined within sales trade agreements.

Delivery Date Control Options for a Sales Order The four options for a delivery date control policy are summarized in Figure 11.4, along with comments about the implications of each option. The bottom of Figure 11.4 displays an additional approach for the sales lead time option, where you calculate a shipment date using CTP logic based on a net change explosion. Separate subsections provide suggestions for using each option.

Delivery Date Control Option	Scenario	Comments
Sales Lead Time	Use Basic Rules or Quoted Lead Time	Auto-assign requested dates based on basic rules Enforce basic rules for manually entered dates* Analyze supplies using ATP form or Supply Overview form
ATP	Stocked End-Item	Auto-assign requested dates based on basic rules + ATP logic Enforce basic rules + ATP logic for manually entered dates* Analyze supplies using ATP form or Supply Overview form
CTP	MTO/CTO End-Item	Auto-assign requested dates based on basic rules + CTP logic Enforce basic rules + CTP logic for manually entered dates*
None	Allow assignment of unrealistic dates	Ignore basic rules for manually entered dates
Sales Lead Time with CTP Logic via Net Change Explosion	MTO/CTO/ETO End-Item	Enforce basic rules for manually entered dates Requires a user-initiated net change explosion, and you can transfer the calculated futures date to the confirmed ship date

* = Display exceptions on *Available Ship and Receipt Dates* form, and transfer a selected set of dates to change confirmed dates (or requested dates)

Figure 11.4 Delivery Date Control Options for a Sales Order

Using Sales Lead Time as the Delivery Date Control Option This option provides automatic assignment of the requested ship and delivery dates, where the dates reflect the basic rules. It also enforces the basic rules for manually entered dates, and automatically displays exceptions in a separate dialogue (termed the Available Ship and Receipt Dates form). The dialogue displays available dates, and you can optionally transfer a selected set of dates to change either the requested dates or the confirmed dates. You can also analyze available supplies for the item using the ATP form or Supply Overview form.

This option provides the simplest approach to delivery promises while enforcing the basic rules. The suggested values for a sales lead time depend on whether it represents a shipment preparation time (for a stocked item) or a quoted lead time (for a make-to-order item).

This option can simply enforce the basic rules for delivery date control, such as a value of 0 or 1 day for the sales lead time. However, some scenarios employ the sales lead time to represent a quoted lead time, so that the sales lead time reflects a larger number (such as 7 days or 14 days).

Using ATP as the Delivery Date Control Option This option typically applies to stocked end-items, where ATP logic just focuses on the salable item. It provides automatic assignment of the requested ship and delivery dates, where the dates reflect the basic rules and ATP logic. It also enforces these rules for manually entered dates, and automatically displays exceptions in a separate dialogue (termed the Available Ship and Receipt Dates form). As previously explained, the dialogue displays available dates, and you can optionally transfer a selected set of dates to change either the requested dates or the confirmed dates. You can also analyze available supplies for the item using the ATP form or Supply Overview form.

The ATP option requires several additional policies about underlying assumptions in order to correctly calculate an available-to-promise date, as summarized below.

- *ATP time horizon.* The ATP time horizon (expressed in calendar days) typically reflects the item's cumulative manufacturing lead time, so that a promise date corresponding to the end of the horizon will be automatically assigned when there is insufficient supply to satisfy the required quantity. In addition, this time horizon constrains the display of

ATP information on the associated inquiry for a sales line (termed the ATP form).

The ATP time fence provides one approach for supporting a quoted lead time, since a promise date corresponding to the end of the horizon will be automatically assigned when there is insufficient supply to satisfy the required quantity

- *Include planned orders.* An item's planned orders should be included in ATP logic when you have defined an S&OP game plan (that drives planned orders), and you actually follow through on the planned orders.
- *Assumptions about the dates for existing orders.* ATP logic requires realistic and up-to-date dates on existing sales orders and supply orders so that promise dates can be correctly calculated. However, some scenarios have orders with incorrect or past due dates so that you must define several assumptions about how ATP logic should handle these. For example, the assumptions (expressed in calendar days) should be defined for considering sales orders with past due dates (termed the backward demand time fence) and supply orders with past due dates (termed the backward supply time fence). The typical values for these time fences depend on how often you update the order dates.
- *Safety lead time via an issue margin.* An additional option for delivery date control is termed "ATP plus issue margin." The issue margin represents a safety lead time expressed in days, so that the promised date reflects the additional days. You define these safety margin days as part of the coverage group assigned to an item.

Using CTP as the Delivery Date Control Option This option typically applies to a make-to-order or configure-to-order item, where CTP logic considers components and operations in its active BOM/Route versions (rather than just focusing on the salable item). It provides automatic assignment of the requested ship and delivery dates, where the dates reflect the basic rules and CTP logic. It also enforces these rules for manually entered dates, and automatically displays exceptions in a separate dialogue (termed the Available Ship and Receipt Dates form). As previously explained, the dialogue displays available dates, and you can optionally transfer a selected set of dates to change either the requested dates or the confirmed dates. It is not as helpful to analyze available supplies using the ATP form or Supply Overview form, since this information only applies to the salable item.

The CTP option considers available inventory and receipts for the end-item and all of the components in its BOM structure, and uses lead times for items when insufficient supplies require replenishment.

Implications of No Delivery Date Control Assigning an option of *none* will disable the rules for delivery date control, thereby allowing assignment of unrealistic dates. As a general guideline, any sales line with this option should be highlighted as an exception requiring follow up.

Using a Net Change Explosion to Calculate a Ship Date This approach typically applies to MTO, CTO or ETO items, and employs delivery date control (for the sales lead time option) to enforce the basic rules. After entering the sales line, you initiate a net change explosion (or explosion for short) in order to calculate a futures date, and you can optionally transfer the futures date to the requested ship date. The net change explosion for an item can also be accessed from other forms, including the Actions, Futures and Requirement Profile form.

This approach requires two sets of master plan data (termed static and dynamic), since the net change explosion can only generate planned orders within the dynamic master plan. A subsequent section describes the use of two sets of master plan data (Section 11.8).

Assignment of a Delivery Date Control Option A delivery date control option can be assigned to a sales order header and each line item. The option for a sales order header is inherited from a company-wide value, and the option for each sales line is typically inherited from an item-specific value. The option can be manually overridden, typically to a value of none in order to disable delivery date control.

Continuous Checking of Sales Order Promise Dates The concept of continuously checking the sales order promise dates is embedded in the futures messages generated by the planning calculations. That is, the futures message warns when a sales order ship date cannot be met, and identifies the projected ship date. When you completely trust the futures messages for an item, you can automatically update the sales order ship dates with the calculated futures dates (as defined by a policy within the coverage group assigned to the item).

11.7 Run Planning Calculations and Analyze Results

Several different approaches can be used for planning calculations and the subsequent analysis of results. For example, the approach varies slightly for scenarios with forecasted requirements or with project-related requirements, or with a multi-company supply chain. For illustrative purposes, this section focuses on a typical business process for make-to-stock products with S&OP game plans based on demand forecasts.[6] The typical business process consists of several steps performed by different roles, as summarized in Figure 11.5 and described below.

Overview As a starting point, the production planner ensures that planning calculations are performed on a regular basis. The planning calculations consist of a forecast scheduling task and a master scheduling task, and they result in a set of forecast plan data and master plan data respectively. The production planner and purchasing agent analyze these results to coordinate supply chain activities for items within their responsibility, such as analyzing an item's planned orders, net requirements and action messages. The production supervisor can also analyze resource requirements when routing data has been defined for manufactured items. These analyses help identify potential material or capacity constraints that require changes to meet the S&OP game plans.

Delete the Existing Planned Orders and Capacity Requirements The production planner determines whether to delete an existing plan, which results in the deletion of existing planned orders and capacity requirements. This step provides a clean starting point for the planning calculations.

Run the Forecast Scheduling Task The production planner ensures that the Forecast Scheduling task is performed on a periodic basis, such as running the task after making any changes to forecasts. The task calculates forecasted demand (within a set of Forecast Plan data) based on forecast plan policies such as a specified forecast model and the desired time horizon. The resulting set of Forecast Plan data provides the basis for further analysis such as analyzing an item's requirements or a resource's capacity requirements.

[6]The business process assumes that you have defined item planning data (Chapter 10) as well as BOM and routing information for manufactured items (Chapters 4, 5 and 6).

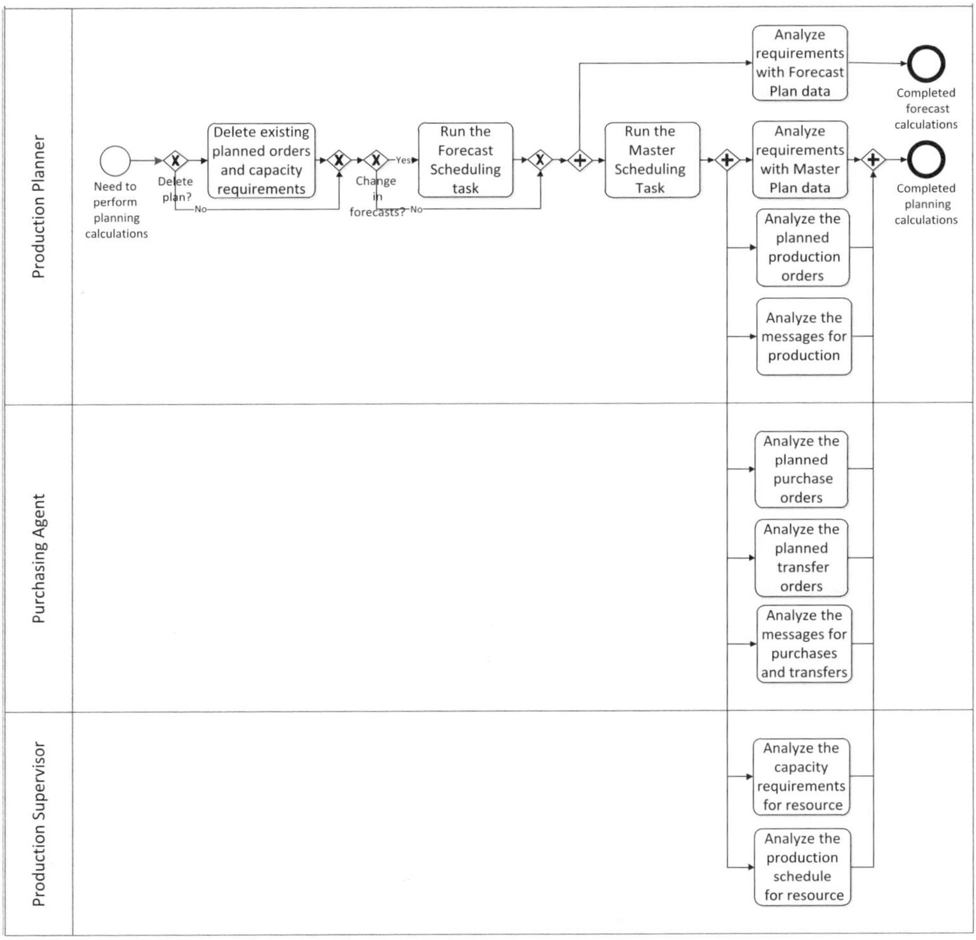

Figure 11.5 Typical Business Process to Run Planning Calculations and Analyze Results

Run the Master Scheduling Task The production planner ensures that the Master Scheduling task is performed on a periodic basis, which represents the primary engine for coordinating supply chain activities. The task generates a set of master plan data based on several master plan policies, such as the identifier for the set of master plan data, the applicable forecast identifier, and several factors affecting the calculations. The resulting set of master plan data provides the basis for further analysis such as analyzing an item's requirements or a resource's capacity requirements. For simulation purposes, the production planner can employ multiple sets of master plan data and associated master plan policies, and then select the desired set when viewing material or capacity requirements.

Analyze Requirements with a Set of Forecast Plan Data The production planner selects the desired set of forecast plan data when analyzing material and capacity requirements, typically in the context of analyzing long-term requirements. For example, you can analyze an item's net requirements or gross requirements for a selected set of forecast plan data.

Analyze Requirements with a Set of Master Plan Data The production planner selects the desired set of master plan data when analyzing material and capacity requirements, typically in the context of coordinating near-term supply chain activities. For example, you can analyze an item's net requirements or gross requirements for a selected set of master plan data.

Analyze the Planned Production Orders The production planner analyzes planned orders about production to help coordinate supply chain activities for those items within their responsibility. The planned orders are typically firmed to execute the S&OP game plans. In a bulk/pack scenario, the production planner typically firms multiple planned orders related to a production run of the bulk item and its various packed items.

Analyze the Messages for Production The production planner analyzes messages about production orders to help coordinate supply chain activities for those items within their responsibility. The production planner employs message filters to eliminate unnecessary messages.

Analyze the Planned Purchase Orders The purchasing agent analyzes planned purchase orders for those items and vendors within their responsibility, and typically firms the planned orders to execute the S&OP game plans.

Analyze the Planned Transfer Orders The purchasing agent analyzes planned transfer orders for those items and warehouses within their responsibility, and typically firms the planned orders to execute the S&OP game plans.

Analyze the Messages for Purchases and Transfers The purchasing agent analyzes messages about purchase orders and transfer orders to help coordinate supply chain activities for those items within their responsibility. The purchasing agent employs message filters to eliminate unnecessary messages.

Analyze the Capacity Requirements for a Resource The production supervisor analyzes the capacity requirements for those resources within their responsibility. The requirements reflect routing data for manufactured items, and planning calculations based on infinite or finite capacity assumptions about the resource. The analysis typically anticipates overloaded periods for bottleneck resources so that adjustments can be made to capacity or to the load stemming from relevant production orders. The aggregate capacity requirements can also be viewed for a resource group consisting of multiple resources.

Analyze the Production Schedule for a Resource The production supervisor analyzes the suggested production schedule for those resources within their responsibility. The suggested schedule can be viewed in different formats, such as tabular or Gantt chart. The production supervisor typically coordinates actual production to meet operation due dates and execute the S&OP game plans.

11.8 Understanding Planning Calculations

The single term *planning calculations* refers to two tasks termed the *forecast scheduling* task and the *master scheduling* task. The forecast scheduling task calculates a set of forecast plan data based on several policies such as a specified forecast identifier. The master scheduling task calculates a set of master plan data based on several policies, such as whether to consider forecasts and the relevant forecast model. Before explaining these two tasks in greater detail, it is helpful to review the demands and supplies considered by the planning calculations.

Sources of Demand and Supply The sources of demand and supply are summarized in Figure 11.6. Several sources of demand such as sales orders, demand forecasts and supply forecasts have been described in previous sections. The optional consideration of sales quotations as demand (based on their win probability) has also been discussed as one of the S&OP approaches.

		Demands (Issues)	Supplies (Receipts)
All Environments		Sales Order	Purchase Order Planned Purchase Order
All Environments		Sales Quotation (Optional) Demand Forecast Supply Forecast	Purchasing RFQ (Optional) On-Hand Inventory Quarantine Inventory
All Environments		Purchase Order Return to Vendor	Sales Order Return from Customer
All Environments		Transfer Order (Ship-from) Planned Transfer Order (Ship-from)	Transfer Order (Ship-to) Planned Transfer Order (Ship-to)
All Environments	Un-posted Inventory Journals	Transfer Journal (Transfer-from) Inventory Adjustment (Negative) Physical Count (Negative)	Transfer Journal (Transfer-to) Inventory Adjustment (Positive) Physical Count (Positive)
Manufacturing	Un-posted Inventory Journals	Picking List Journal (Positive)	Picking List Journal (Negative) Reported-as-Finished Journal
Manufacturing		Component Requirement (aka derived requirement)	Production Order Planned Production Order

Figure 11.6 Sources of Demand and Supply

Planning calculations can selectively include or exclude some of these sources of demand and supply, as defined by the policies assigned to the master plan. For example, these policies determine whether the planning calculations should consider demands related to demand forecasts, supply forecasts and sales quotations. The policies also determine whether to include unposted inventory journals.

Planning calculations ignore inventory identified as non-nettable. A warehouse can be designated as non-nettable (using the Manual Planning flag), and a batch-controlled item can have an inventory batch designated as non-nettable (based on its disposition code policies). Inventory blocking can also identify when the inventory should be treated as non-nettable.

Some sources of demand and supply only apply to project-oriented operations, and are not shown in the figure. These project-specific demands include item forecasts and sales orders for item requirements, and optional consideration of project quotations based on win probability. The project-specific supplies include project purchase orders and project production orders. Chapter 20 provides further explanation of project-oriented operations. Service orders can also identify project-specific demands, as described in Chapter 21.

Master Scheduling Task The master scheduling task represents the primary engine for coordinating supply chain activities. As shown in Figure 11.6, the master scheduling task uses information about demands and supplies and a set of master plan policies to calculate material and capacity requirements within a set of *master plan data (*aka *requirements data*). It also generates planned orders and action messages to synchronize supply chain activities.

Several master plan policies directly affect the planning calculations for a set of master plan data. For example, these policies indicate the forecast identifier and the forecast consumption approach. They also determine the scheduling method, and whether finite or infinite scheduling logic will be used for production orders based on their routing data.

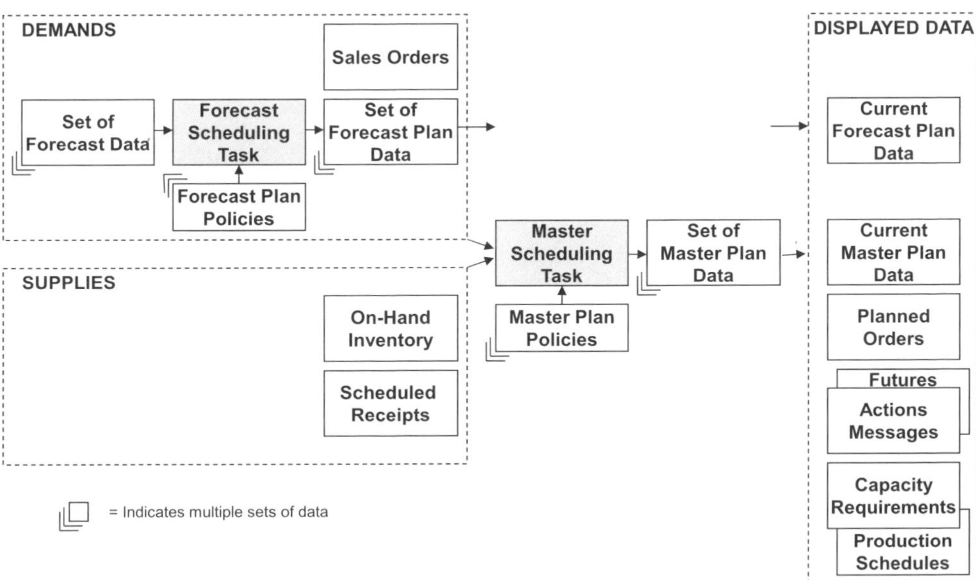

Figure 11.7 Overview of Planning Calculations

For simulation purposes, you can employ multiple sets of master plan data and their associated master plan policies. You can choose the desired set of master plan data when viewing material and capacity requirements, although the default set of displayed data reflects the company-wide policies for the current master plan and forecast plan.[7] Using this displayed data (shown in the right side of Figure 11.7), you can coordinate supply chain activities through planned orders, suggested action messages, and the analysis of material and capacity requirements.

Forecast Scheduling Task The *forecast scheduling task* represents a second coordinating engine, as shown in Figure 11.7 when forecasted demands are applicable. It calculates forecasted demand within set of *forecast plan data* based on several policies such as a time horizon and the relevant forecast identifier. Forecast scheduling must be performed after changing forecast information so that the master scheduling task recognizes forecasted demands. Multiple sets of forecast plan data can be calculated, typically to reflect various scenarios for simulation purposes.

A set of forecast plan data represents gross requirements to support planning of materials and capacity, whereas a set of master plan data represents net requirements to support day-to-day supply chain coordination.

Master Scheduling with Two Sets of Data Most scenarios can employ a single set of data as their current master plan. Some environments are better served by two sets of master plan data—termed the static plan and the dynamic plan—when using net change explosions for calculating sales order delivery promises (described in Section 11.6). The net change explosion generates planned orders when there are insufficient supplies for the end-item or its components. The planned orders immediately communicate the need for replenishment to meet the promised delivery date.

This situation creates difficulties for buyers and planners in determining appropriate actions for planned orders. It becomes even more difficult when using this approach for multiple checks of delivery promise information, or when deleting the sales order because the customer is only asking about delivery promises or finds them unacceptable. The situation results in constant changes to planned orders.

One approach to handling this problem involves two sets of data termed the *static master plan* and *dynamic master plan*. The static master plan

---

[7] These company-wide policies are embedded in the Master Planning parameters.

contains the results of the previous master scheduling task that generated suggestions about planned orders. The dynamic master plan starts with the same set of data, but is continuously updated by new sales order commitments. This approach insulates buyers and planners from planned orders stemming from delivery promise simulations. However, this approach assumes that the delayed communication of planned orders is acceptable (until the next master scheduling task generates a new set of data for the static master plan).

11.9 S&OP Game Plans for a Configurable Item Built from Stocked Components

A configure-to-order or make-to-order product is often built from stocked components to shorten delivery lead times. For illustrative purposes, this section focuses on a typical business process for maintaining the S&OP game plan for a configurable item built from stocked components. The game plan includes supply forecasts for stocked components in order to generate planned orders for replenishment, and it also includes sales orders for the configurable item. The item's configuration technology determines how you define the configuration and its associated BOM version and route version. This information enables CTP logic to provide a delivery promise. The game plans are typically reviewed and updated on a periodic basis. The typical process consists of multiple steps performed by different roles, as summarized in Figure 11.8 and described below.

The business process starts with an analysis of historical and projected demands so that the sales manager can prepare a sales plan and inventory plan for each configurable item, where the inventory plan focuses on stocked components. The production planner uses this information to enter the supply forecasts for stocked components. The customer service rep enters sales orders for the configurable item and defines the configuration, calculates delivery promises for the configuration, and creates the production order linked to the sales order line. After planning calculations have been performed, the production planner analyzes the results to determine the need for adjustments. The production planner firms the master schedule for stocked components and adjusts the final assembly schedule—expressed as production orders for the configurable item.

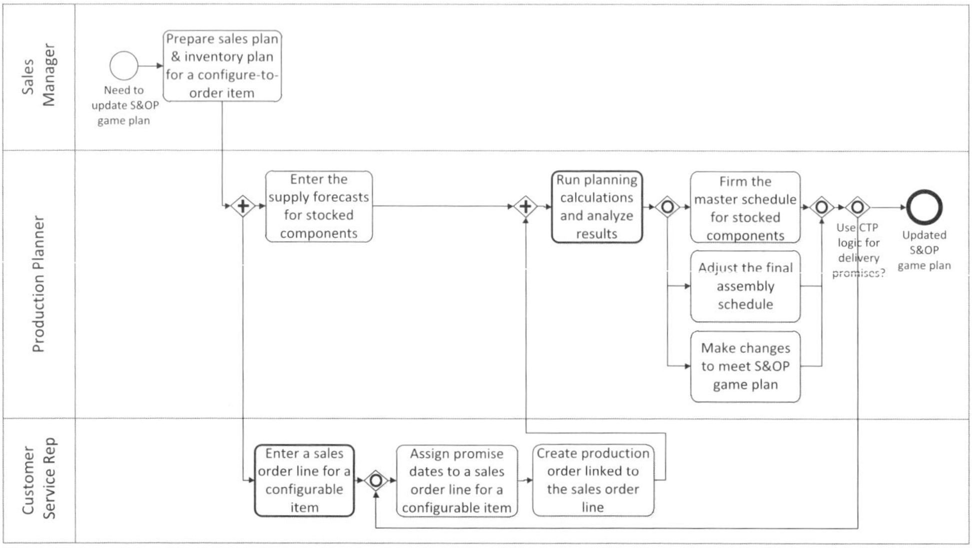

Figure 11.8 Typical Business Process to Maintain S&OP Game Plans for a Configurable Item Built from Stocked Components

Prepare a Sales Plan and Inventory Plan for the Item The sales manager analyzes historical and projected demands for the configurable item in order to prepare the estimated demands for stocked components, typically expressed in monthly increments. The analyses may reflect a statistical forecasting technique or some other method.

Enter the Supply Forecast for Stocked Components The production planner uses the estimated demands as the basis for entering a supply forecast for stocked components, typically expressed in weekly increments (or even daily increments) in the near-term time frame.

Enter a Sales Order Line for a Configurable Item The customer service rep enters sales orders for the configurable item, and defines the configuration using the item's configuration technology. The sales line indicates a quantity, ship-from location, and requested delivery date. The requested ship date may be initially assigned based on a standard quoted lead time.

Assign Promise Date to a Sales Order Line for a Configurable Item The customer service rep calculates a promised ship date based on a net change explosion for the sales line, and transfers it to the requested ship date (if different from the originally entered date). The promised date reflects the S&OP game plan, which helps align actual sales orders to the game plan.

The impact of projected production or material delays on the promised delivery date can be identified by futures messages (generated by the planning calculations). The futures messages provide a continuous check on realistic delivery promises.

Create a Production Order Linked to the Sales Order Line After completing the configuration process, the customer service rep creates a production order from the sales order line, thereby establishing linkage between the orders.

Run Planning Calculations and Analyze Results The production planner ensures that planning calculations are performed on a regular basis. The planning calculations consist of a forecast scheduling task and a master scheduling task. The production planner analyzes the results for manufactured items within their responsibility, whereas the purchasing agent does the same for purchased items and transfer items. In the context of the S&OP planning process, the production planner responsible for the end-items must consider constraints and multiple objectives in maintaining realistic S&OP game plans.

Firm the Master Schedule for Stocked Components The production planner firms the planned orders for manufactured items within their responsibility, especially for those items representing stocked components. Firming a planned order creates a production order with a scheduled status which can be locked to prevent rescheduling.

The purchasing agent performs similar tasks for purchased items and transfer items within their responsibility, especially for those items representing stocked components.

Adjust the Final Assembly Schedule for the Configured Item The production planner schedules the linked production order (created by the customer service rep) as part of adjusting the final assembly schedule.

Make Changes to Meet the S&OP Game Plan The production planner coordinates several types of changes to meet the master schedule. These changes may involve adjusting capacity at bottleneck resources, using alternate routings, or revising production schedules. The changes may involve working with the purchasing agent to expedite purchase orders for components, or they may involve working with the production supervisors to adjust capacity or schedules. When the schedule cannot be met, the production planner may need to work with customer service representatives to delay the promised delivery date on sales orders.

11.10 Using Simulations for S&OP Purposes

A basic simulation approach involves a different set of forecast data with a different forecast identifier. For example, you may define best-case and worst-case scenarios about expected demand with two different forecast identifiers and associated forecast plans. This forecast identifier is specified as one of the policies for a forecast plan, so that the forecast schedule task can generate a set of forecast plan data. You select the forecast plan data when viewing displayed data about material and resource requirements (shown in the right side of Figure 11.5).

A designated forecast identifier is also a key policy for a master plan, and you typically define a separate master plan for simulation purposes. For example, you may choose to ignore demand forecasts (as a master plan policy) so that the master plan data only reflects demands stemming from actual sales orders. Examples of other master plan policies that support simulations include the following.

- Time fences for forecasts, coverage and explosion. The time fences may reflect a long-term time horizon for long range planning.
- Capacity Time Fence. The time fence may reflect a long-term horizon for capacity planning purposes. Alternatively, with a capacity time fence of zero, the fixed lead times for manufactured items will be used by planning calculations.
- Infinite versus finite capacity viewpoint. A master plan with infinite capacity planning can be used to identify overloaded periods, so that available capacity could be adjusted via the calendars assigned to resources.

11.11 Guidelines Concerning S&OP Game Plans

Effective game plans lead to improved firm performance and bottom line results. Metrics include reductions in stock-outs, delivery lead time, missed shipments, partial shipments, and expediting efforts. Metrics also include improvements in customer service. The lack of effective game plans is typically cited as a leading cause of poor ERP system implementations. The following guidelines provide suggestions for improving the effectiveness of S&OP game plans.

The S&OP game plans typically represent a demand pull strategy. A push strategy applies to some types of products. Examples include agricultural-related products that must be picked and processed at certain times of the year, and animal-related industries (such as poultry, beef and pork) requiring a maturation period before the animals can be sent to market. In these examples, the push strategy will be influenced by the raw material availability, and the determination of size and quality upon receipt. It is particularly important for the S&OP game plans to match demands to the incoming supply.

Minimum Planning Horizon for Each Game Plan A saleable item's cumulative lead time represents the minimum horizon for a game plan, and additional months provide visibility for purchasing and capacity planning purposes. This minimum planning horizon should be reflected in the item's time fences, such as the coverage and forecast time fences.

Reviewing and Updating Game Plans The process for reviewing and updating each game plan should be embedded into the firm's regularly scheduled management meetings focusing on demands and supply chain activities. An agreed-upon game plan reflects a balance of conflicting objectives related to sales, engineering, manufacturing, inventory, purchasing and accounting. Periodic revisions to game plans should be reflected in updated forecasts and promised delivery dates.

Primary Responsibility for Maintaining Game Plans The person(s) acting as a master scheduler typically maintains the game plans and obtains management agreement. This role typically requires an in-depth understanding of sales and supply chain capabilities, as well as the political power to achieve agreed-upon game plans. The responsibility for providing sales order and forecast data typically belongs to the sales function, with a hand-off to the master scheduler. The primary responsibility for game plans should be reflected in the planner (and buyer) responsibility assigned to items.

Formulating Realistic Game Plans Realistic game plans require identification of capacity and material exceptions that would constrain the plans, and then eliminating the constraints or changing the plan. Identification of material-related exceptions typically starts with suggested actions, while capacity exceptions are identified using work center load analysis. In many cases, a realistic game plan must anticipate demands and demand variations via forecasts and inventory plans for stocked material. Finite scheduling can also contribute to a realistic game plan.

Enforcing Near-Term Schedule Stability Near-term schedule stability provides one solution for resolving many conflicting objectives, such as improving competitive efficiencies in purchasing and production and reducing exceptions requiring expediting. It provides a stable target for coordinating supply chain activities and removes most alibis for missed schedules. Near-term schedule stability can benefit from inventory plans and realistic order promises about shipment dates. It involves a basic trade-off with objectives requiring fast response time and frequent schedule changes. The critical issue is that management recognizes the trade-offs to minimize near-term changes. An item's freeze time fence represents one approach to support near-term schedule stability, since planning calculations do not suggest planned orders during the frozen period.

Making and Maintaining Realistic Sales Order Promises Realistic delivery promises represent the key link between sales commitments and supply chain activities. You can calculate a realistic promised delivery date during order entry, and also through planning calculations that suggest delayed delivery based on projected completion dates. A key aspect of promised delivery dates is to reduce and isolate the number of exceptions requiring expediting. When available inventory only partially satisfies the sales order requirement, one solution approach involves splitting delivery across two sales order line items with different shipment dates.

Executing Supply Chain Activities to Plan Planning calculations make an underlying assumption that everyone works to plan, and the system provides coordination tools to communicate needed action. For example, it is assumed that procurement will ensure timely delivery of purchased material so that manufacturing can meet production schedules. It is assumed distribution will make on-time shipments because sales made valid delivery promises and procurement and production are working to plan. An unmanageable number of exceptions will impact this underlying assumption and the usefulness of coordination tools.

Reducing Exceptions that Require Expediting The intent of near-term schedule stability, valid delivery promises and shipment dates, realistic game plans, and executing to plan is to reduce the number of exceptions to a manageable level. This improves the usefulness of coordination tools to meet the game plans.

Additional Case Studies

Case 58: Statistical Forecasting The sales management team at a discrete manufacturer used statistical forecasting to calculate future sales demand in monthly increments based on historical data. In addition to shipments, the historical data included customer returns and selected inventory adjustments. Further refinements to the historical analysis included the requested shipment date on sales orders (to give a true picture of demand patterns) in addition to the actual shipment date.[8]

Case 59: S&OP Simulations A manufacturer employed simulations to assess the impact of changing demands and supplies. Using multiple sets of forecast data to represent various scenarios, and a designated set of forecast data for planning calculation purposes, the management team could analyze the impact of changing demands on material and capacity requirements. For example, the planning calculations were first performed using infinite capacity planning to anticipate overloaded periods. After adjusting available capacity and consideration of alternate routings, the planning calculations were performed again using finite capacity and material to highlight unrealistic delivery dates. In this scenario, capacity simulations were especially important because many shelf life products cannot be prebuilt, and refrigerated products have high inventory carrying costs.

[8] See **www.DemandSolutions.com** for further information about their forecast management module for AX 2012.

Case 60: Aggregate Forecasts by Item Group A manufacturing company had thousands of stocked end-items, and wanted to minimize the effort to maintain forecasts for individual items. Items were grouped together for forecasting purposes, with a mix percentage assigned to each item, so that aggregate forecasts could be entered for each group of items. This approach reduced the number of forecasts to be maintained, from thousands of individual items to a few dozen groups.

Case 61: Planning BOM for Stocked Components An equipment company currently forecasts a group of stocked components for a configure-to-order equipment item. The concept of a planning BOM was implemented with an item allocation key, which identified the stocked components and a mix percentage of their typical usage. A supply forecast specified the item allocation key and a quantity reflecting expected sales volume for the CTO equipment.

Case 62: Manual Master Schedule for Medical Devices A medical device company produced a line of medical devices that required a manually maintained master schedule to reflect the planner's decision-making logic about production constraints. The medical devices required an expensive outside operation for sterilization, where multiple end-items could be sterilized at the same time. The scheduling considerations included a cost-benefit analysis about amortizing the fixed fee for sterilization over the largest possible number of end-items subject to a weight maximum, while still building the product mix for customer demands and avoiding excess inventory. A manually maintained master schedule proved most effective for this case.

Case 63: S&OP Based on Sales Quote Pipeline A fabricated products company designed, quoted and built hundreds of one-time products to customer specifications. They used configurable items to model one-level and two-level custom products, and to define the unique BOM and routing for each configuration. This detailed information provided the basis for calculating estimated costs and a suggested sales price for sales quotations. The sales quotation backlog was used as part of the S&OP game plans to anticipate material and capacity requirements.

Executive Summary

The ability to run the company from the top requires a sales and operations planning process that formulates an S&OP game plan for each saleable product. The nature of an S&OP game plan depends on several factors, such as the need to anticipate demand for the item, the item's primary source of supply, and the need for linkage between a sales order and the supply order. It also depends on the production strategy for manufactured items

The starting point for each game plan typically involves identifying all sources of demand such as sales orders and forecasts, and forecast consumption logic determines how the combination of these demands will drive supply chain activities. Planning calculations help formulate and analyze S&OP game plans, especially in using multiple sets of data for simulation purposes. Realistic promises for sales order delivery can be based on the S&OP game plans and delivery date control policies that enforce basic rules such as calendars and transport time. Unrealistic promises can only be made by disabling the delivery date control logic, and the exceptions should require follow-up.

Several scenarios illustrated how to maintain S&OP game plans. Guidelines were suggested to improve S&OP game plans, such as how to formulate realistic game plans, enforce near-term schedule stability, and make realistic delivery promises. The case studies highlighted variations in the use of S&OP game plans, such as a manually maintained master schedule, statistical forecasts, and supply forecasts for stocked components.

Chapter 12

Sales Order Processing

Sales orders capture demands for the firm's products and services. They comprise a key element in two larger contexts: the sales and operations (S&OP) game plan driving supply chain activities, and customer service across the customer relationship life cycle. Sales orders may originate from one or more order streams, such as direct customer communication with sales reps or customer service reps, customer self service via web-based applications, and electronically transmitted customer schedules.

Sales order processing involves a wide spectrum of considerations and many variations. As an explanatory approach, it is easiest to start with a typical business process for sales orders of stocked products. Using the steps in this typical process, we will review the basic model of sales order processing embedded within AX. The basic model provides a foundation for explaining key considerations and major variations for sales order processing, and the definition of customer information. This explanatory approach is reflected in the following sections within the chapter.

1. Typical Business Process for Sales Orders
2. Basic Model of Sales Order Processing
3. Key Considerations in Sales Order Processing
4. Sales Prices and Trade Agreements
5. Sales Agreements
6. Customer Information
7. Special Orders and Direct Orders
8. Customer Returns and RMAs
9. Sales Orders for Configurable Items
10. Sales Quotations
11. Major Variations in Sales Order Processing

12. Sales Analysis
13. Commissions for Sales Orders

12.1 Typical Business Process for Sales Orders

A typical business process for sales orders consists of multiple steps performed by different roles, and provides a context for further explanation. This example starts with a customer placing a sales order with a customer service rep, as illustrated in Figure 12.1 and described below.

The customer service rep initially creates a sales order for a customer, which results in a sales order header. If needed, the rep maintains aspects of the sales order header information, such as designating (or adding) the desired delivery address or delivery mode, or overriding information inherited from the customer master. The customer service rep also creates sales order line items, where each line item identifies a product, quantity, sales price, ship-from location and the requested dates for shipment and delivery. When a line item's requested date cannot be met for a sales line, the promised dates can be automatically assigned based on available to promise logic. When all line items have been defined, the customer service rep generates a sales order confirmation and sends it to the customer.

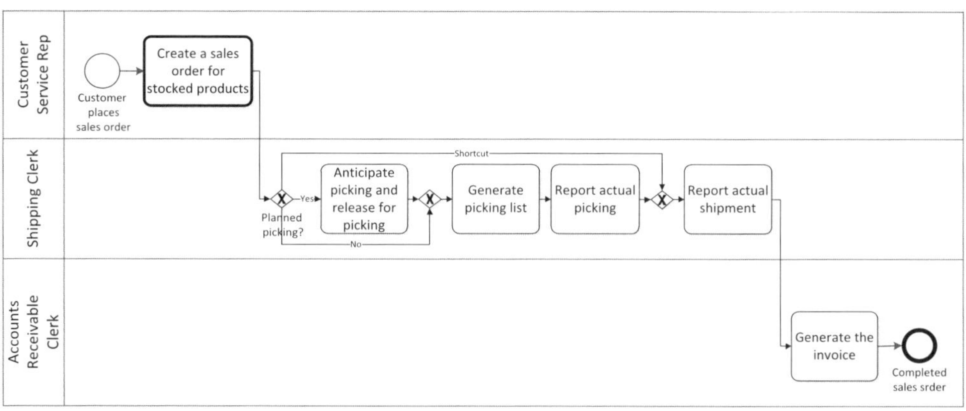

Figure 12.1 Typical Business Process of a Sales Order for Stocked Products

The shipping clerk typically anticipates picking activities by viewing a subset of sales order line items reflecting user-specified criteria, such as a specified ship-from location, shipping date and delivery mode. The shipping clerk can analyze inventory availability, and identify those sales lines (and quantities) which should be released for picking. The release-for-picking step reserves the inventory, and also generates an order-based picking list for each sales order. Each picking list has a unique identifier, and the printed picking list indicates the reserved material that should be picked and shipped. The shipping clerk reports actual picking activities against a picking list identifier, usually by simply confirming completion of the picking list. After completing the picking activities, the shipping clerk prints the paperwork for a sales order shipment and reports actual shipment of a sales order.

The accounts receivable clerk periodically generates the sales order invoices based on the information about which sales lines have been picked and shipped.

12.2 Basic Model of Sales Order Processing

The structure of a sales order consists of header and line item information, and each line item can optionally specify a delivery schedule of quantities and dates. The header identifies the sold-to customer, and optionally identifies a different customer for bill-to purposes. The sold-to customer information provides default values for the sales order header, and header information provides several default values when adding line items. Changes to header information can optionally update the line item information, with a prompt to confirm the mass update.

This section describes a basic model of sales order processing that reflects the typical business process described above and the embedded conceptual models within AX. It provides a framework for explaining major variations. For example, the basic model employs an order-based picking list to communicate picking/shipping requirements, whereas another variation employs a consolidated picking list. The basic model consists of the six steps summarized in Figure 12.2. The figure also indicates short-cut approaches (via a dashed line) allowing you to by-pass steps, such as simply shipping or invoicing a sales order without performing the picking list steps.

Step 1: Create a Sales Order The customer service rep uses the Sales Order form to create a sales order for a selected customer. Each line item

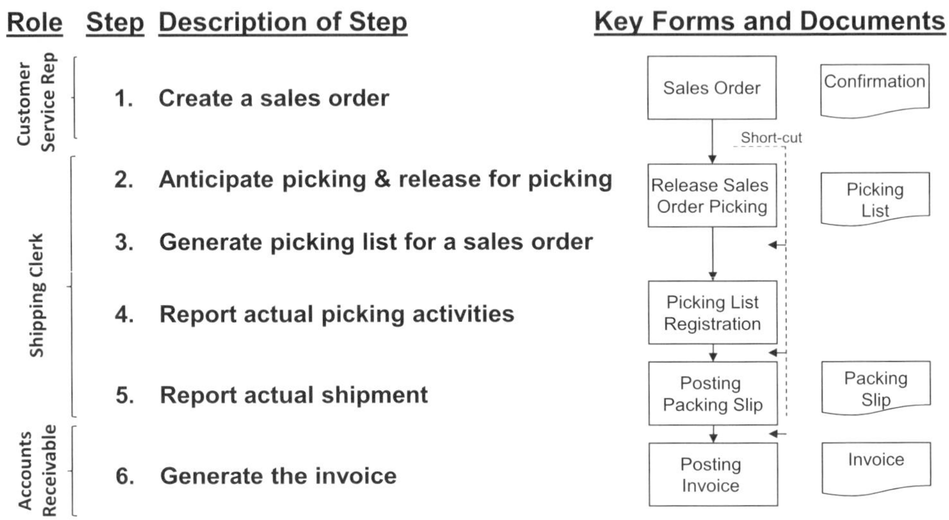

Figure 12.2 Basic Model of Sales Order Processing

identifies a product, quantity, sales price, ship-from site/warehouse and the dates for shipment and delivery. You generate and send a confirmation to the customer after completing the information. As possible short cuts, you can generate the picking list during order entry, or even skip the picking list steps and simply report the actual shipment and/or invoice for the sales order.

In most scenarios, you reserve material as a result of generating a picking list, where the picking list displays the reservations reflecting FEFO (first expired first out) logic. Some scenarios require reservations during order entry.

Step 2: Anticipate Picking Activities and Release for Picking

The shipping clerk uses the Release Sales Order Picking form to view open sales lines that should be released for picking based on actual availability. This helps ensure that you only print picking lists for items actually in stock. The displayed lines can reflect selection criteria to focus attention of warehouse shipping personnel, such as selection criteria about the ship date (e.g., today's date), the ship-from site/warehouse, mode of delivery, customer or the customer's priority (aka customer classification code). After indicating which sales order lines should be picked, you perform the *release for picking* step, which reserves the material and generates the picking list.

Step 3: Generate the Picking List The shipping clerk typically generates an order- based picking list as a result of the release for picking step, although it can also be generated during the order entry process. Each picking list has a system-assigned identifier, and displays the locations of the reserved material. It can be reprinted, and you report actual picking activities against the picking list identifier.[1] More than one picking list can be generated for a sales order when the sales lines specify warehouses reflecting different ship-from sites, or the sales lines specify different customer addresses. The creation of an order-based picking list also creates an associated shipment, uniquely identified by a shipment number.

Step 4: Report Actual Picking Activities The shipping clerk uses the Picking List Registration form to report actual picking activities against a picking list identifier. In most cases, the shipping clerk simply confirms the suggested quantities and locations were picked. Some cases require a correction such as the actual quantity picked.

Step 5: Report the Actual Shipment The shipping clerk uses the Posting Packing Slip form to report actual shipment. The step is commonly termed a packing slip update or posting the packing slip. The form can be accessed from the Sales Order form, thereby inheriting information from the selected sales order. It can also be accessed directly, which means that you must identify which sales order(s) are actually being shipped. As part of the step, you indicate the quantity basis for initially populating the packing slip information (such as the picked quantities) and whether to print the packing list.

Step 6: Generate the Invoice The accounts receivable clerk typically generates invoices on a periodic basis to reflect the actual shipments. The step is commonly termed posting the invoice. As part of the step, you indicate the quantity basis for initially populating the invoice information (such as the packing slip quantities) and whether to print the invoice.

Life Cycle of a Sales Order The life cycle of a sales order consists of several steps represented by a status automatically updated by the system.

---

[1] An item-specific policy can optionally mandate that the item must be picked before reporting actual shipment, thereby preventing a short-cut approach. This policy (termed the Picking Requirements checkbox) is embedded in the Item Model Group assigned to the item.

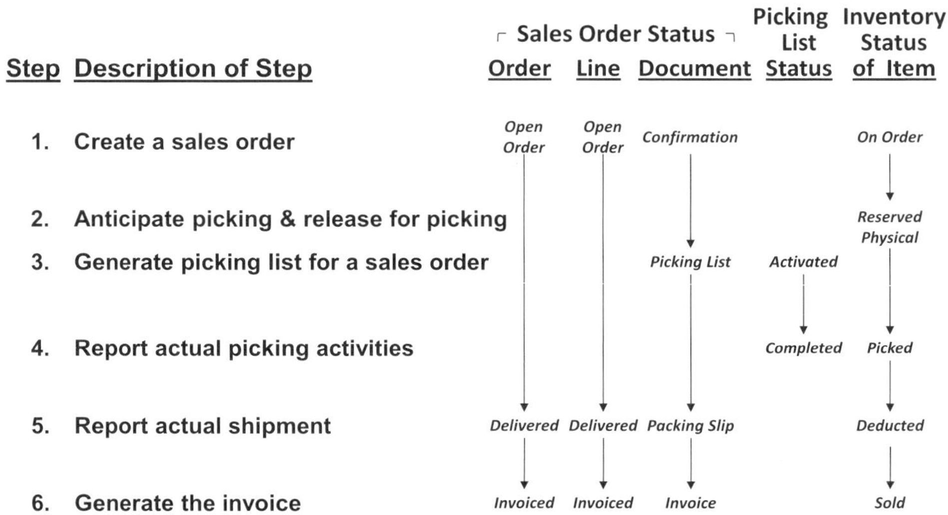

Figure 12.3 Life Cycles Related to a Sales Order

A status applies to the sales order, a sales line and the printed documents, as summarized in Figure 12.3 and described below. An additional status applies to the order-based picking list and to the inventory, as shown on the right side of the figure. Each life cycle and status reflects the embedded conceptual models within AX.

An order status indicates the following steps in the life cycle of a sales order:

- *Open Order.* The status indicates the order has been created.
- *Delivered.* The status indicates all order lines have been shipped.
- *Invoiced.* The status indicates all order lines have been invoiced.[2]

A line status indicates the following steps in the life cycle of a sales order line:

[2]Information about a sales order and/or line item with an invoiced status can be system-deleted immediately or subsequently deleted (by a user-initiated process) based on company-wide policies. Another policy determines whether the system retains manually deleted sales orders as voided orders.

- *Open.* The status indicates the line has been created, and partial shipment or invoicing may have occurred.
- *Delivered.* The status indicates the delivered quantity equals the order quantity. When using delivery tolerances, the delivered quantity can exceed the order quantity or an under-delivery can be flagged as closed.
- *Invoiced.* The status indicates the line item quantity has been completely invoiced, taking into account the over- or under-delivery considerations mentioned above.

A document status indicates the last document printed (aka posted) for the sales order, which includes the following documents.

- *Confirmation.* The status indicates a confirmation (aka order acknowledgement) has been posted.
- *Picking List.* The status indicates a picking list has been created, and it can be reprinted.
- *Packing Slip.* The status indicates the packing skip has been posted, which updates on-hand inventory for the shipped item unless the item's inventory is not being tracked.
- *Invoice.* The status indicates the invoice has been posted.

The status of the order-based picking list is shown on the right side of Figure 12.3, where a newly created picking list is assigned an *activated* status. Reporting actual picking activity (via the Picking List Registration form) changes this status to *completed.*[3]

The inventory status for the item on the sales line is also shown on the right side of Figure 12.3. The steps in sales order processing will change this status from *on order* to *reserved physical, picked*, *deducted* and *sold.*

Other Types of Sales Orders You indicate the sales order type when initially creating a sales order. In addition to a normal sales order, the order types include the following:

[3]Most firms employing a two-step picking process will print the picking list, and then report actual picking activities against the picking list (with an activated status). However, a few firms prefer to assume material has been automatically picked after printing the picking list (with an automatically assigned status of completed), which eliminates the need to report actual picking activities unless there is a correction. The desired approach is defined by a company-wide policy (on the A/R Parameters form) that determines whether printing the picking list will result in a status of activated or completed.

- *Returned Order.* A sales order with a type of returned order is automatically created for an RMA (returned material authorization), and handles the arrival, receipt and credit note for the returned goods (via a negative quantity line item). It also supports sending the returned item back to the customer. A subsequent section provides further explanation of customer returns and RMAs.
- *Journal (or Draft).* A journal sales order does not represent a demand. It is typically used to capture information early in the sales cycle, and you change the order type to sales order upon placement by the customer.
- *Subscription.* A subscription sales order represents a demand, and the system automatically recreates it after invoicing.
- *Item Requirement.* An item requirement represents a project-specific sales order, and must be created from a project. The sales order shipment does not require sales order invoicing, since invoicing (if required) is handled through the project. The chapter about projects explains the significance of item requirements (Section 20.4).

Sales quotations reflect a separate construct, and not a different type of sales order. A sales quotation can be confirmed, thereby generating a sales order with linkage back to the sales quotation.

12.3 Key Considerations in Sales Order Processing

Several sales order considerations reflect different ways of doing business with customers and different internal procedures. These considerations include order-related text, sales order dates for shipment and delivery, delivery addresses, calculated weight and volume, and alternative items, as described below.

Order-Related Text Many situations require textual explanations or additional descriptive information about the sales order and line items. Order-related text can be specified in several ways.

- *Carry Forward of Item Text to Line Item.* The item master allows each item to have an unlimited amount of descriptive text that automatically carries forward to the sales order line item, where it can be optionally overridden.

- *Document Handling Capabilities*. Documents containing descriptive text (defined as a document type of note) can be defined for the sales order header and/or each line item and flagged for internal or external purposes. The system can print the external notes on each sales document. These note documents can be previously defined for customers and items but do not automatically carry forward to the sales order; they must be explicitly copied and pasted to the sales order header and lines. Other types of documents such as Word files, Excel spreadsheets, and images can also be defined.
- *Printing Descriptive Information*. The setup policies for A/R forms determine the extent to which each printed form includes descriptive information. For example, the printed packing slip can identify the external item number, the serial and batch numbers of shipped material, and the note documents.

Sales Order Quantity and UM The item's standard sales order quantity and UM act as default values when entering an order and can be overridden. The system provides a soft warning if the entered quantity does not conform to the item's order quantity modifiers for a minimum, maximum and multiple. When a partial shipment is anticipated, entering a separate "deliver now" quantity can simplify the posting process for deliveries. Partial shipments for a line item can be explicitly forbidden using the ship complete flag to indicate the delivery quantity must match the order quantity exactly.

The shipped quantity can be greater or less than the ordered quantity as long as it is with the specified delivery tolerances. Over- and under-delivery tolerances are expressed as a percentage, and the values assigned to an item act as defaults for a sales order line item.

Alternative Approaches to an Item's Sales Price An item's sales price can be defined several different ways. As summarized in Figure 12.4, the four major approaches include a sales agreement, sales price trade agreements, the inherited sales price from a source document, and a standard sales price.

As the simplest approach, an item's standard sales price can be defined on the item master along with its default sales UM. It represents a company-wide sales price that acts as the default on a sales line when other sources of pricing information do not exist. This standard sales price can be manually specified or calculated, and the calculations differ for a purchased item versus a manufactured item. With a purchased item, the item's standard pur-

Source of the Sales Price on a Sales Order		Factors	Significance of the Item's Sales Price
Sales Agreement	Sales Agreement for a product quantity commitment	Committed quantity Minimum release quantity Validity period	Companywide or Site/Warehouse-specific Sales Price for the item
Sales Trade Agreement	Sales Price Trade Agreement Special Case: Calculated Sales Price based on Commodity Pricing	Customer or Customer Group Unit of Measure Quantity Breakpoints Effectivity Dates Delivery Lead Time	Companywide or Site/Warehouse-specific Sales Price for the item
Source Document	Sales Quotation	N/A	Inherit Sales Price from Source Document
	Copy a Sales Order		
Standard Sales Price	Manually entered Standard Sales Price	N/A	Companywide Sales Price for the item
	Calculated Standard Sales Price for a purchased item	Markup Percentage or Contribution Ratio	
	Calculated Standard Sales Price for a manufactured item	Markup Percentages for Material, Labor and Overhead	

Figure 12.4 Alternative Approaches to an Item's Sales Price

chase price and a specified markup percentage (or contribution ratio) can be used to calculate its standard sales price. This will be continuously recalculated based on changes to the item's standard purchase price as the result of the last vendor invoice. With a manufactured item, the standard sales price can be updated by activating an item's sales price record, where the sales price has been calculated based a cost-plus-markup approach for its purchased components, routing operations, and overhead formulas. Section 8.10 previously described the calculation of manufactured item's sales price.

As the second approach, the sales price on a sales order can be inherited from a source document. Examples of a source document include a sales quotation converted to a sales order and copying information into a sales order.

The third approach involves sales price trade agreements, which can represent company-wide or site/warehouse-specific sales prices for an item. They can also reflect customer-specific prices, different sales UM, validity dates, and quantity breakpoints. As noted in Figure 12.4, the sales price trade agreements also support the special case of item's sales price that has been calculated based on commodity pricing. Subsequent sections provide further explanation of sales trade agreements and also commodity pricing.

The fourth approach involves a sales agreement, which specifies the item's sales price based on a commitment quantity over a validity period. Releases against the sales agreement create a sales order, and the item inherits the specified price. Sales agreements can also define a discount percent (rather than a purchase price), and a subsequent section provides further explanation.

Sales Order Dates for Shipment and Delivery A sales order header has a requested ship date and a requested delivery date, where the difference represents the transportation time (termed transport days) between the ship-from warehouse and the delivery address. It also has a confirmed ship date and confirmed receipt date. These dates within the sales order header will be initially inherited by the sales lines, and changes in the header dates can optionally update information for the sales lines. The confirmed ship date for a sales line (if specified) will drive planning calculations, otherwise planning calculations use the requested ship date.

Several basic rules can be enforced for the shipment and delivery dates on a sales order header and for each line item, but only when the header and line items have been assigned any one of the three major options for delivery date control. The three major options for a delivery date control policy include sales lead time, available-to-promise (ATP) and capable-to-promise (CTP). The relevant policy depends on the scenario and S&OP approach. All three options enforce basic rules to help ensure realistic promise dates. A fourth option (labeled none) disables the enforcement of the basic rules, thereby allowing assignment of unrealistic dates. This fourth option is also referred to as disabling delivery date control. The previous chapter provided detailed explanations of these approaches for assigning delivery promises to a sales order (Section 11.6).

Delivery Schedule for a Sales Order Line A sales order line item normally consists of a single quantity and its associated ship and delivery dates. You can optionally specify a delivery schedule for a sales line, where each schedule line consists of a quantity and its associated dates. The total quantities within the delivery schedule lines must equal the quantity for the sales line, or the system will automatically adjust the sales line quantity.

Analyzing Supply Options for Making Delivery Promises You can view alternative supply options (using the Supply Overview form) for a sales order line item. These options include inventory and scheduled receipts at different sites and warehouses, quarantined inventory, an alternative item (if specified on the item master), and lead times to obtain the item from various sources.

Delivery Address by Sales Order Line Item Each line item inherits the delivery address from the sales order header, and it can be overridden. When printing a document such as a picking list or packing list, a separate document can be printed for each delivery address. The separate documents correctly communicate which line items are being sent to the delivery address.

Customer Pickup for a Sales Order A customer pickup must be designated as a policy for a user-defined delivery mode, and you assign this delivery mode to a sales order. A typical name for the delivery mode would be Customer Pickup. The Sales Pickup form displays sales orders having one or more line items with a delivery mode for customer pickup, and provides a short-cut approach for reporting shipment and invoicing transactions.

Reserving Material for a Sales Order Line Item Most scenarios employ reservations at the time you release a sales line for picking, and the picking list communicates these reservations. Some scenarios require reservations at the time of order entry. Reservations can be made manually or automatically, and reservations can be made against an item's scheduled receipts.[4] Other scenarios require reservations of specific batches.

Identifying an Alternate Item for a Sales Order Line Item When an alternate item has been defined for an item, the system automatically suggests the alternative item during order entry and replaces the originally entered item number. An item-specific policy determines whether the system always suggests replacement or only when available inventory is insufficient to cover the ordered quantity.

Versions of a Sales Order Posting a sales order confirmation results in automatic assignment of a version number. Each version is identified by

[4]The policy concerning reservations defaults from the sales order header, which defaults from the company-wide policy embedded in the A/R parameters. An additional company-wide policy determines whether reservations can be made against scheduled receipts.

the sales order number and a numeric suffix (such as -1 and -2). A sales order may be changed and the confirmation reposted in order to track versions of a sales order and communicate the changes to customers. The version number is displayed on a printed sales order confirmation. These historical versions can be viewed as part of inquiries about posted confirmations for a sales order. The system uses the existing sales order data (regardless of the assigned version number) for the purposes of the picking list, packing list and invoice.

The existing sales order data can revert to a previous version via the *Copy from Journal* function. You select from the displayed list of versions, and specify to delete lines from the existing order, so that the existing sales order data gets updated. You can optionally repost the sales order confirmation to assign a new version number.

Case 64: Comparing Versions of an EDI Sales Order

The majority of incoming sales orders for a manufacturing company were handled via EDI. Many of the incoming EDI sales orders did not reflect correct pricing, especially during periods reflecting changes in the effectivity dates for price lists. It was important to capture the sales prices specified by the customer, so that they could be compared with the correct assignment of sales prices. As the baseline, the incoming EDI sales orders did not have a specified price group, and the sales order confirmations were automatically posted. The applicable price group was then specified for each EDI sales order so that sales prices were correctly updated, and the sales order confirmations were posted a second time. The two versions of sales order confirmations were then compared to identify changes in prices.

Creating a Sales Order via the Copy Function A copy function (termed Copy from All) can be used to create line items from an existing sales order and other sources such as quotes and invoices. For example, you can select the desired sales order and the desired line item(s) from a displayed list of all existing orders. You can also select from versions of sales orders, or from sales quotations, packing lists and invoices. You indicate how to update the existing order, such as appending information to the existing line items and recalculating prices for the new line items.

Backorders in Sales A backorder represents a sales order line item that is not yet delivered to a customer. Backorders can be viewed by item or customer in order to answer customer inquiries and help prioritize use of available inventory for picking and shipment.

Month End Revenue Recognition of Sales Order Shipments Not Yet Invoiced Certain month-end situations require revenue recognition based on shipments prior to actual invoicing. In this case, the shipment (recorded via the packing slip update transaction) can update a revenue account that will be cleared upon invoice generation. The *post physical revenue* policy (embedded in the Item Model Group assigned to the item) indicates that shipments should update the *packing slip revenue* account and a *packing slip revenue offset* account (defined in the Item Group assigned to the item).

Totals for a Sales Order The system calculates several order totals, including revenue, cost and margin, discounts and taxes, and total weight and volume. Order totals can be displayed for order quantities, picked quantities, or shipped quantities. The total volume and weight can be used for truckload planning purposes.

12.4 Sales Prices and Trade Agreements

A sales trade agreement represents predefined information for selling products to customers, such as published list prices, customer-specific prices, and/or discount schemes. There are four types of sales trade agreements—bout the sales price, line discount, multi-line discount and/or total discount—and further explanation focuses on the sales price aspects. The different types can be used in combination with each other, such as defining the sales price and a discount.

Sales Price Trade Agreement Sales price trade agreements provide the primary approach for defining a named price list for different groups of customers. Synonyms of a price list include a price book. A key construct—termed the Price Group—typically represents a named price list such as a price group for Direct Sales or Distributors. Price groups are user-defined, and you assign a price group to relevant customers so that it is automatically inherited by sales orders for the customers.

	Factor	Sales Price	Line Discount	Multi-line Discount	Total Discount
	Warehouse-Specific Information			N/A	N/A
	Companywide Information				
			Types of Discounts		
Item	Item and UM	X	X	N/A	See item policy about including item value
Item	Group of Items	N/A	X Line Discount Group	X Multi-line Discount Group	N/A
Item	All Items		X	X	
Sold-To Customer	Customer	X	X	X	X
Sold-To Customer	Group of Customers	X **Price Group**	X Line Discount Group	X Multi-line Discount Group	X Total Discount Group
Sold-To Customer	All Customers	X	X	X	X
Other Factors	Validity Period	X	X	X	X
Other Factors	Currency Code	X	X	X	X
Other Factors	Order Quantity Breakpoints	X	X	X	Order Value Breakpoint
Other Factors	Delivery Days Price Charge	X X	N/A	N/A	N/A
	Policies	Price Group Policy: Price includes sales tax			Item Policy: Include item value for total discount purposes

Figure 12.5 Sales Trade Agreement Entries

Price trade agreements are expressed as multiple entries that identify the price group, the applicable items and their prices, and the effectivity dates. Other factors may include a different sales price based on the item's sales UM or for a quantity breakpoint on a sales order line. These factors affecting sales price trade agreement entries are summarized in Figure 12.5 and described below.[5] The following description focuses on the column labeled Sales Prices and the use of the Price Group to represent a named price list.

- Pricing for a named price list as identified by the Price Group field. The price group typically reflects a group of similar customers.
- Pricing for a specific customer. The sales pricing can be for a specific customer, but a Price Group is still typically used to identify the named price list.

[5] A set of company-wide policies (embedded in the *Activate Price/Discount* form within A/R setup) determines whether the system recognizes these factors.

- Pricing with validity period, for supporting periodic price updates or seasonal price promotions. A company-wide policy determines whether the sales price assignment reflects the order entry date on a sales order, or the requested ship date or receipt date for sales order lines.[6]
- Pricing by item and unit of measure, such as different prices per piece and per case.
- Pricing by currency type, such as separate pricing for foreign sales.
- Pricing with quantity breakpoints for the sales line quantity.
- Pricing based on delivery days. A higher price may apply for faster delivery, or the delivery lead time could vary by ship-from site/warehouse.
- Pricing involves an additional charge, such as a charge for fast delivery, small order quantity or freight.

As noted earlier, price trade agreements are expressed as one or more entries that identify the applicable factors. A simple pricing scheme that represents this year's price list for Distributors, for example, would be expressed as one entry for each saleable item. Every entry would also identify the price group (representing the Distributor price list) and the effectivity dates. Additional entries would be required for each site/warehouse when using site- or warehouse-specific pricing. Figure 12.5 illustrates the site/warehouse factor as a third dimension, since pricing can be company-wide or site/warehouse-specific.

During order entry, the price group assigned to the sales order determines the applicable trade agreement entries. This price group represents the named price list, and is initially inherited from the sold-to customer but can be overridden. The system uses the trade agreement information to automatically assign an item's price using the lowest price of applicable trade agreement entries.[7] The system also assigns the delivery lead time and the charge associated with the price. You can view available prices during order entry, such as viewing quantity breakpoints or future pricing to guide customer decisions.

[6]You define this company-wide policy as part of the A/R parameters about sales prices.

[7]The logic for finding the lowest applicable price requires an additional policy for each trade agreement record – termed the *find next* checkbox – otherwise the search will stop at the first applicable record.

Case 65: Sales Prices Based on Total Order Weight

A manufacturer employed the standard AX functionality for sales price trade agreements as the foundation for supporting their price lists based on total order weight. Each item had a lower sales price when total order weight exceeded a breakpoint. For example, the Distributor price list had two different prices for an item based on the weight brackets of less than and greater than 10,000 pounds. Within AX, this involved two different price groups labeled "Distributor-LT10k" and "Distributor-GT10k." Each trade agreement record identified the price group, item number and sales price, so that a given item had two trade agreement records reflecting the different sales prices for the two brackets. During order entry, the customer service rep (CSR) might initially specify the price group corresponding to the lower weight bracket as the basis for assigning sales prices. In those cases where total order weight exceeded 10,000 pounds, the CSR changed the Price Group in order to automatically re-price the sales order line items for the higher weight bracket.

Types of Sales Discounts in Trade Agreements The types of sales discounts can be related to a single line item, multiple lines, the order total value, or a combination of these approaches.

- ❖ *Line Discount.* The line discount is expressed as a fixed amount or a percentage or both. In particular, the percentage discount can be expressed as a single value or as two values (e.g., using a 10% discount for both values results in a 19% discount). In the case where both a fixed amount and a percentage discount are applied, the system applies the discount percentage after reducing the price by the fixed discount amount. Line discounts often reflect one or more of the factors shown in Figure 12.5, and a line discount can be company-wide or site/warehouse-specific.
- ❖ *Multi-Line Discount Based on Total Quantity.* The multi-line discount reflects a discount based on total quantity for multiple line items. It is expressed the same way as a single line discount— as a fixed amount or a percentage or both. The trade agreement entries can reflect the factors shown in Figure 12.5, such as a discount that applies to a group of customers or a group of items. Two different group codes (both termed

the *Multi-line Discount Group*) can be predefined—one for items and one for customers—and then assigned to relevant items and customers. A multi-line discount only reflects company-wide information, and can only be defined for a group of items or all items. You must initiate calculation of multiline discounts on a sales order after all line items have been entered.

The combination of a line discount and multi-line discount can be handled different ways, as defined by a company-wide policy (embedded in the A/R parameters). A typical approach views the two values as additive. An alternative approach views the two percentages as multiplicative, or indicates use of the lowest value or highest value, or indicates use of only one of the values.

- *Discount (or Surcharge) Based on Total Order Value.* The total discount reflects a discount based on total order value. It is expressed the same way as a single line discount—as a fixed amount or a percentage or both. Expressing the fixed amount as a negative value represents a surcharge based on total order value. The trade agreement entries can reflect the factors shown in Figure 12.5, such as a discount with order value breakpoints that apply to a group of customers. Note that a different group code—the *Total Discount Group*—can be assigned to relevant customers. An item-related policy determines whether the system includes or excludes the item in calculating total order value. You must initiate the calculation of the total discount on a sales order after all line items have been entered.[8]

Maintaining and Viewing Sales Trade Agreement Information

Information about sales trade agreements must be prepared beforehand and then used to update trade agreement information. Preparing data beforehand (using the Price/Discount Agreement Journal and its associated line items) offers several advantages in data maintenance. For example, you can create a new journal for preparing next year's sales price trade agreements, and then initially populate the entries with information about existing sales price agreements for selected items or customers. The information can then be manually maintained prior to posting the journal. In addition, you can perform mass changes to the entries (such as increasing the sales price a specified percentage or amount), or copy the entries in order to prepare price agreements for another item, customer, validity period or currency.

[8] Alternatively, the total discount can be automatically calculated (based on a company-wide policy embedded in the A/R parameters).

Use the Sales Prices report to view sales price trade agreement information, or a subset of information based on the report's selection criteria (such as the selected items, customers or currency). Use the Price/Discount List report to view all types of price and discount trade agreement information. Use the Price List report to view a comprehensive list of item sales prices, or the Customer Price List report to view the comprehensive list for each customer. Each report has selection criteria to view a subset of information.

Agreements about Supplementary Items Some sales environments involve predefined agreements about supplementary items such as "buy one and get an additional item free" which result in additional line items on a sales order. Supplementary items can also represent related items that should be sold together, or opportunities for up-selling or cross-selling. The definition of supplementary items can be tied to a customer or item or both, so that information about the relevant supplementary items can be viewed during order entry. The definition of each supplementary item includes an item number and quantity which can be designated as mandatory or optional, and chargeable or free-of-charge. The rules may also include date effectivities, a minimum order quantity and/or a one-time-only offer.

Agreements about Charges Some sales environments involve predefined agreements about charges, such as handling charges for selected items or customers. These charges can be embedded in the sales price trade agreement information, or they can be specified separately as *auto charges.* These auto charges can be applied to an entire sales order or to individual line items, and expressed as a fixed amount, an amount per piece, or a percentage of value.

- *Order-Level Charges.* Charges related to the entire sales order can be defined for a single customer, all customers or a group of customers (identified by the *Customer Charges Group* assigned to relevant customers). Examples of an order-level charge include order preparation costs for selected customers.
- *Line item charges.* Charges related to the sales order line item can be defined by customer and item, such as charges for a single item, all items, or a group of items (identified by the Item Charges group assigned to

relevant salable items).[9] Examples of a line item charge include a setup fee for producing selected items for a customer.

12.5 Sales Agreements

Sales agreements define a commitment to sell products to a customer over a time period in exchange for special prices or discounts. Synonyms include a blanket sales order.[10] The various types of a commitment include a total quantity for a specific product (with a specified sales price and/or discount percent), or a total value for a specific product, a category of products, or all products/categories (with a specified discount percent). After defining the sales agreement, you change its status to "effective" in order to allow usage, such as creating sales orders linked to the sales agreement.

The type of commitment is defined in the header information for a sales agreement, which then affects the information for each line item, as summarized below.

- *Create a line item for a product quantity commitment.* You define the total commitment quantity and the sales price and/or discount percent for a specified item. An optional minimum or maximum release quantity may also be defined.
- *Create a line item for a product value commitment.* You define the total commitment value and discount percent for a specified item. An optional minimum or maximum release amount may also be defined.
- *Create a line item for a product category value commitment.* You define the total commitment value and discount percent for a specified category of items. Section 3.1 (and Figure 3.3) previously explained categories and a category hierarchy for sales purposes. An optional minimum or maximum release amount may also be defined.
- *Create a line item for a value commitment.* You define the total commitment value and discount percent that will be applicable to all items or categories sold to the customer. An optional minimum or maximum release amount may also be defined.

[9] Two policies (embedded within the A/R parameters) indicate whether the system recognizes auto charges for the entire order and for line items.

[10] Previous versions of Dynamics AX provided a function termed "blanket sales order" which did not really support commitments over a validity period.

As part of the header information, you indicate whether the maximum should be enforced on related sales orders. Additional terms and conditions may also be specified—such as the payment terms and mode of delivery—which will be inherited by related sales orders.

Several different approaches are used to link a sales order to a sales agreement, as summarized below. As a result of these approaches, you can view the sales orders linked to a selected sales agreement or generate the equivalent report.

- *Release a sales order from a sales agreement.* You create the sales order by starting from a selected sales agreement, and specify the item and quantity for a sales order line item. The sales order header inherits the terms and conditions from the sales agreement, and a line item inherits the applicable sales price or discount percent from the sales agreement.
- *Manually create a sales order linked to a sales agreement.* You specify the identifier of the applicable sales agreement when manually creating a sales order. The sales order header inherits the terms and conditions from the sales agreement, and a line item inherits the applicable sales price or discount percent from the sales agreement.

You can also unlink a sales order currently linked to a sales agreement, which means the sales price or discount percent for the line item will no longer reflect the sales agreement.

12.6 Customer Information

A subset of customer information directly relates to sales order processing. Each customer is defined in a customer master file by a unique identifier. Sold-to and bill-to customers require unique identifiers.[11] The following data elements have particular significance to sales order processing.

Preferred Ship-From Site/Warehouse Each sold-to customer can have a preferred ship-from site/warehouse which acts as the default value in sales order header information.

[11] The concepts of a sold-to and bill-to customer represent a basic viewpoint representative of many situations. The sold-to customer determines the applicable sales trade agreements, whereas the bill-to customer determines the applicable credit management policies. Each sold-to customer can have multiple delivery address (ship-to) locations which determine the applicable sales taxes. More complex situations often require additional information, such as the corporate entity associated with various sold-to customers, or the end-user associated with a delivery address.

Ship-to Addresses A sold-to customer can have one or more addresses for delivery purposes, and a delivery address can be assigned to each sales order line item. When defining additional addresses, you can designate one as the default delivery address and others as alternates. During sales order entry, the system displays the default delivery address but you can select (transfer) an alternate to the order or create an order-specific delivery address. You can optionally designate (move) the order-specific delivery address as customer master information.

Bill-To Customer and Invoicing Considerations Each customer can optionally have a designated bill-to customer (termed the *invoice account* customer) that acts as a default on sales orders. The system supports a customer-specific numbering sequence for invoices. An invoice can be generated for each sales order or for multiple orders (e.g., with the same bill-to customer and currency) as a summary invoice.

Attributes Related to Pricing and Discounts The sold-to customer determines applicable pricing and discounts for a sales order. Sales prices in trade agreements can be based on the *price group* assigned to the sold-to customer. Discounts in trade agreements can be based on three other groups assigned to the sold-to customer—the *line discount*, *multi-line dis*count, and *total discount group*. A previous section described sales trade agreements.

Attributes Related to G/L Account Number Assignment General ledger (G/L) account number assignments (such as revenue and cost of sales) are based on a combination of customer and item characteristics. For example, the revenue account can reflect sales based on customer group and item group.

Financial Dimensions for a Customer The financial dimension(s) assigned to a customer provide a means to analyze sales by customer type. It can be used in conjunction with financial dimensions assigned to other entities, such as items, sales campaigns and sales persons, to provide multi-dimensional sales analyses.

One-Time Customers and Creating Customers during Order Entry When initially entering a sales order, the sold-to customer can be created on the fly by indicating a one-time customer. You enters the customer name and address information as part of creating the sales order, and the system automatically creates a new customer that is flagged as a one-time customer. Additional information defaults from an existing customer designated as the source of one-time customer information. The customer information can then be manually maintained, including the removal of the one-time customer flag.

Customer Hold Status A customer hold status (termed the *Invoicing and Delivery On Hold* policy) can prevent all transactions from being recorded, or prevent shipments and invoicing to the customer.

Language for a Customer The language assigned to each customer determines which language version should be displayed on printed documents and other customer interactions. For example, the assigned language determines the language version for an item description on a printed packing slip or invoice.

Intercompany Trading Partner Some enterprises have multiple companies defined within a single Dynamics AX instance, and trading between the companies. A sister company can act as a vendor (or customer) for intercompany trading purposes. A vendor (or customer) must be defined that represents the sister company. A subsequent chapter explains intercompany orders (Section 17.5).

Customer Calendar of Work Days Assigning a calendar to a customer and related delivery addresses enables delivery dates to reflect the available hours of operation (when using the delivery date control capabilities). The delivery dates are based on the company-wide calendar when a customer calendar is not specified.

Credit Management Policies The bill-to customer can have no requirement for a credit check, or a mandatory credit limit check with an associated credit limit amount. A company-wide policy (embedded in the A/R parameters) defines the basis for credit limit comparisons, such as the customer's current balance, shipments not yet invoiced, and open sales orders. You can check credit limit information during order entry, and the system prevents further transactions such as confirmations and shipments when the credit limit has been exceeded. A periodic task must be performed to enforce a credit limit consistency check on open orders when you change the basis for credit limit comparisons.

Summarized Information Summarized information about a customer can be viewed in several ways. A customer's statistics inquiry provides summarized data by monthly increments, such as the number and value of invoices and payments. Transaction detail can also be viewed by type of sales document, such as outstanding quotes, sales orders, and return orders.

12.7 Special Orders and Direct Orders

Many distribution companies sell products as a special order or direct order in addition to selling stocked items. For a given sales order, you can selectively designate which lines should be treated as a special order or direct order. Both types require close coordination of sales order and purchase order processing, as described in the following sections. The explanation briefly covers the purchase order implications, since the next chapter provides in-depth explanations.

Special Orders One or more lines on a sales order can be designated as a special order, which results in a corresponding special purchase order (aka special PO for short). A basic model for special order processing contains several steps for the sales order and the corresponding purchase order, as illustrated by the numbered steps in Figure 12.6 and described below. These numbered steps reflect the basic models for sales order processing (Figure 12.2) and purchase order processing (Figure 13.2).

- *SO Step 1: Create a sales order.* You create the sales order for a customer using the Sales Order form, where each line item identifies a product, quantity, sales price, the ship-from site/warehouse, and the dates for shipment and delivery. The shipment date should reflect the purchasing lead time for a special order item, such as calculating a shipment date based on capable-to-promise logic using the item's lead time. A bin location representing a "special order receipt" may also be specified on the sales line, which provides one method for communicating cross-dock receipt for the special PO.[12]

[12]When using a bin location for communicating a cross dock receipt, you must define some additional information about the bin location and its use as the item's default picking location, as described in Chapter 16.

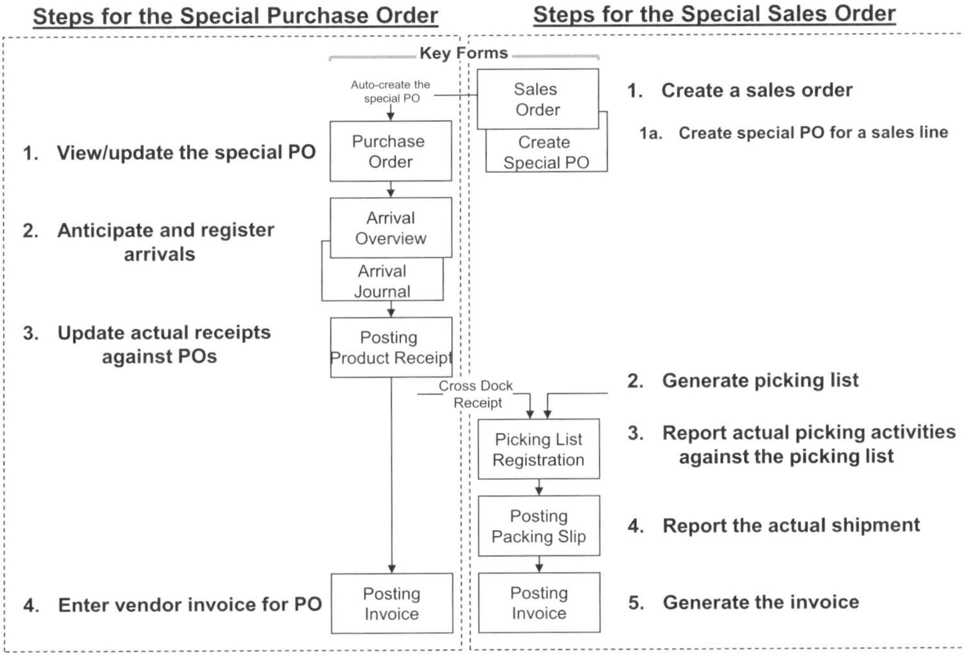

Figure 12.6 Basic Model of Special Order Processing

- *SO Step 1a: Create the special PO for a sales line.* After completing the sales order information, you access a separate form (termed Create Purchase Order) to indicate which sales lines should create a corresponding special PO. The selected lines inherit the item's preferred vendor and purchase price, and the sales order quantity, and these values can be overridden prior to indicating completion. Using a checkbox, you can optionally indicate that the quantity on the automatically created PO should reflect the item's order quantity modifiers (for a minimum, multiple and maximum related to purchases). Indicating completion will automatically create the corresponding special PO, and the PO number will be identified as reference information for the sales line. A special PO may contain multiple line items sourced from the same vendor.

  As an alternative approach, you can start from a purchase order and then select the applicable sales order for creating a special order.
- *PO Step 1: View/update the special PO.* The Purchase Order form displays a newly created special PO. You can optionally update informa-

tion, and then confirm the PO. Each line item indicates the linkage to the originating sales order.

- *PO Step 2: Anticipate and register arrivals.* The Arrival Overview form displays anticipated arrivals, and you can designate the purchase orders (or lines) that have arrived in order to create an Arrival Journal. By accessing the Arrival Journal form, you can report the actual quantity received, putaway location and batch numbers (if applicable) for each PO line item, and then post the journal. The putaway location typically reflects a bin location for cross-dock receipt of a special order.
- *PO Step 3: Update actual receipts against the POs.* Actual receipts and the vendor's packing slip number can be reported on the Posting Product Receipt form, typically by using the results of a completed Arrival Journal (termed a product receipt ready journal).
- *SO Steps 2 and 3: Generate the picking list and report actual picking activities against the picking list.* These represent optional steps, because you can directly report the actual shipment for the special sales order.
- *SO Steps 4 and 5: Report the actual shipment and generate the invoice.*
- *PO Step 4: Post the vendor's invoice for the PO.*

Direct Orders One or more lines on a sales order can be designated as a direct order, which results in a corresponding direct purchase order (aka direct PO for short). A basic model for direct order processing contains several steps for the sales order and the corresponding purchase order, as illustrated by the numbered steps in Figure 12.7 and described below.

- *SO Step 1: Create the sales order.* You create the sales order for a customer using the Sales Order form, as described above for a special order.
- *SO Step 1a: Create the direct PO for a sales line.* After completing the sales order information, you access a separate form (termed Create Direct Delivery) to indicate which sales lines should create a corresponding direct PO. The selected lines inherit the item's preferred vendor and purchase price, and the sales order quantity, and these values can be overridden. You can optionally indicate that the quantity on the automatically created PO should reflect the item's order quantity modifiers. Indicating completion will automatically create the corresponding direct PO, and the PO number will be identified as reference information for the sales line. A direct PO may contain multiple line items sourced from the same vendor.

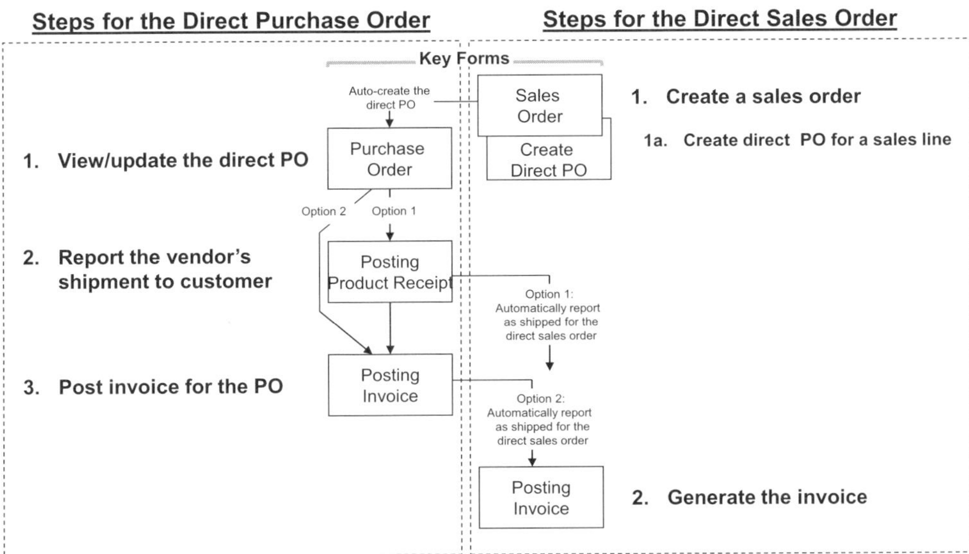

Figure 12.7 Basic Model of Direct Order Processing

With a direct PO, the delivery address on the sales order (including addresses by line item) will be automatically transferred to the purchase order. In addition, changes to the sales order line can update the direct PO (such as a change in quantity) prior to any receipt transactions.

- *PO Step 1: View/update the direct PO.* The Purchase Order form displays a newly created direct PO. You can optionally update information, and then confirm the PO. Each line item indicates the linkage to the originating sales order.
- *PO Step 2: Report the vendor's shipment to the customer.* You report the vendor's shipment and packing slip number on the Posting Product Receipt form. This also updates the shipment for the direct sales order, as shown by Option 1 in the figure. Alternatively, you can skip this step and just post the vendor's invoice, which also updates the shipment for the sales order, as shown by Option 2 in the figure.
- *PO Step 3: Post invoice for the PO.* As noted above, the posted invoice can also represent the vendor shipment to the customer.
- *SO Step 2: Generate the invoice.* The invoice reflects the vendor's shipment to the customer, whether the shipment was indicated by Option 1 or Option 2.

The concept of a direct PO also applies to a manually created PO, where there is no corresponding sales order. A typical example would be a purchased item that the vendor directly ships to a designated person or company.

12.8 Customer Returns and RMAs

Customer returns generally require an authorization, termed a returned material authorization (RMA) number. In a simple situation, for example, the customer wants to return a defective product and obtain a credit. The company creates an RMA and provides the RMA number to the customer, who returns the item. The company subsequently records receipt of the returned item and creates a credit note for the customer. RMA situations can become more complex with variations in handling a returned item, its replacement, and the related financial transactions. Each variation involves different steps and considerations.

RMA processing builds on sales order functionality. Each RMA has an associated sales order (termed the *return order*) for handling returns, and an optional second sales order (termed the *replacement order*) for handling replacements. Both sales orders have the same order number (but a different order type) with linkage to the originating RMA number.

- *Return Order.* Every RMA has an associated sales order (with a sales order type of return order) to only handle the arrival, receipt and credit note for the returned item. Creation of an RMA automatically creates the associated return order, which represents a mirror image of the RMA. Changes to the RMA information automatically change information on the return order; you cannot directly maintain data on the returned order.
- *Replacement Order.* An RMA can have a second associated sales order when a replacement must be shipped to the customer. This replacement order can be created from the RMA to support immediate shipment, or created after an RMA line item (with a disposition indicating replacement) has gone through arrival. This replacement order has all the functionality previously described for sales orders.

A typical business process will be used to explain customer returns and RMAs, as summarized in Figure 12.8 and described below.

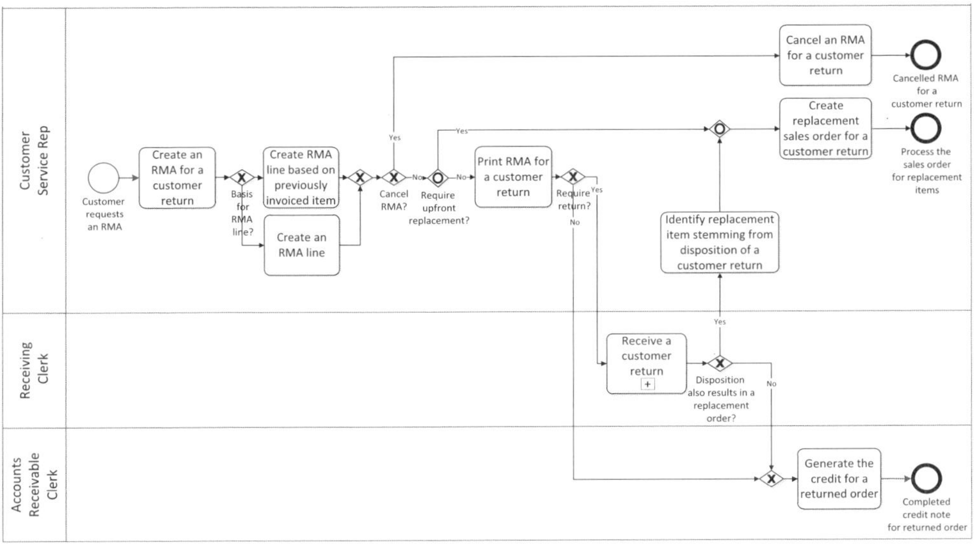

Figure 12.8 Typical Business Process for a Customer Return (RMA)

Create an RMA for a Customer Return The customer service rep initially creates a return order for a specified customer, which results in a return order header identified by a sales order number and a system-assigned RMA number. The return order provides the means to handle actual customer returns and credit notes. As part of the dialogue for creating the return order, the customer service rep can specify the return reason code, the return deadline, and the return-to location. The header information can also be maintained after initial creation.

Create an RMA Line Based on Previously Invoiced Item The customer service rep creates an RMA line by finding a previously invoiced sales order for the bill-to customer, and selecting the line item(s) and quantity being returned. The search can be based on the item number or sales order number. Each selected line item creates a line item on the return order, along with the original cost and the sales price (which acts as the credit amount). For each RMA line, the customer service rep can optionally specify a return reason code and unlimited text, such as a description of damaged goods. The customer service rep can also assign a disposition code indicating that the material does not require actual return.

Create an RMA Line for a Customer Return The customer service rep creates an RMA line item by specifying the item number, quantity, cost and credit amount. The cost defaults to the item's inventory cost, and the credit amount defaults to the item's current sales price. The credit amount may be adjusted to reflect partial credit.

Print RMA for a Customer Return After completing the RMA information, the customer service rep can optionally print a return order and send it to the customer.

Create Replacement Sales Order for a Customer Return (RMA) When the customer requires upfront replacement, the customer service rep creates a separate replacement order identified by a sales order number (with a reference to the RMA number). Only one replacement order is created for a return order. The line items on the replacement order initially reflect the RMA information, and further processing of the replacement order is just like a sales order. For example, the customer service rep can maintain information or add lines to the replacement order. The replacement order can also be created (or added to) after reporting the disposition of a returned item, and identifying the desired replacement item(s).

Identify Replacement Item Stemming from Disposition of a Customer Return After reporting the disposition of a returned item that involves "replace," the customer service rep can identify the desired replacement item in order to create (or add to) the replacement order.

Cancel an RMA for a Customer Return The customer service rep can cancel a return order at any time prior to receipt of returned items or invoicing. A cancelled returned order does not affect the related replacement order (if applicable), so that the replacement order may require deletion.

Receive a Returned Order for a Stocked Item The receiving clerk anticipates the arrival of returned orders based on selection criteria, such as the expected return location, arrival date and delivery mode. The anticipated arrivals provide the basis for estimating the handling time and the total weight/volume/pieces. The receiving clerk generates a list of the anticipated arrivals (with a system-assigned identifier), and then registers actual arrivals of the returned orders against the list, including the lot number of lot-controlled items. The receiving clerk also reports the disposition code assigned to the returned material. The disposition code determines whether the receiving clerk places the material in inventory or disposes it. It can also determine whether a replacement should be sent, so that the customer service rep can identify the desired replacement item in order to create (or add to) the related replacement order.

Generate the Credit for a Returned Order The accounts receivable clerk generates a credit note for the customer return, where the RMA may not require actual return of the material. The credit note reflects the credit amount specified on the return order.

12.9 Sales Order for a Configurable Item

A configurable item provides the starting point for configuring a custom product, typically in the context of a line item on a sales order or sales quotation. Dynamics AX provides three different configuration technologies to support configurable items, as previously described (Section 7.1). With each approach, the configuration process results in a configuration ID, and the combination of item number and configuration ID provides a unique identifier.

The configuration process varies based on the configuration technology. With the constraint-based configuration technology, for example, the process reflects a product configuration model assigned to the configurable item. The item may have multiple models reflecting different versions with different validity dates, so that the order date determines the relevant version. The configuration process results in creation of a configuration ID and its associated BOM and route versions. The configuration process can also calculate a sales price and delivery date, which can automatically populate the information on the sales line.

12.10 Sales Quotations

A sales quotation represents a key step in the life cycle of many customer relationships. A sales quotation can be converted into a sales order, or identified as lost or cancelled. The structure and life cycle of a sales quotation provide a foundation for explaining variations. The variations include the use of price simulations, the relationship between multiple quotations, and versions of a sales quotation.

Structure and Life Cycle of a Sales Quotation The basic structure consists of a header and line item information. The header identifies the sold-to business account contact and related customer (if applicable). Several aspects of the header information act as defaults for the line items, such as the requested ship date. Each line item minimally specifies an item, quantity, ship date, price, and ship-from site/warehouse.

The life cycle of a sales quotation consists of three basic steps (create, send, and disposition), with three possible dispositions (confirmed, lost or cancelled), that are represented by five statuses.

- *Created.* The quotation has been created. It can be sent to or confirmed with the business relation contact.
- *Sent.* The quotation has been sent to the business account (via the *Send Quotation* update). The specified business relation cannot be changed. The quotation can be updated to a disposition of confirmed, lost or cancelled.
- *Confirmed.* The quotation has been converted into a sales order (via the *Confirmation* update), and all quote line items are converted into line items on the new sales order. The system identifies the link between the quotation and sales order.
- *Lost.* The quotation has been identified as lost (via the *Quotation Lost* update).
- *Cancelled.* The quotation has been identified as cancelled (via the *Quotation Cancelled* update).

The system allows changes to created or sent quotations, and creation of a customer from the specified business relation (via the *Convert to Customer* function). When updating the disposition of a quotation, you can optionally record a win/loss reason code. Changes cannot be made to a quotation after it has been updated with a disposition.

Similarities and Differences with a Sales Order A sales quotation shares many similarities to a sales order, but there are also several differences, as described below.

- *Similarities.* The sales trade agreement information applies to quotations, and you can also calculate discounts and supplementary items. You can define a custom product configuration, perform an order-specific calculation for a suggested sales price, and transfer the suggested sales price to the quotation. You can optionally employ delivery date control capabilities for the requested ship and delivery dates.

- *Differences*. A sales quotation can be defined for a business relation that does not have to be a customer. A promised delivery date cannot be calculated via a net change explosion. Previous quotes can be copied into a sales quotation, but previous sales orders cannot be copied into a quotation. The price simulation capabilities only apply to quotations.

Converting a Business Relation into a Customer A customer can be created from the business relation specified on a quotation (via the *Convert to Customer* function). After creating the customer, the system displays the customer master form so that additional information can be entered.

Converting a Sales Quotation into a Sales Order A sales quotation can be converted into a sales order (via the *Confirmation* update), and all quote line items are converted into line items on the new sales order. The system prevents conversion unless the business relation reflects a customer. The system identifies the link between the quotation and sales order.

Planning Calculations and the Sales Quotation Win Probability A win probability can be assigned to a sales quotation and its line items.[13] Planning calculations can optionally include demands stemming from sales quotation line items with a win probability greater than a specified percentage. Treating these as demand makes sense in situations where the pipeline of quotations comprises 100% of the projected demand. Quotations do not consume a demand forecast. In situations where quotations and demand forecast are both considered as demand, the forecast may require manual adjustment to reflect the incremental demand not already in the pipeline of quotations and sales orders.

Price Simulations in Support of Price Negotiation Efforts Price simulations can be used to support the salesperson's efforts to negotiate prices with the customer while still retaining visibility of the desired margins and contribution ratio. For example, the impact of a discount percentage, a

[13] The win probability for a sales quotation is actually assigned to the related opportunity. An opportunity will be automatically created for a sale quotation based on a company-wide policy (on the Sales and Marketing Parameters form).

discount amount, or a specified price can be evaluated. A price simulation can be performed for individual line items or for the entire quotation, and then saved as a scenario with a user-defined description. Multiple scenarios can be saved. You can optionally apply a saved scenario to the quotation.

- *Price Simulation for a Line Item.* You can enter a discount percent, a discount amount, and/or a specified price, and the price simulation displays the impact on margin and contribution ratio. Alternatively, you can enter a specified margin (or contribution ratio) and the price simulation displays the impact on price. Applying a saved scenario updates the price, discount percent and amount on the quotation line item.
- *Price Simulations for an Entire Quotation.* You can enter a discount percent, and the price simulation displays the impact on margin and contribution ratio. Alternatively, you can enter a margin (or contribution ratio) to view the impact on discount percentage. Applying a saved scenario updates the discount percent in the quotation header.

Relationship between Multiple Sales Quotations Multiple sales quotations may be required in certain situations, such as quotes for different quantity breakpoints. Other examples would be quotes for multiple phases or for different groups of items such as basic versus optional. You establish the relationship by starting with a parent quotation, and then assigning the child quotation(s) using the *Alternative Quotations* function. The same function displays alternative quotations that have already been defined.

Versions of a Sales Quotation A sales quotation may be changed and then resent to the business relation in order to communicate the changes. The system automatically tracks each time a quotation is sent, and assigns a numeric suffix to the quotation identifier (such as -1 and -2) for each version. These historical versions can be viewed on the quotation inquiry and the Quotation Journal Inquiry. The system uses the latest version as the basis for confirming a quotation to create a sales order.

Sales Quotation Follow-Up Date and Expiration Date Each sales quotation has a follow-up date and an expiration date. The dates provide reference information and the basis for selectively viewing sales quotations.

Mass Creation of Sales Quotations Using a Template Certain situations may require the mass creation of sales quotations, such as providing the same quote to several different contacts or customers. An initial quote must be created and then designated as an active template (with a user-defined template name). The periodic task for *Mass Create Quotations* can then be used with the specified template and a user-defined selection of business relations. The system creates a sales quotation for each business relation.

Deleting Sales Quotations Quotations are not automatically deleted by the system since win/loss analysis requires historical data. Periodic deletion of quotations should reflect the desired data retention policies. Use the Delete Quotations task to select quotations to be deleted based on criteria such as the status, creation date, and/or expiration date.

12.11 Major Variations in Sales Order Processing

Sales order processing in manufacturing and distribution environments often involves variations to the basic model. Some of these variations are described below.

Generating a Production Order from a Sales Order You can immediately generate a production order when the line item represents a make-to-order manufactured product requiring a link to order. As part of the dialogue for creating the production order, you can view the item's BOM and routing information, and override suggested values. After creating the production order, you can view and maintain information on the Production Order, such as immediately scheduling the order. The sales order line item is linked to the associated production order (and vice versa), as indicated by the reference fields on each order.

Performing Tests (via Quality Orders) during Picking/Shipping of a Sales Order Quality guidelines can be established for automatically creating a quality order as part of the picking or shipping steps for a sales order. A quality order communicates the need to perform tests, and provides a mechanism for reporting results against the tests. The automatic creation of a quality order can reflect a particular site, item, or customer, or a combination of these conditions. You can also create a quality order manually. The test results can then be reported against the quality order, and validation of the test results determine a pass or fail status of the quality order. The actual test results provide the basis for printing a certificate of analysis. A subsequent chapter (Section 17.4) provides further explanation of quality orders.

Printing Test Results as a Certificate of Analysis to Accompany a Sales Order Shipment A printed certificate of analysis may be needed to accompany the material being shipped to a customer. As noted in the previous point, the actual test results for a quality order provide the basis for printing a certificate of analysis.

Printing a MSDS Document to Accompany a Sales Order Shipment for Hazardous Material When entering a sales order line for an item designated as hazardous material, an infolog warning will be displayed about sending the latest active MSDS document to the customer. This infolog warning occurs when the customer has not yet received the item's MSDS document, or when a newer version (defined by the document's effective date) needs to be sent. You can optionally print the relevant MSDS documents when posting the packing list or invoice for the sales order, and even prevent posting when a document's expiry date has been exceeded. A subsequent chapter (Section 17.8) provides further explanation of MSDS documents.

Restricted Sales Order Transactions Based on Item Policies The sales order transactions for an item can be stopped, either as a company-wide or site-specific policy (specified on the Default Order Settings or Site Specific Order Settings form). The stopped flag means that transactions cannot be entered for an item's existing sales orders, and that new sales orders cannot be created for the item. An additional policy can mandate that sales order transactions be limited to a single site (and warehouse) that actually sells the item. The mandatory site (and warehouse) acts as a default value when manually creating a sales order line item for the item.

Restricted Sales Order Transactions Based on the Batch Disposition Code The disposition code assigned to a batch can restrict its usage in sales order processing. That is, the policies associated with the disposition code can prevent reservations, picking, or shipment of the inventory. Changing the assigned disposition code to "available" means that the sales order restrictions no longer apply.

Selling a Kit of Material Items The BOM version for a manufactured item can represent a kit of components, and the kit can be sold as individual components. During sales order entry, you can view and select the components for a specified line item (using the function *Explode BOM*). The system automatically adds a line item for each selected component, with pricing based on the component item and quantity. The original line item is displayed on the form but not on printed documents.

Customer Self-Service and the Enterprise Portal One aspect of the Enterprise Portal involves the customer role, which is referred to as customer self-service. This customer role enables a customer to browse the product catalog, add items to a shopping basket, and create sales orders. The customer can add items to a shopping basket without ordering them, and then return at a later time to finish the order. Other features of the shopping basket can be defined as policies, such as enforcement of the sales order minimum, multiple and maximum quantities, and displaying the customer's balance.

12.12 Sales Analysis

Requirements for sales analysis information vary significantly between firms and decision makers within a firm. Dynamics AX includes a number of standard sales analysis inquiries and reports, as illustrated below. Each company tends to develop customized reports to meet their unique requirements.

Sales Analysis for Individual Sales Quotations and Orders The summarized data for a sales order or quote include calculated totals for revenue, cost, margin and contribution ratio.

Sales Analysis for Individual Customers The statistics window for a customer displays period totals for invoices and payments, including the number and value. It also displays information about the last invoice and payment. The Customer Turnover report displays the total value of sales orders or invoices by customer. The Top Customers report displays total revenue, margin and quantity for each customer, with optional sequencing based on any of the three totals. A pivot table inquiry provides multidimensional sales analysis, such as sales by item group and customer group.

Sales Analysis for Individual Items The statistics window for an item displays period totals for purchases and sales, including the number of orders, quantity and value. It also displays information about the last purchase order and sales order.

Sales Analysis by Customer and Item The Customer/Item Statistics report summarizes the items sold to each customer (in terms of quantity, revenue and margin) over a specified date range, and optionally provides a comparison with another date range. The Item/Customer Statistics report displays the same information for customer sales grouped by item. The Business Statistics inquiry summarizes the sales units and revenue by type of item and customer, in tabular and graphic format.

Data Warehouse and Sales Analysis Sales analysis often requires summarized data for large volumes of detailed transaction data. This data summarization requires periodic data extractions into a data warehouse. Dynamics AX includes an installation wizard and population tools to support out-of-the-box data warehouse functionality with minimal technical expertise and implementation effort. The cubes within the data warehouse reflect several business areas, including customers, sales, inventory, vendors, purchasing and general ledger information. They also reflect the financial dimensions employed within Dynamics AX. A number of predefined reports are based on an analysis of best practices, and end-users can easily develop ad hoc customized reports—presented as graphs, maps, charts and objects.

12.13 Commissions for Sales Orders

Sales commissions often involve a complex business process in many companies. The many variations in sales rep assignments and commission plans contribute to this complexity. This section provides an overview of the sales commission capabilities within AX.

A commission sales group (or sales group for short) identifies one or more sales reps. The sales group assigned to a customer acts as a default for a sales order, which then acts as a default for line items. The sales group represents a primary factor in calculating commission amounts for the sales order, along with the customer and products being sold. The calculated commission amount reflects a specified commission percentage times the sales order value (such as the gross revenue or net margin). Figure 12.9 illustrates

			Scenario #1	Scenario #2
			Single rep obtains 10% commission for all sales to customer	Split commission of 10% based on type of product and customer
Factor	Item	Item		
		Group of Items (Commission Item Group)		X
		All Items	X	
	Sold-To Customer	Customer	X	
		Group of Customers (Commission Customer Group)		X
		All Customers		
	Sales Group*	Sales Group With One Rep	100% for Rep #1	
		Sales Group With Multiple Reps		60% for Rep #1 40% for Rep #2
Commission Percentage			10%	10%
Commission Rules		Value basis: Revenue vs Margin	Revenue	Revenue
		Value basis: Net vs Gross	Gross	Gross
		Date Effectivity	Current year's Commission plan	Current year's Commission plan
		Applicability Search	One Entry	Multiple Entries

* = The sales group indicates the applicable sales reps and split commission information.

Figure 12.9 Examples of Sales Commission Calculations

these factors affecting commission calculations along with two scenarios. The first scenario can be defined by a single entry in the commission setup. It represents a single rep obtaining a 10% commission on all product sales to a given customer based on gross revenue value and this year's commission plan. An additional entry could define next year's commission plan. The second scenario represents a 10% commission split between two sales reps based on the type of product and customer. Multiple entries in the commission setup would be needed to define the various combinations of item groups and customer groups.

Commission calculations are normally based on the most specific entry related to a commission percentage, such as an entry for a specific item and customer rather than groups. With searching enabled, the system uses all of the applicable entries (when multiple entries exist) for calculating commissions. Commissions are calculated (with associated G/L entries) after posting a sales order invoice.

Additional Case Studies

Case 66: Commission Calculations A manufacturing company defined the commission plans (termed a commission sales group) for each sales rep, and tracked commissions based on sales order invoices. The commission plan identified the sales rep, the applicable items and customers, the effectivity dates, and the basis for commission calculations such as net versus gross and revenue versus margin. The commission plan could also define split commissions when there are multiple sales reps, brokers or managers involved in the sale. Commissions were calculated (with associated G/L entries) after posting a sales order invoice.[14]

Case 67: Sales Quotations A manufacturing company typically created and sent a sales quotation to customers and prospects (aka business relations) when initially conducting business with them. Each line item minimally specified an item, quantity, ship date, price, ship-from site/warehouse, and a win probability. The pipeline of sales quotations with a high win probability (above 90%) was used by planning calculations to drive supply chain activities. When the quote was accepted by the customer, it was converted to a sales order, which sometimes required prior conversion of the prospect information to a customer master record. When not accepted, the sales quotation was identified as lost or cancelled along with a reason code. Each sales quotation had a follow-up date and an expiration date to support these follow-up activities.

Sales quotations often involved negotiated prices. In these situations, the sales person employed price simulations (for individual lines or all lines) to evaluate the impact of a specified price, a discount percentage or a discount amount on the desired margins and contribution ratio. A price simulation could be saved with a user-defined description, and multiple scenarios could be saved, so that the sales person could optionally apply a saved scenario to the quotation.

[14]The variations in commission calculations often require customizations or an add-on module, such as the add-on functionality from **www.RedMaple.com**.

Case 68: EDI for Sales Order Processing A supplier to retail chains needed to communicate details of their product lines, and process the subsequent sales orders for fulfillment from various locations around the world. The price/sales catalogs were produced as EDI 832 documents and used to update a customer-accessible global product catalog. Customers could place sales orders for delivery to a single store, multiple stores, or a regional distribution center, and the product could be marked with the customer's retail information including pricing. The fulfillment locations were based on the ship-to locations and product availability. An add-on module provided integration and crucial business process mapping for each type of business transaction, and easily supported additional trading partners while leveraging the value of standardized procedures and systems.[15]

Case 69: Automotive Tire Outlets A firm specializing in automotive tires required customized sales order processing to match the business processes at their outlets. The typical customer contact starts with a telephone inquiry about the options, pricing and availability about a given tire type, and proceeds through several steps including a quotation, sales order, work order and invoice. As part of the customizations for the quotation process, the system displayed alternative items with availability, pricing, and profitability along with highlighting to steer the customer's decision toward corporate promotions and higher margins. The system also suggested additional sales order line items about related services (such as tire installation and balancing) and indicated prior business with the customer. The quotation could be converted to a sales order and a work order with scheduling based on tire availability. When inventory was unavailable at the local outlet, the system checked availability across all outlets and recommended an inventory transfer, or generated a purchase order to the tire manufacturer. Many of the customizations represented work simplification and advanced decision support, with extensive prototyping to ensure ease-of-use, user acceptance and security considerations.

Case 70: Mobile Order Entry via Hand-Held Devices A manufacturing company had field sales representatives that wrote orders on paper forms that were faxed to the home office for manual re-keying. This manual system was replaced with hand-held devices (with a built-in bar-code

[15]See **www.ColumbusGlobal.com** for further information about their Trading Post Central (TPC) add-on module for AX, and **www.GraceBlood.com** for their integrated approach for implementing EDI.

scanner) that allowed sales reps to enter quotes, orders and invoices, and print them via a portable printer. At headquarters, the sales documents were seamlessly and automatically posted into Dynamics AX during each user's synchronization. The solution increased order efficiency and reduced errors, and allowed the average order size to grow significantly.

Case 71: Rules-Based Pricing A distribution company employed several types of rules-based pricing when selling their products to retailers. The approaches included a surcharge for a small order and discounts for a large order (based on total order value), as well as discount percentages and supplementary items based on total quantity ordered for different items within a product line. A miscellaneous charge was added to items requiring faster-than-normal delivery lead time.

Case 72: Tiered Sales Prices Based on YTD Sales A manufacturing company required tiered sales pricing based on year-to-date quantities specified in a contract. For example, the contract price was $10 for a YTD quantity up to 999, $9.50 for 1000-1999, and $9.00 for a YTD quantity of 2000 or greater. A contract consisted of multiple line items, specifying the item, the contract period (expressed as from- and to-validity dates), and the price for each quantity breakpoint. The cumulative sales were tracked for sales orders linked to the contract, with a complete transaction history for each sales order line.

Executive Summary

Sales orders capture demands for the firm's products and service, and comprise a key element in the larger contexts of customer relationship management and the S&OP process. This chapter described a basic model of sales order processing and a typical business process. The basic model provided the foundation for explaining major variations in manufacturing scenarios. The chapter covered sales pricing approaches and additional considerations such as order-related text and making delivery promises. The case studies highlighted several aspects of sales order processing, such as quotations, commission calculations and EDI.

Chapter 13

Purchase Order Processing

A primary responsibility of procurement is to coordinate and execute the supply chain activities driven by the firm's S&OP (sales and operations planning) game plans. Purchased material represents the dominant concern in distribution environments and in many manufacturing environments. Procurement activities can significantly impact the firm's bottom-line performance in terms of reduced material costs and inventories, improved quality and lead time agility, and fewer disruptions stemming from stock-outs or delivery problems. In addition, purchases of indirect material often constitute a large proportion of procurement activities.

Purchase order processing represents a key business process within procurement, and involves a wide spectrum of considerations and variations. This chapter primarily focuses on purchase orders for replenishing stocked items, with requirements driven by the S&OP game plans. This focus excludes several other topics that generally do not apply to trade goods such as purchase requisitions and workflow approval processes. The chapter briefly covers these other topics.

As an explanatory approach, it is easiest to start with a typical business process for purchase order processing which includes quality control activities for testing received material. Using the steps within this typical business process, we will review the basic model of purchase order processing embedded within AX. The basic model provides a foundation for explaining key considerations and major variations for purchase order processing, the definition of vendor information, and the coordination of procurement activities. This explanatory approach is reflected in the following sections within the chapter:

1. Typical Business Process for Purchase Orders
2. Basic Model for Purchase Order Processing
3. Approved Vendors for a Purchased Item
4. Key Considerations for Purchase Order Processing
5. Purchase Trade Agreements
6. Purchase Agreements
7. Vendor Information
8. Major Variations in Purchase Order Processing
9. Workflows and Purchase Order Approval
10. Purchase Order Returns
11. Coordinate Procurement Activities

13.1 Typical Business Process for Purchase Orders

A typical business process for purchasing stocked items consists of multiple steps performed by different roles, and provides the context for further explanation. As shown in Figure 13.1, the business process starts with a purchase requirement and the purchasing agent role.

The purchasing agent analyzes and firms the planned purchase orders that reflect requirements stemming from the S&OP game plans and the item's planning data. Alternatively, the purchasing agent manually creates a purchase order and its line items. The purchasing agent confirms a purchase order when information has been completely entered.

The receiving clerk typically anticipates arrivals by viewing a subset of open purchase order line items reflecting user-specified filters, such as filtering for a ship-to location, delivery date and delivery mode. The receiving clerk analyzes the estimating handling time and total weight/volume/pieces by selecting purchase orders within this subset, and then generates a list of the anticipated arrivals from the selected orders. Alternatively, the receiving clerk manually creates an arrival list for an unplanned arrival. Using the arrival list, the receiving clerk typically confirms each item's quantity and the suggested put-away location, and reports exceptions such as overriding a quantity or suggested location, or removing line items not actually received. In addition, batch-controlled material require assignment of an internal batch number, as well as details about the vendor's batch number. The receiving clerk posts the updated arrival list after completing the information (which

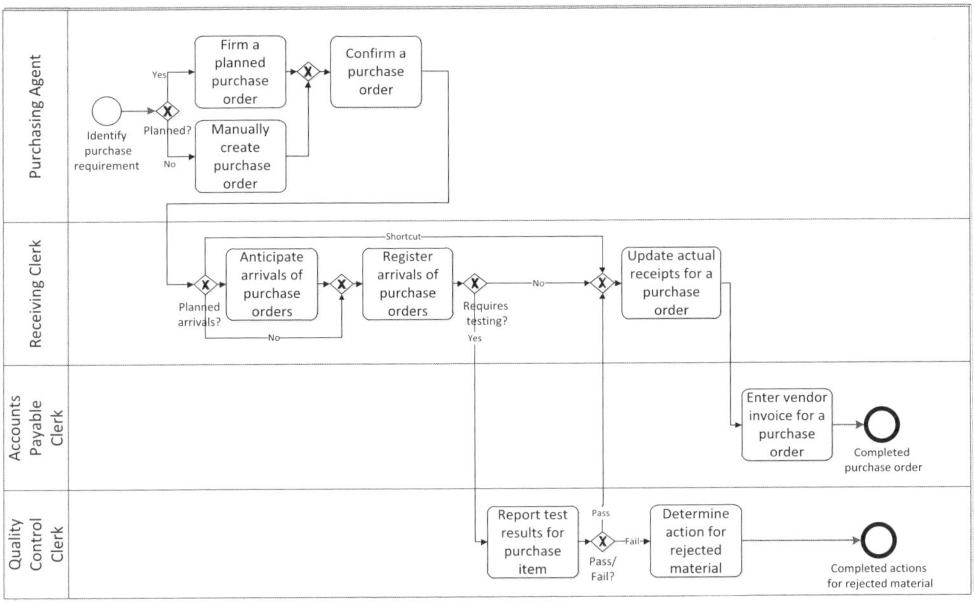

Figure 13.1 Typical Business Process for a Purchase Order

places the items into on-hand inventory), and uses the same information to update actual receipts against purchase orders. When applicable, the receiving clerk reports a separate put-away transaction for arrivals placed in a bin location representing a receiving or inspection area.

The quality control clerk reviews an automatically generated quality order (triggered by the arrival) to identify an item's testing requirements and the sample quantity. As part of the testing requirement, the system can optionally block further transactions for the material until actual test results have been reported and validated. The quality control clerk reports the actual test results against the quality order, and then validates the test results to determine pass/fail status. With a failed status, the quality control clerk determines the action for rejected material, such as a scrap transaction or a return to vendor.

The accounts payable clerk records the vendor's invoice against a purchase order, and typically populates the invoice lines based on the reported receipt quantities.

13.2 Basic Model for Purchase Order Processing

The structure of a purchase order consists of header and line item information, and each line can optionally specify a delivery schedule of quantities and dates. The header identifies the buy-from vendor, and optionally identifies a different vendor for pay-to (invoice) purposes. The buy-from vendor information provides default values for the purchase order header, and header information provides several default values when adding line items. Changes to header information can optionally update the line item information, with a prompt to confirm the mass update.

This section describes a basic model for purchase order processing using AX forms and functionality, where the basic model reflects the typical business process (described above) and the embedded conceptual models within AX. The basic model provides a foundation for explaining key considerations and major variations in purchase order processing. The basic model consists of the seven steps summarized in Figure 13.2. It focuses on purchase orders created by manual entry, or by firming up planned purchase orders, as shown by the large arrows in the figure. The figure also indicates (via a dashed line) the short-cut approaches allowing you to by-pass steps, such as reporting actual receipt (without reporting arrival) or posting the vendor invoice (without reporting actual receipt beforehand).[1]

The short-cut approach for reporting actual receipt, for example, typically involves printing a list of expected receipts for a purchase order (aka Posting the Receipts List) as a turnaround document, and then entering the information about material actually received (aka Posting the Product Receipt). Each receipts list is automatically assigned a unique identifier, and the resulting document (termed a receipts list journal) can be viewed and reprinted.

Step 1: Create a Purchase Order The purchasing agent uses the Purchase Order form to manually create a purchase order, or to maintain an order created by firming a planned purchase order. The process of firming a planned purchase order is explained in a subsequent section about coor-

[1]The short-cut approaches can be prevented by two item-specific policies. The first policy can mandate that item arrival must be registered before you can report actual receipt, and the second policy can mandate that the actual receipt must reported before you can post the vendor invoice. These two policies—termed the *Registration Requirements* policy and the *Receiving Requirements* policy—are embedded in the Item Model Group assigned to the item.

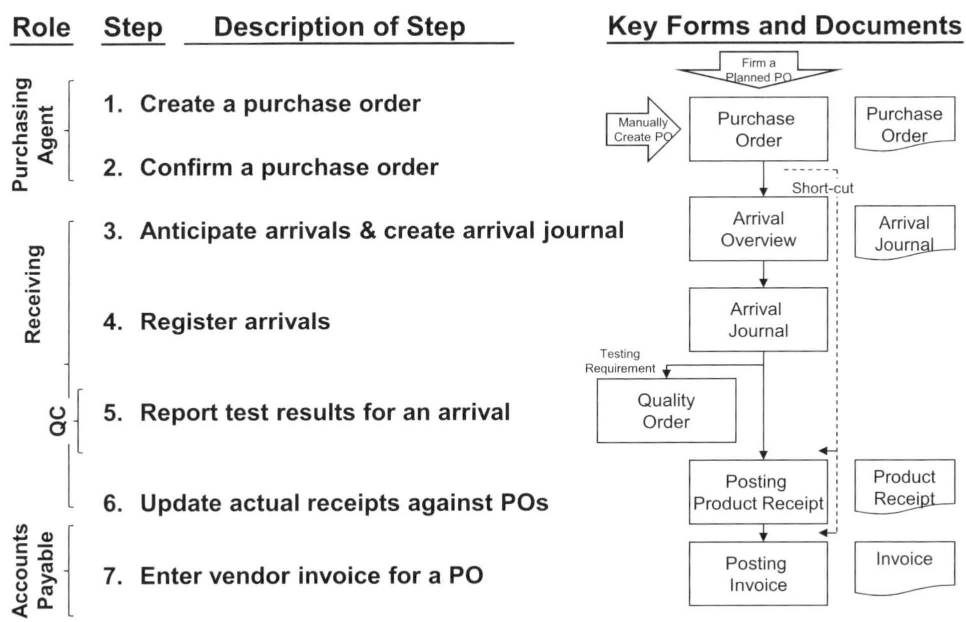

Figure 13.2 Basic Model of Purchase Order Processing

dinating procurement activities. Each line item identifies an item, quantity, purchase price, ship-to site/warehouse and a delivery date. For a given line item, you can optionally define delivery schedule lines that specify a date and quantity. The total quantity for delivery schedule lines must equal the order quantity for the line item.

Other sources of creating a purchase order include a release against a purchase agreement, a special or direct purchase order (described in the previous chapter), and an intercompany sales order. A purchase order can also be created from an approved requisition or an accepted reply to a RFQ (request for quote). In manufacturing environments, a buy-to-order component or a buy-to-order subcontracted service can have an automatically generated purchase order after you update the status of production order for its parent item. The steps within the basic model also apply to these other sources of creating a purchase order.

Step 2: Confirm a Purchase Order The purchasing agent confirms a purchase order after completing the information, using either the Purchase

Order form (for a selected order) or the Confirm Purchase Order form (for multiple orders satisfying the query criteria). The confirmed order can be sent to the vendor, and the confirmation enables subsequent processing steps such as receipts. Changes to a confirmed purchase order require an additional confirmation. Each confirmation creates a history record so that you can view historical versions of a purchase order.

Step 3: Anticipate Arrivals and Create Arrival Journal The receiving clerk uses the Arrival Overview form to view open purchase order line items that represent anticipated arrivals. You can filter the displayed information to view the desired subset, such as the time window of expected deliveries (expressed as a number of days forward and back), the vendor, the ship-to site/warehouse, and the delivery mode. After selecting relevant line items, the Arrival Overview summarizes the associated workload expressed in terms of total quantity, volume, weight, and estimated handling time.[2] The selected line items can then be used to create an arrival journal that provides a list of expected arrivals.

As noted earlier, short-cut approaches allow you to by-pass steps (such as reporting actual receipt without reporting arrival) or use an alternative approach. As one example of an alternative approach, you can generate a printed receipts list for a purchase order (which indicates the expected items and quantities) and then use it as a turnaround document for reporting actual receipts.

Step 4: Register Arrivals An Arrival Journal is typically created and populated based on selections from the Arrival Overview form, with each line item reflecting the item's expected quantity and suggested put-away location.[3] Each arrival journal has a unique identifier. The Arrival Journal and its line items can also be created manually, typically to handle unplanned arrivals. The quantity reflects the UM for the purchase line.

The receiving clerk simply confirms the information in many cases, whereas exceptions require additional entry to reflect actual arrivals, such as overriding the quantity or put-away location, or removing lines items not actually received. The internal batch numbers are automatically assigned to

---

[2]Each item's typical volume, weight, and arrival handling time (expressed in minutes or hours) can be defined on the item master.

[3] The bin location on an arrival journal line item can initially default to the item's default receipt bin location within a warehouse (as specified in the item's setup information about warehouse policies), to the warehouse's default bin location for receipts, or to the bin location specified in the header information for an arrival journal.

batch-controlled items, and details about the vendor's batch number can be reported. You can also identify the vendor's packing slip number associated with the received material.

The receiving clerk posts an arrival journal after completing the information, which changes inventory status to registered. The arrival journal is now termed *product receipt ready*, and the actual quantities and inventory placement cannot be overridden. The concept of *product receipt ready* means that the same information can now be used to update actual receipts against purchase orders.

Optional Step 5: Report Test Results for an Arrival An item's testing requirements can result in the automatic generation of a quality order, such as generation of a quality order after posting the arrival journal. The quality control clerk reviews the quality order to identify an item's testing requirements and the sample quantity. As part of the testing requirement, the system can optionally block further transactions for the material until actual test results have been reported and validated. The quality control clerk reports the actual test results against the quality order, and then validates the test results to determine pass/fail status. With a failed status, the system provides a warning on subsequent transactions such as entering the vendor's invoice. After the validation step, the quality control clerk can optionally reopen a quality order in order to revise the test results or the validation. A subsequent chapter (Section 18.4) provides further explanation of quality orders.

The quality control clerk determines the action for rejected material at the time of purchase order arrival. The decision typically occurs in the context of a failed quality order reflecting the testing results. The possible actions include scrapping the material or assigning a batch disposition code with restricted usage policies, or initiating a return to vendor to obtain a credit (which may or may not involve an actual return of material).

Step 6: Update Actual Receipts for a Purchase Order The receiving clerk uses the Posting Product Receipt form to update actual receipts for purchase orders, typically in the context of reusing information already recorded for an arrival journal. That is, you access it from the Arrival Journal form (or the Arrival Overview form) after posting an arrival journal, which is now termed *product receipt ready*. This updates the actual receipts for all related purchase orders, and represents the simplest approach. As an alternative approach, the Posting Product Receipt form can be accessed directly (and populated via query criteria) or from the Purchase Order form (thereby inheriting information from the selected purchase order). With either approach, you can optionally print product receipt information.

The vendor's packing slip number can be recorded at the time of reporting arrival or updating product receipts. The entry of a duplicate packing slip number generally indicates a mistake, such as a typographic error or duplicate entry. A company-wide policy (on the A/P Parameters form) determines whether entry of a duplicate number will be accepted or result in a warning or a rejection communicated via an infolog.

Step 7: Post the Invoice for the Purchase Order The accounts payable clerk uses the Posting Invoice form to record the vendor's invoice number and invoice information. The form can be accessed from the Purchase Order form, thereby inheriting information from the selected purchase order. It can also be accessed directly, which means that you must identify the applicable purchase order(s) for the vendor invoice(s). As part of the step, you indicate the quantity basis for initially populating the invoice information (such as the product receipt quantities) and whether to print the invoice.

Life Cycles Related to Purchase Order Processing The basic model for purchase order processing reflects the embedded conceptual models within Dynamics AX. For example, AX employs several related constructs—for a purchase order, an arrival journal, a quality order, and the inventory status of an item—to support a typical business process, and each construct has a life cycle with associated statuses. The seven steps within the basic model represent a change in status for one or more constructs, as summarized in Figure 13.3 and described below in more detail.

An order status indicates the following steps in the life cycle of a purchase order:

- *Open Order.* The status indicates the order has been created.
- *Delivered.* The status indicates all order lines have a delivered status.
- *Invoiced.* The status indicates all order lines have an invoiced status. .
- *Cancelled.* The status only applies to a returned order, where all order lines have been returned to the vendor and a credit note generated.

A line status indicates the following steps in the life cycle of a purchase order line, or a line within the delivery schedule for a purchase order line:

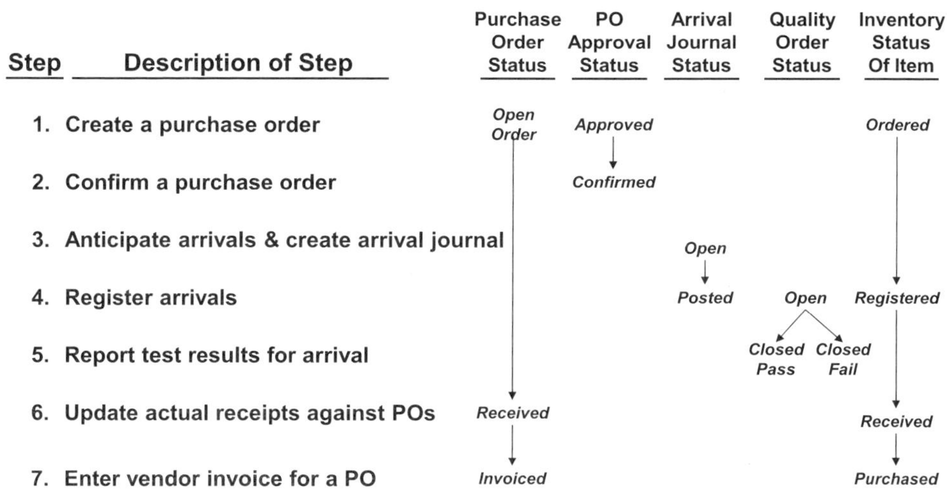

Figure 13.3 Life Cycles Related to Purchase Order Processing

- *Open Order.* The status indicates the line has been created, and partial receipts or invoices may have been entered.
- *Delivered.* The status indicates that the delivered quantity equals the order quantity. When using delivery tolerances, the delivered quantity can exceed the order quantity or the under-delivery can be flagged as closed during the posting process. Over- and under-delivery delivery tolerances are expressed as a percentage, and the values assigned to an item act as defaults for the purchase order line item.[4] However, a line item can be flagged as receive complete so that the system only allows delivery and invoice transactions that exactly match the order quantity.
- *Invoiced.* The status indicates the line item quantity has been completely invoiced, taking into account the over- or under-delivery considerations mentioned above.

A document status indicates the last document printed (aka posted) for the purchase order, as described below. The document status is not shown in the figure.

[4]Company-wide policies (embedded in the A/P parameters) determine whether over- and under-deliveries will be allowed for purchase orders.

- *None.* The status indicates that the purchase order has not been printed.
- *Purchase Order.* The status indicates a purchase order has been posted.
- *Product Receipt.* The status indicates a product receipt has been posted for all lines.
- *Invoiced.* The status indicates the vendor's invoice has been posted.

The purchase order approval status indicates whether the order has been confirmed, as described below. Other statuses (for *Draft* and *In Review*) pertain to purchase orders requiring an approval process and also to purchase requisitions. Purchase requisitions fall outside the primary focus of this chapter.

- *Approved.* The status indicates the purchase order needs to be confirmed.
- *Confirmed.* The status indicates the purchase order has been confirmed.
- *Draft.* The status indicates creation of a purchase order that must go through an approval process, where the purchase order has not yet been submitted for approval.
- *In Review.* The status indicates a purchase order going through an approval process, where the order has been submitted but not yet approved.

The arrival journal status indicates the following steps in its life cycle:

- *Open.* The status indicates that the arrival journal has been created.
- *Posted.* The status indicates the arrival journal has been posted, and information cannot be changed. A posted arrival journal is termed *product receipt ready*, so that you can easily reuse the information to update actual receipts for related purchase orders.

The quality order status indicates the following steps in its life cycle. A subsequent chapter (Section 18.4) provides further explanation of quality orders.

- *Open.* The status indicates that the quality order has been created. You can view/maintain the tests and report actual test results.
- *Closed – Pass.* The status indicates that the validation process has been performed, and the actual test results passed the required AQL (acceptable quality level).
- *Closed – Fail.* The status indicates that the validation process has been performed, and the actual test results failed the required AQL (acceptable quality level).

The inventory status for the item on a purchase line is also shown on the right side of Figure 13.3, since the steps in purchase order processing will change this status from ordered to registered, received and purchased.

13.3 Approved Vendors for a Purchased Item

A purchased item can have one or more approved vendors, as defined on the Approved Vendor List form (accessed from the item master). You also define the start and expiration dates for an item's approved vendor. You can anticipate upcoming expiration dates using the Approved Vendor List Expiration form. The expiration date indicates when a vendor is no longer approved. An item's approved vendor represents a company-wide policy.

Most companies will enforce the use of an item's approved vendor, as defined by an item-specific policy termed the *approved vendor check method*. This policy designates whether the approved vendor information will (1) be ignored, (2) prevent entry or (3) provide a warning. The policy is initially inherited from the Item Model Group assigned to the item. Enforcement of the approved vendor policy applies to several situations, as summarized in the following list. The list also identifies the relevant section number (in parentheses) within the book.

- Specify the item's preferred vendor in coverage planning data (Section 10.1)
- Manually create a purchase order line for the item (Section 13.2)
- Firm a planned purchase order for the item (Section 13.11)
- Define a purchase trade agreement for the item (Section 13.5)
- Define a purchase agreement for the vendor and item (Section 13.6)
- Create a purchase order from a sales order line for the item (Section 12.7)
- Create a purchase order from an accepted RFQ reply (Section 13.8)
- Specify the preferred vendor for a buy-to-order component in a BOM line or in an order-dependent BOM (Sections 4.4.and 4.5)
- Specify the preferred vendor for a subcontracted service in a BOM line (Sections 4.4 and 16.4)

As noted in the above list, the approved vendors for an item should include those vendors identified as the preferred source, and also those with purchase trade agreements or purchase agreements.

13.4 Key Considerations for Purchase Order Processing

The basic model of purchase order processing provides a foundation for explaining key considerations and different ways of doing business with vendors and with different internal procedures. For example, these variations may involve the use of textual explanations, delivery dates, delivery schedules, pricing, and discounts.

Order-Related Text Many situations require textual explanations or additional descriptive information about the purchase order and line items. Order-related text can be specified in several ways, such as text carried forward from the item master or document handling capabilities.

- *Carry Forward of Item Text to Line Item.* The item master allows each item to have an unlimited amount of descriptive text that automatically carries forward to the purchase order line item, where it can be optionally overridden.
- *Document Handling Capabilities.* Documents containing descriptive text (defined as a document type of note) can be defined for the purchase order header and/or each line item and flagged for internal or external purposes. The system can print the external notes on each purchase document.

  These note documents can be previously defined for the vendor and items but do not automatically carry forward to the purchase order; they must be explicitly copied and pasted to the purchase order header and lines. Other types of documents such as Word files, Excel spreadsheets, and images can also be defined.
- *Printing Descriptive Information.* The setup policies for A/P forms determine whether each printed form includes descriptive information. For example, the printed purchase order can identify the external item number and the note documents.

Purchase Order Quantity and UM The item's standard purchase order quantity and UM acts as default values when manually entering a purchase order. The system provides a soft warning if the entered quantity does not conform to the item's order quantity modifiers for a minimum, maximum and multiple. When a partial delivery is anticipated, entering a separate "receive now" quantity can simplify the posting process for deliveries.

Partial deliveries of a line item can be explicitly forbidden using the *receive complete* flag to indicate the delivery quantity must match the order quantity exactly. With purchase order delivery tolerances, the system allows the received quantity to be greater or less than the ordered quantity as long as it is with the specified tolerances. Over- and under-delivery tolerances are expressed as a percentage, and the values assigned to an item act as defaults for a purchase order line item.

Alternative Approaches to an Item's Purchase Price An item's purchase price can be defined several different ways. As summarized in Figure 13.4, the four major approaches include a purchase agreement, purchase price trade agreements, the inherited purchase price from a source document, and a company-wide standard purchase price.

Source of Purchase Price on a Purchase Order		Factors	Significance of Item's Purchase Price
Purchase Agreement	Purchase Agreement for a product quantity commitment	Committed quantity Minimum release quantity Validity period	Companywide or Site/Warehouse-specific Purchase Price
Trade Agreement	Purchase Price Trade Agreement	Vendor Unit of measure Quantity breakpoints Validity period Delivery lead-time	Companywide or Site/Warehouse-specific Purchase Price
Source Document	Purchase Requisition	N/A	Inherit Purchase Price From Source Document
	Accepted RFQ Reply		
	Copy a Purchase Order		
Standard Purchase Price	Manually Entered Standard Purchase Price	N/A	Companywide Purchase Price
	Updated by Last Purchase Invoice		

Figure 13.4 Alternative Approaches to an Item's Purchase Price

As the simplest approach, an item's standard purchase price can be defined on the item master along with its default purchase UM. It represents a company-wide purchase price that acts as the default on a purchase line when other sources of pricing information do not exist. This standard purchase price can be manually specified or automatically updated by the last purchase invoice.

As the second major approach, the purchase price can be inherited from a source document used to create the purchase order. Examples of a source document include an approved requisition, an accepted RFQ reply, and copying information into a purchase order.

The third major approach involves purchase price trade agreements, which can represent company-wide or site/warehouse-specific purchase prices for an item. They can reflect different purchase UM, validity dates, and quantity breakpoints. A subsequent section provides further explanation of purchase trade agreements.

The fourth major approach involves a purchase agreement, which specifies the item's purchase price based on a commitment quantity over a validity period. Releases against the purchase agreement create a purchase order, and the item inherits the specified price. Purchase agreements can also define a discount percent (rather than a purchase price), and a subsequent section provides further explanation.

Delivery Schedule for a Purchase Order Line A purchase order line item normally consists of a single quantity and its associated ship and delivery dates. You can optionally specify a delivery schedule for a purchase line, where each schedule line consists of a quantity and its associated dates. The total quantities within the delivery schedule lines must equal the quantity for the purchase line, or the system will automatically adjust the purchase line quantity.

Significance of a Confirmed Delivery Date Each purchase order line (and a line within a delivery schedule) has a delivery date and a confirmed delivery date. The confirmed delivery date is initially blank, and should be updated to reflect actual conditions, such as a delayed delivery communicated by the vendor. Planning calculations employ the confirmed delivery date as the basis for suggested actions, such as a projected delay in meeting a sales order shipment date.

Versions of a Purchase Order Different versions of a purchase order can identify the history of changes. The system assigns a version number each time you confirm a purchase order, where the version reflects a numeric suffix (such as -1 and -2) to the purchase order number. Hence, each confirmation provides a history of changes. The version appears on a printed purchase order confirmation, and the historical versions can be viewed and compared. The most recent version is used for planning calculations and the reporting of arrivals/receipts and vendor invoices. Two versions of a purchase order confirmation can be compared in order to identify differences.

You can revert to a previous version via a copy function (termed the *Copy from Journa*l function) on a purchase order. Select from the displayed list of versions, and specify to delete lines from the existing order, so that the existing purchase order data gets updated. After making the updates, you should reconfirm the purchase order to assign a new version number.

Creating a Purchase Order via the Copy Function A copy function (termed Copy from All) can be used to create line items from a previously entered purchase order. For example, you can select the desired purchase order and the desired line item(s) from a displayed list of all previous orders. You can also select from versions of purchase orders, or packing lists and invoices. You indicate how to handle updates, such as appending line items and recalculating prices for the new line items.

Generating a Credit Note from a Purchase Order Some situations require creation of a credit note while in the midst of purchase order entry. One approach employs a negative quantity for the purchase order line item. When posting the receipt or vendor invoice, the system will subtract the value from the invoice and record an issue rather than a receipt.

A second approach (termed the *create credit note* function) acts like the copy order function, since you must select the applicable order from the displayed list of the vendor's previously invoiced purchase orders. This requires historical information but supports access to the original information such as purchase price. Just like the copy function, the selected line item can then be added to the purchase order (with a negative quantity).

Changing the Buy-From or Pay-To Vendor on a Purchase Order Changes to the buy-from or pay-to vendor can be made prior to posting receipts, but the changes have several impacts. For example, changing the buy-from vendor may result in a new pay-to vendor. After changing the buy-from vendor, you can respond to prompts about updating information impacted by the change, such as prices and discounts that reflect purchase trade agreements with the new vendor.

Totals for a Purchase Order The system calculates several order totals, including a total amount, weight and volume. Order totals can be displayed for order quantities or received quantities. For example, the volume and weight of order quantities can be used for truckload planning purposes.

Restricted Purchase Order Transactions based on Item Policies The purchase order transactions for an item can be stopped, either as a company-wide or site-specific policy, as specified on the Default Order Settings or Site-Specific Order Settings form for the item. The stopped flag means that transactions cannot be entered for an item's existing purchase orders, and that new purchase orders cannot be created for the item. An additional policy can mandate that purchase order transactions be limited to a single site (and warehouse) that actually purchases the item. The mandatory site (and warehouse) acts as a default value when manually creating a purchase order line item for the item.

13.5 Purchase Trade Agreements

A purchase trade agreement represents predefined information for buying material from suppliers, such as published list prices, negotiated purchase prices, and/or discount schemes. There are four types of purchase trade agreements—about the purchase price, line discount, multi-line discount, and/or total discount—and further explanation focuses on the purchase price aspects. The different types can be used in combination with each other, such as defining the purchase price and a discount.

Purchase Price Trade Agreements A purchase price trade agreement indicates the purchase price for an item. The purchase price typically reflects one or more of the factors shown in Figure 13.5 and illustrated below.[5] The agreement also defines the delivery lead time and an optional charge. For example, a different purchase price or a charge could be defined for a shorter delivery lead time.

[5] A set of company-wide policies (embedded in the Activate Price/Discount form) determines whether the system recognizes these factors.

	Factor	Purchase Price	Line Discount	Multi-line Discount	Total Discount
	Site or Warehouse-Specific Information			N/A	N/A
	Companywide Information				
			Types of Discounts		
	Factor	Purchase Price	Line Discount	Multi-line Discount	Total Discount
Item	Item and UM	X	X	N/A	See policy about including item value
Item	Group of Items	N/A	X Line Discount Group	X Multi-line Discount Group	N/A
Item	All Items		X	X	
Buy-From Vendor	Vendor	X	X	X	X
Buy-From Vendor	Group of Vendors	X Price Group	X Line Discount Group	X Multi-line Discount Group	X Total Discount Group
Buy-From Vendor	All Vendors	X	X	X	X
Other Factors	Date Effectivity	X	X	X	X
Other Factors	Currency Code	X	X	X	X
Other Factors	Quantity Breakpoints	X	X	X	Order Value Breakpoint
Other Factors	Delivery Days Price Charge	X X	N/A	N/A	N/A
	Policies	Price Group Policy: Price Includes Sales Tax			Item Policy: Include item value for total discount purposes

Figure 13.5 Purchase Trade Agreement Entries

- Pricing by item and unit of measure, such as different prices per piece and per dozen.
- Pricing by currency type, such as separate pricing for foreign purchases.
- Pricing with date effectivities, for supporting annual price updates or seasonal price promotions. Price assignment reflects the order date on a purchase order.
- Pricing with quantity breakpoints.
- Pricing based on delivery days.
- Pricing that involves an additional charge, such as a charge for fast delivery or small order quantity.

Price trade agreements are expressed as one or more entries that identify the applicable factors. A simple pricing scheme that represents a single purchase price, for example, would require one entry for each item purchased from the vendor. Additional entries would be required for defining next year's price, quantity breakpoints, and variations in the items' purchase UM.

Additional entries are also required for each site and warehouse when using site- and warehouse-specific pricing. Figure 13.5 illustrates the site/warehouse factor as a third dimension, since pricing can be company-wide or site/warehouse-specific.

When manually creating a purchase order, or firming a planned purchase order, the system uses the trade agreement information to automatically assign an item's price using the lowest price of applicable trade agreement entries. The system also assigns the delivery lead time and charge associated with the price. You can view available prices during purchase order entry, such as viewing quantity breakpoints or future pricing to guide purchase decisions.

There are several considerations with respect to purchase price trade agreements:

- Trade agreements for an item's purchase price and line discounts can represent either company-wide or site/warehouse-specific information, based on an item-specific policy (embedded in the dimension group assigned to the item).
- Master scheduling logic can suggest a vendor for planned purchase orders based on lowest price or delivery lead time.[6]
- The price trade agreement information for purchased components can be used for calculating the planned cost of a manufactured item (described in Section 8.9).

An additional consideration involves the system logic when there are multiple trade agreement entries that apply to a situation. Each trade agreement entry can optionally specify whether the system should search for other applicable entries. The system normally uses the most specific entry possible, such as a vendor-specific purchase price rather than one associated with a vendor group.

Types of Purchase Discounts in Trade Agreements Purchase discounts are calculated after the line item prices have been identified on a purchase order. The discounts can be related to a single line, multiple lines, the order total value, or a combination of these approaches.

[6] A company-wide policy (embedded in the master planning parameters) determines whether planning calculations consider trade agreement information for planned purchases and whether the criterion should be lowest price or lead time.

- *Line Discount.* The line discount is expressed as a fixed amount or a percentage or both. In particular, the percentage discount can be expressed as a single value or as two values (e.g., using a 10% discount for both values results in a 19% discount), and the system applies the discount percentage after reducing the price by the fixed discount amount. Line discounts often reflect one or more of the factors shown in Figure 13.5 and illustrated below.
  - Discounts for a single item, all items, or a group of items (based on the *Line Discount Group* assigned to relevant items). For example, the groups could represent different product lines. Two different group codes (both called the *Line Discount Group*) can be predefined —one for items and one for vendors—and then assigned to relevant items and vendors.
  - Discounts based on date effectivities, quantity breakpoints, and currency code for foreign purchases.

  A simple discount scheme involving a discount percent by group of items, for example, would require one trade agreement entry for each group. Note that a line discount can be company-wide or site/warehouse-specific, as illustrated in Figure 13.5.
- *Multi-Line Discount Based on Total Quantity.* The multi-line discount reflects a discount based on the total quantity for multiple line items. It is expressed the same way as a single line discount (as a fixed amount or a percentage or both). The trade agreement entries can reflect the factors shown in Figure 13.5, such as a discount that applies to a group of items. Two different group codes (both called the *Multi-line Discount Group*) can be predefined—one for items and one for vendors—and then assigned to relevant items and vendors. You must initiate calculation of multiline discounts on a purchase order after all line items have been entered.

  The combination of a line discount and multi-line discount can be handled different ways, as defined by a company-wide policy embedded in the A/P parameters. A typical approach views the two values as additive. However, you could specify the policy as use the lowest value or highest value, use only one of the values, or treat them as multiplicative.
- *Discount (or Surcharge) Based on Total Order Value.* The total discount applies to the total order value. It is expressed the same way as a single line discount—as a fixed amount or a percentage or both. Expressing the fixed amount as a negative value represents a surcharge. The trade agreement entries can reflect the factors shown in Figure 13.5, such as a

discount with order value breakpoints. An item-related policy determines whether the system includes or excludes the item in calculating total order value for the purpose of a total discount. You must initiate calculation of the total discount on a purchase order after all line items have been entered, or the total discount can be automatically calculated (based on a company-wide policy embedded in the A/P parameters).

Maintaining and Viewing Purchase Trade Agreement Information Information about purchase trade agreements must be prepared beforehand and then used to update trade agreement information. Preparing data beforehand (using the Price/Discount Agreement Journal and its associated line items) offers several advantages in data maintenance. For example, you can create a new journal for preparing next year's purchase price trade agreements, and then initially populate the entries with information about existing purchase price agreements for selected items or vendors. The information can then be manually updated prior to posting the journal. In addition, you can perform mass changes to the entries (such as increasing the price a specified percentage or amount), or copy the entries in order to prepare price agreements for another item, vendor, validity period or currency. The concept of preparing data beforehand is employed within the request for quotes (RFQ) business process, so that a vendor reply can be used to prepare purchase trade agreement information.

Use the Purchase Price report to view purchase price trade agreement information, or a subset of information based on the report's selection criteria (such as the selected items, vendors or currency). Use the Price/Discount List report to view all types of price and discount trade agreement information, or a subset based on the report's selection criteria.

Agreements about Supplementary Items Some purchase environments involve supplementary items, such as "buy one and get an additional item free," which result in additional line items on a purchase order. Supplementary items can also represent related items that should be purchased together, thereby providing a reminder to the purchasing agent. A supplementary purchase item and quantity can be designated as mandatory or optional, and chargeable or free-of-charge. The rules may also include validity dates, a minimum order quantity and/or a one-time-only offer. The supplementary item information can be associated with a specific item or vendor, where you define a group code (termed the *Supplementary Item Group*) and assign it to relevant items and vendors.

During the process of entering purchase order line items, you initiate a calculation that displays the applicable supplementary items. The items are segmented into mandatory and optional (with user selection of the optional items), and acceptance results in additional purchase order line items.

Agreements about Charges Some purchase environments involve predefined agreements about charges, such as handling or freight charges for selected items or vendors. These charges can be embedded in the purchase price trade agreement information, or they can be specified separately as *auto charges*. These auto charges can be applied to an entire purchase order or to individual line items, and expressed as a fixed amount, an amount per piece, or a percentage of value.

- *Order-level charges*. Charges related to the entire purchase order can be defined for a single vendor, all vendors or a group of vendors (identified by the *Vendor Charges Group* assigned to relevant vendors). Examples of an order-level charge include order preparation costs for selected vendors.
- *Line item charges*. Charges related to the purchase order line item can be defined by vendor and item, such as charges for a single item, all items, or a group of items (identified by the Item Charges Group assigned to relevant purchased items). Examples of a line item charge include a setup fee for purchasing selected items from a vendor.

13.6 Purchase Agreements

Purchase agreements define a commitment to buy products from a vendor over a time period in exchange for special prices or discounts. Synonyms include a blanket purchase order.[7] The various types of a commitment include a total quantity for a specific product (with a specified purchase price and/or discount percent), or a total value for a specific product, a category of products, or all products/categories (with a specified discount percent). After defining the purchase agreement, you change its status to "effective" in order to allow usage, such as creating purchase orders linked to the purchase agreement.

[7] Previous versions of Dynamics AX provided a function termed "blanket purchase order" which did not really support commitments over a validity period.

The type of commitment is defined in the header information for a purchase agreement, which then affects the information for each line item, as summarized below.

- *Create a line item for a product quantity commitment.* You define the total commitment quantity and the purchase price and/or discount percent for a specified item. An optional minimum or maximum release quantity may also be defined.
- *Create a line item for a product value commitment.* You define the total commitment value and discount percent for a specified item. An optional minimum or maximum release amount may also be defined.
- *Create a line item for a product category value commitment.* You define the total commitment value and discount percent for a specified category of items. The concept of product categories and a category hierarchy for purchasing purposes was previously explained in Section 3.1. An optional minimum or maximum release amount may also be defined.
- *Create a line item for a value commitment.* You define the total commitment value and discount percent that will be applicable to all items or categories purchased from the vendor. An optional minimum or maximum release amount may also be defined.

As part of the header information, you indicate whether the maximum should be enforced on related purchase orders. Additional terms and conditions may also be specified—such as the payment terms and mode of delivery—which will be inherited by related purchase orders.

Several different approaches are used to link a purchase order to a purchase agreement, as summarized below. As a result of these approaches, you can view the purchase orders linked to a selected purchase agreement or generate the equivalent report.

- *Release a purchase order from a purchase agreement.* You create the purchase order by starting from a selected purchase agreement, and specify the item and quantity for a purchase order line item. The purchase order header inherits the terms and conditions from the purchase agreement, and a line item inherits the applicable purchase price or discount percent from the purchase agreement.
- *Firm planned purchase orders with grouping by purchase agreement.* You firm the planned purchase orders with grouping by purchase agreements, which results in a purchase order with multiple line items.

Regardless of the grouping preference when firming planned orders, each resulting purchase order will inherit information from the applicable purchase agreement.

- *Manually create a purchase order linked to a purchase agreement.* You specify the identifier of the applicable purchase agreement when manually creating a purchase order. The purchase order header inherits the terms and conditions from the purchase agreement, and a line item inherits the applicable purchase price or discount percent from the purchase agreement.

You can also unlink a purchase order currently linked to a purchase agreement, which means the purchase price or discount percent for the line item will no longer reflect the purchase agreement.

13.7 Vendor Information

A subset of vendor information directly relates to purchase order processing. Each vendor is defined in a vendor master file by a unique identifier. Buy-from and pay-to vendors require unique identifiers, and a buy-from vendor can optionally have one or more ship-from addresses. The following data elements have particular significance to purchase order processing.

Vendor Calendar of Work Days When purchase lead times are expressed in working days, the calculation of a purchase order start date and/or delivery date can be based on a specified calendar of the vendor's working days. The calculations use the company-wide calendar as the default when a vendor calendar is not specified.

Language for a Vendor The language assigned to each vendor determines which language version should be displayed on printed documents and other vendor interactions. For example, the assigned language determines the language version for an item description on a purchase order confirmation.

Attributes Related to G/L Account Number Assignment General ledger (G/L) account number assignments (such as trade payables and purchase price variances) are based on a combination of vendor and item characteristics. For example, the trade payables account updated by a purchase order receipt can be based on the vendor group and item group assigned to the vendor and item respectively.

Financial Dimensions for a Vendor The financial dimension(s) assigned to a vendor provide a means to analyze purchases by vendor type. They can be used in conjunction with financial dimensions assigned to other entities such as items to provide multi-dimensional purchase analyses.

One-Time Vendors and Creating Vendors during Purchase Order Entry When initially entering a purchase order, the buy-from vendor can be created on the fly by indicating a one-time vendor. You enter the vendor name and address information as part of creating the purchase order, and the system automatically creates a new vendor that is flagged as a one-time vendor. Additional information defaults from an existing vendor designated as the source of one-time vendor information. The vendor information can then be manually maintained, including the removal of the one-time vendor flag.

Vendor Hold Status A vendor hold status can prevent all transactions from being recorded, or only prevent invoices or payments from being entered for the vendor. You assign the vendor hold status by explicitly accessing the *change vendor status* function from the vendor master. Optional information about the hold status includes a hold release date and the assignment of a user-defined reason code. An additional policy only applies to a multi-company scenario (in which the same vendor has been defined in multiple AX companies within one AX instance), so that you can optionally assign the vendor's hold status to all companies.

Same Vendor Defined for Multiple Companies Some multi-company scenarios involve the same vendor serving multiple companies. In this case, you can define the vendor in one company, and then add the vendor to another company along with an applicable vendor group and vendor hold status. After accessing the database for the other company, you must define all other aspects of vendor information.

Intercompany Trading Partner Some enterprises have multiple companies defined within a single Dynamics AX instance, and trading between the companies. A sister company can act as a vendor (or customer) for intercompany trading purposes. A vendor (or customer) must be defined that represents the sister company. A subsequent chapter explains intercompany orders (Section 17.5).

Summarized Information by Vendor Summarized information about a vendor can be viewed in several ways. A vendor's statistics inquiry provides summarized data in monthly increments, such as the number and value of invoices and payments. Transaction detail can also be viewed by type of purchase document, such as outstanding purchase orders, receipts, invoices, and backorder purchase lines.

13.8 Major Variations in Purchase Order Processing

Purchase order processing in a manufacturing or distribution environment involves many of the above-mentioned considerations and a few additional ones. These additional variations include special orders, direct orders, buy-to-order components, purchases of subcontracted service, receiving inspection, returns to vendor, requests for quotes, and purchase requisitions.

Handling Special Orders A special order reflects a purchase order directly linked to a sales order, with cross-dock receipts shipped to the customer. The previous chapter (Section 12.7) described the basic model of special order processing, and the impact on purchase orders.

Handling Direct Orders A direct order (aka direct delivery order) reflects a purchase order directly linked to a sales order, with material directly shipped to the customer. The previous chapter (Section 12.7) described the basic model of direct order processing, and the impact on purchase orders.

Handling a Buy-to-Order Component When the BOM for a manufactured item contains a buy-to-order component (identified by a component type of vendor), a scheduled production order for the manufactured item automatically generates a linked purchase order for the purchased component. The purchase order is automatically created for the component's preferred vendor (if defined) or the item's preferred vendor. The reference field information identifies the linkage in each order and the system reserves the scheduled receipt for the production order. Changes to the scheduled date for the production order can automatically update the schedule date for the linked purchase order (aka the reference order).

Handling Purchases of a Subcontracted Service A subcontracted service represents one example of a buy-to-order component, as described above. Chapter 16 explains subcontracted production and the purchase of subcontracted services.

Request for Quote (RFQ) A request for quote (RFQ) provides a structured approach for soliciting and using purchase quotations. RFQs are oftentimes used as an extension of purchase requisition activities, or in the context of sourcing an item with a planned purchase order. In addition, an RFQ can be manually created with the intent of creating a purchase agreement or a single purchase order. These represent three different starting points for creating an RFQ. The RFQ business process consists of several basic steps to create an RFQ and handle the vendor-specific replies. A vendor reply can be accepted or rejected, and the impact of an accepted reply depends on the starting point. For example, an accepted reply can update the originating purchase requisition.

Purchase Requisition Purchase requisitions generally apply to many types of indirect materials, where procurement is triggered by a user request and involves an approval process before items can be purchased. However, a purchase requisition approval process sometimes applies to direct material items with requirements driven by S&OP game plans, such as sourcing a new item from a new vendor. The approval process employs the workflow management capabilities within Dynamics AX, where you define one or more workflows for purchase requisition approval. A purchase order can be automatically created for an approved requisition.

13.9 Workflows and Purchase Order Approval

Some scenarios require a purchase order approval process when buying trade goods. An approval process is not typically required when purchasing trade goods based on requirements driven by S&OP game plans, as indicated by planned purchase orders. Within AX, an approval process does not apply to purchase orders that have been created by firming a planned order. Hence, an approval process only applies to a manually created purchase order.

The term *change management* refers to use of an approval process for purchase orders. The associated policy—termed *activate change management*— can be company-wide, vendor-specific or order-specific. Use of change management requires the definition of a purchase order approval process, which identifies the steps and responsibilities for approval. A detailed explanation of this setup information falls outside the book's scope because of book length considerations.[8]

When an approval process applies to a manually created purchase order, an approval status of *draft* is initially assigned to the order. This approval status automatically changes to *in review* after you submit the order for approval, and it subsequently changes to *approved* after successful completion of the approval steps. The status can then be changed to confirmed, as previously described in the basic model of purchase order processing (Section 13.2).

13.10 Purchase Order Returns

Returning material to a vendor typically involves a different type of purchase order (termed a returned order), but it can also be handled via a purchase order line item with a negative quantity. These two approaches are summarized below, along with a typical business process for returns to vendor.

Purchase Order Type of Returned Order When creating a purchase order, you designate the order type as returned order and enter the vendor RMA (Return Material Authorization) number. The line items for a returned order are expressed with a negative quantity. Line items can be manually entered, or the original purchase order information can be copied precisely (via the *Copy from All* function or the *Create Credit Note* function) with an inverted quantity. A user-defined reason code (termed *return action* code) can be specified for each line item. A scrap checkbox indicates the material does not warrant an actual return to vendor. After returning the item, the printed invoice reflects a credit note.

Negative Quantity for Purchase Order Line Item A line item with a negative quantity can indicate a return to vendor, rather than using a

[8]The training materials provided by Microsoft, especially the e-learning courses, provide an excellent explanation of the setup information for approval processes.

separate purchase order type of returned order. The additional line item typically reflects situations where quality or delivery problems require an immediate return, or an incorrect receipt quantity must be reversed.

Typical Business Process for Purchase Order Returns The typical business process reflects an approach using a purchase order type of returned order, as illustrated in Figure 13.6 and summarized below.

The purchasing agent creates a returned order for a specified vendor, and identifies the vendor's RMA number. The purchasing agent also creates a line item for each returned item, where the line item identifies an item, a negative quantity, purchase price, ship-from location and the requested ship date. The line item information can also be created by selecting lines from a previously invoiced purchase order, which helps identify the original purchase price. The purchasing agent confirms a purchase order when information has been completely entered. The shipping clerk reports the item(s) being sent back for a returned order. The accounts payable clerk creates the vendor's credit note based on the quantity of each item returned, or based on the returned order quantity when there is no return.

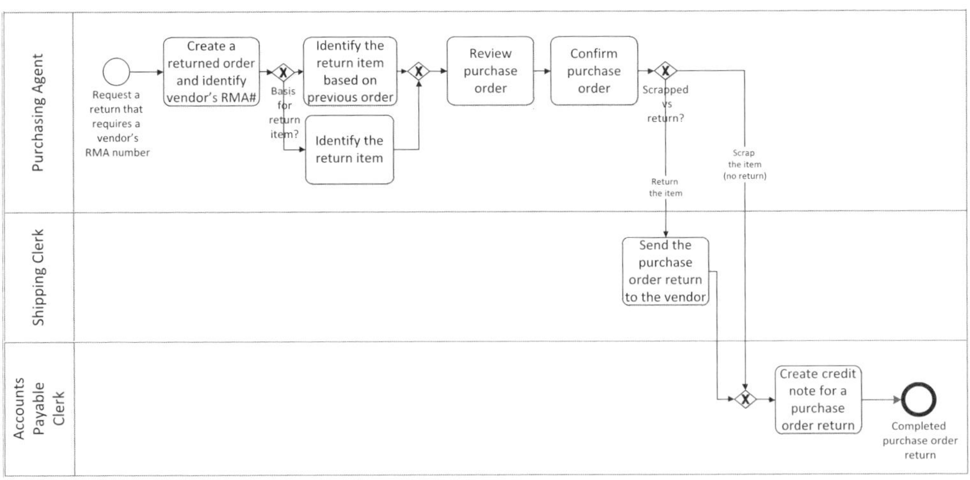

Figure 13.6 Typical Business Process for a Purchase Order Return

13.11 Coordinate Procurement Activities

A firm's S&OP game plans for saleable products and services provide the primary driver of purchasing activities for material items. The game plans define item demands that form the first step in every purchase cycle. Planning calculations synchronize supplies to meet these demands, as expressed through several coordination tools. The primary coordination tools consist of planned purchase orders and suggested action messages generated by planning calculations. The planned orders and action messages reflect the planning data for purchased material (described in Chapter 10) and the planning calculations (Chapter 11).

Suggestions for Planned Purchase Orders The suggestions can be viewed on the *Planned Purchase Orders* form or the *Planned Orders* form. The displayed information typically represents the current master plan.[9] You can also manually add a planned order. Purchase orders can be created from selected planned orders via a function termed *firming planned orders*.

- *Selecting and firming planned orders.* You select planned orders via a marking check box. Planned orders can be viewed and optionally selected based on attributes such as the buyer, order date, and planned order status. You can assign a status to planned orders (unprocessed, processed and approved) to indicate those that have been analyzed, but this status only represents reference information. The form does not retain marked orders if you exit the form before firming.

  The firming function creates purchase orders for selected planned orders that have a specified vendor. The system creates single-line purchase orders unless you indicate grouping preferences (via the firming dialogue when you select more than one planned order).[10] With grouping by vendor, the system can create multi-line purchase orders from selected planned orders within a daily, weekly or monthly period. An alternative grouping option can be based on purchase agreements, resulting in a multi-line purchase order with all lines related to the same purchase agreement.

[9] You can view information based on a selected set of master plan data or forecast plan data. For simplicity's sake the explanation focuses on the set of data representing the current master plan.

[10] The default values for grouping preferences (when firming planned purchase orders) are defined as part of the master planning parameters.

Execution of the firming function automatically deletes the selected planned orders, and creates a log for tracking which planned orders have been firmed and by whom.

- *Analyzing and editing planned orders.* Buyers often need to understand the rationale and impact of a planned purchase order, and the system supports several analysis approaches.
  - Related action messages. The form displays action messages related to a planned order, such as expediting the planned order.
  - Understanding the sources of demand and supply. You can view single-level pegging information about the source of demand for a planned order. Additional inquiries display single-level pegging to all supplies and demands for an item (via a Net Requirements inquiry), and the multi-level pegging information about supplies and demands for a planned order (via an Explosion inquiry).

  The analysis efforts often lead to needed action, and several actions can be implemented on the planned orders form.
  - View and select from alternative vendors (via the selection list for the vendor field). Identification of alternative vendors reflects the approved vendor list, purchase price trade agreement information, or vendor item information. The trade agreement information provides the basis for selecting a vendor based on purchase price, delivery lead time, quantity breakpoints, and validity dates.
  - Change quantity and/or delivery date for the planned purchase order.
  - Split the planned purchase order using a specified quantity and date.
  - Group together several selected planned orders for the same item, where the delivery date of the firmed order reflects the currently selected planned order.
  - Assign the planned order to an existing purchase order so that the firming process adds a line item to the existing order.
  - Convert the planned order to a request for quote.
  - In some cases, the item can be sourced via transfer or production, so that you change the planned purchase order to a planned transfer order or production order to indicate an alternate source of supply.

Time Fences for Automatic Firming and a Frozen Period

The use of planned purchase orders is affected by two time fence policies regarding minimum turnaround time and automatic creation of purchase orders. These time fence policies are embedded in the coverage group assigned to an item.

Freeze Time Fence The freeze time fence represents the shortest possible turnaround time to obtain material with a new purchase order, so that planning calculations will place planned orders at the end of the frozen period. An item's freeze time fence represents expedited delivery whereas the purchase lead time represents normal delivery.

Firm Time Fence The firm time fence enables the system to automatically create purchase orders, thereby eliminating the effort to manually firm planned orders. However, automatic firming only works when planned orders have a suggested vendor (e.g., based on the item's preferred vendor or purchase price trade agreements). The system uses the company-wide grouping preferences to create multi-line purchase orders, such as creating a multi-line order for planned orders with the same vendor and within a weekly period. To be effective, the automatic firming time fence should be slightly greater than the item's purchase lead time and reorder cycle.

The firm time fence also applies to intercompany purchase orders, where automatically firmed up purchase orders communicate requirements across a multi-company supply chain. In this case, an effective time fence must consider the desired visibility of intercompany requirements.

Action Messages Planning calculations generate two types of action messages termed actions and futures, as previously explained in Chapter 10. An actions message indicates a suggestion to advance/postpone an order's delivery date, to increase/decrease an order quantity, or to delete an order. A futures message indicates that the projected completion date for supply chain activities (based on realistic scheduling assumptions) will cause a delay in meeting a requirement date such as a sales order shipment. These messages are displayed on two different forms termed the *Actions* form and *Futures* form. Users cannot take action on these inquiry forms, but can readily access the relevant master table for the referenced order to indicate their action.

Additional Case Studies

Case 73: Purchase Requisitions A manufacturer used purchase requisitions for many types of indirect materials, where various types and amounts of purchases required an approval process. They wanted to use the workflow management capabilities within Dynamics AX. A typical approval process involved the following steps.

1. Create a purchase requisition for one or more items. The identity of the requisitioner (and their position within the organizational hierarchy) can limit the items being requested, and impact an approval process based on organizational hierarchy.
2. Submit the purchase requisition. After submission, the workflow should define additional steps related to task completion and approval.
3. Report a task as completed. A typical task involves an RFQ, and an accepted RFQ reply represents completion of the task.
4. Approve or reject the purchase requisition. The approval process can contain one or more approval steps. A simple approval process might contain a single approval step and a specified user as the assigned approver. Alternatively, the assigned approver for an approval step can reflect the organization hierarchy or a group of users.
5. Create the purchase order for an approved purchase requisition.

Case 74: Purchasing RFQs A manufacturer used an RFQ (request for quote) as a structured approach for soliciting and using vendor responses to purchase quotations. RFQs were used for purchase requisitions of MRO items, and for sourcing planned orders for new items. The RFQ business process has three starting points (a purchase requisition, a planned PO, and manual creation) and several basic steps. These steps are summarized below.

1. Create an RFQ for the desired items and the applicable vendors.
2. Send the vendor-specific RFQs (to applicable vendors) to obtain reply information.
3. Receive a reply for a vendor-specific RFQ.
4. Prepare purchase price trade agreement based on a reply.
5. Accept or reject a reply.
6. Update information based on an accepted reply. The starting point affects the updated information, such as updating the purchase requisition or creating a purchase orders.

Case 75: Landed Costs for Purchased Items An equipment company incurred several types of landed costs for purchased items (such as freight and pallet charges) and employed a standard costing approach. These incremental landed costs were included in an item's standard cost, and also identified as charges on purchase orders. The cost accountant wanted to identify the different types and amounts of these landed costs for an item, and also obtain a comparison of standard versus actual costs for each type. The cost accountant was considering an add-on module to support these requirements.[11]

Case 76: Supplier Coordination via E-Commerce A manufacturer wanted to improve coordination via several e-commerce initiatives with their suppliers. The e-commerce initiatives included Biztalk and electronic marketplace capabilities. They communicated purchase order releases and changes to their suppliers, and received confirmations and changes from the suppliers. Automating these basic business processes improved coordination and reduced data entry errors and time. Additional capabilities included a common baseline of vendor performance metrics (such as delivery quantities/dates and tolerances), tracking of in-transit materials, and replenishment of vendor-managed inventory.

Case 77: Vendor Performance A manufacturing company wanted to enhance vendor performance analysis beyond the standard reports for quantity and cost variances. They wanted an overall score for each vendor based on the metrics described below, where the metrics reflected receipts during a specified time period.

- *Delivery Timeliness.* The scoring percentage reflected the number of on-time receipts divided by the total number of receipt transactions. On-time receipts reflected the line item's confirmed date and delivery tolerances expressed in days.
- *Delivery Quantity.* The scoring percentage reflected the number of correct quantity receipts divided by the total number of receipt transactions. The correct quantity receipts reflected the line item's order quantity and delivery tolerances in percentages. This metric required the ability to accept receipts outside of tolerances.

[11] See **www.scalable.com.au** for additional information about their Import Costing module.

- *Quality.* The scoring percentage reflected the total good quantity divided by the total received quantity. This metric required linkage between the reporting of good and scrapped material to the originating purchase order receipt.
- *Price.* The scoring percentage reflected a standard costing approach, with the total value of purchase price variances divided by the total value of received items.

Case 78: Invoice Matching Using Quality Results The accounts payable function at a manufacturer performed invoice matching against the purchase order, receipts, and actual quality of the received material. The actual quality was reported via a quality order, which identified the test results to determine whether the material passed or failed.

Executive Summary

Purchase order processing represents a key business process in distribution and manufacturing environments, and involves a wide spectrum of variations and considerations. This chapter described a basic model for purchase order processing, which provided the foundation for explaining major variations. It covered sourcing and agreement information for purchased items, including the preferred vendor and agreements about purchase prices. Planning calculations help coordinate procurement activities by communicating the need for planned orders and suggested changes to existing orders. The case studies highlighted variations in purchase order processing, including vendor coordination via e-commerce initiatives.

Chapter 14

Production Order Processing

Production orders provide a key coordination tool for scheduling and reporting production activities in most discrete manufacturers. Some mixed mode scenarios also use batch orders to coordinate production, and a previous chapter explained batch orders and the related formula information (Chapter 5). The majority of software capabilities for production orders and batch orders are exactly the same, so that terminology represents the primary difference. For explanatory purposes, this chapter focuses on the use and terminology of production orders. It also covers several aspects of batch orders (such as co/by-products) for handling special cases in discrete manufacturing. This approach avoids duplicate explanations for the two types of coordination tools, and avoids the use of combined terms such as a production/batch order and an order-dependent BOM/formula.

The production order for a stocked item is typically generated by firming a planned production order, whereas the production order for a make-to-order product can be generated from the related sales order. In addition, the production order for a make-to-order component will be automatically generated. Each production order goes through several life cycle steps.

A basic model of production order processing provides the starting point for further explanation of the order life cycle, scheduling, production reporting and costing. These topics are reflected in the following sections:

1. Significance of a Single Production Order
2. Typical Business Process for a Production Order
3. Basic Model of Production Order Processing
4. Life Cycle of roduction Order
5. Considerations about Production Orders

6. Significance of Picking Lists
7. Significance of Route Cards and Job Cards
8. Report Finished Quantity of a Parent Item
9. Rework Order for a Finished Quantity
10. Scheduling an Individual Order
11. Coordinate Production via Planned Orders
12. Coordinate Production via Action Messages
13. Coordinate Production via Production Schedules
14. Costing for a Production Order

14.1 Significance of a Single Production Order

The significance of a single production order can vary in different scenarios, especially those involving manufactured items with batch tracking. It may represent a single production run in some scenarios, or it may represent multiple production runs within a day or week in other scenarios. The terms for a "production run" may differ between companies, such as a single physical batch or other synonym. This chapter primarily employs the term production run. One aspect of the production order's significance concerns the order quantity, as described below.

Single Order Represents One Production Run When a single order represents one production run, the entire order quantity would typically be reflected in the started quantity, the generation and posting of picking lists about material usage, and the generation and posting of route cards about operation time. The start date of the order typically represents the due date for components. However, the component due dates may reflect an operation start date in scenarios with a multistep routing involving lengthy processing times and material usage tied to an operation number.

With a batch-controlled parent item, you would typically assign a single batch number to the finished quantity. One advantage of this approach concerns batch tracking, since the batch numbers of components can be traced to a single batch number of the parent item. Other approaches do not provide this granularity in batch tracking.

Single Order Represents Multiple Production Runs When a single order represents multiple production runs, the following considerations apply to the started quantity and the finished quantity.

- *Reporting the started quantity.* In most scenarios, you would report a started quantity that corresponds to a single production run. Each additional production run would involve an additional started quantity.

  The started quantity has an additional consideration, since it can trigger the automatic generation of a picking list populated with suggested quantities and locations of components. The picking list can reflect all components, or only those components assigned a flushing principle of start. You can report actual material usage against the picking list, and then post the picking list to update inventory balances. The reported usage can indicate the initially picked quantities, or the final consumption quantities, since you can post the picking list at any time. If needed, an additional picking list may be manually created to indicate adjustments to the consumed material.

  The started quantity can also support the concept of forward flushing material, which involves automatic generation and posting of a picking list. You identify automatic posting as part of the policies for starting an order quantity.

  In a similar fashion with routing data, the started quantity can also trigger the automatic generation of a route card reflecting the operations, and also support the concept of forward flushing resource usage.
- *Reporting the finished quantity.* The finished quantity consists of a good quantity and an optional scrapped quantity. It can be reported during or after completion , of each production run.

  The finished quantity has an additional consideration, since it can trigger backflushing of components that have a flushing principle of finish. More specifically, the finished quantity results in automatic generation and posting of a picking list for these components. The finished quantity can also trigger a similar process for automatic generation and posting of a route card about resource usage, where the relevant operations have been assigned a flushing principle of automatic route consumption.

With a batch-controlled parent item, the assignment of unique batch numbers must be reflected in how you report finished quantities for the order. You would typically assign a unique batch number when reporting the finished quantity for each production run. Multiple batch numbers can also be reported in a single transaction by registering the different quantity associated with each batch prior to posting the finished quantity. Alternatively, you could assign a single batch number to all production runs. The choice

A Single Order Represents	Significance of the Batch Number
One Production Run	One Batch Number for the Production Run
Multiple Production Runs within One Shift/Day/Week	Unique Batch Number per Batch or Same Batch Number for all Batches

<u>Additional Considerations:</u>
Report the Finished Quantity for an order
Report the Started Quantity for an order
Generate a Picking List to report material usage
Generate of a Route Card to report resource usage
Quantity breakpoints for the item's route versions

Figure 14.1 Significance of a Single Order and its Related Batch Numbers

of how to assign batch numbers (and the batch number mask) can be embedded within the batch tracking policies for the manufactured item, as described in a previous chapter (Section 9.2).

Summarizing the Significance of a Single Order The basic variations in the significance of a single order number and its related batch numbers are summarized in Figure 14.1. The figure also lists some of the additional considerations, such as how to report finished quantities and started quantities for an order, the automatic generation of picking lists and route cards, and the quantity breakpoints for the item's route versions.

14.2 Typical Business Process for a Production Order

This business process focuses on the production of a stocked item, where a single production order represents one production run and the picking list

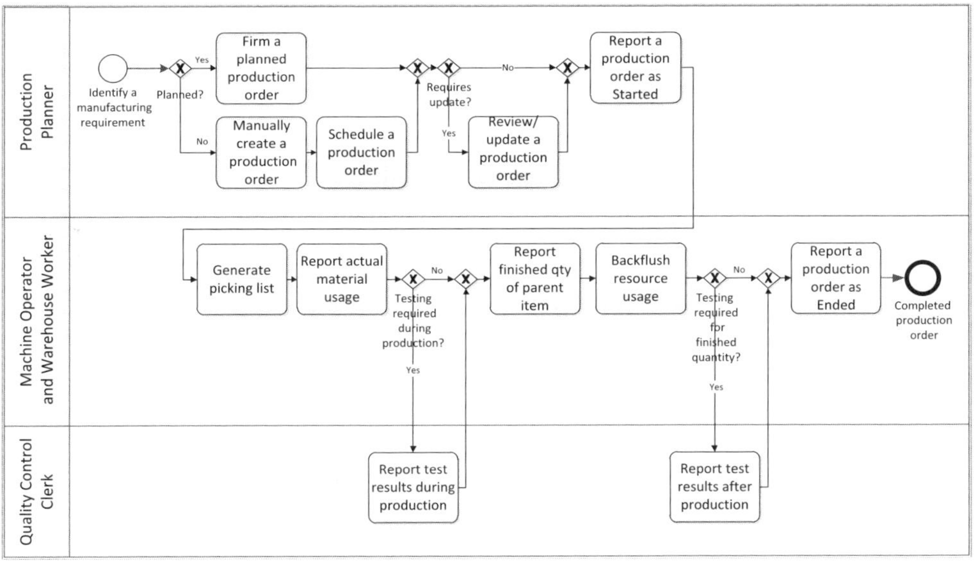

Figure 14.2 Typical Business Process for a Production Order

reflects the entire order quantity. The typical business process consists of multiple steps performed by different roles, as illustrated in Figure 14.2 and described below. The typical business process would vary when a single production order represents multiple production runs.

The production planner analyzes and firms a planned production order that reflects requirements stemming from the S&OP game plans and the item's planning data. Alternatively, the planner manually creates and then schedules a production order, typically to meet an unplanned requirement or as part of a manually maintained master schedule. The production planner reviews the production order and optionally updates it, such as changing the order quantity, rescheduling the order, or locking the order. The production planner reports the order as started (for the entire order quantity), where the started quantity automatically generates a picking list.

Starting the order represents an authorization to report actual production activities. This includes the reporting of picking and receiving activities, and the reporting of test results. The reporting of a finished quantity for the parent item results in automatic assignment of a unique batch number, and also triggers backflushing of resource usage. The production process may also generate a co/by-product which requires reporting of a finished quantity.

The machine operator reports the production order as ended when all activities have been reported.

Firm a Planned Production Order The production planner analyzes and firms a planned production order that reflects requirements stemming from the S&OP game plans and the item's planning data. The production planner can analyze the source of requirements and action messages for the planned order, and optionally edit the order—such as changing the suggested quantity or date.

Manually Create a Production Order The production planner manually creates a production order, typically to meet an unplanned requirement or as part of a manually maintained master schedule. When creating the order, the planner may optionally override the inherited value for the item's active route version or BOM version, such as indicating use of a different routing.

Schedule a Production Order The production planner schedules a manually created production order so that planning calculations recognize the requirements for the components and resources. The scheduling logic assigns the start/end dates to the production order, and also the operation start/end times when using routing data.

Review/Update the Production Order The production planner may need to review and update the production order. For example, the production planner may change the order quantity or the order-dependent BOM, schedule the production order on different dates, or lock the order to prevent rescheduling. When using routing data, the production planner can review the detailed schedule of operation start/stop times in tabular or Gantt chart format, and optionally assign an operation to a different resource.

Report a Production Order as Started The production planner reports a production order as *started*, along with a started quantity representing the entire order quantity. This automatically generates a picking list for the started quantity, where the picking list can be optionally segmented by operation number.

Generate the Picking List for a Production Order A picking list can be automatically generated based on the started quantity, and it indicates the suggested quantity and location for each component. The machine operator can also manually generate an additional picking list, typically to report adjustments or corrections to component usage.

Report Actual Material Usage against a Picking List Using the picking list, the machine operator can report actual usage by confirming or overriding the suggested information. As noted previously, the machine operator may manually generate an additional picking list in order to report adjustments or corrections to component usage.

Report Test Results during Production As part of reporting production for an operation, the system can automatically generate a quality order identifying the item's testing requirements and the sample quantity. The quality control clerk reports the actual test results against the quality order, and then validates the test results to determine pass/fail status. After the validation step, the quality control clerk can optionally reopen a quality order in order to revise the test results or the validation.

Report Finished Quantity of the Parent Item The machine operator reports the parent item's finished quantity after completion of a production run, with automatic assignment of the internal batch number. The finished quantity also triggers backflushing of resources. If reporting partial or multiple receipts, the machine operator also indicates when the last receipt is being recorded so that order status will be updated.

Back Flush Resource Usage The finished quantity of the parent item triggers automatic generation and posting of a route card journal which will back flush resource usage. The resource usage provides the basis for calculating remaining work for the production order.

Report Test Results after Production As part of reporting a finished quantity, the system can automatically generate a quality order identifying the item's testing requirements and the sample quantity. The testing requirement can optionally block further transactions for the material until actual test results have been reported and validated. The quality control clerk reports the actual test results against the quality order, and then validates the test results to determine pass/fail status. After the validation step, the quality control clerk can optionally reopen a quality order in order to revise the test results or the validation.

Report a Production Order as Ended The machine operator reports the end of a production order, indicating that no additional transactions need to be reported. When there are missing transactions, the system provides warning messages and does not change the order status to *ended*, although specifying an override will force an ended status. After ending the production order, the variances are automatically calculated for a standard cost item.

14.3 Basic Model of Production Order Processing

This section summarizes a basic model of production order processing that reflects many aspects of the typical business process described above. The basic model consists of the major steps illustrated in Figure 14.3, which highlights the key forms, documents and order status associated with each step. The figure's numbered steps result in a change to order status, whereas other steps do not change order status.

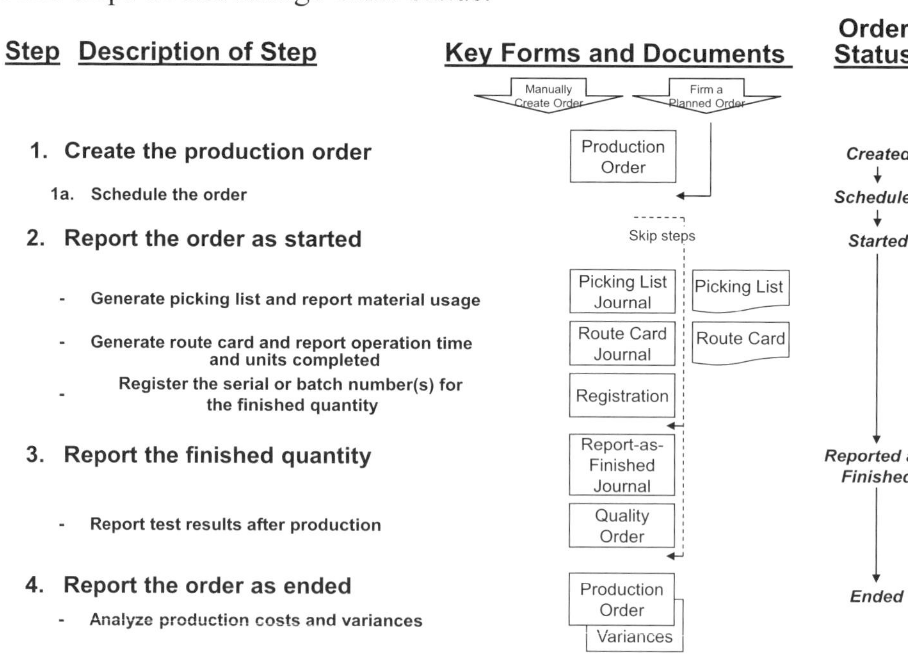

Figure 14.3 Basic Model of Production Order Processing

The basic model provides a framework for explaining major variations in system usage for managing internal production. For example, subsequent sections describe variations in using picking lists and route cards, scheduling orders, reporting finished quantities and coordinating production. The next section provides more comprehensive explanations of the possible life cycle steps and how you change order status via a user-initiated task and related dialogue.

Step 1: Create the Production Order The Production Order form is used to manually create an order, or to maintain an order that was generated by firming a planned order.

- *Manually create an order.* When you manually create a production order, the system displays the Create Production Order dialogue so that you can specify the relevant information. The relevant information includes the parent item, quantity, delivery date and the deliver-to site/warehouse/bin. Based on this information, the dialogue displays the active BOM version and route version, and these can be optionally overridden prior to order creation. Completion of the dialogue results in the creation of a production order (with a *created* status) and an order-dependent BOM and routing.
- *Maintain an order created from a planned order.* The firming process results in a production order with an assigned order status.[1] Most scenarios employ an assigned status of *scheduled*, which enables planning calculations to recognize requirements associated with the order-dependent BOM and routing. A subsequent section provides further explanation about firming planned orders.

Steps in the order status can be skipped, as shown by the dashed lines in Figure 14.3 For example, you could simply jump from the created status to the report-as-finished status in order to record the parent receipts, with auto-deduction of components and routing operations. The ability to skip steps is determined by company-wide or site-specific policies.[2]

[1]The status assigned to a production order generated by the firming process reflects an item-specific policy embedded in the coverage group for the item. A scheduled status reflects a commonly used policy.

[2]The ability to skip steps can be defined as a company-wide policy (on the Status Tab of the Production Control Parameters form) or as a site-specific policy (on the Status Tab of the Production Control Parameters by Site form).

Step 1a: Schedule the Order A production order with a created status must be scheduled so that planning calculations recognize the requirements associated with the order-dependent BOM and routing. Firming a planned order typically results in a scheduled status, whereas a manually created order has a created status that must be changed to a scheduled status. For example, when you initiate the schedule order task for a production order, the system displays a dialogue so that you can specify relevant information. The two choices for the schedule order task—termed operations scheduling and job scheduling—will be discussed in a subsequent section. Completion of the dialogue results in a *scheduled* order status.

Step 2: Report the Order as Started A production order must have a started status in order to report actual production activities such as material usage, operation time and parent receipts. When you initiate the start order task for an order, the system displays a start order dialogue so that you can specify relevant information. The relevant information includes the started quantity and policies about automatic generation of picking lists and route cards. Subsequent sections provide further explanation of picking lists and route cards. Completion of the dialogue results in a *started* order status.

Generate Picking List and Report Material Usage You typically generate and print a picking list as part of starting an order and then report actual material usage against the picking list. Each picking list has a unique identifier. You report actual usage using the Picking List Journal form, and then post the picking list. The same form can also be used to manually generate a picking list, typically to report and post adjustments to material usage. A subsequent section provides further explanation of picking lists.

Generate Route Card and Report Operation Time and Units Completed In many scenarios, operation time will be back flushed based on the finished quantity for the parent item. That is, the finished quantity automatically generates and posts a Route Card Journal. In other scenarios, you generate a Route Card Journal as part of starting an order. You report actual operation time and unit completions, and then post the journal. Reporting unit completions at the last operation can optionally update the finished quantity of the parent item. A subsequent section provides further explanation of route cards.

Register the Batch Number(s) for the Order When a single production order represents multiple production runs, and you report the finished quantity for multiple production runs as a single transaction, you can register the separate batch numbers (and their quantities) as part of reporting the finished quantity. The registration step is not typically used when separately reporting the finished quantity for each production run. The registration step updates the item's inventory balance, where the inventory has a registered status.

Step 3: Report the Finished Quantity You indicate the finished quantities of a parent item using the Report as Finished Journal, typically as part of the report-as-finished task for the order. The report-as-finished task is also used for reporting co/by-product receipts. When you initiate the report-as-finished task, the system displays a reported-as-finished dialogue so that you can specify relevant information such as the good quantity. The order status changes to *report-as-finished* after flagging the order as complete using the *end job* flag. The reported-as-finished status means that the system ignores remaining component/routing requirements and expected parent receipts, but additional transactions can be reported. A subsequent section provides further explanation about reporting finished quantities for the parent item.

Report Test Results after Production When testing requirements have been defined for the finished quantity of the parent item, the system automatically generates a quality order. You report the actual test results against the quality order, and then validate the test results to determine pass/fail status. A subsequent chapter provides further explanation of quality orders (Section 18.4).

Step 4: Report the Order as Ended When you initiate the end order task, the system displays an end dialogue so that you can specify relevant information, such as how to allocate scrap costs. Completion of the dialogue results in an order status of *ended*, and further transactions cannot be reported.

Analyze Production Costs and Variances You can view the details underlying actual versus estimated production costs for the order, and also view the variances related to standard cost items.

14.4 Life Cycle of a Production Order

The life cycle of a production order consists of several steps represented by an order status.[3] The order status represents a linear progression that affects order behavior, such as the ability to report actual production activities. Steps in the linear progression can be skipped. Steps can also be reversed by resetting order status.

Each step involves a user-initiated update task (and an associated dialogue) and results in a change to order status. For example, changing order status to *started* involves a start task and an associated start dialogue, and default values can be defined for many of the dialogue fields. The life cycle steps first require an understanding of these update tasks, since the update tasks provide the context for understanding order status. The types of update tasks and their significance are summarized in Figure 14.4 and explained below. The figure also indicates the ability to define dialogue default values, and the option to include reference orders linked to the production order.

Create Order Task The critical information in the create order dialogue includes the item, quantity, delivery date, and the deliver-to site/warehouse. Based on this information, the dialogue displays the active BOM version and routing version, but these can be optionally overridden. Once the order has been created, the order-dependent BOM and routing initially reflect the specified versions, and they can be manually maintained.

Estimate Order Task The estimate order task calculates the order costs based on the order-dependent BOM and routing, the related cost information, and the order quantity. A price calculation inquiry displays the order's per-unit costs. The estimate order task represents an optional step when you need to calculate estimated costs prior to scheduling or starting an order. It is typically performed automatically as a result of updating order status to a higher status such as scheduled or started.

[3]Those readers familiar with the concept of a production order life cycle in other ERP packages often ask for clarification about the differences with AX. In Dynamics AX, for example, a planned production order represents a separate construct so there is no order status called planned. The process of firming a planned production order generates a production order with a designated order status such as scheduled or started; there is no order status called firmed. The started status (rather than the released status) indicates an authorization to report production activities. The reported-as-finished status means that the system ignores remaining component requirements and expected parent receipts, but additional transactions can be reported without re-opening the production order. Changing the order status to ended prevents any further transactions, and results in the calculation of production variances for standard cost items. The order status can be reset at any time prior to ended status, and the system will automatically reverse all associated transactions.

Type of Update Task	Significance of Update Task	Dialogue Default Values	Option to Include Reference Orders
Create	Initially create a new batch/production order	N/A	N/A
Estimate	Initially perform (if needed) to calculate material requirements Perform (if needed) cost-plus-markup calculation of a sales price Perform again (if needed) to recalculate order costs based on updated information	Yes	Yes
Schedule	Initially schedule material and capacity requirements Perform again (if needed) to reschedule order based on updated information	Yes	Yes
Release	Perform (if needed) to print shop traveler of routing operations	Yes	Yes
Start	Indicate started quantity (and selected operations) Perform again (if needed) to define additional started quantity (and selected operations) Perform again (if needed) to indicate completion of all picking and/or all operations	Yes	Yes
	Report Related Activities: Generate picking list and report material usage via the picking list journal Report unit completions by operation via the report-as-finished journal Report time and unit completions by operation via the route (or job) card journal	N/A	N/A
Report as Finished	Report receipts, and optionally indicate completed order, picking, or all operations Perform again (if needed) to report additional receipts or indicate completed order Perform again (if needed) to indicate completion of all picking and/or all operations	Yes	N/A
End	Change status to ended , thereby preventing further transactions Calculate variances for standard cost items	Yes	N/A
Reset Status	Change order status to created, thereby allowing deletion of order Change order status, thereby reversing all associated transactions	Yes	Yes

Figure 14.4 Update Tasks for Production Orders

Schedule Order Task There are two scheduling methods—termed operation scheduling and job scheduling – to choose from. The scheduling method is only relevant when using routing data, and the choice depends on how you assign resource requirements to an operation (described in Section 6.10). Job scheduling must be used when resource requirements are defined in terms of resource capabilities or employee competencies.

When scheduling an order using either method, you specify the critical information in a schedule order dialogue, such as the scheduling direction and several scheduling policies. The scheduling direction, for example, could be forward from today's date or backward from a specified scheduling date. The scheduling policies can optionally include consideration of finite capacity and material. A subsequent section provides further explanation about scheduling individual orders. The schedule order task must be repeated after changing the order quantity or the order-dependent BOM and routing.

You can optionally specify that an order is locked, thereby preventing rescheduling by planning calculations or by the schedule order task.

Release Order Task The release order task and its dialogue can be used to print shop traveler paperwork (related to routing information) prior to starting production activities. The release order task represents an optional step.

Start Task Starting an order quantity (via a start order dialogue) represents an authorization for reporting actual production activities. The relevant information depends on the significance of a single order, as described in a previous section. In some scenarios, you will start the entire order quantity and all operations. In other scenarios, you will start a partial order quantity or selected operations. You can also indicate completion of all picking activities or routing operations so that planning calculations ignore remaining requirements.

The reporting of actual production activities—shown in Figure 14.4 for informational purposes—includes component material usage, time and unit completions by operation, and finished quantities. Unit completions at the last operation can optionally update the finished quantity for the parent item.

Report as Finished Task The report-as-finished task provides one approach for reporting parent receipts and co/by-product receipts, expressed in terms of the good quantity and scrap quantity (termed *error* quantity). As part of the report-as-finished dialogue, you can optionally indicate completion of all picking activities or routing operations, so that planning calculations ignore remaining requirements. The order status changes to report-as-finished after flagging the order as complete using the end job flag. The reported-as-finished status means that the system ignores remaining component/routing requirements and expected parent receipts, but additional transactions can be reported. The report-as-finished journal contains these transactions for parent receipts and co/by-product receipts.

Order status will not change to reported-as-finished when transactions are missing unless you indicate that errors will be accepted (as part of the report-as-finished dialogue). Missing transactions may include expected parent receipts or remaining requirements for components and operations.

End Task The end task changes the order status to ended. The end dialogue also indicates how to handle costs associated with a scrap quantity, either by allocating scrap costs to actual parent receipts or by charging them to a specified G/L account.

Under certain conditions the end task can be performed instead of the report-as-finished task (via the reported-as-finished flag in the end task dialogue), where the system assumes the entire order quantity will be reported as finished.

Reset Status Task A production order can be reset to a previous status, and you indicate the desired order status on the reset order dialogue. For example, order status may be changed to created to allow deletion, or changed to released from started so that the system automatically reverses all transactions about actual production activities.

Update Tasks and the Option to Include Reference Orders Several update tasks for a production order have an option to include reference orders, as indicated in the right-hand column of Figure 14.4. A reference order reflects a buy-to-order or make-to-order component. The reference orders can be included in cost calculations, scheduling, releasing, and the authorization to start production activities. For example, the estimate task will always generate reference orders, and the schedule order task can optionally include reference orders and even synchronize them. Resetting order status can apply to reference orders. Deleting an order can optionally delete the reference orders. The update tasks can also be performed for a production order that represents a reference order.

Significance of Production Order Status The update tasks provide a context for understanding the order status of a production order. The update tasks allow you to skip steps in the order status, since the system automatically performs the intervening update tasks based on default values for each dialogue. For example, you could manually create an order and then change status to started, and it would be automatically estimated and scheduled. As another example, the firming process can generate a production order with a scheduled status or started status. The order status also affects several aspects of system behavior, as illustrated in Figure 14.5 and summarized below.

The order status determines whether planning calculations recognize expected parent receipts and co-product receipts, and the requirements for components and operations. It also affects the ability to modify the order-dependent BOM and routing, generate a picking list or shop paperwork, report actual production activities, split an order quantity, reset order status, and delete an order.

<table>
<tr><th colspan="3"></th><th>Created</th><th>Estimated</th><th>Scheduled</th><th>Released</th><th>Started</th><th>Reported as Finished</th><th>Ended</th></tr>
<tr><td rowspan="15">Significance of the Current Status</td><td rowspan="4">Planning Calculations</td><td>Recognize Expected Parent Receipt</td><td colspan="5">Yes</td><td colspan="2">No</td></tr>
<tr><td>Recognize Expected Co-Product Receipt</td><td colspan="5">Yes</td><td colspan="2">No</td></tr>
<tr><td>Recognize Component Requirements</td><td>No</td><td colspan="3">Yes</td><td>Yes*</td><td colspan="2">No</td></tr>
<tr><td>Recognize Operation Requirements</td><td colspan="2">No</td><td colspan="2">Yes</td><td>Yes*</td><td colspan="2">No</td></tr>
<tr><td colspan="2">Status Option for Firming a Planned Order</td><td colspan="2">No</td><td colspan="3">Yes</td><td colspan="2">No</td></tr>
<tr><td colspan="2">Modify Order-Dependent Formula/BOM or Routing</td><td colspan="5">Yes</td><td colspan="2">No</td></tr>
<tr><td colspan="2">Timing Option for Automatic Reservations</td><td>No</td><td colspan="2">Yes</td><td>No</td><td>Yes</td><td colspan="2">No</td></tr>
<tr><td colspan="2">Copy BOM/Formula or Routing to Order</td><td colspan="2">Yes</td><td colspan="5">No</td></tr>
<tr><td colspan="2">Generate Shop Paperwork for Routing Operations</td><td colspan="3">No</td><td colspan="3">Yes</td><td>No</td></tr>
<tr><td colspan="2">Generate Picking List</td><td colspan="3">No</td><td colspan="3">Yes</td><td>No</td></tr>
<tr><td colspan="2">Report Actual Production Activities</td><td colspan="4">No</td><td colspan="2">Yes</td><td>No</td></tr>
<tr><td colspan="2">Change or Split Order Quantity</td><td colspan="5">Yes</td><td colspan="2">No</td></tr>
<tr><td colspan="2">Register the Batch Numbers for Order Output</td><td colspan="5">Yes</td><td colspan="2">No</td></tr>
<tr><td colspan="2">Reset Order Status</td><td>N/A</td><td colspan="5">Yes</td><td>No</td></tr>
<tr><td colspan="2">Ability to Delete Order</td><td>Yes</td><td colspan="5">No</td><td>Yes</td></tr>
</table>

* = Remaining component requirements are ignored after reporting a picking list as completed, and remaining operation requirements are ignored after reporting an operation as completed

Figure 14.5 Significance of Production Order Status

When firming a planned order, an item-specific policy (embedded in the coverage group assigned to the item) determines the order status of the resulting production order. In most cases, you should employ the option for a scheduled status.

When using automatic reservations for the components of a production order, an order-related policy determines when the reservations will be performed. In most cases, you should employ the option for a scheduled status.

Life Cycles Related to a Production Order The life cycle of a production order consists of several steps represented by an order status automatically updated by the system, as previously described. Several other constructs and their life cycles are related to an order, such as a picking list,

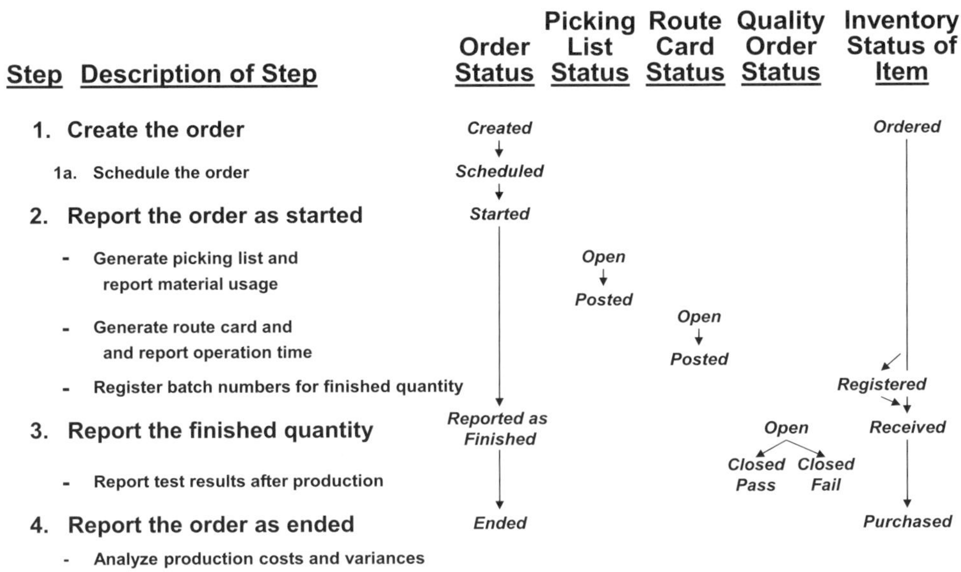

Figure 14.6 Life Cycles Related to a Production Order

route card, quality order and the inventory status of the parent item. Figure 14.6 summarizes these related life cycles in terms of the basic model of production order processing.

14.5 Considerations about Production Orders

The basic information for a production order includes the item, quantity, delivery date and the deliver-to site/warehouse. Additional information includes the order-dependent BOM and routing, the location for component material, and other factors.

Order Quantity Considerations Order quantity modifiers apply to the creation dialogue when manually creating an order, or when manually overriding the quantity for a planned order or existing order. In addition, when manually creating an order for an item with quantity-sensitive formulations, the manually entered quantity may also result in a different active version for the BOM or routing.

Picking Lists and the Order-Dependent BOM The order-dependent BOM initially reflects the BOM version used to create the order. You can manually maintain the information, but the system does not recognize the changes until you perform the scheduling (or estimation) task for the order. The order-dependent BOM also provides the foundation for generating picking lists to report material usage, as described in a subsequent section.

Route Cards and the Order-Dependent Routing The order-dependent routing initially reflects the routing version used to create the order. You can manually maintain the information, but the system does not recognize the changes until you perform the scheduling task for the order. The order-dependent routing also provides the foundation for generating route cards to report operation time and unit completions, as described in a subsequent section.

Splitting a Production Order Splitting a production order results in a new order for the specified quantity and delivery date. The split order quantity must be less than the originating order quantity, and you can split an order prior to a started status. A started production order can be split, but only for a quantity that has not yet been reported as started. This approach avoids the complications associated with allocations of issued components and reported operation times to the split orders.

Production Lead Time The planning calculations will calculate a variable production lead time based on routing data, or use a fixed lead time when no routing data applies. An item's fixed production lead time can be specified as a company-wide value and overridden for a site/warehouse, as previously described (Section 10.3). The calculation of a variable lead time reflects the order quantity, the resource requirements for routing operations, and the available capacity of resources.

Prevent Order Rescheduling A production order can be flagged as locked to prevent rescheduling, and then unlocked when desired.

Identifying Order Linkage to a Demand A production order can be directly linked to a demand, either a sales order line item or another production order's component. The system indicates direct linkage in the reference fields for a production order, and also in the corresponding demand (such as a sales order line item).

The significance of the reference type field can become confusing, since an additional system capability termed *marking* also employs the reference fields. A primary purpose of marking is to support cost tracking and reservations by linking receipt transactions to issue transactions. Marking automatically applies to a production order with direct linkage, which also involves a hard reservation. It can optionally apply to orders with indirect linkage. For example, you can manually mark an existing order so that costs can be tracked to one or more demands. As another example, the firming process for planned orders can assign marking based on pegging information. Marking does not provide direct linkage, but it can update the value of the reference type field. The dual use of the reference type field can lead to confusion. For simplicity's sake the explanation focuses on the significance of the reference fields related to direct linkage. The Reference List inquiry for a production order identifies the linked reference orders.

Summarized Information The summarized information includes estimated and actual costs for a production order. Access to detailed information includes actual component issues, parent receipts and routing operations; batch and serial tracking, and related reference orders.

14.6 Significance of Picking Lists

Material usage can only be reported through a picking list. There are multiple variations for generating a picking list, where the variations reflect differences in modeling the business process. This section summarizes the variations and the starting point of an order-dependent BOM.

Order-Dependent BOM The order-dependent BOM provides the foundation for generating a picking list. Creation and maintenance of this information was previously described for a production order (Section 4.5). Several factors have particular relevance to picking lists, as summarized below.

- Warehouse location assigned to components
- Operation number assigned to components
- Flushing policy assigned to a component item
- Reservation policy for the order and the suggested batch numbers for batch-controlled components
- Impact of a phantom component

– Impact of a make-to-order or buy-to-order component resulting in a reference order

Common Scenarios for Picking Lists The common scenarios for picking lists typically reflect variations in the significance of a single order and its related production runs, as previously described. When the order represents a single production run, the common scenarios include the following:

- Single picking list for all components
- Multiple picking lists reflecting components by operation number
- One picking list for reporting actual material usage, and one picking list for auto-deduction of material
- Additional picking list for reporting adjustments and corrections

Reserving Component Inventory for a Production Order Some scenarios require reservations of component inventory for a production order. A reservation policy assigned to the order determines whether reservations will be made manually or automatically, and the timing of automatic reservations can reflect an order status of estimated, scheduled or started. The reservation policy is inherited from a company-wide or site-specific default value. The reservations for a component will be reflected in the picking list.

The use of automatic reservations involves several additional item-specific policies embedded in the Item Model Group assigned to the component item. With batch-controlled material, for example, one policy determines whether first-in-first-out (FIFO) logic will be used for automatic reservations.

Variations in Generating and Posting Picking Lists A picking list can be generated using several different approaches, where the approach also determines how it is populated and posted. The different approaches are summarized below.

❖ *Automatically generate a picking list based on the started quantity.* A typical example would be to populate the picking list with components assigned a flushing principle of start. The approach reflects the policies in the Start Order dialogue.[4]

---

[4]The policies within the Start dialogue (and the dialogues for other update tasks) can be specified for each order, and default values can also be defined—as shown in the right side of Figure 14.5.

- *Automatically generate and immediately post a picking list based on the started quantity.* This approach is commonly termed forward flushing because the picking list is automatically posted. The approach reflects the policies in the Start Order dialogue.
- *Automatically generate and immediately post a picking list based on the finished quantity.* A typical example would be to populate the picking list with components assigned a flushing principle of finish. This approach is commonly termed back flushing because the picking list is automatically posted. The approach reflects the policies in the Report As Finished dialogue.
- *Manually generate a picking list.* This approach starts from the Picking List Journal where you specify the basis for automatically populating a picking list via a Create Lines dialogue. For example, you can automatically create lines based on a specified quantity or the order's started quantity. You post the picking list after reporting actual material usage. The approach ignores the flushing principle assigned to component items.
- *Reverse the entries for a previously posted picking list.* When manually generating a picking list (described above), the basis for automatically populating the picking list can reflect reversing entries for a previously posted picking list. This approach is typically employed to record adjustments or corrections.
- *Issue unexpected components to an order.* This approach starts from the Picking List Journal where you manually add a line item for issuing the component. A manually created line item represents an unexpected component which will be added to the order-dependent BOM with a required quantity of zero. It will also result in a material substitution variance for a standard cost item. It does not represent an additional quantity for an existing component.

Definition of Remaining Requirements for a Component A material shortage represents the remaining requirements for a component in the order-dependent bill for a started production order. The system ignores the components' remaining required quantity under several conditions: when a specific component has been flagged as completely picked; when picking for all components has been flagged as complete; when an operation linked to the material has been flagged as complete; or when the production order status becomes reported-as-finished. The system displays shortages on the Material Stock-out List inquiry.

14.7 Significance of Route Cards and Job Cards

Reporting for an internal operation involves unit completions and/or operation time, and only applies to orders with routing data. A route card or job card can be used for reporting purposes.[5]

- *Reporting Operation Time.* Operation time is reported on the route card journal. Each journal line indicates the operation number, resources, time element (such as process or setup time) and actual hours expended. The route card journal provides several user options, such as overriding the basis for costing and indicating the employee performing the work. You can optionally create a picking list journal from the route card journal, which may be useful when the operator is responsible for reporting component usage at the operation.
- *Reporting Unit Completions by Operation.* Units completions by operation are reported on the route card journal for an order, and units can be reported without a time entry. Unit completions are reported as a good quantity, with an incremental quantity for scrapped units and an optional reason code. You can indicate the operation is completed so that remaining requirements are ignored. The route card journal provides several other user options, such as overriding the basis for costing unit completions.

  Reporting unit completions for the last operation has special significance. The good unit completions can optionally update parent receipts by designating the report-as-finished flag. Additional information may need to be recorded about batch and serial numbers based on the item's quality management policies.

The unit completions and processing hours provide one measure of progress against the routing operation. The system automatically calculates a completion percentage based on actual versus expected process hours as one indicator of remaining work. The completion percentage can be manually overridden. The completion percentage is used in planning calculations to calculate remaining work.

[5]The approach for reporting operation time depends on the scheduling method. The route card journal applies to production orders scheduled via either method, whereas the job card journal only applies when orders have been scheduled via the job scheduling method. The two reporting approaches are similar. The job card differs slightly, since it also supports calculation of reported time based on specified start- and end times. For simplicity's sake further explanation focuses on using the route card journal for reporting unit completions and operation time.

Order-Dependent Routing The order-dependent routing provides the foundation for generating a route card. Creation and maintenance of this information was previously described (Section 6.11). Several aspects have particular relevance to route cards.

- Operation number assigned to the operation
- Resource assigned to the operation
- Warehouse location assigned to components based on the resource
- Automatic consumption policy assigned to an operation
- Significance of the operation's time elements (defined in the Route Group)
- Impact of a phantom component on the order-dependent routing

Automatic Consumption Policy for an Operation Time expended for an operation's run time and setup time can be manually reported or auto-deducted; likewise for unit completions. These represent different aspects of a routing operation. A routing operation has several policies (embedded in the routing group) indicating whether each aspect should be manually reported or auto-deducted.

The auto-deduction policies for routing operations are slightly different than the ones for material, since they do not differentiate between a flushing principle of forward or finish. Hence, a fundamental decision is typically made about using either forward or backward flushing, so that auto-deduction does not result in doubled-up reporting.[6] The same triggers for automatically generating picking lists also apply to generating route cards, as described below.

❖ *Start Trigger*. The start quantity and specified operation(s) determine how the system generates a route card journal, where journal lines identify the auto-deducted routing operation transactions. Policies embedded in the start order dialogue determine whether it is posted immediately. Reviewing the route card journal prior to posting allows you to make corrections.

[6]The decision about forward- versus backward-flushing is embedded in the *automatic route consumption* policy associated with the start order and report-as-finished tasks (and associated dialogues), where the policy is specified as *never* for one task. When using a backward-flushing approach, for example, the policy would be *never* for the start task and *routing group dependent* for the report-as-finished task. Conversely, the policy would be *never* for the report-as-finished task when using a forward-flushing approach.

- *Finish Trigger.* The quantity of good plus scrapped items determines how many auto-deducted hours will be in the route card journal, and the journal is posted immediately without an option to be reviewed.

Remaining Time Requirements for an Operation The remaining time requirements for a routing operation can be ignored under several conditions: when the operation has been flagged as complete, when the entire routing has been flagged as complete; or when the order status becomes reported-as-finished.

Labor Data Collection and the Manufacturing Execution System (MES) Module The Manufacturing Execution System (MES) module supports data collection for reporting unit completions and operation time via clock-in and clock-out registrations for specific production orders and operations. Based on this registration information, the system automatically accumulates the times and unit completions by operation, which can then be used to create line items in route card (or job card) journals. This functionality builds on the time and attendance capabilities within the module, and also supports preparation of payroll data from a single source of labor data. The typical business process to report labor for production orders using the MES approach is summarized in Figure 14.7 and described below.

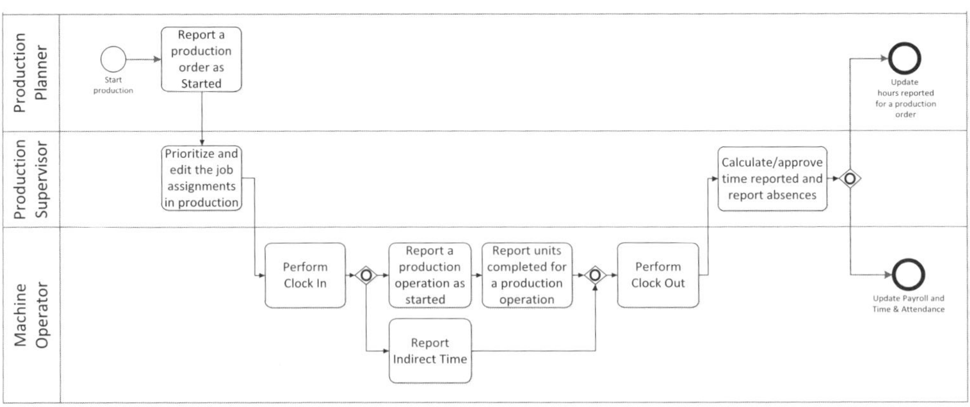

Figure 14.7 Report Labor for Production Orders Using MES Approach

As the first step, the production planner indicates the production orders that are released or started, which triggers the generation of route cards and picking lists.

Prior to reporting production, the production supervisor uses a key form (termed the Edit Job List) to fine-tune the daily schedule, such as re-sequencing or moving jobs, assigning available resources, and designating high priority jobs. This form provides information about each production order, the material availability, and capacity loads to support decision making about efficiency and on-time completions. The resulting job list provides the machine operators the sequence to perform their daily tasks.

When reporting production, a machine operator uses a touch-enabled screen (termed the Job Registration form) to "clock in" to a resource group or a specific resource. The operator is presented up-to-date job information and related documents such as drawings and process specifications. The operator can start a specific job or start a bundle of multiple jobs, or indicate indirect time such as meetings. The operator provides feedback about units completed (including the scrap quantity) and updates the status of the operation, such as completed or stopped. The operator can "clock out" when done working at a resource, or done for the day.

The production supervisor reviews and analyzes the reported time throughout the day, such as reviewing who has clocked in, correcting time entries, or shifting jobs to different machines or operators. At the end of the day, the supervisor performs a calculation to determine elapsed hours from the clock in/clock put times. The production supervisor may enter adjustments, and then approve the information in order to update the hours reported for the production order. The approved information can also be transferred to a payroll or time-and-attendance system.

The MES capabilities require setup information, and a detailed explanation of this setup information falls outside the book's scope because of book length considerations.

14.8 Report Finished Quantity of a Parent Item

The finished quantity of a production order is also termed a parent receipt.[7] Reporting the finished quantity involve identification of the good quantity, with an incremental quantity for scrapped units and an optional reason code. Parent receipts can be recorded three different ways.

- *Report-as-finished task.* This update task provides one method for reporting parent receipts when routing data does not exist, and it generates a report-as-finished journal. As part of the task dialogue, you can also indicate the completion of all picking or all routing operations, or completion of the entire order.
- *Report-as-finished journal.* The journal can be accessed directly in order to create line items for reporting the finished quantity.
- *Route card journal for reporting unit completions at the last operation.* When routing data exists, reporting the unit completions at the last operation can generate and post the report-as-finished journal.

You indicate completion of a production order using either the report-as-finished task or the report-as-finished journal, which changes order status to reported-as-finished. However, the system prevents changing order status when missing feedback or errors exist, as described below.

- All component quantities must be issued.
- Each operation must be reported as completed.
- Parent receipts must equal the good unit completions at the last operation.
- Parent receipts must be less than or equal to the quantity started.

The system provides warnings about these conditions. You can override these warnings by using the *accept errors* flag on the report-as-finished task.

[7]The term reported-as-finished has several contexts within Dynamics AX that can lead to confusion. These contexts include the update task for a production order, a journal for reporting unit completions by operation, report-as-finished flags when reporting production activities, and the status of a production order. Hence, the term parent receipt is used for clarification purposes.

14.9 Rework Order for a Finished Quantity

Rework may be necessary for the finished quantity of a production order that has not been reported as scrapped. The approach for managing this rework is summarized in Figure 14.8 in terms of the basic model for production order processing. The key differences involve the creation step for the rework order, and subsequent steps (shown in grey) follow the basic model.

- *Rework using a production order.* You manually create a new production order, but with an unspecified BOM version so that you must manually define the parent item as a component of itself in the order-dependent BOM. After updating the order status to scheduled (or estimated), you must explicitly reserve this component. The reservation step is especially important for a batch-controlled item, as explained above.

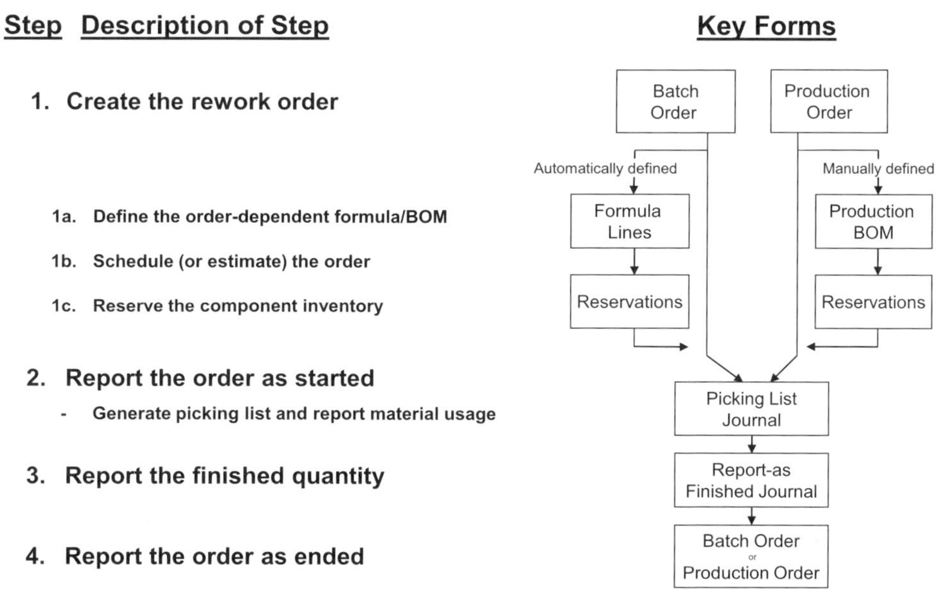

Figure 14.8 Rework for the Finished Quantity of a Production Order

In both scenarios, you report the order as started, and then report consumption of the component and any other material used in rework. Upon completion, you report the finished quantity of good items (and a scrap quantity if applicable) and update the order status to ended. Additional considerations may apply, such as the definition of a routing version for rework (which can be assigned when you create the rework order) and the reporting of actual time expended on rework. It may also be helpful to assign a production pool (to rework orders) that represents rework, which helps filter the orders related to rework.

14.10 Scheduling an Individual Order

Scheduling an individual production order has several considerations. It can change order status to scheduled, or update an already scheduled order, so that requirements for resources and materials will be correctly recognized and scheduled. The resource requirements and related scheduling logic only apply when using routing data. The considerations include the scheduling method, the scheduling direction and several scheduling options, as described below.

Choosing a Scheduling Method There are two scheduling methods —termed operation scheduling and job scheduling—to choose from. The scheduling method is only relevant when using routing data, and the choice depends on how you assign resource requirements to an operation (described in Section 6.10). Job scheduling must be used when resource requirements are defined in terms of resource capabilities or employee competencies.

Scheduling Direction Both scheduling methods support different scheduling directions. The basic scheduling directions are forward and backward as of a given date, such as the requirement date. Figure 14.9 summarizes the variations in scheduling directions for both scheduling methods. Fewer options are available for rescheduling a planned order.

Scheduling Options Scheduling logic for individual orders can optionally include finite capacity and finite material, the use of properties (for block scheduling purposes), and reference orders. Another option can exclude selected time elements, such as queue and transit time, to calculate the fastest possible production throughput.

<table>
<tr><th colspan="3"></th><th colspan="3">Applicability</th></tr>
<tr><th colspan="2"></th><th>Other Parameter</th><th>Operations Scheduling</th><th>Job Scheduling</th><th>Reschedule Planned Order*</th></tr>
<tr><td rowspan="13">Variations in Scheduling Direction</td><td colspan="2">Forward from today</td><td rowspan="12">Yes</td><td rowspan="12">Yes</td><td rowspan="3">No</td></tr>
<tr><td colspan="2">Forward from tomorrow</td></tr>
<tr><td colspan="2">Forward from a planned start date</td></tr>
<tr><td>Forward from a specified schedule date</td><td rowspan="2">Specify a Schedule Date</td><td rowspan="2">Yes</td></tr>
<tr><td>Backward from a specified schedule date</td></tr>
<tr><td colspan="2">Backward from the delivery date</td><td>No</td></tr>
<tr><td colspan="2">Backward from the planned end date</td><td rowspan="3">Yes</td></tr>
<tr><td colspan="2">Backward from the calculated action date</td></tr>
<tr><td colspan="2">Backward from the calculated futures date</td></tr>
<tr><td colspan="2">Schedule according to last scheduling date</td><td rowspan="3">No</td></tr>
<tr><td>Forward from a specified job</td><td rowspan="2">Specify a Job Identifier</td></tr>
<tr><td>Backward from a specified job</td></tr>
<tr><td colspan="2">Forward from order date</td><td colspan="2">No</td><td>Yes</td></tr>
</table>

* = Planned orders are initially scheduled using backward scheduling from the requirement date.

Figure 14.9 Variations in Scheduling Direction

- *Finite Capacity.* When a bottleneck resource has finite capacity, the scheduling logic ensures the scheduled loads do not exceed the available capacity. The consideration of available capacity can be factored down by an operations schedule percentage assigned to the resource, so that the resource is not loaded to 100% of available capacity.
- *Finite Material.* Scheduling logic requires on-hand inventory on the start date of the production order or the relevant operation (if applicable). When there is insufficient inventory of the component item, the scheduling logic uses the item's lead time to determine when it will be available. The components' availability date determines when the order can be started.
- *Finite Property and Block Scheduling.* The finite property approach represents a form of block scheduling for grouping similar operations to minimize setup time, and performing them during a predefined block of time in the calendar assigned to a resource.

❖ *Reference Orders.* You can optionally schedule and synchronize reference orders related to the selected order, thereby synchronizing downstream (and upstream) orders via forward (and backward) scheduling.

14.11 Coordinate Production via Planned Orders

Planning calculations synchronize supplies to meet demands and provide several coordination tools. Chapter 11 previously explained planning calculations. The coordination tools consist of planned orders and suggested action messages, plus capacity analysis and production schedules when routing data has been defined. This section focuses on planned orders.

Suggestions for planned orders reflect the S&OP game plans and the planning data for manufactured items. These suggestions can be viewed on the Planned Orders form or the Planned Production Orders form.[8] You can create production orders from selected planned orders via a function termed firming planned orders. This function involves selecting and firming planned orders. It may also involve analyzing and editing planned orders, and time fence policies about automatic firming and a frozen period.

Selection of Planned Orders There are several methods to select planned orders for firming. For example, orders can be individually marked or block-marked. Planned orders can also be viewed and optionally selected based on attributes such as the buyer, order date, and a separate status for planned orders. You can assign this separate status to planned orders (unprocessed, processed and approved) to indicate those that have been analyzed, but this status only represents reference information. The form does not retain marked orders if you exit before firming.

Firming the Selected Planned Orders The firming function generates production orders for selected planned orders. The generated orders have an assigned order status based on an item-related policy (embedded in the coverage group assigned to the item). A status of scheduled is a typical

[8]You can view information for a selected set of master plan data or forecast plan data. For simplicity's sake the explanation focuses on the set of data representing the current master plan data.

policy. The system automatically deletes the suggestion for a planned order after execution of the firming function. It also creates a log for tracking which planned orders have been firmed and by whom.

The Planned Orders form provides one starting point for firming planned orders. The same form can also be accessed in the context of making sales order delivery promises by exploding the requirements for the end item.

Analyzing and Editing Planned Orders Planners often need to understand the rationale and impact for a planned order, and the Planned Orders form supports the following approaches.

- *Related action messages*. The form displays action messages related to a planned order, such as expediting the planned order or delaying delivery because of the projected completion date.
- *Understanding the sources of demand and supply*. The form displays single-level pegging information about the source of demand for a planned order. Additional inquiries display single-level pegging to all supplies and demands for an item (via a *Net Requirements* inquiry), and the multi-level pegging information about supplies and demands for a planned order (via an *Explosion* inquiry).

  The Explosion form provides additional functionality to calculate a projected delivery date (termed a futures date) for completing the planned order quantity. You can also take action to firm planned orders for all components in the multi-level product structure.
- *Understanding requirements for components*. The component requirements can be viewed along with action messages related to each component.
- *Understanding requirements for routing operations*. The routing operations can be viewed along with the scheduled start/end dates for each operation.

The analysis efforts often lead to needed action, and the following actions can be implemented on the Planned Orders form.

- Change quantity and/or delivery date for the planned order.
- Reschedule the planned order using a specified scheduling method and scheduling direction, with optional consideration of finite material and capacity.

- Split the planned order using a specified quantity and date.
- Group together several selected planned orders for the same item, with a total quantity for a single production order. The delivery date reflects the currently selected planned order.
- Change the planned production order to a planned purchase order or transfer order to indicate an alternate source of supply.

Automatic Firming and a Frozen Period The use of planned orders is affected by two item-specific time fence policies regarding near-term schedule stability and automatic firming of production orders. These time fence policies are embedded in the coverage group assigned to an item.

- *Freeze Time Fence.* The freeze time fence provides one approach to support near-term schedule stability, since planning calculations will place planned orders at the end of the frozen period.
- *Firm Time Fence.* The firm time fence enables the planning calculations to automatically firm production orders, thereby eliminating the effort to manually firm the planned orders. To be effective, the automatic firming time fence should be slightly greater than the item's production lead time and reorder cycle.

14.12 Coordinate Production via Action Messages

Planning calculations generate two types of action messages termed actions and futures, as previously explained in Chapter 10 (and Figure 10.3). These messages are summarized below.

- *Actions Message.* An actions message indicates a suggestion to advance/postpone an order's delivery date, to increase/decrease an order quantity, or to delete an order. Suggested advancement of an existing order reflects the item's rescheduling assumption, so that the system suggests expediting rather than a new planned order to cover a requirement.
- *Futures Message.* A futures message indicates that the projected completion date for supply chain activities (based on realistic scheduling assumptions) will cause a delay in meeting a requirement date such as a sales order shipment.

Dynamics AX displays actions and futures messages on two different forms termed the *Actions* form and *Futures* form. You cannot take action on these inquiry forms, but you can readily access the relevant master table for the referenced order to indicate the action.

14.13 Coordinate Production via Production Schedules

When using routing data, planning calculations can provide a capacity load analysis for resources and suggested production schedules. The visibility of these resource requirements is constrained by a capacity time fence expressed in days, which is normally defined as part of the policies assigned to a master plan. For example, the capacity time fence may reflect several months for long-term capacity analysis, or it may reflect a few weeks for near-term scheduling purposes.

Capacity Analysis Capacity analysis reflects a comparison between a resource's available capacity and the requirements stemming from production orders. You can optionally include or exclude requirements stemming from planned orders based on company-wide policies embedded in the production control parameters. The nature of capacity analysis depends on three major factors: the definition of an operation's resource requirements, consideration of finite capacity limits and the set of master plan data.

- *Definition of an operation's resource requirements.* The resource requirements for an operation can be defined in several ways, as previously described in Chapter 8. For example, they may be specified for a single resource, a resource group, or a resource capability.
- *Consideration of finite capacity.* A resource's available capacity can be viewed as infinite or finite. An infinite capacity viewpoint means that scheduling of each operation's duration considers the available working hours at a resource, but an unlimited number of orders can be scheduled concurrently. This means capacity analysis can identify overloaded periods.

  A finite capacity viewpoint typically means that only one order can be scheduled concurrently during working hours, and that scheduling logic considers existing loads. Scheduling logic only considers a finite capacity limit for resources centers designated as having finite capacity.

- *Set Master Plan data.* Capacity analysis can be viewed for a specified set of master plan data or forecast plan data. The current dynamic master plan acts as a default.

With these factors in mind, capacity analysis can be viewed for a resource (or a resource group) using a tabular or graphic format.

- *Tabular Format for Capacity Analysis.* The Capacity Load Inquiry provides a tabular format for load analysis of one resource or a resource group. It displays total load hours in daily increments and automatically highlights overloaded days. You can view detailed reference information about routing operations comprising a daily load. A separate form (termed Capacity Reservations) provides a tabular format about all routing operations for the resource.
- *Graphical Format for Capacity Analysis.* The Capacity Load Graphical Inquiry provides a setup dialogue that determines how to display the information. For example, the information can be displayed in hours or percentages, and in specified increments (such as daily, weekly or monthly) for a specified range of dates. These time increments represent the continuum of aggregate to detailed capacity analysis, and the percentage viewpoint can highlight overloaded periods.

  Additional variations include displaying loads for a range of resources, either as multiple graphics or as a single graphic with an accumulated load. Selected sources of loads can be excluded, such as loads stemming from planned orders. You cannot access detailed reference information about the operations comprising a resource load.

Production Schedules The nature of a production schedule depends on the three major factors mentioned above—the definition of an operation's resource requirements, the consideration of capacity limits, and the set of master plan data. A production schedule identifies each routing operation performed in the resource. It consists of the same detailed reference information as the load analysis drill-down, but is presented in a format more appropriate for communicating the needed action. In particular, it provides visibility of production orders at various order statuses so that production personnel can finish those already started as well as anticipate those that need to be started.

Production schedules can be displayed in different formats, such as tabular or Gantt chart. Each firm tends to customize their production schedule to fit their operations, but a typical tabular format can be described. A production schedule in tabular format identifies operations in a priority sequence with the hottest operations listed first. The simplest sequencing rule is based on operation start (or ending) date and time. Operation information includes the remaining units and time and also the units completed to-date. It may include other information that proves useful to the planner or production personnel, such as the prior and next operation, the expected operation scrap percentage, and the operation description. Much of the information may be identified by the shop paperwork for each order, thereby minimizing the need for including it in the production schedule. The Operations List Inquiry provides one example of a production schedule.

14.14 Costing for a Production Order

The estimated costs for a production order can be initially calculated by performing the *estimate order task*, where the calculated costs reflect the order quantity and the order-dependent BOM and routing. The estimate order task may be used to recalculate estimated costs after changes, such as changes to components or operations, or changes to the active cost records for items, labor rates, or overhead formulas.

The actual costs (termed realized costs) for a production order are automatically calculated based on reported production activities, such as actual material usage and operation times. You can view detailed transactions about reported activities on the Production Posting inquiry for a production order. Several reports summarize reported activities for all current orders, including the raw materials in process report, the work in process report (for routing transactions), and the indirect costs in process report (for overheads incurred).

You can analyze estimated and actual costs using the price calculation inquiry for the order. Cost information is shown for each component, operation, and applicable overhead formula.

Updating an Item's Actual Cost With an actual cost item, it's actual cost will be updated based on a production order that has been ended.

Calculated Variances for a Standard Cost Item Variances are calculated after ending a production order for a standard cost item. The variances reflect a comparison between the reported production activities and the item's standard cost calculation (not to the order's estimated costs).[9] Four types of variances are calculated: lot size variance, production quantity variance, production price variance, and production substitution variance. Figure 14.10 identifies these four variances that account for the difference between an order's actual costs and the item's standard cost. Similar variances are also calculated for co/by-products.

The common sources of order variances are shown in the bottom half of Figure 14.10, such as a different quantity issued or received.

You can analyze order variances using the Production Variances inquiry or report. You can use the report options to view detailed variances by item, resource or cost group, or to view summarized variances. The cost break-

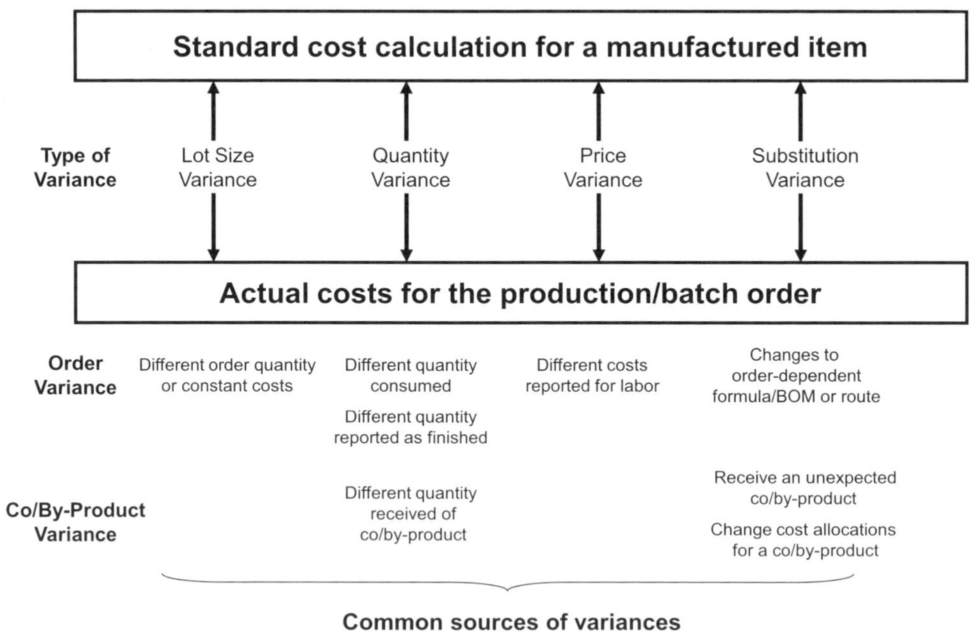

Figure 14.10 Order Variances for Production

[9]The calculated standard cost for a manufactured item reflects the specified BOM version, route version, quantity, calculation date, and active cost records as of the calculation date. Calculation of a manufactured item's cost was previously explained in Chapter 8 (Section 8.7).

down policy within the inventory parameters determines whether variances will be tracked by cost group. The Standard Cost Transactions inquiry provides another approach to analyzing order variances. For example, you can identify the variances associated with every production order for an item. In order to anticipate variances prior to ending a production order, you can analyze the detailed information provided on the Cost Estimates and Costing report.

Use the Variance Analysis Statement report to view production variances (and purchase price variances) during a specified time period, such as the current period or current year. You can use the report options to view variances by item, production order or cost group, with a summary or detailed breakdown of variances.

Additional Case Studies

Case 79: Production Reporting via Wireless Devices The production workers at a discrete manufacturer employed wireless devices to report actual production of networking technology equipment. When using the device, the five basic menu options included (1) Start Production, (2) Report Material Usage, (3) Report Hours Worked, (4) Report Finished Quantity and (5) End Production. For example, the material usage option enabled workers to identify the component serial numbers and report scrap. The finished quantity option also enabled workers to report the serial numbers of completed items, and the actual put-away locations. The ability to scan bar codes increased data accuracy, and the immediate updates improved inventory visibility and serial traceability.

Case 80: Advanced Planning and Scheduling (APS) Integration A fabricated products company required APS capabilities to minimize setups and avoid additional equipment purchases for its line of extruded plastic products. Multiple extrusion machines produced plastic pipes of varying diameters and colors. Scheduling considerations included sequence-dependent setup time (based on pipe diameter and color), and machine capabilities for handling different products. Scheduling considerations also included machine-specific run rates, and secondary resources for tooling and skilled operators. To integrate an APS application, additional attributes were required for resources (e.g., machine capabilities), routing operations (e.g., setup attributes) and calendars (e.g. available crew size by shift).[10]

Executive Summary

Production represents the distinctive competency of many manufacturers. Production activities can be coordinated and reported using production orders, and the significance of a single order affects these activities. Several considerations apply to production orders, such as the order status within the order life cycle, the order-dependent BOM and routing, and the production order lead time. Production activities can be reported against started orders, such as picking material, reporting operation time, and receiving parent items and co/by-products. Coordination of production activities is based on suggestions for planned orders, action messages and production schedules by resources. The case studies highlighted variations in manufacturing environments, such as using a graphical planning board and a manufacturing execution system.

[10]See **www.Preactor.com** for additional information about their Advanced Scheduler module, and see **www.DemandSolutions.com** for further information about their Advanced Planning & Scheduling module.

Chapter 15

Transitioning from Traditional to Lean Manufacturing

The primary focus so far has been on using AX 2012 for supply chain management in traditional manufacturing environments. AX 2012 also supports lean manufacturing approaches within a single system. However, the lean approaches involve a significant reconceptualization about new constructs such as production flows and kanban orders, and there are just as many variations of lean environments as traditional environments. Therefore it is difficult to explain how AX handles these new constructs and variations in just a few pages. By way of example, my previous books about AX 2009 required approximately 400 pages for explaining traditional approaches and 200 pages for explaining the lean approaches. Book length considerations mandate a separate book for comprehensive explanations of AX 2012 functionality for lean manufacturing.[1]

This chapter summarizes the lean manufacturing capabilities within AX 2012. It explains and illustrates the new constructs—such as kanban orders, production flows and coordination via kanban schedule boards – and the S&OP approaches for lean scenarios. It also highlights the many impacts on the conceptual models for traditional manufacturing. This reconceptualization can guide you through the early maturity stages of lean manufacturing. The chapter starts with common scenarios in lean manufacturing and includes the following sections:

[1]The separate book covering *Lean Manufacturing Using Microsoft Dynamics AX 2012* was not yet completed at the time of publication for this book. The lean manufacturing functionality within AX 2012 represents a significant change from the functionality within AX 2009, which was previously described in the book *Lean Manufacturing Using Microsoft Dynamics AX 2009*.

1. Common Scenarios for Lean Manufacturing
2. Typical Business Process for a Manufacturing Kanban
3. Coordination Tools for Kanban Orders
4. Some Key Aspects of the Lean Manufacturing Approach
5. S&OP Approaches for Lean Scenarios
6. Impacts on the Conceptual Models for Traditional Manufacturing
7. Maturity Stages in Lean Manufacturing

15.1 Common Scenarios for Lean Manufacturing

Several common scenarios represent a large proportion of lean manufacturing environments, such as the scenarios for make-to-stock and make-to-order products. This section summarizes some of the most common scenarios.

Make-to-Stock Products with a Small Finished Goods Inventory This scenario reflects the classic Toyota system approach with a short order-to-ship lead time and a short manufacturing cycle (ranging from hours to 1 or 2 days). Finished goods inventory can be stocked in a shipping area or at the final work cell, where the inventory levels typically reflect a day of supply (depending on the volatility of demand). When stocked at the final work cell, transfer kanbans (for the sales order quantity) can be used to move inventory to the shipping area. One benefit of locating the finished goods inventory at the final work cell is that production personnel can easily see their inventory position and act accordingly.

Make-To-Order Products with No Finished Goods Inventory This scenario reflects the Dell Computer approach where sales order visibility exceeds the manufacturing cycle. The customer provides forward visibility by placing sales orders with future delivery dates or by accepting a promised sales order delivery date in the future. The kanban orders typically reflect the precise quantity and mix of products specified in the sales orders. As an alternative, the sales quantity can be satisfied by multiple kanbans reflecting the item's normal handling unit.

Make-to-Order Products Built from Stocked Components Many make-to-order products are built from stocked components, where the stocked components may be purchased or manufactured. The stocked components are typically placed in a stockroom (or kept at the producing work cell) based on fixed kanbans, and then pulled to the relevant work cell based on sales order demands. This approach employs event withdrawal kanbans to move a stocked component to its point of use.

MTO and MTS Products at a Final Assembly Work Cell This scenario involves a final assembly work cell that produces both make-to-order and make-to-stock items. The sales event kanbans for MTO products have a higher priority than the fixed kanbans for the MTS products. The sales event kanbans are typically planned automatically for the first available time periods, whereas the fixed kanbans are manually planned to take advantage of unused capacity. Case 82 illustrates this common scenario.

Partial Implementation of Kanban Orders Within the Product Structure (aka Mixed Mode Manufacturing) This scenario is often characteristic of the early stages of maturity in lean manufacturing, as described in a subsequent section (Section 15.7). The scenario has two major variations. The first variation reflects kanban orders for the top of the product structure (such as a final assembly work cell for finished goods), with production of lower level components coordinated by production orders. The second variation is just the reverse, with kanban orders coordinating production of lower level components. Other variations include the use of kanban orders for all items within one entire product structure, and production orders for another product structure. These scenarios are often termed mixed-mode manufacturing.

Case 81: Kanban Orders for Printed Circuit Boards in a CTO Product

A manufacturer of electronic control units produced configure-to-order products consisting of several printed circuit board (PCB) assemblies placed in a frame and enclosure. Each sales order defined a configuration of different PCB assemblies. Many of the PCB assemblies had high-volume demand and some had infrequent demand. The typical product structure and routing for one of their CTO products were described in a previous case study (Case 9).

The company was transitioning from traditional to lean manufacturing. This involved definition of a production flow and its activities, as illustrated in the top half of Figure 15.1. As a prerequisite step, they defined the work

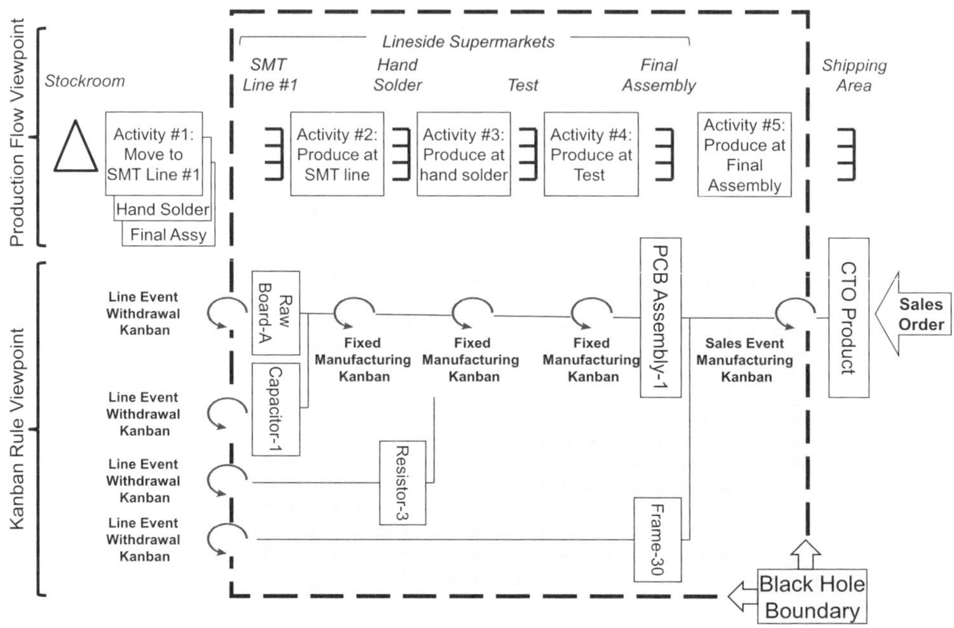

Figure 15.1 Kanban Orders for Printed Circuit Boards in a CTO Product

cells and the warehouse/bin information for their lineside supermarkets. The production flow identified one process activity for the final assembly work cell, and three process activities (and their associated work cells) for producing PCB assemblies. The production flow also identified the transfer activities for moving material from the stockroom to the various lineside supermarkets.

The production flow information provided the foundation for defining kanban rules for items within the product structure. As shown in the bottom half of Figure 15.1, the kanban rules included (1) a sales event manufacturing kanban for the CTO Product, (2) fixed manufacturing kanbans for each step in producing the high-volume PCB Assembly-1, and (3) line event withdrawal kanbans for moving components to lineside supermarkets. These withdrawal kanbans are triggered by the manufacturing kanbans.

The figure also illustrates the concept of a black hole boundary, also known as the costing boundary. Kanban orders simply coordinate production (with no impact on inventory) within the boundary, and inventory gets updated as kanban orders cross the boundary. For example, issuing components across the boundary will update the equivalent value in the WIP account for the production flow, and receiving a finished item will deduct the item's standard cost from the WIP account. This approach provides the foundation for production flow costing, as further explained in a subsequent section (Section 15.4).

15.2 Typical Business Process for a Manufacturing Kanban

One type of kanban order consists of a manufacturing kanban trigged by a sales order line item. Coordination of these manufacturing kanbans involves two graphical planning tools termed the Kanban Schedule Board and the Kanban Board for Process Jobs. These coordination tools are used in the typical business process for manufacturing kanbans, as illustrated in Figure 15.2 and summarized below.

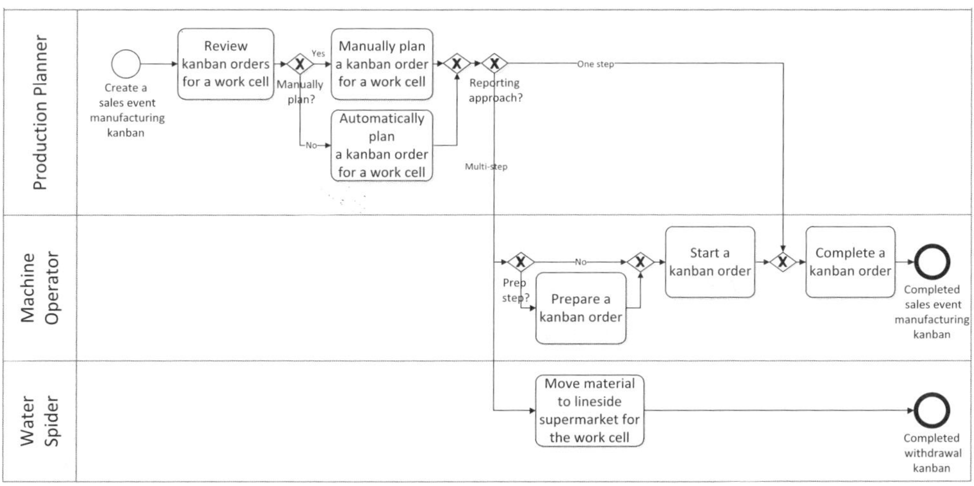

Figure 15.2 Typical Business Process for a Sales Event Manufacturing Kanban

The production planner uses the Kanban Schedule Board to review and plan the kanban orders for a selected work cell. The manufacturing kanbans reflect automatically created sales event kanbans in this specific example, but they may stem from other replenishment strategies such as fixed kanbans. The planner can review load versus capacity for each daily period, and manually load an unplanned kanban in a period with available capacity. This changes the kanban job status from unplanned to planned. Alternatively, a manufacturing kanban can be automatically planned based on a policy within the item's kanban rule.

The machine operator uses the Kanban Board for Process Jobs to review the kanban orders for a selected work cell, and report actual production for selected kanban orders. The reporting approach may involve a single step indicating completion of the kanban order, or multiple steps indicating when it has been prepared, started and then completed. For example, the prepare step typically represents preparation of the work cell and component materials, where component materials may need to be moved to the lineside supermarket for the work cell. These movements are typically coordinated through withdrawal kanbans which can be reported on the same form. The start step can trigger forward flushing of material, and the complete step can trigger backflushing of materials (based on the components' flushing principle).

The water spider uses the Kanban Transfer Board to coordinate and report withdrawal kanbans, such as withdrawals to replenish lineside supermarkets for a work cell. A withdrawal kanban can be reported with a single "Complete" step, or with two steps to "Start" and then "Complete" the transfer.

15.3 Coordination Tools for Kanban Orders

The coordination tools for kanban orders are distinctly different than those for production orders. Coordination tools for production orders were described in the previous chapter, including planned orders, action messages and production schedules by resource. The differences reflect the different types of kanban orders, and the unique life cycles for each type of kanban replenishment strategy. The differences also reflect a graphical orientation for coordination of kanban orders. This section illustrates the primary coordination tools for kanban orders.

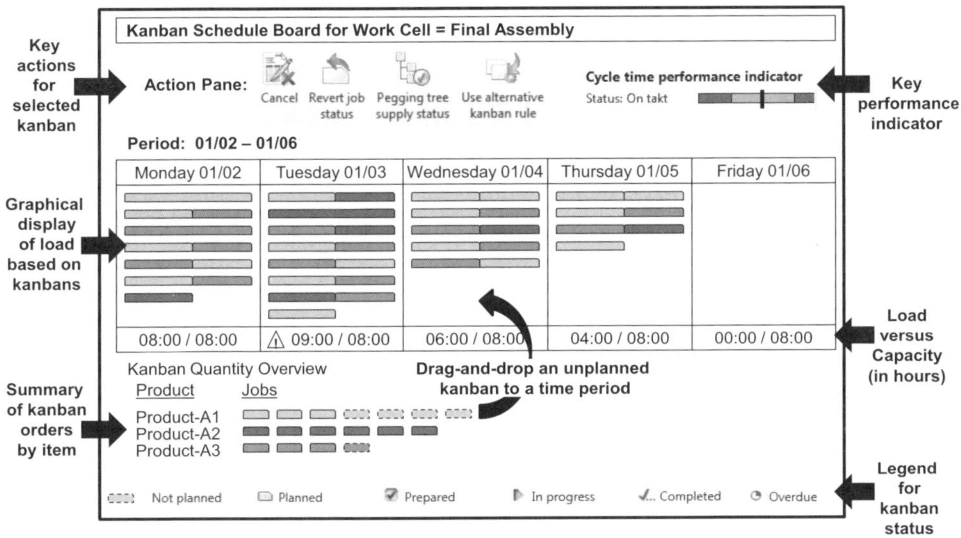

Figure 15.3 Example of the Kanban Schedule Board

Kanban Schedule Board Use of the Kanban Schedule Board supports several steps in the typical business process for a manufacturing kanban, as described in the previous section. The key aspects of the Kanban Schedule Board are illustrated in Figure 15.3 and described below.

A production planner uses the Kanban Schedule Board for a selected work cell in order to review and plan load versus capacity for each daily period. The comparison of load versus capacity will be expressed in equivalent units or in hours (as shown in the figure) depending on whether the production flow model expresses capacity in throughput units or hours. The load reflects kanban orders assigned to a daily period, and the form provides a graphical display of these kanban orders. A cycle time performance indicator displays whether work needs to speed up or slow down at the work cell.

For an unplanned kanban order, the production planner can manually assign the load by dragging and dropping it to a daily period, which also changes its status to planned. Alternatively, the kanban order can be automatically planned based on a policy within the item's kanban rule. A related policy (for the production flow) determines whether it is automatically assigned to the requested date, or distributed across several dates (or even postponed) to reflect constraints in available capacity.

Other possible actions for the production planner include cancelling a kanban order, reverting the status of a kanban order in order to manually re-plan it, assigning the kanban order to a different work cell (by selecting an alternate kanban rule), and viewing the pegging tree supply status of all related kanban orders.

Kanban Board for Process Jobs The key aspects of the Kanban Board for Process Jobs are illustrated in Figure 15.4 and described below. This form is normally used by the machine operator to review the planned kanban orders for a work cell, and report actual production for selected kanban orders. A cycle time performance indicator displays whether work needs to speed up or slow down at the work cell.

As mentioned in the typical business process, the reporting approach may involve a single step indicating completion of the kanban order, or multiple steps indicating when it has been prepared, started and then completed. The form displays these key actions on separate tabs for "Pick" and "Manufacture," and the figure illustrates the Start and Complete actions on the "Manufacture" tab.

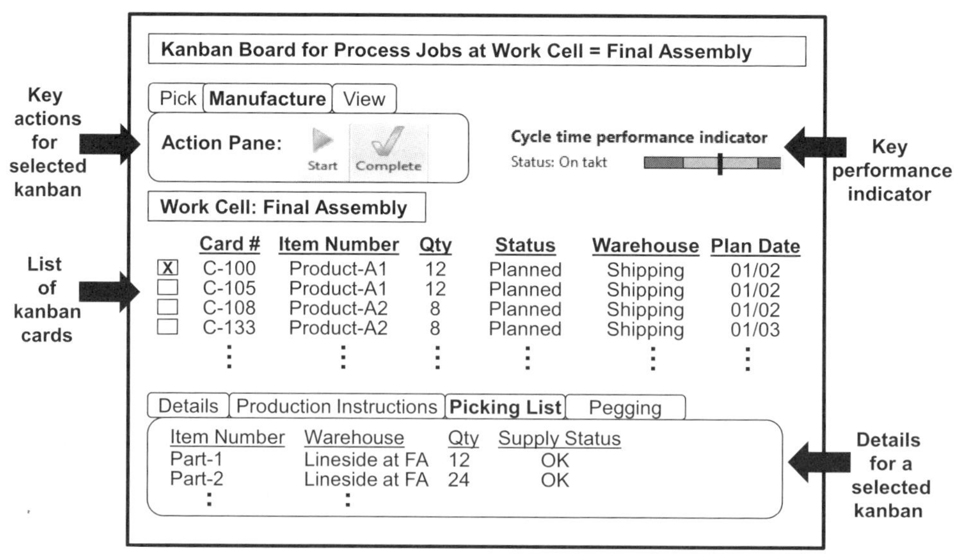

Figure 15.4 Example of the Kanban Board for Process Jobs

The bottom half of the form provides an additional set of tabs that provide details for a selected kanban. The figure displays the details related to the "Picking List" tab, which identifies the required components and their supply status. The component materials may need to be moved to the lineside supermarket for the work cell. These movements are typically coordinated through withdrawal kanbans, and the withdrawal kanbans can be reported on the same form. They can also be reported on the Kanban Transfer Board, as described on the next subsection.

Kanban Transfer Board The information displayed on the Kanban Transfer Board identifies withdrawal kanbans that reflect the desired filtering option, such as the from or to location or a selected production flow. A water spider typically uses the Kanban Transfer Board to coordinate and report withdrawal kanbans to transfer material, such as replenishing lineside supermarkets for a work cell, or transferring material from a work cell to a shipping area for fulfill sales order demand. A withdrawal kanban can be reported with a single "Complete" step, or with two steps to "Start" and then "Complete" the transfer.

15.4 Some Key Aspects of the Lean Manufacturing Approach

The lean manufacturing approach involves a significant reconceptualization for the coordination of production activities and the related setup information. Book length considerations preclude a complete explanation of these topics. This section highlights some of the key aspects of the lean manufacturing approach. These key aspects include the basis for work cell capacity and requirements, the definition of work cells, the definition of a production flow and its activities, the definition of kanban rules for items, and the related concepts of a black hole boundary and production flow costing.

Model of Work Cell Capacity and Requirements: Hours Versus Thoughput Units The model of work cell capacity and requirements represents a key policy for a production flow. The model can be based on two different approaches termed the hours approach and the throughput units approach. Only one approach can be assigned to a production flow and its related work cells.

- *Hours Approach.* The hours of operation represent one approach to modeling work cell capacity.[2] The requirements for producing an item at the work cell are also expressed in hours. Each item can require a different number of hours, such as one item requiring twice the time as another item. The "hours" approach is conceptually familiar to most people, since it has been traditionally used in routing operations. The time requirements provide the basis for costing using the hourly costs for the work cell.
- *Throughput Units Approach.* An alternative approach employs throughout units (rather than hours) as the basis for work cell capacity and requirements. The work cell's capacity is defined in terms of the average throughput quantity (and related UM) for a standard workday.[3] Changes in the average throughput quantity can be modeled by assigning a different quantity and its validity date.

  A throughput ratio defines the requirements for producing an item at the work cell. A ratio of 1 indicates a standard part. A ratio greater than 1 indicates the part consumes more time, and a ratio less than 1 indicates consumption of less time. The "throughout units approach" reflects the fundamental concept of a drumbeat. However, you still specify time requirements for a process activity, since they provide the basis for costing using hourly costs for the work cell.

The choice between the hours versus throughout units approach is labeled the *throughput model* policy within a production flow model.

Work Cells A resource group must be defined for each work cell, and explicitly designated as a work cell. There are several impacts of this work cell designation, since it introduces some new information and eliminates some previous capabilities for a resource group. Some capabilities stay the same.

- *New information.* Each work cell requires additional information about the defaults for its input and output warehouse/bin locations. In addition,

[2]The hours of operation are defined by the calendar assigned to the work cell.

[3]The duration of a standard workday is defined as part of the calendar assigned to the work cell, and the same duration applies to any working day in the calendar (whether it consists of 1 minute or 24 hours). Hence, this approach provides an approximation of thoughput capacity. Changes in the duration of a standard workday can be modeled by assigning different calendars and their validity dates to a work cell.

the relevant production flow model(s) must be assigned to the resource group, where a throughput approach requires additional information about the average throughput quantity for a standard workday.

- *Eliminate some capabilities*. The policies concerning master scheduling logic no longer apply (such as the policies for scheduling and capacity), and planning calculations no longer calculate the capacity requirements for the resource group. The concept of resources within a resource group no longer applies.[4]
- *Same capabilities*. These include the hourly rates (defined by the assigned cost categories) and financial dimensions for a resource group.

Production Flow and its Activities A production flow defines the flow of material through work cells and locations for a specific scenario. The flow consists of a sequence of process activities (at work cells) and transfer activities.[5] All kanban rules for items are directly connected to this predefined structure of a production flow.

A production flow replaces the use of routing information. In addition, the calculation of value-added costs for a manufactured item is now based on its related production flow rather than its route version.

An activity within a production flow can represent production (or transfer) of items at different levels in a bill of material. It can also represent different steps in the production process of an item, which are commonly termed semi-finished items. For example, the process activity representing the first step in an item's production process will "receive" the semi-finished item, and the second step will "pickup" the semi-finished item. This approach avoids the need for multiple BOM levels for supporting an item's kanban orders.

A simple scenario for a production flow consists of a linear sequence of activities. More complex scenarios may involve optional activities, alternate activities (such as an alternate work cell) and parallel activities (including those related to production of co/by-products). Multiple production flows can also be linked together, such as a production flow representing a feeder line that is linked to other production flows.

---

[4]The concept of resources within a resource group still applies in just one scenario—for subcontracted production using kanban orders—because the resources can identify the different vendors performing the subcontracted service.

[5]The activities for a production flow are not the same thing as the activities defining a work breakdown structure for a project (described in Section 20.2).

Kanban Rules and Types of Kanbans The kanban rules for items are directly connected to the predefined structure of a production flow. The definition of kanban rules requires an understanding of the different types of kanbans and their replenishment strategy. Within current AX, the two types of kanbans consist of a manufacturing kanban and a withdrawal kanban.[6] A manufacturing kanban is assigned to a process activity (and its associated work cell) within a production flow, whereas a withdrawal kanban is assigned to a transfer activity (along with the from- and to-locations). Several replenishment strategies apply to these two basic types of kanbans, as summarized in Figure 15.5 and described below. The primary replenishment strategies (summarized in the top half of the figure) include a fixed kanban for stocked items, and event kanbans that are only created by a related demand.

	Replenishment Strategy	Kanban Type		Special Cases of Replenishment Strategy
		Manufacturing	Withdrawal	
Primary Strategies	Fixed Kanban	Yes	Yes	Single Use Fixed Kanban Stock Replenishment Event Kanban
Primary Strategies	Sales Event Kanban	Yes	Yes	Large sales order triggers sales event kanban (for an item with fixed kanbans)
Primary Strategies	Line Event Kanban	Yes	Yes	Withdrawal kanban from a remote site
Other	BOM Line Event Kanban	Yes	Yes	Comment: Create a kanban order for production order components that are sourced from a production flow
Other	Scheduled Kanban	Yes	No	Comment: Planning calculations generate a planned kanban order (rather than a planned production order), and firming the order creates a "scheduled kanban"

Figure 15.5 Summary of Kanban Types and Replenishment Strategies

[6] A purchasing kanban represents a third type of kanban. It is not currently supported in standard AX 2012 functionality, but can be implemented using an add-on module as described in Case 86.

- *Fixed Kanban.* A fixed kanban applies to both types of kanbans and typically employs circulating cards, where the printed card physically circles between the item origin and the point of consumption. Its handling unit (aka container size) determines the fixed quantity, and the suggested number of circulating cards can be calculated. Both of these quantities are defined as part of the kanban rule. An emptied kanban serves as the trigger for replenishment.

  A single use fixed kanban represents a special case for a replenishment strategy. It is typically used to cover exceptional demand situations for an item, and an emptied kanban does not trigger replenishment

  Another special case involves a stock replenishment event kanban in a quick turning environment, with automatic creation of the kanban when the item's inventory falls below a specified minimum quantity. This approach provides an immediate reaction to depletion of safety stock in comparison to recalculating and increasing the number of kanbans in slower turning environments.
- *Sales Event Kanban.* A sales order line item can trigger automatic creation of a manufacturing kanban (to produce or package the item), or a withdrawal kanban (to move the item to a shipping area).

  As a special case, a large sales order quantity for a manufactured item with a fixed kanban rule can also trigger a sales event kanban. A typical example involves fixed kanbans for defining the item's buffer inventory in a finished goods warehouse, so that an exceptionally large sales order quantity would deplete the entire buffer. This special case requires an additional kanban rule for the item, where the kanban rule defines use of a sales event kanban when the order quantity exceeds a specified minimum.
- *Line Event Kanban.* A kanban line event applies to a component, and gets triggered by a manufacturing kanban for its parent item. It pulls the required component to a downstream manufacturing process much like a picking list. The line event kanban applies to both types of kanbans. For example, it can trigger a withdrawal kanban to move the item from the stockroom to a lineside supermarket, or it can trigger a manufacturing kanban to produce the item and place it in the designated location.

  A special case for using a line event withdrawal kanban involves sourcing the material from a physically remote site. In this case, the withdrawal kanban is "started" when shipped from the remote site, and then "completed" when received and correctly put away. An additional policy for the withdrawal activity (defined within the production flow) indicates whether it is freighted by the shipping or receiving site, or by a carrier.

Several other replenishment strategies are summarized in the bottom half of the figure. They are typically used in the early maturity stages of lean manufacturing or in mixed-mode environments.

- *Production BOM Line Event.* This replenishment strategy only applies to mixed-mode environments using a combination of production orders for parent items and kanban orders for components. A production order can trigger creation of kanban orders for its components supplied by a production flow. The actual trigger occurs when updating the production order to an estimated status or a higher status. The kanban rule for these production order components is termed a Production BOM Line Event, or BOM Line Event for short. The kanban rule can apply to manufacturing or withdrawal kanbans. For example, the withdrawal kanbans for components can simply represent the picking list for a production order, such as moving material from the stockroom to a lineside supermarket.
- *Scheduled Kanban.* This replenishment strategy typically applies to early maturity stages of lean manufacturing, where you simply replace planned production orders with planned manufacturing kanbans. More specifically, you define the item's planned order type as kanban order (rather than production order) so that planning calculations will generate planned kanban orders. Other aspects of the item's coverage planning data still apply, such as replenishment based on period lot size or min-max logic. These planned kanban orders can be automatically firmed (based on the firming time fence) or manually firmed, where firming results in creation of a *scheduled kanban*. The manual firming approach typically starts from the Supply Schedule form because the information is not displayed on the planned order forms. After firming, the scheduled kanban appears on the Kanban Schedule Board just like other manufacturing kanbans.

The terminology for different types of kanban orders and their replenishment strategies has been shortened for explanatory purposes. For example, the terminology for "a manufacturing kanban with an event-based replenishment strategy triggered by a sales event" has been shortened to a "sales event manufacturing kanban."

Manual Versus Automatic Planning for a Manufacturing Kanban The Kanban Schedule Board displays manufacturing kanbans for a selected work cell, and enables the production planner to manually "load" or "plan" an unplanned kanban in a daily period. As an alternative, the kanban rule for a manufacturing kanban can specify automatic planning, so it is automatically "loaded" in the first available daily period. It can also be automatically distributed over several daily periods based on capacity availability.

Production Flow Costing and the Black Hole Boundary The concept of a black hole boundary (aka costing boundary) provides the foundation for production flow costing. Kanban orders simply coordinate production (with no impact on inventory) within the boundary, and inventory gets updated as kanban orders cross the boundary. For example, issuing components across the boundary will update the equivalent value in the WIP account for the production flow, and receiving a finished item will deduct the item's standard cost from the WIP account.

The actual boundary is defined within each activity of a production flow. With a transfer activity, you indicate whether a withdrawal kanban will update inventory upon pick or receipt. With a process activity, you indicate whether completion of a manufacturing kanban will update inventory.

Production flow costing involves an end-of-period calculation (termed a backflush costing calculation) for valuing the work in process within the black hole boundary. It accounts for the in-process and unused quantities that are still within the black hole boundary at the end of the period, and calculates production variances to standard cost.

15.5 S&OP Approaches for Lean Scenarios

This section summarizes several common S&OP approaches to lean manufacturing, and explains the use of planning calculations to support these approaches. The common S&OP approaches build on the primary replenishment strategies for manufacturing kanbans that were described in the previous section.

Common S&OP Approaches for Lean Scenarios The nature of the S&OP approach depends on the lean manufacturing scenario. The common S&OP approaches consist of fixed kanbans for stocked items and event kanbans for MTO/CTO items, as illustrated in Figure 15.6 and described below.

	Scenario	S&OP Approach	Comments	Basis of Delivery Promises
No Link	Stocked Item	Fixed Kanbans	Calculate suggested number of fixed kanbans based on demand plan Large sales order quantity can generate a sales event kanban	CTP
Link to Order	MTO/CTO End-Item	Sales Event Kanban	Automatic creation of the sales event kanban for a sales order line	
	MTO/CTO Component	Line Event Kanban	Automatic creation of the line event kanban	

Figure 15.6 Common S&OP Approaches for Lean Scenarios

- *S&OP approach with fixed kanbans.* The suggested number of fixed kanbans for a stocked item can be calculated based on the demand plan. The demand plan typically reflects a demand forecast within AX. Other approaches for the demand plan include the combination of sales orders and demand forecast, and the supply forecasts for stocked components. Further explanation focuses on use of a demand forecast, and the next subsection describes the kanban quantity calculations and the associated calculation policies.

  As noted in the comments section of Figure 15.6, the use of fixed kanbans for a salable end-item may not apply in a scenario with large sales order quantities, since the demand would deplete the buffer inventory. You can define an additional kanban rule so that a large sales order quantity for the item (greater than a specified minimum quantity) will generate a sales event manufacturing kanban.
- *S&OP approach with sales event kanbans for an MTO/CTO end-item.* A sales order line results in the automatic creation of a sales event kanban for the end-item, either as a single kanban order (reflecting the sales quantity) or multiple kanban orders (reflecting the handling unit quantity).
- *S&OP approach with line event kanbans for MTO/CTO components.* The creation of a sales event manufacturing kanban can automatically trigger the creation of line event kanbans for MTO/CTO components.

Periodic Calculation for the Suggested Number of Fixed Kanbans The suggested number of fixed kanbans for an item can be periodically calculated using the Kanban Quantity Calculation task, which employs the set of calculation policies assigned to the item's kanban rule. In summary, the suggested number of fixed kanbans equals the average daily demand multiplied by the lead time (in days), and divided by the product quantity per handling unit. The calculation policies indicate the applicable demand plan (such as a specified set of forecast plan data) and the applicable time window for considering demand. The time window may include historical demands or future demands or both. It can be expressed as specified dates, or as the number of days before and after the current date.

In order to anticipate demand variations via an inventory plan, you can optionally include safety stock requirements with the demand plan, or specify a multiplier (termed the safety factor) to inflate the demand plan considered by the Kanban Quantity Calculation task.

Typical Business Process to Run Planning Calculations and Analyze Results for Lean Scenarios The typical business process shown in Figure 15.7 illustrates use of the forecast scheduling task and the kanban quantity calculation task to suggest the number of fixed kanbans for an item. It also illustrates two other aspects of planning calculations for lean scenarios, as highlighted with shaded boxes. First, planned purchase orders may be used for coordination purposes when not using purchasing kanbans. Second, planned kanban orders may be used as the basis for creating scheduled kanbans, typically in the context of a transition period in coordinating production via kanban orders. A similar diagram illustrated the typical business process for planning calculations in traditional manufacturing scenarios (Section 11.7).

Assign Delivery Promises to a Sales Order Realistic promise dates for sales order shipments and deliveries can help improve customer satisfaction and supply chain coordination, as explained in a previous chapter on S&OP (Section 11.6). In a lean scenario, you normally assign a delivery date control policy of CTP to salable end-items. An additional policy applies to MTO end-items with a kanban rule for sales event kanbans, so that CTP logic applies to the automatically created sales event kanban.

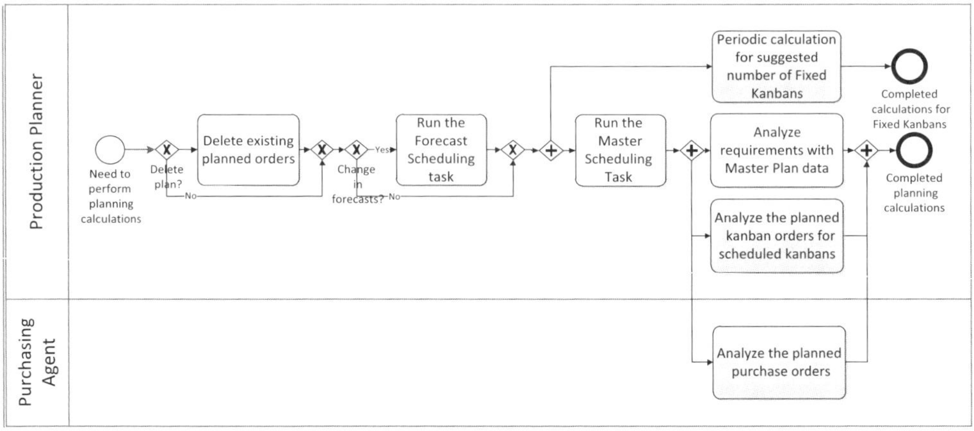

Figure 15.7 Typical Business Process to Run Planning Calculations and Analyze Results for Lean Scenarios

15.6 Impacts on the Conceptual Models for Traditional Manufacturing

The lean manufacturing capabilities involve several significant changes to the conceptual models for traditional manufacturing. For example, the use of a production flow and its activities replace the use of routings and routing operations. The impacts of lean manufacturing on the conceptual models for traditional manufacturing are summarized below. The traditional approaches still apply in a mixed mode scenario.

Impacts on Resources and Routings With lean manufacturing, the constructs for resources, routings and routing operations are replaced by the constructs for work cells, production flows and activities. While you still employ a resource group to identify a work cell, almost all other functionality does not apply. For example, the functionality associated with resource capabilities and employee competencies does not apply, nor do you use master operations, master routings and route versions.

Impacts on BOM Information Lean manufacturing has several impacts on BOM information. First, the significance of a operation sequence number for a BOM line no longer applies because routings have been eliminated.

Second, the options concerning the warehouse source of a component have changed slightly; these options were previously summarized in Figure 4.2. One option employs the resource consumption policy (and a blank value for the warehouse) on a BOM line, so that the source will reflect the work cell for the process activity. This is, the source reflects the default values of the input warehouse/bin location for the work cell. The second option employs the specified warehouse on a BOM line, and the bin location will be inherited from the item's default issue location (if it exists) or from the process activity and its default settings for picking.

Third, a make-to-order component should no longer be identified by its BOM line type (of pegged supply), since this approach has been replaced by the component's kanban rule for a line event kanban.

Finally, the flushing principles of Start and Finish still apply when not using a black hole boundary. For example, the flushing principle determines whether starting a manufacturing kanban will trigger forward flushing of components, and whether completing a manufacturing kanban will trigger back flushing of components.

Impacts on Product Costing The use of kanban orders requires a standard costing approach for all related items. The standard cost calculations for a manufactured item are based on its BOM version and the relevant production flow (rather than a route version), where the relevant production flow is determined by the kanban rule assigned to the item. The kanban rule identifies the relevant process activity within the production flow, and this activity defines the hourly rates and time requirements for the work cell.

Impacts on Serial and Batch Tracking The tracking of an item's serial number or batch number (or both) is restricted to kanban jobs that update inventory. They cannot be tracked inside the black box boundary because inventory transactions no longer apply.

Impacts on Coverage Planning Data for Manufactured Items In most lean scenarios, the coverage planning data for a manufactured item no longer applies because the replenishment logic has been replaced by a manufacturing kanban rule. In addition, withdrawal kanbans have replaced the concept of picking material from a stockroom or using transfer journals to move the material.

Some scenarios still employ the coverage planning data for a manufactured item, as described below

- *Fixed kanbans for stocked items.* The suggested number of fixed manufacturing kanbans can be calculated based on planned orders which reflect the production lead times and order quantity modifiers.
- *Planned kanban orders for scheduled kanbans.* Scheduled kanbans can be created from the planned kanban orders for a manufactured item with a planned order type of kanban (rather than production). The planned kanban orders reflect the item's production lead time and order quantity modifiers.

Impacts on Coverage Planning Data for Purchased Items The coverage planning data for purchased items still applies because current AX capabilities do not support purchasing kanbans. The due dates of planned purchase orders for components will reflect the production lead times for their parent items. Purchasing kanbans can be employed by using an add-on module, as described in Case 86.

Impacts on S&OP Approaches The S&OP approaches for lean scenarios include fixed kanbans for stocked items and sales event kanbans for make-to-order items, as described in a separate section (Section 15.5). The capacity requirements for a work cell are not calculated by planning calculations because routing information does not apply to work cells.

Impacts on Production Some scenarios will employ planned kanban orders that get generated by planning calculations just like planned production orders, where firming a planned kanban order creates a scheduled kanban. The scheduled kanban can then be coordinated via the kanban boards described in a previous section (Section 15.3). In addition, mixed mode environments will still employ production orders.

Impacts on Subcontracted Production The approach to subcontracted production (described in Chapter 16) has been replaced by activities within a production flow. For example, transfer activities can be used to move supplied components to a subcontractor (and also move finished items), and a process activity specifies the work cell representing the subcontractor. The lean manufacturing approach provides inventory visibility for supplied components and the finished item.

Impacts on Quality Management Quality orders and quarantine orders do not apply in a lean manufacturing approach.

Impacts on Projects A project-specific item requirement—which consists of a sales order with an order type of item requirements—can serve as the trigger for creating a sales event manufacturing kanban. In addition, the demands stemming from projects (and service orders) can be included in the kanban quantity calculations for fixed kanbans.

15.7 Maturity Stages in Lean Manufacturing

Most companies begin their lean journey with a pilot project approach, which represents the first of three maturity stages in lean manufacturing.[7] The pilot project focuses on shop floor processes and implementing lean methods at one or more work cells. The project may involve changes in the factory layout based on value stream mapping. Illustrative changes include the definition and design of work cells, lineside supermarkets for floor stock areas, and a reduction in bottlenecks. The pilot project uses manufacturing and withdrawal kanbans, and typically tracks floor stock inventory. The pilot approach identifies a supplier for each purchased item (along with quality at the source initiatives), but purchasing kanbans are not typically used because suppliers are not ready for this type of coordination. Figure 15.8 summarizes this first stage and the other maturity stages of lean manufacturing.

The pilot project stage can also be characterized by several other lean techniques that are summarized in the figure. Once the pilots are working well, the lean methods are rolled out across the plant and into other areas of the business.

With the second stage, the biggest change involves a value stream focus, with production flow costing and the related definition of the black hole boundary. Components are issued to the production flow, and end items are received from the production flow. Inventory is not tracked within the black hole boundary. Other changes include the widespread use of manufacturing kanbans and selective use of purchasing kanbans. The third stage involves organizing the company by value stream, and extending the lean practices throughout the company and with customers/suppliers.

[7]The brief description of maturity stages draws heavily on the comprehensive explanations provided in the book *Practical Lean Accounting* by Brian Maskell and Bruce Baggaley (Productivity Press, 2004).

<table>
<tr><th></th><th>Maturity Stage</th><th>Primary Characteristics</th><th>Other Characteristics</th></tr>
<tr><td></td><td>Preparing for Lean</td><td>Initial efforts to model lean scenarios using traditional approaches
Gain understanding of lean approaches</td><td>Initial efforts to change factory layout</td></tr>
<tr><td>Stage #1</td><td>Lean Pilot Projects</td><td>Focus on shop floor processes
Use of kanbans for manufacturing
No purchasing kanbans for suppliers
Visual coordination tools
Tracking of floor stock inventory</td><td rowspan="3">Making to takt time
Drumbeat scheduling
Quick changeover and SMED
Standardized work
Quality at source and self inspection
Continuous improvement teams</td></tr>
<tr><td>Stage #2</td><td>Manage by Value Stream</td><td>Focus on value stream
Widespread use of kanbans for manufacturing
Use purchasing kanbans for some suppliers
Eliminate tracking of floor stock inventory
Production flow costing</td></tr>
<tr><td>Stage #3</td><td>Lean Enterprise</td><td>Organize company by value stream
Extend lean practices throughout company
Extend lean practices with customers/suppliers</td></tr>
</table>

Figure 15.8 Maturity Stages of Lean Manufacturing

These three maturity stages are reflected in variations of using the lean manufacturing functionality within Dynamics AX. For example, the current AX functionality supports the transition from traditional SCM approaches to lean, the transition to production flow costing, and the transition from detailed tracking to no tracking of floor stock inventory. The current AX 2012 functionality does not support purchasing kanbans, but these can be supported by an add-on module (see Case 86).

Additional Case Studies

Case 82: Final Assembly Work Cell for MTO and MTS Products

A manufacturing company produced make-to-order and make-to-stock products at the same final assembly work cell. In terms of the S&OP approaches, the demand plan consisted of sales event manufacturing kanbans for the make-to-order products, and fixed kanbans for the make-to-stock products. The production characteristics are summarized below.

- *Make-to-Order Products*. The make-to-order products represented more than 80 percent of the production volume, and consisted of 50,000 different configurations with 3 to 10 day lead times. Sales order delivery promises were based on capable-to-promise logic. The stocked components of these make-to-order products were managed by fixed kanbans.
- *Make-to-Stock Products*. The make-to-stock products represented less than 20 percent of the production volume, and consisted of 1,500 different configurations that were stocked at the final assembly work cell. When emptied, the fixed kanbans for end items were manually planned on the kanban schedule board when there was available capacity at the final assembly work cell.

Case 83: Farm Trailers A manufacturer of customized farm trailers used kanban orders and kanban schedule boards to coordinate final assembly and other work cells in the production flow. Final assembly actually consisted of three sequential steps in three adjacent work cells (termed bays), where a given farm trailer was moved through the three bays. Each step required 40 minutes and a team of five workers. A sales event kanban coordinated production for the third step, and line event kanbans coordinated production for the first two steps. The lower level components included high volume items managed by fixed kanbans, and line event kanbans coordinated production of unique items.

Case 84: Automotive Parts An automotive parts manufacturer used fixed kanbans to coordinate production of several variations of a windshield wiper at a final assembly work cell. The customer provided visibility of actual and anticipated demand (via a sales schedule) so that the suggested number of fixed manufacturing kanbans could be periodically calculated for each item in the three-level product structure. Based on this information, the existing number of an item's fixed kanbans was manually adjusted. Engineering changes also required new fixed kanbans for new components, and deletions of kanban orders for phased-out components.

Fixed manufacturing kanbans acted as the pull signal for the final assembly work cell, and for the supporting work cells that produced components. A graphical schedule board was used to coordinate production at a work cell, and purchasing kanbans coordinated deliveries from suppliers. The purchased components were received into a stockroom, and moved to the relevant floor stock area based on withdrawal kanbans. The floor stock areas were treated as a black hole so that inventory was not tracked through production. Explicit kanban empty transactions (and kanban complete transactions) were used to report and coordinate production activities. Completion of the manufacturing kanban for the end-item deducted the item's standard cost from WIP for the production flow, and WIP was valued based on production flow costing.

Case 85: Customized Electric Motors An electric motor manufacturer produced custom products from stocked components and several make-to-order components. The factory layout involved a U-shaped final assembly work cell and several supporting work cells, as reflected in a two-level product structure. The daily production volume was approximately 500 units (a takt time of 10 minutes per unit), and the similarity of custom products meant they could be treated as equivalent units. Use of a product configurator during order entry generated a configuration id, and also a unique BOM version for the item number representing a custom product, and for the item numbers representing customized assemblies.

The item number representing a custom product was assigned a kanban rule for a sales event manufacturing kanban. As a result, each sales order for a custom motor generated a corresponding sales event manufacturing kanban for the end-item's configuration ID. The kanban orders were manually planned for the final assembly work cell, and this step triggered generation of line event kanbans for the make-to-order components produced at supporting work cells.

Case 86: Purchasing Kanbans and the Vendor Portal The procurement manager at a discrete manufacturer wanted to implement purchasing kanbans with key suppliers, and was considering the capabilities within an add-on module for AX.[8] These capabilities extended the production flow to include purchasing kanbans, where each purchasing kanban represented a release against a blanket purchase order. The key coordination tools included a kanban board for purchased material, and a vendor portal to support communication with suppliers. The vendor portal was integrated directly through the .NET framework into Dynamics AX, where all business logic and data access occurs. Another coordination tool involved a purchase schedule of projected requirements.

[8]See **www.ebecs.com** for further information about their Purchasing Kanban Management capabilities for Dynamics AX 2012.

Executive Summary

This chapter summarized the lean manufacturing capabilities within AX 2012. It explained and illustrated the new constructs such as kanban orders, production flows and coordination via kanban schedule boards. It also highlighted the many impacts on the conceptual models for traditional manufacturing. This reconceptualization can guide you through the early maturity stages of lean manufacturing. The chapter included several case studies for using kanban orders in different industries, such as printed circuit boards, automotive parts and electric motors.

Chapter 16

Subcontracted Production

Subcontracted production and internal production share many similarities in the use of basic constructs like bills of material and production orders. However, subcontracted production involves significant differences and several variations that merit a separate explanation. One key difference stems from the AX approach to modeling subcontracted production, which requires a unique item representing the subcontracted service, and a BOM line specifying the item as a buy-to-order component of a parent item. As a result, scheduling a production order for the parent item automatically creates the purchase order for the subcontracted service.

Subcontracted production has many different variations. A basic issue concerns the inventory visibility of supplied components and the finished item, and there are two major solution approaches. One solution approach provides visibility of this inventory. The other solution approach provides no visibility of this inventory, since it employs a production order picking list to "send" supplied material and then "receive" a completed operation. A combination of the two approaches can provide partial visibility.

This chapter focuses on the full visibility approach to subcontracted production, and includes a section on the alternative approaches with no visibility. The chapter also covers several other variations for modeling subcontracted production, and consists of the following sections:

1. Variations in Subcontracted Production
2. Modeling Subcontracted Production
3. Define an Item Representing the Subcontracted Service
4. Define the BOM for a Subcontract Manufactured Item
5. Planning Data for a Subcontract Manufactured Item
6. Typical Business Process for Subcontracted Production

7. Subcontracted Production with Partial or No Inventory Visibility
8. Considerations about Subcontracted Production

16.1 Variations in Subcontracted Production

One of the major solution approaches to subcontracted production provides full visibility of the inventory of supplied components and the finished item. As part of this solution approach, you define a single-level bill of material for the finished item that defines the supplied components and a component representing the subcontracted service. Another part of this solution approach involves the significance of a single production order for the finished item, since it may represent a single production run or the desired output for a time period. The significance of a single order affects the approach for reporting started quantities and finished quantities, and the use of picking lists to report usage of supplied material. There are several variations of this solution approach, as summarized in Figure 16.1 and described below. The bottom of the figure also displays the solution approach with no visibility of inventory at the subcontractor, and a subsequent section provides further explanation.

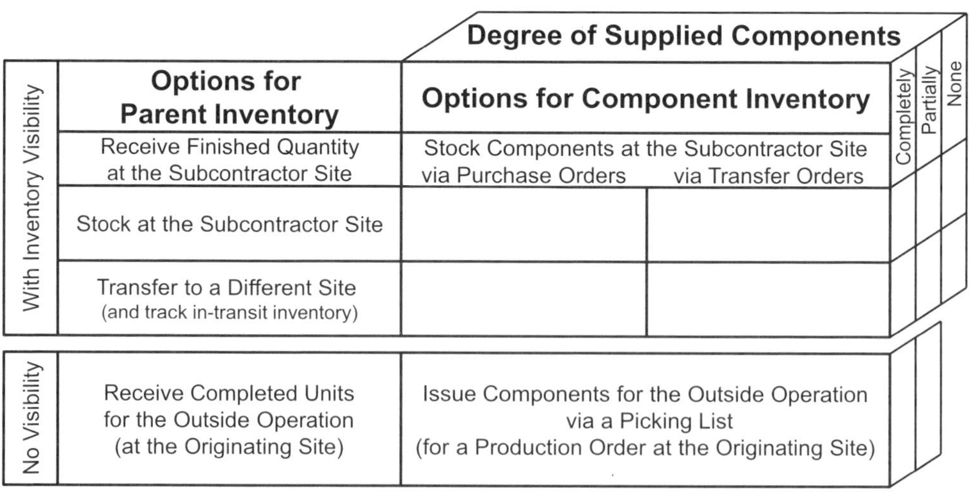

Figure 16.1 Variations in Subcontracted Production

Degree of Supplied Components A subcontracted production scenario may involve completely supplied, partially supplied, or no supplied components, where the supplied components are defined in the BOM version for the parent item. When no components are supplied, the parent item is often termed a turnkey item. A turnkey item can be coordinated through a simple purchase order.

As a corollary to the degree of supplied components, it can be helpful to identify components provided by the subcontractor. These are sometimes termed reference components. The information can be used for calculating aggregate requirements to negotiate agreements with suppliers, as well as calculating theoretical usage for reconciling a subcontractor's claims about actual usage of a reference component.

Subcontractor Location Identified by an AX Site and Warehouse Each subcontractor must be identified by an AX site and warehouse in order to track inventory of supplied components and parent items. Most scenarios identify the subcontractor location as a unique AX site, while some scenarios simply identify it as unique AX warehouse. The choice affects possible options for managing inventory of the supplied components and the parent item, since the warehouse source for components and the deliver-to warehouse for the production order must be within the same AX site.

Identifying a subcontractor as a separate AX site supports production of the same item at different subcontractors with site-specific BOM versions and site-specific costs. The site-specific costs also apply to the supplied components and the items representing the subcontracted services. Identifying a subcontractor as a separate AX warehouse (rather than an AX site) precludes the above-mentioned advantages. The next chapter provides further explanation of the AX solution approaches for multisite operations (Section 17.1).

Options for Component Inventory When supplied components are stocked at the subcontractor, the two basic options include purchase orders delivered to the subcontractor and transfers from another site/warehouse (with tracking of in-transit inventory). With either option, it is important to indicate the relevant warehouse source of component inventory in the BOM information, and the relevant planning data for replenishing component inventory at the subcontractor location.

Options for Parent Inventory When the production order is reported as finished, the two basic options include stocking the finished quantity at the subcontractor (for subsequent sales order fulfillment) and transferring it to another location (with tracking of in-transit inventory).

16.2 Modeling Subcontracted Production

The AX approach to subcontracted production involves a unique item representing the subcontracted service, where you define this item as a component of a manufactured item.[1] It can be termed a *subcontracted service item* or an *outside operation component*. The item defines the value-added costs for the subcontracted service, and provides the basis for defining approved vendors and purchase price agreements. The purchase order for this subcontracted service item is closely linked to the production order for the manufactured item. That is, the purchase order is automatically generated when you schedule the production order, and the dual constructs—of a purchase order and a production order—coordinate the supply chain activities for subcontracted production. The dual constructs require two separate receipt transactions, where the purchase order receipt indicates what you are willing to pay for, and the finished production quantity indicates the good and scrapped quantity of the parent item. Either transaction can trigger backflushing of supplied components.[2]

A subcontracted service item is defined as a component within the BOM version for a subcontract manufactured item. Figure 16.2 illustrates this BOM information, where a subcontractor produces Product A using the supplied material of Component #1 and Component #2. The left-side of the figure also highlights the dual constructs of a production order and the purchase order for coordinating subcontracted production.

[1]The approach to modeling subcontracted production varies by ERP software package. Two common approaches involve a routing operation or a component to represent the subcontracted service and its associated costs. Both of these approaches typically require the dual constructs of a production order and purchase order to coordinate subcontracted production.

[2]The finished quantity for a production order normally triggers backflushing of components and resources. However, you can specify a company-wide or site-specific policy so that backflushing is triggered by the purchase order receipt for a subcontracted service. This makes sense in some scenarios for subcontracted production, especially when using a multistep routing with an outside operation. You define this company-wide policy on the Production Control Parameters form for automatic updates related to purchase order receipts.

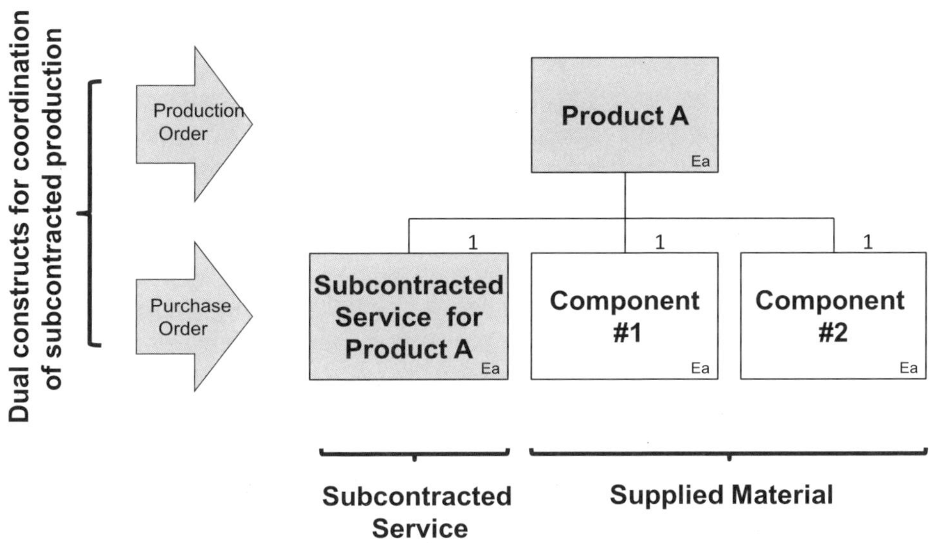

Figure 16.2 Example BOM for a Subcontract Manufactured Item

16.3 Define an Item Representing the Subcontracted Service

You define a unique item number to represent a subcontracted service. As a rule of thumb, each parent item produced by a subcontractor typically requires a unique item number to represent the associated service. The typical business process for defining a subcontracted service is very similar to the process for defining a material item. Figure 16.3 summarizes a typical business process and provides an organizing focus for highlighting key considerations.

Define Enterprise-Level Data for the Item The enterprise-level data includes the product type and subtype, the product number and the product name. Several considerations apply to an item representing a subcontracted service.

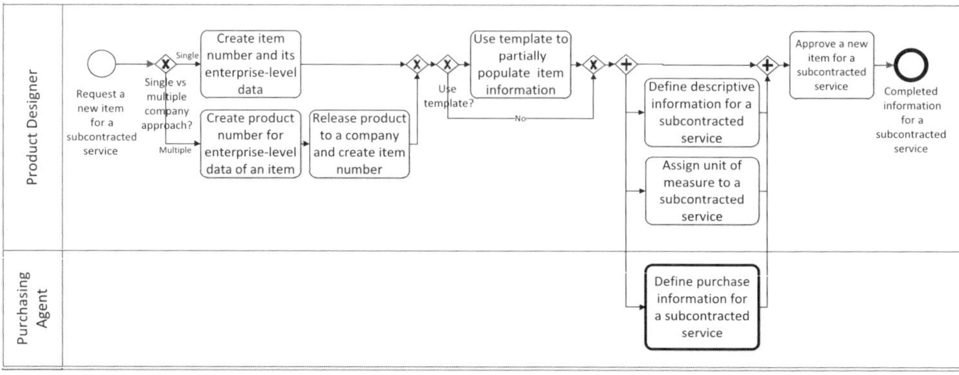

Figure 16.3 Typical Business Process to Define Item Information for a Subcontracted Service

- *Product Type of Service Versus Item.* The item number representing a subcontracted service is frequently defined with a product type of *Service*. When defined as a service, you must employ actual costing as an inventory valuation method.[3] In standard cost environments, you can still create an item cost record for this service item in order to calculate the standard cost of the subcontract manufactured item. However, purchase price variances will not be calculated for the item representing the subcontracted service.

  In order to support purchase price variances, the product type must be designated as *Item* and the Inventory Model must be Standard Costs. Further explanation uses the term *subcontracted service item* regardless of the product type assigned to the item.

  An additional policy also seems counter intuitive. Regardless of the product type, AX prevents use of a "not stocked product" as a component, so that the item number representing the subcontracted service must be designated as a stocked product.[4]
- *Product Subtype of Product.* This policy indicates that the subcontracted service will be identified by an item number rather than an item number and variant code.

[3]The inventory valuation method is defined by the Inventory Model field within the Item Model Group assigned to the item.

[4]The policy for a stocked product is embedded within the Item Model Group assigned to the item.

- *Product Name.* The product name will appear on the purchase order for the subcontracted service item, so that the product name typically matches the name of the parent item being produced by the subcontractor.

Use Template to Partially Populate Item Information A template can be employed as a short-cut approach to partially populate item information for a subcontracted service, either when creating a new item or by applying it afterward.

Define Units of Measure for a Subcontracted Service You typically assign an inventory UM and purchase UM that match the UM of the parent item being produced by the subcontractor.

Define Purchase Information for a Subcontracted Service The following aspects of purchase information reflect key considerations for a subcontracted service.

- *Approved Vendors.* You define the approved vendors for a subcontracted service just like any other purchase item, as previously described (Section 13.3).
- *Preferred Vendor.* The item's preferred vendor will be assigned when the system automatically creates a purchase order as a result of updating the related production order. The preferred vendor can be defined as a company-wide or site/warehouse policy, or it can be defined within the component information in a BOM line. A third option only applies when using routing data, where you specify the preferred vendor as part of the resource representing the subcontractor.[5] The system prevents automatic purchase order creation when a preferred vendor does not exist in any of the three options.
- *Agreements about Purchase Prices.* You define agreements about purchase prices just like any other item, as previously described (Sections 13.5 and 13.6).
- *Item Group.* You define a unique item group for subcontracted service items, which defines the relevant G/L account numbers. A typical name for the item group would be Subcontracted Service.

[5] These three options represent increasing levels of specificity, so that the suggested vendor on a purchase order reflects the highest level specified.

- *Cost Group.* You define a unique cost group for subcontracted service items to support cost segmentation in the calculated cost of a subcontract manufactured item. The designated cost group type for this cost group depends on the Product Type assigned to the subcontracted service item. When the Product Type is service, the designated cost group type should be Direct Outsourcing, whereas it should be Undefined when the Product Type is Item.
- *Other Aspects of Planning Data.* Several aspects of planning data do not apply to an item representing a subcontracted service, since its purchase order will be automatically created for the production order that coordinates subcontracted production. These aspects include the coverage code, coverage group policies, purchase lead time and order quantity modifiers.
- *Standard Cost.* In standard cost scenarios, you typically assign a standard cost to the item representing the subcontracted service. The standard cost is site-specific, so that multiple item cost records may be required when the subcontracted service is performed at different sites representing different subcontractors.
- *Flushing Principle.* You typically assign a flushing principle of Finish, so that reporting the finished quantity of a production order will trigger back flushing of the subcontracted service item.

Requirements for batch tracking and testing are specified for the parent item, and do not typically apply to the item representing the subcontracted service.

16.4 Define the BOM for a Subcontract Manufactured Item

The BOM version for a subcontract manufactured item contains one line item for the subcontracted service item, and other line items reflecting the degree of supplied components. Figure 16.4 summarizes a typical business process to define the BOM version for a subcontract manufactured item, and provides an organizing focus for further explanation. The figure reflects the similarities in the typical business process for defining an item's bill of material (described in Section 4.2).

Define BOM Version Policies The BOM version is typically site-specific because each subcontractor represents a different site.

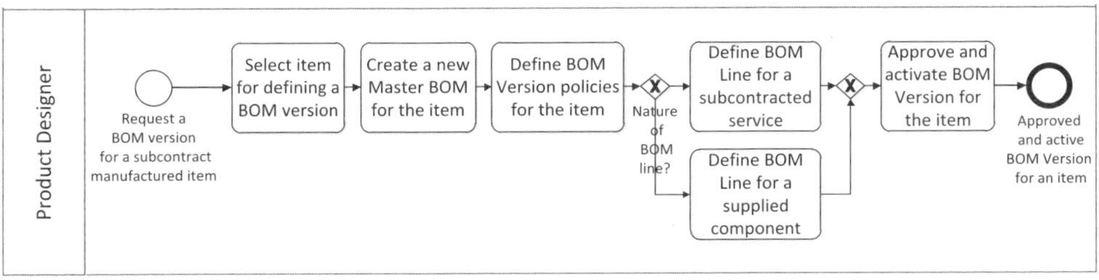

Figure 16.4 Typical Business Process to Define the BOM for a Subcontract Manufactured Item

Define BOM Line for the Subcontracted Service The line defines the subcontracted service item, a required quantity of one, a warehouse source that reflects the relevant subcontractor, and a line type of vendor indicating the buy-to-order service. When using routing data, you also specify the related operation number and flag the line as due at the end of the operation (aka the due date of the related production order).[6] You also assign a flushing policy of finish.

Define BOM Line for a Supplied Component A separate line defines each supplied component, its required quantity, and a warehouse source that reflects the desired option for supplied components. You also assign a flushing policy of finish so that the finished quantity of the parent item will trigger automatic generation and posting of a picking list.

Some scenarios also identify the material purchased by the subcontractor, also known as reference components. A separate BOM line defines each reference component, its required quantity and a warehouse source. In addition, you indicate the BOM line should not be included in cost rollup calculations. An item representing a reference component is typically assigned a manual flushing policy (so it will not be back flushed) and a manual coverage planning code (so that planned supply orders will not be generated).

[6]The current AX design forces you define routing data to correctly align due dates of the purchase order and production order for subcontracted production. A customization provides the alignment without the need for routing data.

16.5 Planning Data for a Subcontract Manufactured Item

The planning data for a subcontract manufactured item is exactly the same as the data for an internally manufactured item, as previously described in Section 10.3. One aspect of planning data involves the significance of a single production order, and the interpretation of production lead time. For example, the production lead time might be a week for a production order representing a weekly period of desired output, where the one-week lead time would be fixed regardless of order quantity. The associated order start date defines when supplied components must be available at the subcontractor. The production order due date should also be reflected in the purchase order for the subcontracted service. The alignment of these order due dates generally requires the use of routing data, as described in a subsequent section on considerations for subcontracted production.

16.6 Typical Business Process for Subcontracted Production

A typical business process reflects several assumptions about the subcontracted production scenario. In this example with partially supplied components, a single production order represents a weekly time period, the subcontractor's location is identified as a unique AX site, and the inventory of supplied material and the parent item are stocked at the subcontractor's location. In addition, the supplied material and the subcontracted service are defined within the BOM version for the parent item with a flushing principle of finish, so that parent receipts will trigger backflushing based on theoretical usage. The typical business process is illustrated in Figure 16.5 and described below.

Overview A production planner typically firms a planned order to generate a production order with a scheduled status. Alternatively, you can manually create and then schedule a production order. Scheduling the production order automatically creates a purchase order for the subcontracted service. These two constructs—the production order and its related purchase order—are used to manage subcontracted production activities. The purchasing

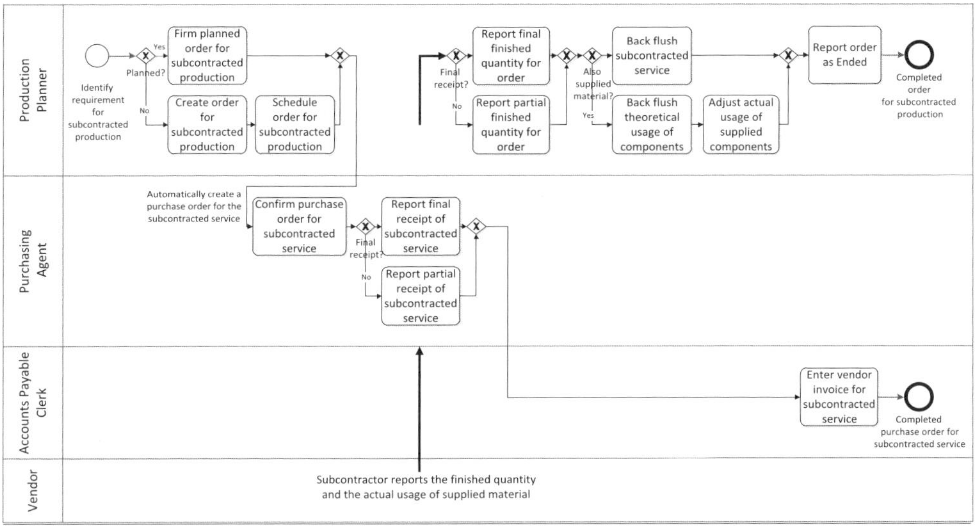

Figure 16.5 Typical Business Process for Subcontracted Production

agent reviews and confirms the purchase order for the subcontracted service, and also reports the quantity completed based on notification provided by the subcontractor.

The notification provided by the subcontractor is also used to report the finished quantity for the related production order. Reporting the finished quantity places the end-item into inventory, and also generates a picking list to automatically deduct the subcontracted service and supplied components. The production planner may create an additional picking list to report adjustments in actual component usage. When all activities have been reported, the production planner ends the production order.

Firm a Planned Order for Subcontracted Production The production planner analyzes and firms a planned order that reflects requirements stemming from the S&OP game plans and the item's planning data. Firming the planned order results in a production order with a scheduled status, and also automatically creates a purchase order for the subcontracted service.

Manually Create and Schedule an Order for Subcontracted Production The production planner creates a production order for the parent item, quantity, due date, and the deliver-to site/warehouse. After creating the order, the production planner schedules the order, which automatically creates a purchase order for the subcontracted service.

Confirm Purchase Order for the Subcontracted Service A purchasing agent typically reviews and confirms the automatically-generated purchase order for the subcontracted service. The purchase order reflects the preferred vendor and price agreements for the subcontracted service. The production order quantity will drive the purchase order quantity, and its due date should be reflected in the purchase order due date.[7]

Report Partial Receipts or Final Receipt of the Subcontracted Service A purchasing agent typically reports the completed quantity of the subcontracted service based on information provided by the subcontractor. The final receipt should be explicitly identified using the Closed for Receipt flag.

Report Partial or Final Finished Quantity for the Production Order Using the same information about the completed quantity, the production planner initiates the Report as Finished task and employs the related dialogue to report the finished quantity. This places the item into inventory and generates a picking list to automatically back flush the supplied components (and subcontracted service) based on theoretical usage.

Adjust Actual Usage of Supplied Components Based on information provided by the subcontractor, the production planner creates an additional picking list in order to report differences between the theoretical usage and actual usage of supplied material.

Report Order as Ended The production planner reports the end of a production order, indicating that no additional transactions need to be reported. When there are missing transactions, the system provides warning messages and does not change the order status to *ended*, although specifying an override will force an ended status. After ending the order, the variances are automatically calculated for a standard cost item.

[7] The purchase order due date will reflect the start date of the production order unless you employ routing data to correctly align the dates, or customize the software functionality.

16.7 Subcontracted Production with Partial or No Inventory Visibility

A basic issue in subcontracted production concerns the inventory visibility of supplied components and the finished item. Inventory visibility is limited when using a production order picking list to "send" supplied material and then "receive" a completed operation, typically at the originating warehouse. Within AX, this approach can employ a special version of the printed pick list (termed a *vendor delivery note*) when a routing operation has been defined. The printed picking list indicates the delivery address for the vendor. The approach does not track inventory of the supplied components or the in-transit inventory, nor does it track in-transit inventory of the completed item.

Several additional considerations apply to this approach. For example, the subcontracted service may represent an intermediate operation in a multi-step routing, so that a partially finished item (without an item number) constitutes the supplied material. Other supplied components should have the same operation sequence number as the subcontracted operation. A multi-step routing with multiple outside operations becomes even more complex for supply chain coordination.

It is possible to obtain partial visibility by stocking components at the subcontractor, or by receiving the finished quantity at the subcontractor. However, these approaches may be constrained by the implications of using different AX warehouses within one AX site.

16.8 Considerations about Subcontracted Production

The considerations for subcontracted production include the need for routing data and the use of coordination tools.

Need for Routing Data The fundamental design of AX requires routing data to correctly align the purchase order due date (for the subcontracted service) with the due date of the production order. The use of routing data involves additional complexity. A customization avoids the need for routing data, as described in Case 87. Definition of the routing data for subcontracted production involves the following steps.

- *Define a resource group and a vendor resource for each subcontractor.* This is required when each subcontractor location represents a unique AX site because resources are site-specific. You can also identify the vendor associated with a vendor resource, which represents one option for indicating the preferred vendor for purchasing a subcontracted service.
- *Define a master operation for each subcontractor.* The master operation identifies the resource requirement for the relevant vendor resource. The time requirements indicate the expected lead time (such as 7 days) using the *queue after* time element. No costs are assigned to the operation.
- *Define a route version for each subcontract manufactured item.* The route version policies include a specified site, so that multiple route versions may be required when producing the same item at different subcontractors. A route version contains a single operation number for the relevant master operation.
- *Assign operation number to BOM components.* The operation number should also be reflected in the BOM line for the component representing the subcontracted service, where you indicate that the due date occurs at the end of the operation.

The use of routing data provides an additional option for reporting and viewing production activities. For example, reporting unit completions for the operation (when it is the last operation) can update the finished quantity for the parent item. The Operations List can also be used to view production orders, where you filter on the master operations associated with subcontracting.

Identifying a Production Order That Involves Subcontracted Manufacturing The Subcontractor Work form displays scheduled orders with a linked purchase order for any buy-to-order component. The buy-to-order component represents a subcontracted service in scenarios with subcontracted production. The form displays information about purchase order status, and enables you to update the production order status via the start task and report-as-finished task.

A production order can be designated with an order type of vendor (rather than standard), but this only provides reference information for filtering purposes.

Additional Case Studies

Case 87: Subcontracted Production Without Routing Data A manufacturing company employed subcontractors to produce several different products, and wanted to model subcontracted production without routing data. The solution approach involved a customization so that the purchase order due date for the subcontracted service automatically aligned with the due date of the production order for the parent item. As the starting point for the customization, they identified the component requirement (for the subcontracted service) occurring at the "end" of production. Using the linkage between automatically-generated purchase order (for the subcontracted service) and the production order, the customization correctly aligned the purchase order due date.

Case 88: Single Receipt Transaction for Reporting Subcontracted Production A manufacturing company employed subcontractors to produce several different products, which involved the dual constructs of a purchase order (for the subcontracted service) and the production order. The dual constructs required two separate receipt transactions, where the users reported the purchase order receipt (to indicate what they would pay for) and then the finished production quantity (to indicate the good and scrapped quantity, and to trigger backflushing of supplied components). The users wanted a single transaction to minimize keystrokes. The suggested solution approach involved a customization that built on the linkage between the two orders. The customization provided a single form that captured relevant information for both constructs, such as the batch numbers and their quantities produced by the subcontractor. After becoming familiar with the system capabilities for hot-keying to the related order (which minimized keystrokes), the users reconsidered the requirement for the customization.

Case 89: Multiple Subcontractors Build Same Item A manufacturing company employed multiple subcontractors to produce the same item, where the supplied components were stocked at each subcontractor. Each subcontractor's location was identified as a unique AX site, and site-specific BOM versions for a parent item defined the supplied components for each subcontractor. A subcontracted service item was defined for each parent item. Since the company was using standard costs, different site-specific standard costs were assigned to the subcontracted service item and to the supplied components. This approach also entailed the calculation of site-specific standard costs for the parent item.

Executive Summary

Subcontracted production and internal production share many similarities in the use of basic constructs like bills of material and production orders. However, subcontracted production involves significant differences about inventory visibility and multisite coordination, and supply chain coordination via the dual constructs of a production order and a purchase order. The AX approach to modeling subcontracted production involves a unique item representing the subcontracted service, where you define this item as a component of a manufactured item. The chapter explained the typical business processes for subcontracted production, and case studies illustrated some of the variations.

Chapter 17

Managing Transfers in Multisite Operations

Many businesses involved in manufacturing and distribution have inventory at multiple physical sites. The multiple sites can serve different purposes. A site may reflect proximity to suppliers or customers, transportation or production cost considerations, or availability of raw materials and human resources. There may be political, technological or competitive considerations for multiple locations. A site may represent an acquisition or internal growth, or a subcontractor location. The sites may operate as autonomous business units with no requirements for transfers, or transfers may be required.

Transfers between sites can be managed using transfers orders or intercompany orders, depending on the grouping of physical sites into companies. The basic variations of multisite operations, and the prescriptions for solution approaches, provide a starting point for further explanation. The chapter contains the following sections.

1. Solution Approaches for Multisite Operations
2. Transfer Orders
3. Considerations about Transfer Orders
4. Coordinate Transfer Orders
5. Intercompany Orders
6. Master Scheduling Across a Multicompany Supply Chain
7. Other Multisite Variations

When modeling physical sites in a multisite operation, you can use AX sites or AX warehouses or both. In this chapter, we will use the terms *AX site* and *AX warehouse* when explaining system-specific functionality, and the generic terms of *multisite* and *physical site* for conceptual explanations.

17.1 Solution Approaches for Multisite Operations

The wide variety of multisite operations can be distilled into five basic variations. Several factors differentiate the nature of these multisite variations, such as the need for transfers between sites. Autonomous sites do not require inventory transfers. A distribution network, on the other hand, could be exemplified by a vertically integrated supply chain with transfers between manufacturing plants and distribution centers. The term distribution network refers to the need for transfers. Other distribution network examples include replenishment of a remote warehouse, space within a contract warehouse, a customer location (for stocking material prior to customer usage), a subcontract vendor location (for stocking supplied components or the completed parent), a customer service center and delivery vans.

In addition to the need for transfers, other differentiating factors for multisite operations include the grouping of sites into companies, the AX approach to modeling physical sites, and the use of another AX instance or another ERP system by a sister company. Figure 17.1 summarizes how these factors influence the AX solution approach for supporting the basic variations in multisite operations.

The prescriptive nature of Figure 17.1 identifies the AX solution approach for each multisite variation. Subsequent sections explain the use of transfer orders and intercompany orders. An explanation of the Application Integration Framework falls outside the book's scope.

AX Approaches for Modeling Physical Sites The choice of an AX approach for modeling physical sites involves several considerations, and there are two basic options.[1] Physical sites can be modeled as multiple AX warehouses with an AX site or as multiple AX sites. Figure 17.2 summarizes these two AX approaches for modeling physical sites and provides an organizing focus for further explanation. The figure also summarizes the costing and production factors that differentiate the AX solution approaches.

- *Multiple AX Warehouses within a Single AX Site.* This solution approach makes sense when costs for items, labor rates and overhead formulas do not vary by warehouse, the same item is not produced at multiple warehouses, and financial reports by warehouse are not required.

[1] A historical capability within previous versions of AX— of multiple AX warehouses without an AX site—represented a third option, but is no longer available with AX 2012.

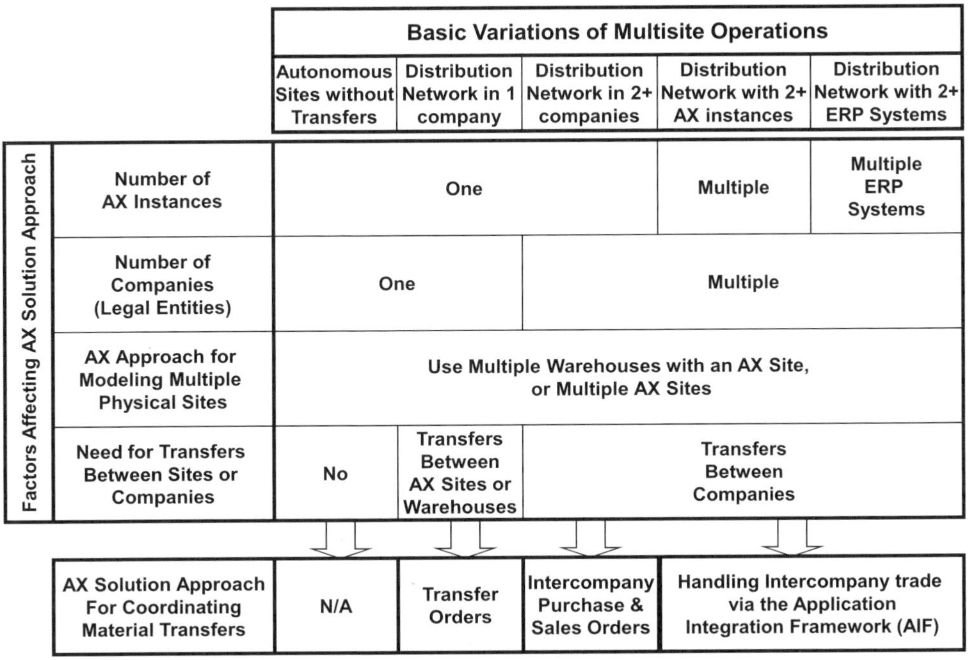

Figure 17.1 Basic Variations of Multisite Operations

❖ *Multiple AX Sites*. A solution approach using multiple AX sites provides several advantages, as illustrated in the right hand column of Figure 17.2. In terms of costing factors, for example, it supports an item's site-specific standard costs, site-specific labor rates and overhead formulas, and financial reporting by site. One caveat involves the single-site considerations for cost calculations.

The significance of an item's company-wide versus site/warehouse information was previously summarized in Section 3.10.

17.2 Transfer Orders

Transfer orders support the coordination of supply chain activities for material flows between two sites/warehouses in the same company. A planned transfer order communicates requirements for moving material from one

		AX Approaches for Modeling Physical Sites	
		Multiple Warehouses Within a Single AX Site	Multiple AX Sites
Costing Factors	Financial Reporting by Site	No	A financial dimension can be assigned to a site, thereby supporting financial reporting by site
Costing Factors	Standard Costing	Supports standard costing	Supports standard costing An item's standard cost can vary by site
Costing Factors	Labor Rates in Manufacturing	Supports labor rates with date effectivities and simulation capabilities	Supports labor rates with date effectivities and simulation capabilities Labor rates can vary by site
Costing Factors	Calculation of Overhead Costs for Manufactured Items	Supports calculation of material- and routing-related overhead costs, and also supports date effectivities and simulation capabilities	Supports calculation of material- and routing-related overhead costs, and also supports date effectivities and simulation capabilities Overhead formulas can vary by site
Costing Factors	Cost Calculations and Inquiries for Manufactured Items	Cost calculations and inquiries apply to the entire product structure	Cost calculations and inquiries only span a single site when a product structure spans 2+ sites
Production Factors	Manufacturing Plants Produce the Same Item	Partially supported by using different Formula/BOM and Route versions for the item	Fully supported by using site-specific (or companywide) formula/BOM versions, and site-specific route versions
Production Factors	Other Production Considerations	N/A	A route version must be site-specific Resources in a routing must be within same site A formula/BOM can be site-specific or companywide Components must be from warehouses within the same site
Production Factors	Other Production Considerations	The warehouse location of auto-deducted components can be linked to the resource that requires the components	The warehouse location of auto-deducted components can be linked to the resource that requires the components

Figure 17.2 AX Approaches for Modeling Physical Sites

site/warehouse (the transfer-from location) to replenish inventory at another site/warehouse (the transfer-to location). Firming a planned transfer order creates a transfer order for actually recording the transfer. In addition, a manually created transfer order can be used to report unplanned transfers between sites/warehouses. Whether created automatically or manually, the transfer order represents a two-step approach to transfer material between warehouses. The two-step approach means that one transaction records the shipment and a second transaction records the receipt, with tracking of in-transit inventory in a transit warehouse.[2] A one-step approach can also be used, typically when a short transportation time does not require tracking of in-transit inventory. The one-step approach means that one transaction records the shipment, with automatic receipt of the shipped quantity.

[2] A transit warehouse must be assigned to each normal warehouse for tracking in-transit inventory shipped from the warehouse. Both the normal and transit warehouses must be within the same site. When inventory is also tracked by bin location, at least one bin must be defined for the transit warehouse (e.g., labeled the intransit bin). The bin location must be defined as the transit warehouse's default issue and receipt bin, since this bin location cannot be specified on a transfer order.

Planning calculations use distribution requirements planning logic (DRP) to suggest planned transfer orders to meet demand based on site/warehouse-specific planning data. The following subsections explain the life cycle of a transfer order, variations in the transfer order process, and the use of planned transfer orders for coordinating transfer activities. A previous chapter covered the planning data for transfer items.

Significance of a Single Transfer Order The basic structure of a transfer order consists of header and line item information. The transfer order header identifies the ship-from and ship-to site/warehouse. Each line item identifies an item and quantity. Shipment of a line item is tracked in a transit warehouse associated with the ship-from warehouse.

A single transfer order usually represents a single shipment and the line items reflect the shipment contents. It sometimes represents a container with a unique identifier, and the transfer order number could be manually assigned to reflect the container identifier.

Basic Model of Transfer Order Processing The basic model of transfer order processing consists of the three major steps illustrated in Figure 17.3. Each step is represented by a transfer order status automatically updated by the system. Each step is also tracked by an inventory status of the item, as it moves from the ship-to warehouse to the in-transit and ship-to warehouses, as shown on the right side of the figure.

- ❖ *Step 1: Create a transfer order.* The Transfer Order form is used to manually create a transfer order, or to maintain an order created by firming a planned transfer order. You can optionally print a document (titled Transfer Order) to assist the picking activities for line items on a transfer order.
- ❖ *Step 2: Ship the transfer order.* Actual shipment is reported on the Transfer Order Shipment form, accessed directly or from the Transfer Order form. You can identify the quantity basis for initially populating the shipped quantities for each line item, and update the actual shipment quantities, locations and batch numbers (if applicable).[3] The actual quantity may be subject to over- and under-delivery tolerances (expressed as

[3]The Transfer Order Shipment form employs two policies to display line items (the Edit Lines policy) and display information about bin location, batch number and serial number for line items (the Explode Lines policy).

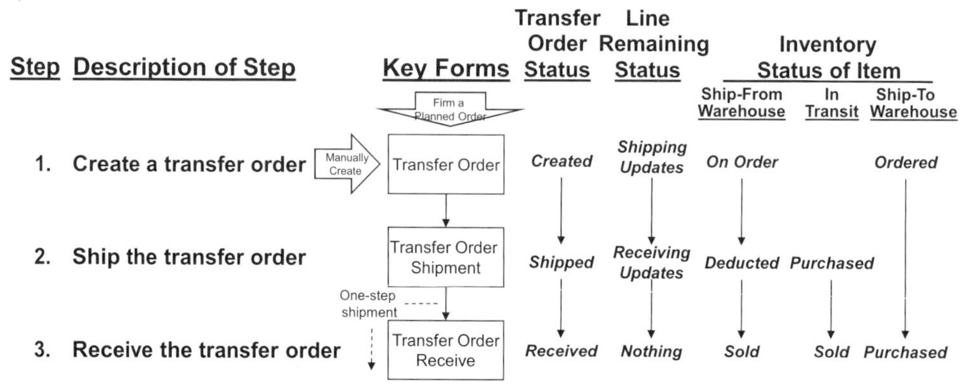

Figure 17.3 Basic Model of Transfer Order Processing

a percentage) specified for the line item.[4] A line item can be short shipped and flagged as closed.

You can optionally specify a tracking number for a transfer order and print an associated document (titled the Transfer Order Shipment) to accompany the transferred material. Posting the shipment will transfer the material to the in-transit warehouse associated with the originating warehouse.

Some scenarios employ a one-step shipment process for a transfer order (shown in the figure) which means there is no tracking of in-transit inventory and no receipt transaction. You indicate this policy (termed the auto-receive policy) when posting a transfer order shipment.

Several variations in business processes may apply to transfer order shipments, such as reservations, the anticipation of picking activities, and the use of picking lists. A subsequent section describes these considerations.

❖ *Step 3: Receive the transfer order.* Actual receipt is reported on the Transfer Order Receive form, accessed directly or from the Transfer Order form. You can identify the quantity basis for initially populating the received quantities for each line item, and update the actual received quantities and scrap quantities (if applicable). The entire quantity shipped must be reported as received or scrapped in order to complete the

[4] A company-wide policy (embedded in the Inventory Parameters form) determines whether over- and under-deliveries will be accepted on transfer orders. The delivery tolerances for a line item initially default from the item.

transfer order. You can optionally print an associated document titled the Transfer Order Receipt to accompany the received material.

Several variations in business processes may apply to transfer order receipts, such as the anticipation and registration of arrivals. A subsequent section describes these considerations.

Life Cycle and Status for a Transfer Order The right side of Figure 17.3 displays the status associated with each step in the basic model, where the system automatically updates the status. The significance of transfer order status is described below.

- *Created.* A created status means that line items can be added and data maintained on a transfer order.
- *Shipped.* All lines have been shipped.
- *Received.* All lines have been received. Information cannot be changed for transfer orders with a shipped or received status.

The remaining status applies to transfer order line items, as described below.

- *Shipping Updates.* The line has only been created or the line has not been completely shipped.
- *Receive Updates.* The line has been completely shipped but not yet completely received.
- *Nothing.* The line has been completely shipped and received.

Each transaction for a transfer order line item will update the item's inventory status, as shown in the right side of the figure.

17.3 Considerations about Transfer Orders

Several considerations apply to transfer orders, including the significance of shipment and receipt dates, the transportation time between warehouses, and reservations. Some business processes will entail the anticipation of transfer order picking, generation of picking lists, and the anticipation of arrivals for transfer orders.

Transfer Order Dates for Shipment and Receipt The transfer order header specifies a shipment date and receipt date, along with the ship-from and ship-to site/warehouses and a mode of delivery (such as air or truck). The difference between the two dates reflects the transportation time (expressed in days) between the two locations. Each line item can also have shipment/receipt dates and a mode of delivery.

The assignments of shipment and delivery dates are affected by the delivery date control policy assigned to the transfer order header and to each line item. A similar policy applies to dates on sales orders, as previously described in Section 11.6. This policy can help enforce several basic rules, such as the transportation time between a pair of warehouses, the working calendar for both warehouses and the delivery mode, the concept of an order entry deadline, and a sales lead time to prepare items for shipment. As summarized in Figure 17.4, the two major options for a delivery date control policy include sales lead time and ATP. An additional option (labeled None) disables the enforcement of the basic rules, thereby allowing assignment of unrealistic dates. This additional option is also referred to as disabling delivery date control.

After manually entering a date that represents an exception to the basic rules, the system automatically displays the exception in a separate dialogue (termed the Available Ship and Receipt Dates form). The dialogue displays available dates, and you can optionally transfer a selected date to change the ship date. You can also analyze available supplies for the item using the ATP form or Supply Overview form.[5]

Using a sales lead time option provides the simplest approach to enforcing the basic rules for dates on transfer orders. The ATP option requires several additional policies about underlying assumptions in order to correctly calculate an available-to-promise date. These additional ATP policies were previously explained in the context of sales orders (Section 11.6). Assigning an option of *none* will disable the rules for delivery date control, thereby allowing assignment of unrealistic dates. As a general guideline, any transfer order or line item with this option should require follow up.

The delivery date control option for a transfer order header is inherited from a company-wide value, and the option for each line item is typically inherited from an item-specific value. The option can be manually overridden, typically to a value of none in order to disable delivery date control.

[5]The two forms are not currently accessible from the Transfer Order form, but they can be accessed from Released Products form or the On Hand Inquiry form.

Delivery Date Control Option	Scenario	Comments
Sales Lead Time	Use Basic Rules	Auto-assign dates based on basic rules Enforce basic rules for manually entered dates*
ATP	Stocked End-Item	Auto-assign dates based on basic rules + ATP logic Enforce basic rules + ATP logic for manually entered dates*
None	Allow assignment of unrealistic dates	Ignore basic rules for manually entered dates

* = Display exceptions on *Available Ship and Receipt Dates* form, and transfer a selected date to change the ship date
Analyze supplies for the item using the *ATP* form or *Supply Overview* form, accessed from the Released Products form or the On-hand Inquiry form

Figure 17.4 Delivery Date Control Options for a Transfer Order

Transportation Time Between Warehouses The transportation time between warehouses can be defined with two different approaches that reflect a warehouse viewpoint versus an item viewpoint.

- *Transportation time based on a warehouse viewpoint.* This viewpoint defines the typical transportation time between a pair of ship-from and ship-to warehouses. The transportation time must be defined for each warehouse pair. This transportation time will be used in planned transfer orders, and in manually entered transfer orders with enforcement of delivery date control rules. Most situations will employ the warehouse viewpoint for defining transportation time.
- *Transportation time based on an item viewpoint.* This viewpoint supports an item-specific transportation time between a warehouse pair, thereby supporting unusual situations not handled by the warehouse viewpoint. You define this transfer time as part of an item's site/warehouse-specific coverage planning data, which also defines the primary refilling warehouse (aka the ship-from warehouse).

Planning calculations will use the transportation time associated with the warehouse viewpoint unless the item viewpoint has been defined.

Cost Change Variances on Transfers With a standard cost item, the item's site-specific standard costs can differ between two sites. The difference frequently reflects a higher standard cost at the ship-to site because of freight or other landed costs. Transferring the item will result in a cost change variance when the costs differ between two sites, where the variance is generated upon receipt at the ship-to site.

Order-Related Text for Transfer Orders Some situations require textual explanations or additional descriptive information about the transfer order and line items. Order-related text can be specified in several ways, such as documents attached to the header or line items of a transfer order, or the item's descriptive text on a line item.

Reserving Material for a Transfer Order Shipment Some scenarios require reservations of the material to be transferred, using either manual or automatic reservation approaches. The reservations will be communicated on picking lists, and they can also serve as the basis for populating the information for suggested shipment. With a manual approach, you access the Reservation form to view existing inventory and select the desired inventory to be reserved. The Reservation form can be accessed from several places during the process, such as after order creation, during picking list registration, or during shipment. Figure 17.5 illustrates the use of reservations in the basic model for transfer order processing.

An automatic reservation policy can be assigned to a transfer order[6] The use of automatic reservations involves several additional item-specific policies embedded in the Item Model Group assigned to an item. For example, one policy determines whether first-in-first-out (FIFO) logic will be used for automatic reservations.

Using Picking Lists for Transfer Orders A picking list provides an alternative to the Transfer Order document for preparing material to be shipped on a transfer order, using either an order-based picking list or a consolidated picking list.[7] This explanation focuses on order-based picking lists, since most firms employ this approach for transfer orders. You access the Posting Picking List form to indicate the quantity basis for initially populating the picking list (such as the order quantity, the available quantity

---

[6]The automatic reservation policy for a transfer order can be inherited from the company-wide policy (defined on the Inventory and Warehouse Management Parameters form) and optionally overridden.

[7]An item-specific policy can optionally mandate that an item must be picked before reporting actual shipment. This policy (termed the Picking Requirements checkbox) is embedded in the Item Model Group assigned to the item.

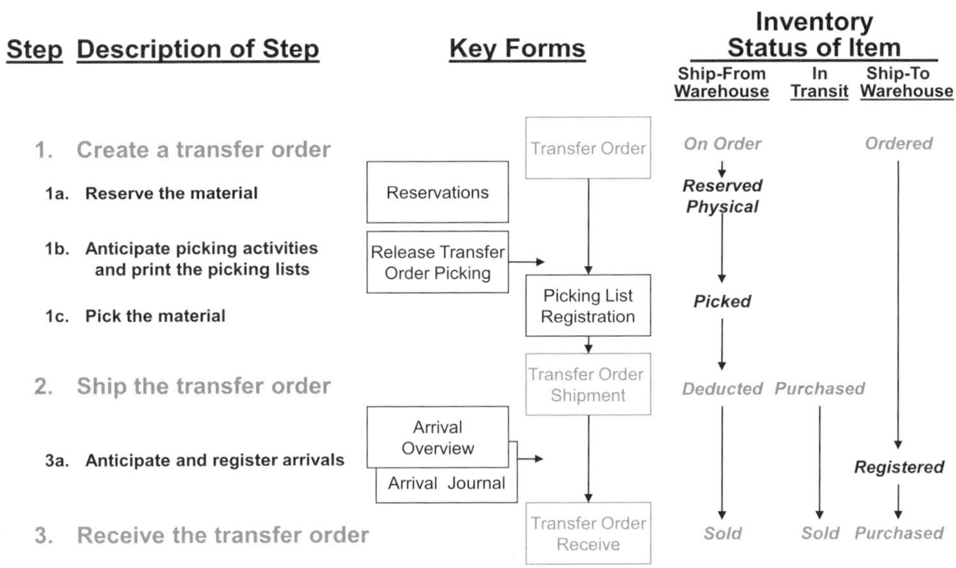

Figure 17.5 Variations for Basic Model of Transfer Order Processing

or the reserved inventory quantity) and to print the document. It can be accessed directly or from the Transfer Order form. This creates a picking list with a unique identifier, and the picking list can be reprinted. You can optionally indicate manual reservations as part of the process.

Actual picking activities are reported against the picking list identifier. This step is termed picking list registration, and you access the Picking List Registration form to report the actual quantities, locations and batch numbers that were picked. Figure 17.5 illustrates the use of picking lists as a variation to the basic model for transfer order processing.

Anticipate Picking Activities for Transfer Orders The anticipated picking activities are summarized on the Release Transfer Order Picking form, which allows you to select those line items that should be released for picking based on actual availability. This helps ensure that you only print picking lists for items actually in stock. The displayed line items can reflect selection criteria to focus attention of warehouse shipping personnel, such as selection criteria about the ship date, ship-from/ship-to warehouses, delivery mode or some item characteristic. If applicable, you can view and change reservations for line items. After you indicate which line items should be picked, the system displays the Posting Picking List form (described above) so that you can print the related picking lists.

Anticipate and Register Arrivals for Transfer Orders This step involves two forms—the Arrival Overview and the Arrival Journal—that work closely together in order to anticipate and register arrivals. The step was previously described for purchase order arrivals.

The Arrival Overview displays transfer order line items that represent anticipated receipts (i.e., with a status of Receiving Updates). You can filter the displayed information to easily select relevant line items that have actually arrived. For example, the filters can highlight line items for the ship-to warehouse and today's delivery. After selecting relevant line items, the Arrival Overview summarizes the associated workload expressed in terms of total quantity, volume, weight, and estimated handling time. The selected line items can then be used to create an arrival journal. After creating an arrival journal, the Arrival Overview summarizes the associated workload for these "line in process." Figure 17.5 illustrates the use of arrival journals in the basic model for transfer order processing.

An arrival journal contains line items that are initially populated with the selected items, their expected quantities, and the suggested putaway locations.[8] This information can be maintained on the Arrival Journal form. For example, you can override a line item's quantity and location to indicate actual arrivals, and delete line items not actually received. You post an arrival journal after completing the information, which changes inventory status to registered. The receipt can then be reported on the Receive Transfer Order form, where the quantity basis reflects the registered quantities and locations. After posting an arrival journal, the Arrival Overview no longer displays the associated line items.

Receiving Inspection for Transfer Orders The approaches for receiving inspection include quarantine orders and quality orders, as described in the next chapter about quality management. In terms of transfer order receipts, a quarantine order (if needed) must be manually created after receipt or automatically created as part of reporting arrival with an arrival

[8]The bin location on an arrival journal line item can initially default to the item's default receipt bin location within a warehouse (as specified in the item's setup information about warehouse items), to the warehouse's default bin location for receipts, or to the bin location specified in the setup information on the arrival overview form.

journal. Quality orders cannot be automatically generated for transfer orders, so that a quality order (if needed) must be manually created after receipt.

Batch Disposition Codes and Restricted Usage for Transfer Orders The batch disposition code assigned to a batch number may restrict its usage for transfer orders, as defined by the policies associated with the code. The policies can prevent reservations, picking and/or shipping of the batch number.

When to Use the Transfer Journal Versus a Transfer Order

A transfer order generally applies to inventory movements between two physical sites, where in-transit inventory must be tracked. You can optionally employ a one-step shipping process when not tracking in-transit inventory.

The transfer journal generally applies to inventory movements within a given physical site. It represents a one-step process for transferring an item between locations, and a simple approach for recording unplanned transfers. It serves other purposes related to variant codes and batch numbers.

- Change or combine batch numbers. You can change or combine the batch number for an inventory quantity, much like you would change or combine inventory in a bin location. You transfer the inventory quantity from one batch number to another (when combining batches), or to a newly created batch number (when changing batch numbers).
- Change variant codes. You can change the variant code for an item's inventory. For example, with an item number that represents an animal or plant, and a variant code that represents the item's age, you can transfer a one-year old variant to a two-year old variant.

17.4 Coordinate Transfer Orders

A firm's S&OP game plans for saleable products and services provide the primary driver of transfer activities for material items. The game plans define item demands at a given site/warehouse. Planning calculations synchronize supplies at the sourcing warehouses to meet these demands, as expressed through several coordination tools. The primary coordination tools consist of planned transfer orders and suggested action messages generated by planning calculations.

Planned Transfer Orders Suggestions for planned transfer orders can be viewed on the *Planned Transfer Orders* form or the *Planned Orders* form. A planned transfer order identifies the item's preferred refilling warehouse. You can also manually add a planned transfer order. Transfer orders can be created from selected planned orders via a function termed firming planned orders.

- *Selection of planned transfer orders.* You select planned orders via a marking check box. For example, orders can be individually marked or block-marked. Planned orders can also be viewed and optionally selected based on attributes such as the ship-from warehouse, buyer, order date, and planned order status. You can assign a status to planned orders (unprocessed, processed and approved) to indicate those that have been analyzed, but this status only represents reference information. The form does not retain marked orders if you exit before firming.
- *Analyzing and editing planned orders.* Planners often need to understand the rationale and impact for a planned transfer order. For example, you can view action messages related to a planned order. You can also view single-level pegging information about the source of demand for a planned order. Additional inquiries display single-level pegging to all supplies and demands for an item (via a *Net Requirements* inquiry), and the multi-level pegging information about supplies and demands for a planned order (via an *Explosion* inquiry).

The analysis often leads to needed action, and several actions can be implemented on the planned orders form.

- Change quantity and/or delivery date for the planned transfer order.
- Split the planned transfer order using a specified quantity and date.
- Group together several selected planned orders for the same item.
- Change the ship-from warehouse, thereby indicating an alternate source of supply. You can view inventory availability at other sites to support decisions about changing the source of supply.
- Change the planned transfer order to a planned purchase order or production order to indicate an alternate source of supply.
- Assign the planned order to an existing transfer order so that the firming process adds a line item to the existing order.

Firming Planned Transfer Orders The firming function creates transfer orders for selected planned orders. The system creates single-line transfer orders unless you indicate a grouping preference (via the firming dialogue when you select more than one planned order). The grouping preference can reflect a day, week or month.[9] With grouping by week, for example, the firming function can create multi-line transfer orders containing planned orders between a warehouse pair. Execution of the firming function automatically deletes the marked planned orders, and creates a log for tracking which planned orders have been firmed and by whom.

Planned orders can be automatically firmed, or automatically delayed to the end of a frozen period, based on time fence policies (embedded in the coverage group assigned to an item).

- *Firm time fence.* The firm time fence enables the planning calculations to automatically create transfer orders, thereby eliminating the effort to manually firm planned orders. The system uses the company-wide grouping preferences to create multi-line transfer orders, such as creating a multi-line order for planned orders within a weekly period. To be effective, the automatic firming time fence should be slightly greater than the item's transfer lead time and reorder cycle.
- *Freeze time fence.* The freeze time fence represents the shortest possible turnaround time to obtain material with a new transfer order, so that planning calculations will place planned orders at the end of the frozen period. The freeze time fence represents expedited delivery whereas the transfer lead time represents normal delivery.

Special Case for Suggested Transfers between Warehouses at an AX Site Warehouses within a given AX site often reflect close proximity, so that actual transfers between warehouses are generally handled through a transfer journal rather than a transfer order. In this case, planned transfer orders can be used to communicate requirements, but firming the planned orders should generate a transfer journal which can be subsequently posted after physically moving the material. This approach requires a site-specific policy termed "Use transfer journals for movements within site" otherwise firming a planned order results in a transfer order.

[9]The company-wide default values for grouping preferences (when firming planned transfer orders) are defined in the Master Planning Parameters form.

Other Coordination Tools for Transfer Orders The action and futures messages provide one tool for coordinating transfer orders to meet the S&OP game plans. Planning calculations generate these two types of messages, as previously explained in Chapter 10 (Figure 10.3). Additional tools include the visibility of picking activities using the Release Transfer Order Picking form, and the visibility of arrivals using the Arrival Overview form.

Case 90: Landed Costs for Transfer Orders

A manufacturing company with multiple sites incurred significant costs in transporting products between sites. They also used standard costs to support site-specific costs for an item. These incremental landed costs were included in an item's site-specific standard cost. The cost accountant wanted to identify the different types and amounts of these landed costs for an item, and also obtain a comparison of standard versus actual costs for each type. The cost accountant was considering an add-on module to support these requirements.[10]

17.4 Intercompany Orders

Trading between two companies involves a customer-to-vendor relationship. Intercompany orders can be used when both companies exist within the same Dynamics AX instance. Placing a purchase order with an intercompany vendor will automatically create a corresponding sales order in the sister company, and vice versa. The origin of an intercompany order identifies whether it was manually or automatically created, as indicated by the origin field in the order header. The origin field can have a value of *source* or *derived* respectively. The origin field is blank for all other sales orders and purchase orders.

Intercompany orders require setup information about items and also about the vendors and customers representing the sister companies. The setup information will be briefly summarized, and then we'll review several variations of intercompany orders.

[10] See **www.scalable.com.au** for additional information about their add-on module for handling landed costs for transfer orders.

Setup Information for Items A product must be released to both companies in order to support intercompany trading, and the item's company-level information must be defined in both companies. Chapter 3 previously described item definition. Given the automatic creation of a corresponding order, the following aspects of item information may be critical.

- Default ship-from site/warehouse for an automatically created sales order. The default values can be defined for an item or for a customer.
- Default ship-to site/warehouse for an automatically created purchase order. The default values can be defined for an item or for a vendor.
- Item information (at the selling company) should include a standard sales price and/or sales agreements that determine prices on the intercompany sales order and purchase order. Pricing information at the selling company normally dictates the price on the corresponding intercompany purchase order.

Setup Information for an Intercompany Vendor Vendor information is defined within each company. Hence, a vendor number must be defined within the buying company so that you can identify the associated sister company. At the same time, you can also identify the corresponding customer number within the selling company.

Several policies must be defined about the trading practices between a pair of purchasing and selling companies. For example, the policies determine the ability to change prices and discounts on the derived order.

Setup Information for an Intercompany Customer Just like vendors, the customer information is defined within each company. Hence, a customer number must be defined within the selling company so that you can identify the associated sister company. At the same time, you can also identify the corresponding vendor number within the buying company. You can also maintain the policies about the trading practices between the companies.

Variations of Creating Intercompany Orders There are several variations of creating intercompany orders, as illustrated by the following examples. The examples involve a distribution company that purchases products from a manufacturing company. Sales orders and purchase orders were previously explained in Chapters 12 and 13 respectively, and intercompany orders reflect the same functionality.

- *Manually Create an Intercompany Purchase Order.* A basic scenario consists of a manually created purchase order (in the distribution company) to an intercompany vendor (the manufacturing company). This results in an intercompany purchase order and automatic creation of an intercompany sales order at the manufacturing company. This is termed a two-legged order because it reflects transactions between the two related companies.

  The converse situation involving the creation of an intercompany sales order will generate an intercompany purchase order when it represents a special order or direct order, as discussed in a subsequent example.
- *Firm a Planned Intercompany Purchase Order.* Firming a planned purchase order to an intercompany vendor will automatically create an intercompany purchase order and a corresponding intercompany sales order (at the manufacturing company).
- *Release an Intercompany Purchase Order from a Blanket Order (aka Purchase Agreement).* A purchase agreement can be defined for an intercompany vendor, where the type of commitment must reflect a purchase quantity commitment. Each line item identifies an item, quantity and the purchase price or discount. You can then generate and view the equivalent sales agreement for the intercompany vendor. Releasing an order from the blanket (for a specified line item, quantity and date) creates an intercompany purchase order and a corresponding intercompany sales order at the manufacturing company. Section 13.6 previously described purchase agreements.
- *Create an Intercompany Purchase Order from a Sales Order (aka Special Order).* A special order can be created for a sales order line, which results in an intercompany purchase order and sales order when the vendor is a sister company. This is termed a three-legged order because the sales order to an external customer reflects the third leg. Changes on the originating sales order can automatically update the derived order, such as changes to the quantity, delivery date or delivery address. Special orders were previously described in Section 12.7.
- *Create a Direct Delivery Intercompany Purchase Order from a Sales Order (aka Direct Order).* A direct order can be created from a sales order line, which results in an intercompany purchase order and sales order (when the vendor is a sister company) that will be directly delivered to the customer. In this case, the sales order shipment at the

sister company can automatically update the related orders. Several policies in the setup information only apply to this direct delivery scenario. Direct orders were previously described in Section 12.7.

Other variations for intercompany orders include replenishment of stocked items across a multi-company supply chain, as described in the next section.

17.6 Master Scheduling Across a Multicompany Supply Chain

The sequence for performing the master scheduling task becomes important in a multicompany supply chain involving two or more companies. Planning calculations apply to a single company, which means the master scheduling task should first be performed for the top-tier company. This generates planned intercompany demand that communicates requirements to the second-tier company, which represents an up-stream company within the supply chain.[11] The process must be repeated for additional up-stream companies. The primary coordination approach involves the intercompany master scheduling task.

Intercompany Master Scheduling Task A sequence of companies—termed an intercompany planning group—can be defined for performing the intercompany master scheduling task. You also identify the set of relevant set of master plan data for each company in the sequence. A single intercompany planning group may be sufficient in many scenarios, where the specified sequence often reflects a subset of companies requiring supply chain coordination. You specify the intercompany planning group as part of the dialogue for performing the intercompany master scheduling task.

Some additional information is specified as part of the dialogue for performing the intercompany master scheduling task, such as the number of iterations to correctly support more complex scenarios such as bi-directional trade. The additional information typically specifies regeneration calculations for the first iteration and net change calculations for subsequent

[11]The term upstream provides a relative reference within a supply chain indicating a source of raw material, whereas the term downstream indicates the direction of the end-customer.

iterations. The intercompany master scheduling task can be started in any company, since the sequencing will reflect the specified intercompany planning group.

As part of generating planned purchase orders within one company, the master scheduling task generates demand for an up-stream company. This demand is labeled *planned intercompany demand*, which differentiates it from other types of demand.[12]

The generation of planned intercompany demand requires some additional setup information within the master plan policies. That is, you designate that downstream planned intercompany demand should be included, and you also specify all possible companies (and their related set of master plan data) that could be considered. These settings only apply when the downstream company is not included in the same master scheduling run, such as running intercompany master scheduling where the specified intercompany planning group does not include the downstream company.

Planned Intercompany Demand Inquiries The planned intercompany demand can be viewed from two perspectives—incoming and outbound—that reflect a company's relative position in the supply chain. The outbound perspective identifies planned purchases (to other companies) for a purchasing company, and the incoming perspective identifies planned sales (to other companies) for a selling company.

Intercompany Supply and Demand Inquiry This form shows all orders—both planned and firm—that a company has from upstream and downstream companies. For example, it displays sales order demands and planned intercompany demands for items. Starting from a selected item, you can access a Multilevel Pegging form to view all supplies and demands across the multicompany supply chain and a multilevel product structure.

Intercompany Inventory Inquiry The On-Hand Inquiry form contains a Tab for displaying an item's inventory in multiple companies.

Value of In-Transit Inventory for Intercompany Orders A separate report—termed the Intercompany Goods in Transit Totals report—displays the period beginning balance, period ending balance and net change

[12]The construct for planned intercompany demand replaces the need for firming planned purchase orders to communicate requirements across a multicompany supply chain.

with a period. Information is grouped by vendor, and provides the basis for manually created general ledger entries. An additional report displays the transaction detail about shipments and receipts within a given period.

Example of Multicompany Supply Chain A simplified example of a global manufacturer illustrates a multicompany supply chain. The simplified example was also included as one of the common scenarios for Case 4. As shown in Figure 17.6, the simplified example consists of two different companies representing a manufacturing company and a distribution company. In the manufacturing company, an intermediate item (produced at one manufacturing site) was transferred to another site for producing the end item. The manufacturing company sold the end-item to domestic customers. The end-item was also transferred to a different company's distribution center for sales to foreign customers. The primary coordination tools across the multicompany supply chain consisted of planned intercompany demand as well as intercompany purchase orders and sales orders.

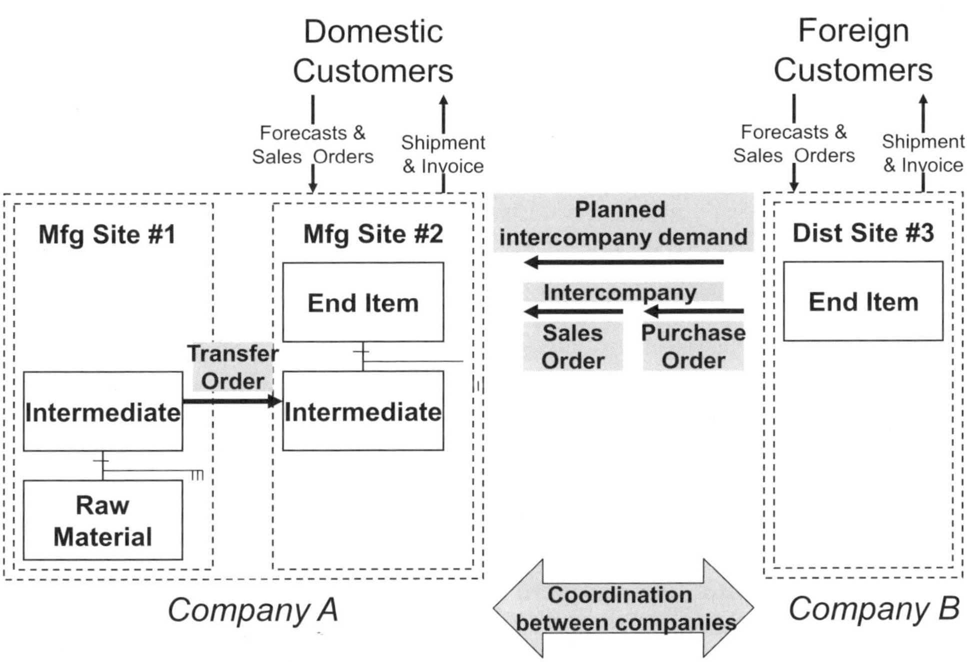

Figure 17.6 Coordination Across a Multicompany Supply Chain

17.6 Other Multisite Variations

Each company with multiple sites tends to have unique requirements. The following variations represent some of these requirements.

Subcontractor Location Identified by an AX Site and Warehouse Each subcontractor must be identified by an AX site and warehouse in order to track inventory of supplied components and parent items. Most scenarios identify the subcontractor location as a unique AX site, while some scenarios simply identify it as unique AX warehouse. The choice affects possible options for managing inventory of the supplied components and the parent item, since the warehouse source for components and the deliver-to warehouse for the production order must be within the same AX site.

Identifying a subcontractor as a separate AX site supports production of the same item at different subcontractors with site-specific BOM versions and site-specific costs. The site-specific costs also apply to the supplied components and the items representing the subcontracted services. Identifying a subcontractor as a separate AX warehouse (rather than an AX site) precludes the above-mentioned advantages.

Multiple Manufacturing Plants that Build Different Items Manufacturing plants that build different products and subassemblies can be modeled as AX warehouses, since there is no requirement for site-specific BOM and routing information. Each manufactured item is only produced in one location, and the BOM lines indicate the relevant warehouse source of components.

Multiple Manufacturing Plants that Build the Same Item Manufacturing plants that build the same products and subassemblies are normally modeled as AX sites, since you can define site-specific BOM and routing information.

Centralized Engineering for Multiple Companies One aspect of centralized engineering involves enterprise-level information about items. As described in a previous chapter (Section 3.1), the enterprise-level information defines the basis for item identification, and the item number and description (aka the product number and product name). This enterprise-level information provides the basis for managing intercompany orders and inventory balances across multiple companies. Other aspects of engineering information—such as BOM and routing information—are maintained as company-level information for an item. Section 3.10 previously summarized the company versus site/warehouse information for an item.

Combined Invoice for Multiple Sales Orders Normal processing generates one invoice for one sales order, but some customers require a combined invoice for multiple sales orders. This is termed a *summary update*. An automatic summary update can apply to all sales orders with the same bill-to customer and currency, and possibly other criteria such as the method of payment and sold-to customer. These criteria must be defined for individual customers, and a summary update designated upon invoicing. The concept of summary updating applies to other sales order documents such as packing slips. It also applies to purchase order documents.

Additional Case Studies

Case 91: Multiple Plants Build Same Item A manufacturer produced the same products in several plants that were modeled as AX sites. They defined a company-wide BOM version for an item to ensure product standardization. They also defined a site-specific routing for each item, along with site-specific labor rates and overhead formulas. The site-specific standard costs for purchased material, labor and overhead were used to calculate site-specific standard costs for each manufactured item. S&OP game plans were defined for each product and site, and planning calculations coordinated supply chain activities for the multiple sites. Financial reports were generated for each site.

Case 92: Home Furniture Outlets A company specializing in home furniture had multiple outlets grouped into various companies. Inventory replenishment was based on outlet-specific min/max quantities. As part of sales order processing, inventory could be checked within a given company's outlets or (if necessary) across all outlets. The system automatically created a transfer order for moving items within a company, or an intercompany order for moving items between companies. When inventory was insufficient, the user could generate a purchase order (to the furniture manufacturer) that was directly linked to the sales order.

Executive Summary

There are many variations of multisite operations. The basic variations reflect requirements for material transfers between physical sites and how the sites are grouped into companies. A planned transfer order supports material coordination between two sites within the same company, whereas intercompany orders support material coordination between sites in different companies. The basic variations also reflect two options concerning the AX solution approach for modeling physical sites.

A basic model of transfer order processing provided the foundation for explaining variations in business processes, such as the use of reservations, picking lists for transfer order shipments, and arrival journals for receipts. The chapter explained the use of planned transfer orders and other coordination tools.

Intercompany orders support the coordination of material transfers between two sites in different companies within a single AX instance. Intercompany orders require setup information in both companies. The chapter described several variations for creating and managing intercompany orders, including special orders and direct orders. It also described master scheduling across a multi-company supply chain and several other multisite variations.

Chapter 18

Quality Management

The concerns of quality management typically extend across every aspect of supply chain management. This broad viewpoint ranges from the definition of item and product structure information through sourcing purchased material, actual production, sales shipments, and returns. These topics have been covered throughout the book. A narrower viewpoint focuses on several aspects of unique functionality for quality management.

The narrower viewpoint includes the definition and enforcement of materials management policies, such as receiving inspection and product testing. Additional aspects include nonconformance reports, the coordination of quality resources to perform inspection and testing, and MSDS documents for hazardous materials. These topics are reflected in the following sections within the chapter.

1. Broad Viewpoint of Quality Management
2. Receiving Inspection and Quarantine Orders
3. Quality Inspection and Inventory Blocking
4. Product Testing and Quality Orders
5. Quality Problems and Nonconformance Reports
6. Using Cases for Quality Management Purposes
7. Coordination of Quality-Related Activities
8. Hazardous Materials and MSDS Documents
9. Sales Order Limitations on Restricted Products
10. Stop Replenishment or Sales of an Item
11. Regulatory Reporting Requirements for Different Countries

18.1 Broad Viewpoint of Quality Management

A wide range of quality management considerations are addressed by out-of-the-box capabilities within Dynamics AX. These capabilities have been covered throughout the book, as summarized below along with the relevant section number in parentheses.

Item and BOM Definition Item and BOM information provide a logical starting point for quality concerns. Some of the major concerns include the following:

- Item identification (Sections 3.1 and 3.3), including the optional use of variant codes as a part of the item identifier (Section 3.14)
- Specify and enforce authorized units of measure for an item (Section 3.6)
- Specify and enforce approved vendors for a purchased item or subcontracted service (Sections 13.3 and 16.3)
- Approval of authorized BOM versions for an item, including the use of electronic signatures for approval (Section 4.3)
- Approval of authorized routing versions for an item, including the use of electronic signatures for approval (Section 6.5)
- Identify quality factors in production, such as planned component scrap for a BOM line and operation scrap percentages in the routing (Sections 4.4 and 6.8)
- Identify planned changes reflecting continuous improvements in production, such as planned changes to BOM and routing information (Sections 4.6 and 6.12)
- Identify the needed documentation for an item, BOM, routing operation, and other key constructs (Section 3.5)
- Define the BOM and routing for a specific configuration of a configurable item (Section 7.1)

Serial and Batch Tracking Many manufacturing companies require serial or batch tracking for purchased and manufactured items (Sections 9.1 and 9.2). Other considerations include batch attributes and batch disposition codes (Sections 9.4 and 9.5), certificates of analysis (Section 18.4) and integration with a laboratory information management system (Case 93).

Purchasing and Production Several aspects of the business processes for procurement and production involve quality management concerns, as summarized below.

- Specify and enforce approved vendors for a purchased item or subcontracted service (Sections 13.3 and 16.3)

- Define and enforce work flow approvals, such as the approval for purchase orders (Section 13.9)
- Identify scrap or returns to vendor for receipts of purchased material (Section 13.10)
- Identify actual scrap or rework options for finished production quantities (Section 14.9)
- Perform receiving inspection and report disposition via quarantine orders (Section 18.2)
- Assign inventory blocking for quality purposes and the expected availability date (Section 18.3)
- Perform testing and report the test results within different business processes, such as during the receipt for a purchase order or during the production process (Section 18.4)
- Identify and track quality problems via nonconformance reports or cases (Sections 18.5 and 18.6)

Sales The business processes associated with sales orders, shipments, and customer returns involve several quality management concerns, as described below.

- Employ configuration technologies during entry of a sales order or sales quote to define the valid BOM and routing for a specific configuration of a configurable item (Section 7.1)
- Enforce restrictions on sales order processing, such as preventing order entry for restricted products or for stopped items (Sections 18.9 and 18.10)
- Provide regulatory reports for sales to different countries (Section 18.11)
- Identify hazardous materials and their MSDS documents, and ensure compliance for sending MSDS documents to customers (Section 18.8)
- Specify RMA disposition codes and related policies for handling customer returns (Section 12.8)

Other quality considerations might include best practices in supply chain management, such as ensuring valid delivery date promises on sales orders (Section 11.6), or the correct assignment of purchase prices on purchase orders (Section 13.4).

18.2 Receiving Inspection and Quarantine Orders

An item's quarantine management policy (embedded within the item model group assigned to the item) enforces 100% inspection for all received material. After purchase order receipt, for example, the system automatically creates a quarantine order for the received quantity. A quarantine order can also be manually created for existing inventory, or selectively created when recording item arrival. A quarantine order prevents material usage until the inspection process has ended. However, planning calculations view the quarantined material as immediately available.

Quarantine orders require the definition of a quarantine warehouse and the bin locations within this quarantine warehouse. A quarantine warehouse can then be associated with each normal warehouse that requires quarantine orders.

A quarantine order only applies to a single item and quantity, and consists of four statuses (created, started, report as finished, and ended). A manually created quarantine order has a created status, and the status can be changed to started. An automatically created quarantine order has a status of started. The optional report-as-finished status supports use of a separate put-away transaction. Each status is summarized below.

- *Created.* A manually created quarantine order represents a directive to move material from the originating warehouse/bin to a quarantine warehouse/bin. The system does not prevent usage, and the quarantine order can be deleted.
- *Started.* The material has been placed in the quarantine warehouse/bin, and cannot be used until the inspection process has been completed. The inspection process can report material as scrapped (via the scrap function), or as having inspection completed. You can split the order quantity in order to report a subset as scrapped or completed. The scrap function immediately reduces inventory and no further action is required. If material must be returned (such as a return to vendor), you can change the status to report as finished (or ended) and subsequently report the returned material.
- *Report as Finished.* This is an optional status to support a separate put-away transaction. By reporting inspection as finished, the system creates a separate arrival journal so you can specify the put-away location before

posting the journal. The user specifies the name of the desired arrival journal, such as the arrival journal for a purchase order.

- *Ended.* The material can be used. The material is placed in the specified site, warehouse, and bin.

Creation of a quarantine order will generate two inventory transactions: a scheduled issue for the normal warehouse (with a status of *on order*) and a scheduled receipt at the quarantine warehouse (with a status of *ordered*). Starting a quarantine order will deduct inventory from the normal warehouse and receive inventory at the quarantine warehouse. Reporting a scrapped quantity (with an immediate reduction in inventory), or reporting a good quantity and ending a quarantine order, will reduce the inventory in the quarantine warehouse.

The Quarantine Order form displays a list of existing quarantine orders, and provides the starting point for manually creating a quarantine order, reporting inspection results and status changes. It also serves as a coordination tool for inspection activities.

Since an item's quarantine management policy represents a requirement for 100% inspection of receipts, it should not be used for items with intermittent or as-required inspection. In these cases, you can selectively indicate the creation of a quarantine order when recording item arrival.

Quarantine Orders for Customer Returns

A customer return can be selectively placed on a quarantine order when recording arrival related to a Return Material Authorization (RMA). An RMA disposition code is initially assigned when recording the arrival, and you can reassign the disposition code on the quarantine order. The disposition code indicates what action should be done with the returned item, such as returning it to stock, scrapping it, or sending it back to the customer. The quarantine order must be split in order to assign different disposition codes to subsets of the returned quantity. Ending the quarantine order will implement the action for the disposition code, such as scrapping the returned material. The logic associated with these RMA disposition codes only applies to quarantine orders for returned items. A disposition code entered for other types of quarantine orders does not have any effect, and is not recognized in the standard RMA reports about disposition codes.

18.3 Quality Inspection and Inventory Blocking

Quality inspection of an item's inventory typically requires blocking of inventory transactions until inspection has been completed. This is termed inventory blocking for short. This section introduces manual assignment of inventory blocking, and the next section covers automatic assignment of inventory blocking in the context of a quality order. The manual assignment of inventory blocking represents a minimalist approach to a quality inspection.

With manual assignment of inventory blocking, you use the Inventory Blocking form to initially identify the blocking and to subsequently remove the blocking. The required information includes the item number, the inventory quantity, and the relevant inventory dimensions such as the site/warehouse/bin and batch number. You also indicate whether you expect the inventory to be usable or scrapped after the inspection process (via an Expected Receipts checkbox), and an expected receipt date when you expect the inventory to be usable. In terms of the item's net requirements, the blocked inventory is treated as a negative quantity, and expected usable inventory is treated as a positive quantity on the expected receipt date. Planning calculations account for the expected receipt date of usable inventory.

The manual blocking must be removed in order to report further inventory transactions, such as an inventory adjustment to scrap the inventory.

The Inventory Blocking form displays existing inventory that has blocking. It also displays the source of the blocking, such as *manual* for manual assignment of inventory blocking. The source can also be a *quality order*, as described in the next section.

18.4 Product Testing and Quality Orders

Product testing entails the use of quality orders to report test results against a group of predefined tests. The explanation of product testing can be segmented into three areas: the definition of tests and test groups, the use of quality orders for reporting test results, and the rules for automatic generation of quality orders. Quality orders have been previously mentioned in the context of typical business processes for purchase orders (Section 13.1) and production orders (Section 14.2), and they can also be employed in other business processes.

Tests and Test Groups There are two types of predefined tests—quantitative and qualitative—and one or more tests can be assigned to a group of tests.

- *Quantitative Tests.* Each quantitative test must be assigned a testing unit of measure, so that acceptable values can be assigned when it is included in a test group. A pressure test, for example, might use pounds per square (PSI) as the unit of measure. The units of measure must be predefined along with the desired decimal precision.
- *Qualitative Tests.* A qualitative test will have an associated test variable (and its enumerated outcomes) when you assign it to a test group. A taste test, for example, may have one test variable for sweetness (with possible outcomes of sweet, sour and okay) and another test variable for color (with possible outcomes of dark, light and okay). You designate whether an outcome represents a pass or failure of the test.

  For both types of tests, you can optionally assign a test instrument and applicable documents that describe the test.

Tests are assigned to a group of tests (termed a *test group*), where the test group has a unique identifier.

- *Test Groups.* For each test group, you assign a sampling plan, an acceptable quality level (AQL), and an indication of whether the tests will require destructive testing of the sample. Destructive testing will result in an inventory reduction of the sample quantity.
- *Sampling Plan* A sampling plan is used to calculate the sample quantity for a quality order, and it can be expressed as an absolute quantity or as a percentage. For example, a sampling plan of 10% for a purchase order receipt quantity of 500 would result in a sample quantity of 50. The sampling plan can optionally require a different sample for each received batch when receiving multiple batches.

  When a quality order has been generated, it also results in inventory blocking for the sample quantity until the testing results have been validated. As described in the previous section, the Inventory Blocking form displays the blocking with a source of quality order, and the validation step removes the blocking. You can optionally specify a policy within the sampling plan so that inventory blocking applies to the entire order quantity rather than just the sample quantity.

- *Acceptable Quality Level (AQL)* An acceptable quality level refers to the percentage of tests which must be passed. An AQL of 90%, for example, means that 9 out of 10 tests must be passed.
- *Tests Within a Test Group.* When assigning a test to a test group, you define the acceptable measurement values for a quantitative test, or the test variable for a qualitative test. Each test can be assigned a sequence number, validity dates, and documents. You can designate which test results should be included in a certificate of analysis report associated with a quality order. An individual test can have its own AQL, referring to the percentage of the sample quantity which must be passed, since test results can be reported for subsets of the sample quantity.

The test group assigned to a quality order provides the initial basis for which tests need to be performed. Tests can be added, deleted, or changed on the quality order.

Use of a Quality Order A quality order defines the tests that need to be performed for an item and a sample quantity of its inventory. It is typically related to a specific order, such as a purchase order, production order or sales order. In addition to communicating the need to perform tests, it provides a mechanism for reporting results against the tests. You can manually create a quality order, or establish quality guidelines within each business process (such as a purchase order receiving process) for automatically creating a quality order. The next subsection explains automatic generation of quality orders.

After reporting the test results for every test within a quality order, you initiate a validation process that assigns a pass or fail status (based on meeting the overall AQL) and closes the quality order. When you try perform the next step in the business process, an infolog warns you when the quality order has failed or has not yet been closed. In addition, you can optionally reopen the quality order and force the validation process to assign a pass status by accepting any error conditions.

You can view information about a quality order (and its test results) from multiple viewpoints. For example, the quality order can be viewed for the related batch number or from the related sales order, purchase order, production order or quarantine order.

You can optionally generate a certificate of analysis that displays the test results for a quality order. A certificate of analysis, for example, could be printed for a batch of material being shipped to a customer. The printed test results will only be displayed for designated tests within the quality order.

You can optionally create a nonconformance report when a quality order identifies defective material. The nonconformance report provides the basis for further investigation, as described in a subsequent section about nonconformance reports.

Automatic Generation of Quality Orders You can define rules (termed *quality association records*) for automatic generation of a quality order for incoming or outgoing material. Each rule defines the set of tests, the acceptable quality level (AQL), and the sampling plan that apply to the automatically generated quality orders. Each rule also defines the event and conditions for automatically generating a quality order within a business process for the item. The business process can be related to purchase orders, quarantine orders, sales orders, or production orders, but not transfer orders. These business processes for a quality order are shown in Figure 18.1 and described below.

Business Process (Reference Type)	Label of the event that triggers a quality order (Execution / Document)	The actual event that triggers a quality order	Conditions: Site	Conditions: Item	Conditions: Other	Destructive Test Allowed
Purchase order	After registration	Post the registration	Site-specific or company-wide	Item-specific, quality group-specific, or all items	Vendor or vendor group	No
	Before receipts list	Initial attempt to post receipts list				No
	After receipts list	Post the receipts list				No
	Before product receipt	Initial attempt to post product receipt				No
	After product receipt	Post the product receipt				Yes
Quarantine order	Before report as finished	Initial attempt to report as finished			N/A	No
	After report as finished	Report the order as finished				No
	Before end	Initial attempt to report as ended				No
	After end	Report the order as ended				No
Sales order	Before picking	Initial attempt to post picking list			Customer or customer group	Yes
	After picking	Post the picking list				Yes
	Before packing slip	Initial attempt to post packing slip				Yes
	After packing slip	Post the packing slip				Yes
Production or Batch order, or Co-product	After registration	Post the registration			N/A	No
	Before report as finished	Initial attempt to report as finished				No
	After report as finished	Update the report as finished				Yes
Route operation	Before report as finished	Create batch/production order			Resource or Group Master Operation or Route Group	No
	After report as finished	Report the operation as finished				No
Inventory	None	None				Yes

Figure 18.1 Rules for Automatic Generation of a Quality Order

The figure summarize the events and conditions for generating a quality order for various business processes (termed the *reference type*). An event is expressed in terms of the relevant document and execution timing, such as after reporting product receipt for a purchase order. These events reflect variations in AX functionality for modeling different business processes. The figure also identifies the actual event that triggers automatic generation of a quality order.

The conditions for generating a quality order can be site-specific or company-wide, and they can apply to a single item, a group of items (based on the quality group assigned to items), or all items. Other conditions depend on the business process, such as vendor-specific conditions for a purchase order or customer-specific conditions for a sales order. A quality order involving destructive tests can only be generated when inventory exists for the event, as shown in the right-hand column of Figure 18.1. The automatic generation of a quality order can be further described for each business process.

- *Purchase Order Process.* The generation of a quality order can occur after posting the registration of received material. It can also occur before or after the posting of a receipts list or product receipt for the received material. A quality order that requires destructive testing can only be generated after posting the registration or product receipt for the received material, because the material must be on-hand in order to automatically deduct it for destructive testing. The need for a quality order can reflect a particular site, item or vendor, or a combination of these conditions.
- *Quarantine Order Process.* The generation of a quality order can occur before or after reporting the quarantine order as finished or ended. A quality order that requires destructive tests cannot be generated for a quarantine order, because it is assumed that the quarantine order functionality will handle scrapping of the destroyed material. The need for a quality order can reflect a particular site, item or vendor, or a combination of these conditions.
- *Sales Order Process.* The generation of a quality order can occur before or after the posting of a picking list or packing slip for the material being shipped. A quality order that requires destructive testing can be generated at any step. The need for a quality order can reflect a particular site, item, or customer, or a combination of these conditions.
- *Production Order Process.* The generation of a quality order can occur after posting the registration of a finished quantity for the parent item.

It can also occur before or after reporting the finished quantity. A quality order that requires destructive testing can only be generated after reporting a finished quantity. The need for a quality order can reflect a particular site or item, or a combination of these conditions.

- *Route Operation for a Production Order* When a production order contains a routing operation, the quality order can be generated before or after reporting the operation as finished. The need for a quality order can reflect a particular site, item or quality group, or a combination of these conditions. The need for a quality order can also reflect a specific master operation or the route group assigned to operations.
- *Inventory.* A quality order cannot be automatically generated for a transaction within an inventory journal (such as a profit/loss or counting journal) or for transfer order transactions. A quality order must be manually generated for an item's inventory quantity, and the selected test group determines what tests will be performed.

A rule must be defined for each variation in a business process requiring automatic generation of a quality order. The validity dates for a quality association record enable you to model planned changes in the business process.

Comparing Quality Orders and Quarantine Orders

Inspection requirements related to receipts and issues are often modeled with a quality order. There are several reasons. Automatic generation can reflect situation-specific conditions in various business processes, and a quality order indicates what should be inspected. A quality order provides a way to record test results and validate the results against the desired AQL. You can designate which test results are included in a certificate of analysis, and which test results should update batch attribute values.

Inspection requirements related to receipts can be modeled with a quarantine order. A quarantine order provides a way to report scrap, and it prevents usage until the quarantine order has been completed. An item's quarantine policy represents a company-wide mandate to perform 100% inspection of received material. However, a quarantine order can be selectively created when reporting the arrival of an item without a mandated quarantine policy. In some cases, a quality order should be used in conjunction with a quarantine order so that the inspectors know what should be tested, and the material cannot be used until completion of the quarantine order.

The inspection results for a batch-controlled item can be used to assign a batch disposition code, regardless of whether quality orders and quarantine orders are actually used. The policies associated with the batch disposition code can restrict material usage, as described in Section 9.5.

18.5 Quality Problems and Nonconformance Reports

A nonconformance report (termed a *nonconformance*) describes an item that has a quality problem, where the descriptive information includes the source and type of problem. The problem source is termed a *nonconformance type*. You assign a problem source and an associated problem type when you create a nonconformance.

Types of Problem Sources for a Nonconformance Report There are five types of problem sources (aka nonconformance types) that can be assigned to a nonconformance report, and each type can have optional source information.

- *Customer problem.* The source information about a customer problem can include the customer number, sales order number, or a lot number of a sales order transaction. For example, the nonconformance could relate to a specific sales order shipment or to customer feedback about product quality.
- *Service Request Problem.* The source information about a service request can include the customer number, sales order number, or lot number of a sales order transaction. For example, the nonconformance could relate to a specific sales order shipment or to a customer's complaint about item quality.
- *Vendor Problem.* The source information about a vendor problem can include the vendor number, purchase order number, or a lot number of a purchase order transaction. For example, the nonconformance could relate to a purchase order receipt or to a vendor's concern about a part that it supplies.
- *Production Problem.* The source information about a production problem can include the production order number or a lot number of a

specific transaction. For example, the nonconformance could relate to a specific batch order.

❖ *Internal Problem.* The source information about an internal problem can include the quality order number or a lot number of a quality order transaction. For example, the nonconformance could relate to the tests that are performed as part of a quality order or to an employee's concern about product quality.

Problem Types The user-definable problem types provide a classification of quality problems for each nonconformance type. For example, the problem types for service requests could reflect a classification of customer complaints, whereas the problem types for an internal nonconformance could represent a classification of defect codes. A problem type can be authorized for one or more nonconformance types (aka problem sources), as defined in the Nonconformance types form. For example, the problem type concerning a defect code could apply to all nonconformance types. You can change the nonconformance type assigned to a nonconformance, and this may require changing the problem type to a valid value for the new nonconformance type.

Use of a Nonconformance Report A nonconformance is initially created with an approval status of *new*, indicating that it represents a request for action. You can approve or refuse a nonconformance (which changes the approval status to *approved* or *refused*) to indicate that you will or will not take action on the nonconformance.[1] You can also close a nonconformance (as indicated by a separate check box) to indicate that you are finished with it, or reopen a nonconformance to indicate that further consideration is required.

Comments can be entered for a nonconformance by using the document handling capabilities. It is generally helpful to define a unique document type about nonconformances (by using the Document Type form) so that you can enter notes for the unique document type. You can then use the Report Setup form to define your policy about printing notes for the unique document type on the nonconformance report and tag.

---

[1] A user cannot approve a nonconformance unless the user has been assigned an employee identifier (via the User relations form). The system tracks the nonconformance history in terms of the employees who changed the status.

A printed conformance report and nonconformance tag can be used to assist material disposition.[2] You can selectively generate reports and tags based on selection criteria, such as the nonconformance number, item, customer, vendor, or status that are associated with a nonconformance.

- *Nonconformance report.* The nonconformance report displays identification information, such as the nonconformance number, item, and problem type. The report displays the related notes based on your report setup policies.
- *Nonconformance tag.* The nonconformance tag displays identification information, such as the nonconformance number and item. The tag displays the related notes based on your report setup policies. The tag also displays the quarantine zone and type (such as restricted usage versus unusable) that you assigned to the nonconformance in order to guide disposition of the defective material.

Options for Nonconformance Reports There are several options for handling the business processes pertaining to a nonconformance report, such as corrective actions, the description of work, additional testing, and related nonconformance reports.

- *Corrective action for a nonconformance report.* You can optionally define one or more corrections for an approved nonconformance. A correction identifies what type of diagnostic should be performed, who should perform it, and a requested date and a planned date for completing the diagnostic. You predefine the user-defined diagnostic types, and assign one to a corrective action. Indicate that you have finished the diagnostic step by changing the status of a correction to end. The status can be reopened. Comments can be entered for a correction by using the document handling capabilities. It is generally helpful to define a unique document type about corrections (by using the Document type form) so that you can enter notes for the unique document type. Use the Report setup form to define your policy about printing notes for the unique document type on the correction report. A printed correction report

[2]The printed nonconformance tag and report will display an assigned quarantine zone (along with information about unusable versus restricted usage) to guide handling of defective material. The zones may or may not correspond to inventory locations or resources. Use the Quarantine zones form to define zones that can be assigned to a nonconformance.

displays identification information about the nonconformance and the related nonconformance notes, as well as the correction information (such as the diagnostic) and related correction notes. The report displays the related correction notes based on your report setup policies.

- *Description of work for a nonconformance report.* You can optionally define one or more related operations for an approved nonconformance. A related operation describes the work that should be performed, expressed as a selected operation (from a predefined list of user-defined quality operations) and descriptive text about the reason for the work. After defining an operation, you can optionally define the miscellaneous charges, items, and time sheet labor hours that are required to perform the work. The calculated costs are shown for the related operation, and the total calculated costs are shown for the nonconformance. The calculated costs and the underlying detail (about items, labor hours, and miscellaneous charges) represent reference information, and they are only used within the quality management function.
- *Defining further tests about a nonconformance report.* You can optionally create a quality order from a nonconformance in order to identify the need for further tests. For example, a quality order may identify the need to test (or retest) the defective material. The newly created quality order displays the linkage to the originating nonconformance.
- *Defining related nonconformance reports.* You can optionally link one nonconformance to another, or create a new nonconformance from an existing one. For example, the linkage can reflect the interconnection between quality problems.

18.6 Using Cases for Quality Management Purposes

A quality issue can be identified by a case, and case management provides a multi-faceted approach to manage issues raised by customers, vendors or employees. Each case is uniquely identified by a Case ID. At its simplest, you manually create a case and a description, and then indicate progress (via the case status of opened, in-process, and closed or cancelled) and case resolution (of accept, reject or none). The optional facets of case management serve several different purposes and involve different types of setup information, as illustrated by the following.

- *Case Category.* A user-defined hierarchy of case categories will reflect the types of issues in a given business situation, and you must assign a case category to each case. As a simple example, the top of one hierarchy may be labeled sales, and consist of several case categories related to sales issues and customer service issues. For each case category, you can optionally define additional information about the need for creating an activity (for a case that is assigned the case category), and the need for a follow-up activity after changing the case status to closed. An activity can be a task, action, event or appointment. You can also identify an associated case process or knowledge article, as described in the next points.
- *Case Process.* A user-defined case process identifies the steps to follow when working on a case. A step can be required or optional. Each step can optionally have a specified activity, priority and responsibility. Linking a case process to a case category enables you to standardize your business processes for different types of issues.
- *Case Details about the Associated Customer, Item or Sales Order.* One or more associations can be defined for a case. In the context of sales, for example, the association may reflect a customer, item or sales order, or even a lead, opportunity, prospect or project. The association may reflect a vendor, item, purchase order or invoice in the context of purchasing. An additional case detail involves the source of information, such as a specified customer, vendor or employee.
- *Knowledge Article.* A knowledge article represents a file or document, or a link to additional information. It provides information for diagnosing or resolving an issue.
- *Service Level Agreement.* A service level agreement can be assigned to case. It indicates the guaranteed response time to an issue, and may also involve reporting time against a case.

Additional facets of case management have broader applications than just the identification of quality issues. For example, cases can be automatically created to identify audit violations based on audit policies. Audit policies consist of rules about purchase orders and vendor invoices (and expense reports), such as invoices to a certain vendor or exceeding a certain amount.

18.7 Coordination of Quality-Related Activities

Dynamics AX provides several coordination tools for quality management personnel, such as schedules, dispatch lists, and recommended actions.

- *Production Schedule for Quality-Related Operations.* The production schedule and job list identify routing operations to be performed by a resource that represents quality resources. The quality resource may include a labor pool of inspectors, a burn-in area, or other resource under quality management control. This may require time reporting (or unit completions by operation) to correctly reflect progress against the routing, availability for the next operation, auto-deduction of material, and actual costs.
- *Dispatch List of Quarantine Orders.* Each quarantine order identifies material placed into inspection or quarantine, but does not indicate what tests must be performed or a scheduled completion date. It may also identify a batch number and the related order (such as a purchase or production order).
- *Dispatch List of Quality Orders.* Each quality order identifies material that requires inspection, and the (remaining) tests that must be performed. It may also identify a batch number and the related order (such as a purchase or production order).
- *List of Inventory Blocking.* The inventory blocking may reflect a quality order or manual assignment.
- *List of Assigned Cases.* The cases assigned to an employee identify the issues raised by customers, vendors and others. The employee can review and take action for each assigned case.
- *List of Nonconformances.* Each nonconformance report (termed a non-conformance) describes an item that has a quality problem, where the descriptive information includes the source and type of problem.
- *List of Corrective Actions (for a Nonconformance).* Each correction identifies what type of diagnostic should be performed, who should perform it, and a requested date and a planned date for completing the diagnostic.

18.8 Hazardous Materials and MSDS Documents

A regulated item requires a Material Data Safety Sheet (MSDS) that can be sent to the customer. The MSDS document for a purchased item may also be received from a vendor. For a selected item, you can define the associated document by accessing the Product Data Safety Sheet form. This form consists of one or more line items uniquely identified by a system-assigned document number. When you add a line item, you define the related information for the item's MSDS document (such as the effective date, expiry date, version number, and an active flag), and use the document handling capabilities to identify the associated file containing the actual descriptive text. The descriptive text for MSDS documents can also be obtained from a subscription service such as Atrion.[3]

The requirements for sending an item's MSDS document may apply to all countries or to selected countries. This item-specific information must be defined on the Material Regulated Countries form.

When entering a sales order line for the item, an infolog warning can be displayed about sending the latest active MSDS document to the customer. This infolog warning occurs when the customer has not yet received the item's MSDS document, or when a newer version (defined by the document's effective date) needs to be sent.[4] An infolog warning can also be generated when an existing MSDS document is about to expire. You can optionally print the relevant MSDS documents when posting the packing list or invoice for the sales order, and even prevent posting when a document's expiry date has been exceeded.[5] The system automatically tracks when an item's MSDS document has been printed for a customer, along with the *last sent date*. The *last sent date* can also be manually entered. The tracking information (about the actual document number, the related sales order number, and the last sent date) can be viewed on the Product Safety Data Sheet Log, accessed from a sales line for the regulated item. The tracking information provides the basis for displaying the infolog warnings described above.

[3]See **www.atrionintl.com/** for additional information about their subscription service.

[4]In the context of sales order entry, the effective date of an MSDS document can be viewed in terms of the sales order delivery date or the current date, as defined by a company-wide policy on the Inventory and Warehouse Management Parameters form.

[5]These two options are displayed on the Posting Packing Slip and Posting Invoice forms, and the values initial default from the company-wide policies defined on the Inventory and Warehouse Management Parameters form.

When entering a purchase order for a hazardous material item, you can view the tracking information about the item's MSDS document. The tracking information (about the actual document number, the related purchase order number, and the last received date) can be viewed on the Product Safety Data Sheet Log, accessed from a purchase order line for the regulated item. An infolog warning can also be generated when an existing MSDS document is about to expire.

18.9 Sales Order Limitations on Restricted Products

Restricted products cannot be entered on a sales order line when the customer's delivery address reflects a non-allowed area, and an infolog warning will be displayed to delete or change the item number on the sales line. As part of setup information, you define a material restriction list for each country (and even the states/provinces within a country), and the item numbers corresponding to the restricted products on the list.

18.10 Stop Replenishment or Sales of an Item

Certain situations require stoppage of all purchasing, sales or inventory activities for an item, such as an obsolete or unsafe item. Three different policies—termed the stop flags—can be used to enforce stoppage.

Stop Purchasing Activities for an Item The purchasing stop flag for an item can be specified as a company-wide policy, and optionally overridden for a specific site. The purchasing stop flag means that an item's existing purchase orders cannot be received, and that new purchase orders cannot be created for the item. The stopped flag does not impact planning calculations, so that planned orders will still be generated. Note that a different stopped flag can also be specified for a purchase order line item, rather than stopping all purchase activities for the item.

Stop Sales Activities for an Item Certain situations require stoppage of all sales activities for an item. The sales stop flag for an item can be specified as a company-wide policy, and optionally overridden for a specific site. The sales stop flag means that an item's existing sales orders cannot be shipped, and that new sales orders cannot be created for the item.

Stop all Inventory Activities for an Item The inventory stop flag for an item can be specified as a company-wide policy, and optionally overridden for a specific site. The inventory stop flag prevents any further receipts or issues. The stopped flag does not impact planning calculations, so that planned orders will still be generated.

18.11 Regulatory Reporting Requirements for Different Countries

Some countries require annual reports about products delivered to the country. As part of setup information, you define a country-specific list of item numbers that need to be tracked, and the start/end dates for the annual report. An inquiry (termed the Regulated Item Reporting Detail form) summarizes the annual usage for an item, such as the yearly quantity used and produced.

Additional Case Studies

Case 93: Integration with a Laboratory Information Management System A manufacturer employed a laboratory information management system (LIMS) to track characteristics of their production processes and product quality. The system was uniquely tailored to their environment, and the batch number within AX provided the primary integration point between AX and the LIMS information.

Case 94: Report Test Results During Production A manufacturer performed different tests during several steps in an item's production process. The required tests were identified by an automatically generated quality order, which also provided the basis for reporting actual test results. The rules for automatic generation of quality orders reflected different operation numbers in the routing, and different tests were performed at each operation. For batch-controlled items (or serial-controlled items), the numbers were preassigned to a newly created production order so that the test results could be recorded against a specific batch number (or serial number).

Case 95: Certificates of Analysis for Sales Order Shipments A manufacturer enclosed a certificate of analysis with sales order shipments of selected items. The certificate reflected the test results reported for the item, where test results were captured as part of a quality order. The contents of a certificate of analysis reflected each customer's requirements for selected test results.

Case 96: Instrument Calibration and Inspection Frequencies The quality manager at a manufacturer wanted a schedule for instrument calibration based on usage and time factors, the tracking of instrument maintenance, and calibration warnings prior to instrument usage. Additional requirements included instrument certificate tracking and risk instrument notifications. The manager also wanted inspection rules about when and how often to perform inspection of incoming material. Some materials required inspection frequencies based on quantities or time factors or both, while other materials required inspection only on the first receipt from the vendor. Skip-lot logic was also required to meet inspection frequency standards for ISO 2859-1, NIST Series 6 and ANSI Z1.4.[6]

Case 97: Nonconformance Reports for Purchased Material The quality manager wanted to track problems related to several purchased items. When a problem was identified, a quality specialist created a nonconformance report that identified the problem source by vendor. The specialist also described the problem (via textual comments), assigned a user-definable problem type that provided a classification of the quality problems, and printed a tag that was attached to the material. When the nonconformance report was approved for further action, it was assigned one or more corrective actions that identified what type of diagnostic should be performed, who should perform it, and the requested date for completion. In some cases, a quality order was also created to capture test results about the material. The status of the nonconformance report was changed to closed after work was completed.

[6]See **www.erpsolutions.biz** for additional information about their quality control applications that support instrument calibration, inspection frequencies, and quality metrics.

Executive Summary

A number of quality management concerns involve the enforcement of materials management practices, such as receiving inspection (via quarantine orders) and required tests (via quality orders). A nonconformance report can identify a quality problem, and drive corrective actions and additional testing. Dispatch lists can help coordinate quality resources to perform inspection and testing. The case studies included certificates of analysis, capturing test results during production and instrument calibration.

Chapter 19

Inventory and Warehouse Management

Warehouse management involves the physical storage and movement of products within and between physical sites, as well as handling outbound and inbound shipments with trading partners. Various terms such as inventory management or distribution management are used to refer to these warehouse management activities, and responsibility for these activities may be assigned to one or several functional areas. For simplicity's sake further explanations use the terms warehouse management function and warehouse personnel.

The requirements for coordinating and reporting warehouse management activities vary from company to company, and between physical sites within a company. They also vary for different types of inventory transactions, such as sales orders, purchase orders, production orders, and transfer orders as well as quarantine and quality orders. Previous chapters have described these transactions.

The explanation of warehouse management starts with the basic functionality. This includes the definition of inventory stocking locations and basic warehouse management policies, as well as basic inventory transactions. Other warehouse activities include handling variations of arrivals and shipments. The basic functionality and some variations in business processes are reflected in the following sections.

1. Basic Functionality for Warehouse Management
2. Handling Arrivals
3. Handling Shipments

19.1 Basic Functionality for Warehouse Management

Warehouse management functionality requires definition of inventory stocking locations and basic warehouse management policies. It also involves several types of basic inventory transactions, including adjustments, transfers, physical inventory counts, and cycle counts.

Sites, Warehouses and Bins Each site has a unique identifier, and an optional financial dimension to support financial reporting by site. A site generally represents a physical site, and consists of one or more warehouses. A site also provides the foundation for site-specific standard costs for items, and site-specific BOMs, routings, labor rates, and overhead formulas for manufactured items.

Each warehouse has a unique identifier, and warehouse information includes its associated bin locations. The identifier for a bin location often reflects its coordinates (consisting of an aisle, rack, shelf level and/or bin), but a different value can be manually assigned. Bin locations can be manually or automatically created. Automatic creation can be based on copying bin locations from another warehouse, or a process that creates bin locations for specified ranges of aisle, rack, shelf level and bin numbers.

A warehouse is designated with a warehouse type of main; a main warehouse is also termed a default or normal warehouse. Two other types of warehouses may be needed to support inspections and transfers at a main warehouse.

- *Quarantine Warehouse.* Each main warehouse requires an associated quarantine warehouse when using quarantine orders to manage the inspection process. A quarantine warehouse has a separate identifier, a warehouse type of quarantine, and its own bin locations. Most situations will employ one quarantine warehouse for each normal warehouse. A minimalist approach would employ one quarantine warehouse per site.
- *Transit Warehouse.* Each main warehouse requires an associated transit warehouse when using transfer orders to ship material from the warehouse. A transit warehouse has a separate identifier, a warehouse type of transit, and at least one bin location that always acts as a default. You need a minimum of one transit warehouse per site, which can be assigned to the main warehouses within the site. Alternatively, a transit ware-

house can be defined for each main warehouse that acts as a ship-from location for transfer orders. The different transit warehouses provide more granular visibility of in transit inventory. Chapter 16 explained the use of transfer orders in a multisite operation.

Several policies serve as the foundation for basic inventory transactions and warehouse management. These policies are defined for each warehouse, bin and item, and include several stop transaction policies, as described in the following subsections.

Warehouse-Related Policies A warehouse can have a default bin location that applies to all receipts, and a second default bin location that applies to all issues. These bin locations serve as a default when item-specific defaults are not specified. These default bin locations for a warehouse should only be specified when a single bin location makes sense, such as a single default bin location for a transit warehouse.

A warehouse can have a specified calendar, and optionally be designated as non-nettable (via the manual planning flag) so that supplies are ignored by planning calculations.

Bin-Related Policies A bin can be designated with a location type that affects usage by warehouse management transactions. The location types include an inbound dock, an outbound dock, a picking location, and a buffer location. These location types are primarily used for palletized items. Given our focus on non-palletized items, we'll primarily use a location type of picking for the inventory transactions covered in this section.

An unusable bin location can be identified as blocked. For example, the bin location may not be ready for use or it may be undergoing repair.

Item-Related Policies The storage dimension group assigned to an item determines whether site, warehouse, and bin must be specified on the item's inventory transactions. The tracking dimension group assigned to an item determines whether batch numbers and/or serial numbers must be recorded for the item's inventory transactions. The negative inventory policies (embedded within the item model group assigned to an item) determine whether the item's physical inventory can be negative. With actual costing approaches (described in Chapter 9), a general guideline would be to prevent negative physical inventory, since this condition creates problems in calculation of actual costs. Negative financial inventory should be allowed, since this allows inventory usage after receipt but prior to financial updates such as posting a vendor's invoice for purchased material.

Items with standard costs must have an active item cost record in order to record inventory transactions. Chapter 9 explained standard costs and item cost records.

An item's inventory unit of measure determines how inventory balances will be maintained and displayed.

An item can have a default bin location within a warehouse—one for receipts and one for issues—that typically represent situations where the item is always stocked in the same location.

Stop Transaction Policies As part of the item master policies, you can use the stopped flags to prevent all inventory transactions for an item, or to selectively prevent item transactions for (1) purchase orders, (2) sales orders (3) intercompany purchase orders, and (4) intercompany sales orders. Transactions can also be stopped for a specified line item on a sales or purchase order, thereby preventing shipment or receipt. In addition, a company-wide policy optionally prevents an item's inventory transactions during the process of cycle counting or physical inventory.

Basic Inventory Transactions Within a Warehouse The basic inventory transactions include inventory adjustments, transfers, and counts related to physical inventory or cycle counting. These basic inventory transactions within a warehouse are summarized in Figure 19.1 and explained in the following subsections. Other basic inventory transactions displayed in Figure 19.1 include sales orders, purchase orders, production orders, transfers to other warehouses in a multisite operation, and quarantine orders.

Inventory Adjustments Inventory adjustments represent one of the basic inventory transactions within a warehouse. They can serve a variety of purposes, such as loading initial inventory balances, reporting inventory corrections, and reporting scrap. Inventory adjustment transactions can be recorded using either the Inventory Adjustment journal or the Movement journal, or the Counting journal (described shortly). The Inventory Adjustment journal employs a predefined G/L account number for an item's inventory adjustments, whereas a Movement journal forces you to specify this offsetting G/L account number for each inventory adjustment transaction. The quantity can be positive or negative, and always reflects the item's inventory UM. The adjustment entries can be maintained and printed

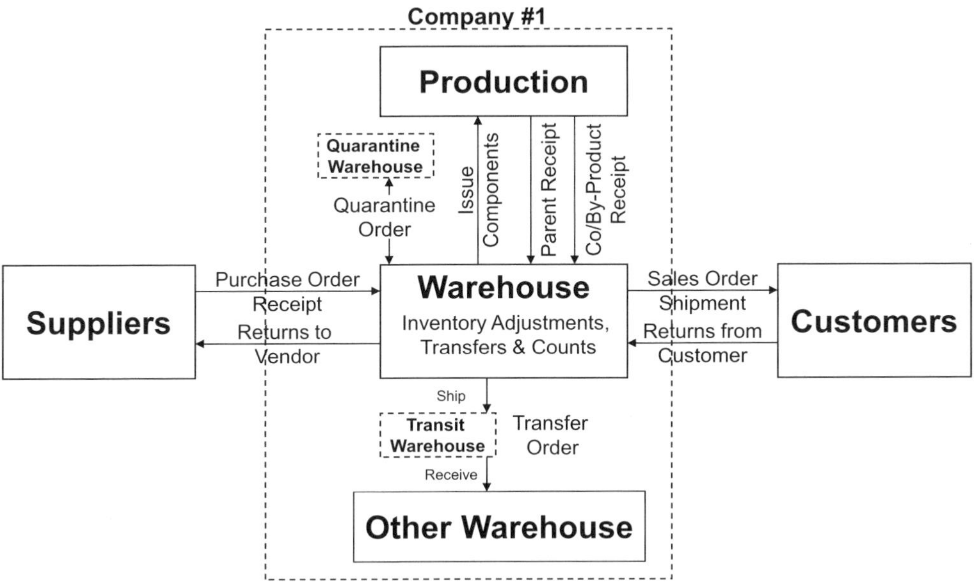

Figure 19.1 Basic Inventory Transactions

prior to posting the journal. Items with an actual costing method require an additional entry about the item's unit cost and possible charges.

Inventory Transfers Inventory transfers between stocking locations are recorded in an inventory transfer journal. Each transfer minimally identifies an item, quantity, and the old and new stocking locations (site, warehouse and bin). The transfer quantity is expressed as a negative, and always reflects the item's inventory UM. The transfer entries can be maintained and printed prior to posting the journal.

Inventory transfers reflect the immediate movement of material, without a requirement for tracking in transit inventory. For example, a transfer journal may be used to move material between two adjacent warehouses. Transfer orders should be used when in transit inventory must be tracked. Chapter 14 explained the use of transfer orders in multisite operations.

An inventory transfer journal also supports the transfer of one variant of an item to another variant, as well as transferring one batch number to another batch number, much like you would transfer inventory from one warehouse to another warehouse.

Physical Inventory and Cycle Counting Physical inventories help ensure valid financial reporting of inventory value. Cycle counting can accomplish the same objective, and help identify the source of inventory errors. The counts for a physical inventory or for a cycle count are recorded in a counting journal. You can manually or automatically create the journal lines identifying the items to be counted, print the journal as a turnaround document, and then record the counted quantity or the adjustment quantity for each journal line. Posting a counting journal updates the inventory balances. This represents a two-step counting process: one step to identify items in the counting journal and a second step to post the journal. A company-wide policy (embedded in the Inventory and Warehouse Management Parameters form) optionally prevents inventory transactions during the counting process.

Automatic creation of journal lines can be based on one or more factors, such as a specified warehouse, a selected range of item numbers or item groups, or the items' cycle counting approach. An item's cycle counting approach (embedded within the *Counting Group* assigned to an item) typically reflects a periodic interval expressed in calendar days. In this case, you specify a "not counted since" date as the basis for automatically creating journal lines. A further refinement can eliminate any items with no inventory transactions since the last count. Alternatively, the approach can reflect a condition such as on-hand inventory reaching zero or the item's minimum quantity, since this approach minimizes the time and effort for performing a physical count.

Some companies employ a control group method in cycle counting, where the same items are counted every day to identify the sources of error immediately. Copying the journal lines from a previous counting journal into the new journal supports the control group method.

Some companies employ tags (with pre-assigned numbers) to conduct a physical inventory, typically with hand-written count information about the quantity and location. A separate tag counting journal can be used to record the tag numbers, tag status (used, voided or missing), and the count information, and then analyze missing tag numbers. This tag counting journal represents an approach to tag control. Posting it results in the creation of a counting journal (with journal lines for used tags), which must be posted to update inventory balances.

An error in an item's inventory balance can be corrected immediately. In a typical scenario, you access the On Hand inquiry for the item to identify the relevant inventory balance, and then access the Counting Journal (via the Quantity Adjustment function) to view and change the quantity.

Dynamics AX Viewpoint of Inventory Transactions

The term *inventory transaction* normally refers to the physical movement of material, such as an inventory adjustment, receipt or shipment. A purchase order and sales order are normally viewed as a scheduled receipt and shipment respectively. Dynamics AX employs a broader view of the term inventory transaction, since it creates an inventory transaction (with an associated inventory status) for various steps in purchase, sales, transfer and production order processing. Figure 19.2 illustrates this broader viewpoint concerning the types and status of an inventory transaction. For example, the system creates an inventory transaction with an inventory status of "ordered" when the user creates a purchase order line item. This status changes to "received" after posting the product receipt; it changes to "purchased" after posting the vendor's invoice.

Status of Inventory Transaction	Type of Inventory Transaction			
	Purchase Order **Receipt**	Sales Order **Shipment**	Inventory Journal* **Receipt**	Inventory Journal* **Issue**
	Ordered Create a PO line item	On Order Create a SO line item	Ordered Create a Journal Line	On Order Create a Journal Line
	Received Post the packing slip	Deducted Post the packing slip	Purchased Post the journal	Sold Post the journal
	Purchased Post the vendor's invoice	Sold Post the customer's invoice		

Status of Inventory Transaction	Batch/Production Order	
	Parent Receipt	**Component Issue**
	Ordered Create a Production Order	On Order
	Received Post report as finished	Sold Post picking list
	Purchased Change Status to Ended	N/A

* = Inventory journals include Inventory Adjustment, Movement, Counting , Transfer, and Project Items journals.

Figure 19.2 Viewpoint of Inventory Transactions

Dynamics AX creates inventory transactions for posted and un-posted inventory journals, as illustrated in the right-hand side of Figure 19.2. With the inventory movement journal, for example, a journal line item for a positive quantity (a receipt) represents an ordered line item prior to posting.

The simplified viewpoint of inventory transactions in Figure 19.2 does not reflect all types of inventory transactions and statuses. A return purchase order, for example, would have statuses of on order, deducted and sold. The system employs additional types of inventory status when using reservations and registration. Examples of inventory status were included in the basic model for sales orders (see Figure 12.3), purchase orders (Figure 13.3), production orders (Figure 14.6) and transfer orders (Figures 17.3 and 17.5).

In summary, the inventory transaction audit trail displays both actual and anticipated receipts and issues. This audit trail includes batch and serial numbers when applicable. You can view additional information about an actual receipt (or issue) concerning the physical and financial vouchers that identify the affected G/L account numbers and values.

Inventory Transaction Audit Trail and Inventory Balances You can view an item's transactions and inventory balances from the item master and from any form involving inventory transactions. You can specify the desired level of detail when viewing inventory balances, such as viewing inventory by warehouse versus viewing inventory for every bin, batch, and serial number. You can also view an item's inventory balances across multiple companies.

Restricted Inventory Transactions based on Batch Disposition Code The policies associated with a batch disposition code can restrict material usage of a batch (described in Section 9.5). These restrictions may apply to transactions related to sales orders, transfer orders or production orders.

19.2 Handling Arrivals

Many inventory transactions represent receipts and arrivals into a warehouse, such as purchase orders, production orders, customer returns, and transfer orders at the ship-to site/warehouse. Previous chapters described these transactions, so that a brief summary is provided below.

Purchase Order Receipts The basic model of purchase order processing (see Figure 13.2) employs the Arrival Overview form to anticipate receipts and create an arrival journal of expected receipts, and then you can report the actual quantities and putaway locations before you register the arrival. You can optionally indicate the need for a quarantine order when recording arrival. Information about the registered arrivals provides the basis for reporting the actual receipts against purchase orders. You can by-pass this registration step using a short-cut approach to directly post the product receipt or vendor invoice.

Purchases related to special orders and direct orders involve slightly different processing steps (described in Section 12.7).

Customer Returns Returned items must first be reported through an arrival journal, typically by selecting the RMA line items on the Arrival Overview form to create the arrival journal. Multiple RMAs and multiple RMA line items can be selected, thereby including them in a single arrival process. Each arrival journal line item must be assigned an RMA disposition code, which determines subsequent processing steps.

Finished Quantities for a Production Order The basic model of production order processing (Section 14.3) employs the Report-as-Finished Journal to report the finished quantities for the parent item. When using routing operations, the parent item can also be received based on units completed at the last operation.

Transfer Order Receipts The basic model of transfer order processing (see Figure 17.3) employs the Transfer Order Receive form to report actual receipts. As a variation (see Figure 17.5), you can use the Arrival Overview form to anticipate receipts, create an arrival journal for selected line items, and report the actual quantities/putaway locations before you register the arrival. You can optionally indicate the need for a quarantine order when recording arrival.

19.3 Handling Shipments

Several inventory transactions represent shipments from a warehouse, such as shipments for sales orders and transfer orders. Previous chapters described an order-based picking list approach for these transactions, so that a brief summary is provided below.

Sales Order Shipments The basic model of sales order processing (Section 12.2) employs an order-based picking list to communicate picking requirements, and a two-step process to report picking and then shipment. Material may be reserved prior to picking. You can use the Release Sales Order Picking form to anticipate picking activities and print the picking lists for selected line items. The actual picking activities are reported on the Picking List Registration form. Information about the picked material provides the basis for reporting actual shipments against sales orders (aka packing slip update). You can by-pass the picking step using a short-cut approach to directly post the packing slip or invoice.

Sales orders involving special orders and direct orders involve slightly different processing steps (Section 12.7).

Transfer Order Shipments The basic model of transfer order processing (see Figure 17.3) employs the Transfer Order Shipment form to report actual shipments. As a variation (see Figure 17.5), you can use the Release Transfer Order Picking form to anticipate picking activities and print the picking lists for selected line items. The actual picking activities are reported on the Picking List Registration form. Information about the picked material provides the basis for reporting actual shipments against transfer orders.

Returns to Vendor Returning material to a vendor typically involves a different type of purchase order (a type of returned order), which requires entry of the vendor's RMA (Return Material Authorization) number. The line items for a returned order are expressed with a negative quantity. You report actual returns by posting the packing slip for the purchase order.

Picking List for a Production Order The picking list for a production order (termed a picking list journal) represents an order-based approach to picking activities, but it differs significantly from the above-described approaches for sales orders and transfer orders. It does not employ the constructs of a shipment, picking route, and output orders to support picking activities. The picking list journal involves additional considerations, such as the definition of components in the order-dependent BOM, segmentation of the printed picking list based on the operation number assigned to components, component auto-deduction policies, and issuing additional components.

Consolidated Picking List for Sales Orders and Transfer Orders A consolidated picking list supports picking activities for multiple sales orders or transfer orders or both. The consolidated picking list approach employs the shipment construct as an organizing focus, and the assignment of output orders to define the shipment contents. Each output order represents a line on a sales order or transfer order, and communicates the need for picking. The grouping of output orders, for example, may reflect the same ship-from site, shipment date, method of delivery, and/or customer. The assigned output orders can then be picked using a picking route and its associated printed pick list. The creation of picking routes for a shipment reflects the *joint packing policy* (order, single customer, or all customers) assigned to the shipment. That is, a picking route can reflect the output orders for a single sales order (similar to the order picking list approach), for a single customer, or for all customers.

Bill of Lading A bill of lading can be automatically created by posting a sales order packing list or invoice. Some information pertaining to the system-assigned bill of lading identifier is automatically updated, such as the customer, sales order number, delivery address, and the shipped items and quantities. Other bill of lading information must be manually maintained, including each package type (such as carton), quantity and weight. Use the bill of lading form for data maintenance and document printing. A bill of lading can be manually created to support other types of shipments (such as office furniture), or to support a master bill of lading (such as shipments to a freight forwarder). After creating a bill of lading identifier, for example, you explicitly designate it as a master bill of lading and also assign the identifier to individual bills of lading associated with it.

Additional Case Studies

Case 98: Advanced Warehouse Management and Distribution A manufacturer of ready-to-assemble furniture had multiple sites and several variations of distribution scenarios.[1] In one scenario, all goods were shipped from a central distribution center. In a second more complex scenario, a

[1]See **www.ColumbusGlobal.com** for more information about their add-on module for Advanced Warehouse Management System that supports these different scenarios.

freight forwarder picked up goods from several warehouses, and the sequence of pickups and deliveries was critical. The transportation planner worked with the freight forwarder to optimize route planning, so that a shipment was created for each truck route and a picking list was created for each pickup warehouse. The shipping manager released all picking lists just prior to the shipment date, and warehouse workers picked the material and placed it in an outbound dock at each warehouse. The material was assigned a staged status after placement in the outbound dock. The status was changed to loaded after the warehouse worker loaded the truck, and all related documentation (such as bills of lading) were prepared after loading the truck at the final pickup warehouse. The truck driver then made deliveries to customer locations.

A third scenario involved an external terminal, where goods were picked up from different warehouses and sent to the carrier's terminal. The carrier sorted, consolidated and shipped the goods, so that the shipments to the carrier terminal also identified the final delivery address.

Case 99: Data Collection System The operations manager for a manufacturing company was considering implementation of an automated data collection system. A key requirement was the use of hand-held devices (such as the Microsoft Pocket PC) for recording all inventory transactions and bar-coded information. The devices also had to support label printing, inventory balance inquiries, and customization of the user interface.[2]

Case 100: ASNs and Bar-Coded Labels A key customer of a manufacturing company required an advanced ship notice (ASN) and bar-coded shipping labels for each shipment. The shipping labels identified the cartons and pallets within a shipment. The ASN information included basic data about the shipment number and customer PO number(s) included in the shipment, as well as content data about the items (for a standard pack approach) or about the pallets, cartons, and items within cartons (for a pick-and-pack approach). These represent the basic variations in the hierarchical data structure for the ANSI X-12 856 transaction for ASNs. The combination of the ASN information and bar-coded labels enables quick and accurate processing of material receipts via bar-code scanning.

[2]Several firms provide data collection support for all transactions within Dynamics AX. One example is **www.rfsmart.com**.

Case 101: UPS Integration Most of the shipments at a marine electronics manufacturing company were sent via UPS. The delivery site was typically to a ship that stopped at different harbors around the world, which required synchronization of deliveries with the ship arrivals and departures. Integrating the UPS capabilities into sales order processing meant that the user could view the available shipping options, and determine the quoted delivery time/date and costs. The shipping quote could then be transferred to the sales order. The customer could be separately invoiced for the transportation costs associated with the UPS shipping invoice, and the UPS tracking numbers provided package tracking. This approach resulted in lower transportation costs while meeting the customer requirements for synchronized deliveries.

Case 102: Consolidated Picking List The shipping manager at a manufacturing company had several major customers with weekly scheduled truck shipments. The contents of a truck shipment reflected the assignment of multiple sales order line items, subject to the truck's weight and volume limitations. A consolidated picking list was used to pick the material and stage it prior to truck arrival. The staged material was then loaded onto the truck, and the loaded material was reported as sent when the truck departed. A packing slip update was generated for all sales order lines within the sent shipment.

Executive Summary

Warehouse management involves the physical storage and movement of products within and between physical sites, and the inbound and outbound shipments with trading partners. It requires the definition of sites, warehouses and bin locations, and accurate reporting of inventory transactions. These transactions include inventory adjustments, transfers, and cycle counting, as well as arrivals and shipments associated with different types of orders. The case studies included advanced ship notices and data collection systems.

Chapter 20

Project-Oriented Operations

Some manufacturing and distribution firms have project-oriented operations. These may be internally focused projects such as new product development, or externally focused projects such as an engineer-to-order (ETO) product where the customer is billed on a fixed price or a time-and-material basis. In any case, a project typically requires a mixture of material, resource time and expenses. It also requires project-specific S&OP game plans to ensure availability of material and resources to meet the requirements.

This chapter focuses on the supply chain management aspects of project-oriented operations, especially the coordination of material and resources. As a result of this focus, the chapter does not cover many aspects of AX software functionality related to other scenarios (such as professional services organizations) or to project accounting (such as an approval process for project budgets). The chapter includes the following sections.

1. Common Scenarios for Using a Project
2. Definition of a Project
3. Project Budget Based on Forecasted Requirements
4. Significance of an Item Requirement for a Project
5. Typical Business Process for an Internal Project
6. Typical Business Process for an External T&M Project
7. S&OP Approaches for Project-Oriented Operations
8. Report Actual Time and Material Against a Project
9. Considerations about Using Projects
10. Typical Business Process for a Project Quotation
11. Project Quotations for External Projects

20.1 Common Scenarios for Using a Project

Common scenarios can help illustrate project-oriented operations in a manufacturing or distribution company. A previous chapter described two scenarios about an external project to design and build an ETO product (Case 2) and an internal project for new product development (Case 3). The following case studies reflect a distributor that employs external projects to coordinate the design and delivery of plumbing/electrical parts, and an engineering manager that employs projects to track each product's R&D costs.

Case 103: External T&M Project to Coordinate Design and Deliveries for a Plumbing/Electrical Distributor

A distribution company sells and installs plumbing and electrical parts for commercial construction sites, and uses external time-and-material (T&M) projects to coordinate design and deliveries. As illustrated by an example in Figure 20.1, an overall project was defined for a specific building (the ACME

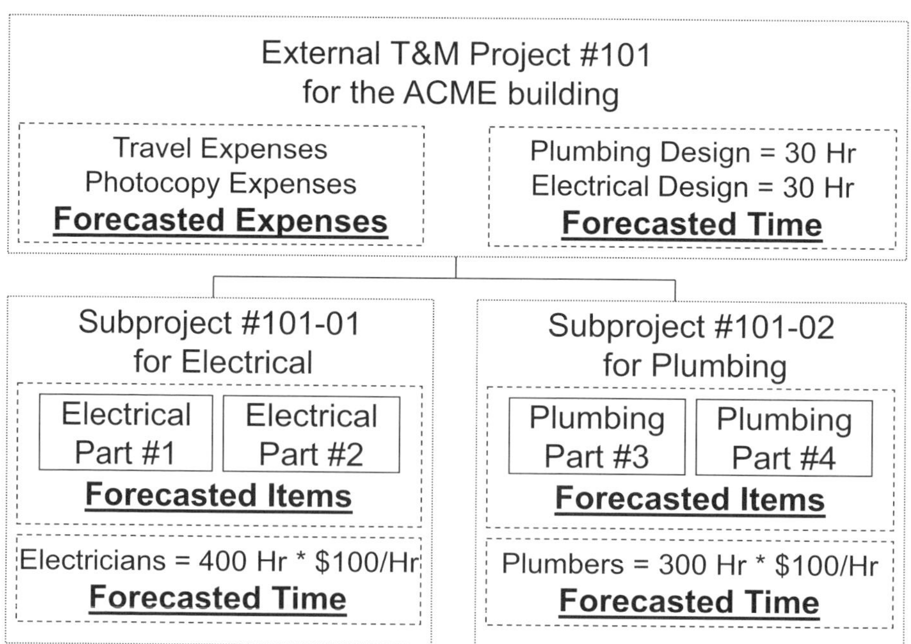

Figure 20.1 External Project to Coordinate Design/Deliveries

building), and the overall project included forecasted expenses and forecasted time. In addition, two subprojects reflected the two major installation phases for electrical and plumbing parts, with forecasted requirements for items and time.

The number and structure of subprojects typically reflected the organizational structure. Using Figure 20.1 as an example, there were separate managers for plumbers and electricians, so that the subprojects reflect their responsibility and reporting requirements. Information can also be accumulated for the general manager responsible for the entire project.

Case 104: Internal Project for Tracking Product R&D

The engineering manager for a manufacturer needed to record and track the R&D costs associated with a product, starting with the initial build and also for each revision. The manager defined an overall project for a product, and subprojects for the initial build and for each revision. Figure 20.2 illustrates the project and subprojects for R&D related to Product XYZ. The figure also shows the anticipated second revision of Product XYZ, which does not yet have a subproject. A detailed work breakdown structure was not employed at this time.

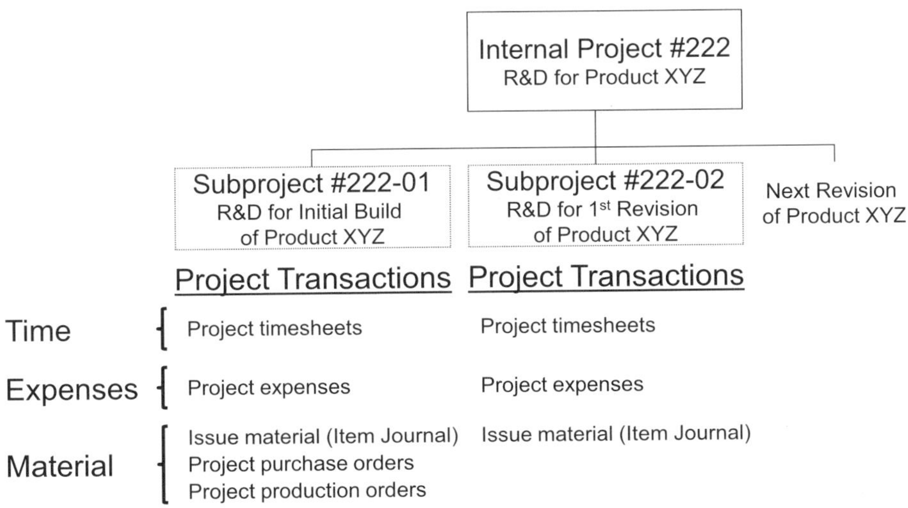

Figure 20.2 Internal Project for Tracking Product R&D

A significant portion of R&D costs were related to engineering time, and various types of engineers were involved throughout the product life cycle. The various types included design engineers, manufacturing engineers, and testing engineers, and each engineer reported their actual time against a subproject via their timesheets. Other types of project transactions were related to expenses and material. Inventoried material could be directly issued to a project via an Item Journal. It could also be purchased or manufactured via project purchase orders and project production orders respectively.

20.2 Definition of a Project

A project is uniquely identified by a project number, which can be manually or automatically assigned. Several key fields define the nature and characteristics of a project, including the project type and a project stage. It may entail the use of subprojects as well as activities within a Work Breakdown Structure (WBS). A project also entails the use of project categories for identifying transactions related to material, resource time and expenses. These key characteristics of defining a project are summarized below.

Project Type A project is either external or internal, and there are several variations of external and internal projects. The major variations are explained below.

External projects require a specified customer and an associated project contract for invoicing purposes. An external project may involve an initial step of a project quotation, and the quote details can be optionally transferred to a project. There are two variations of external projects.

- *Time and Material.* A time-and-material project is invoiced to the customer based upon the incurred costs for material, resource hours, expenses and fees. It may involve project-specific sales orders, where the sales price or discount can be based on project-specific sales agreements.
- *Fixed Price.* A fixed-price project is invoiced to the customer according to the billing schedule. Revenue is recognized on the project based on an assessment principle of either completed contract or a completed percentage. Revenue recognition is handled via an estimation process.

Internal projects do not involve customer invoices or project quotations, but typically have a specified customer (representing an internal customer) in order to support the S&OP approach for item requirements. There are three major variations of internal projects.

- *Internal.* An internal project helps budget and track costs for something that will not be available to capitalize, such as an engineering project or new product development.
- *Investment.* An investment project helps budget and track costs against something that will be available to capitalize, such as the production of a fixed asset.
- *Cost Project.* A cost project is similar to an investment project, but the project costs can only be posted to profit and loss accounts (and they cannot be capitalized).

An additional project type—termed a time project—supports time reporting about miscellaneous activities that do not impact the General Ledger or production resources. For example, it may be used to track vacation or illness, or for time reporting via the Manufacturing Execution System (MES) capabilities within Dynamics AX.

A summary project represents another type of project, and is used to collect information about several projects for budgeting and reporting purposes.

Project Group A project group must be assigned to every project, where a user-defined project group reflects a project type and defines the associated general ledger accounts. Most firms require more than one project group to support different project types or posting to different general ledger accounts.

Project Stage The life cycle of a project consists of multiple stages, such as the three stages of created, in-process and finished. You can optionally employ additional stages for a project, but further explanation focuses on these three stages.[1] A company-wide parameter defines the desired stages for each project type. A basic rule is that the system enforces

[1]The explanation focuses on the minimal number of stages for supply chain management purposes. It is possible to use just two stages of in-process and finished. Some firms may want additional stages for project management purposes. The additional stages can be selected from five predefined stages and three user-definable stages, and these stages can be renamed. The applicable stages must be defined for each of the six project types (e.g., time and material projects) as part of the parameters form for projects.

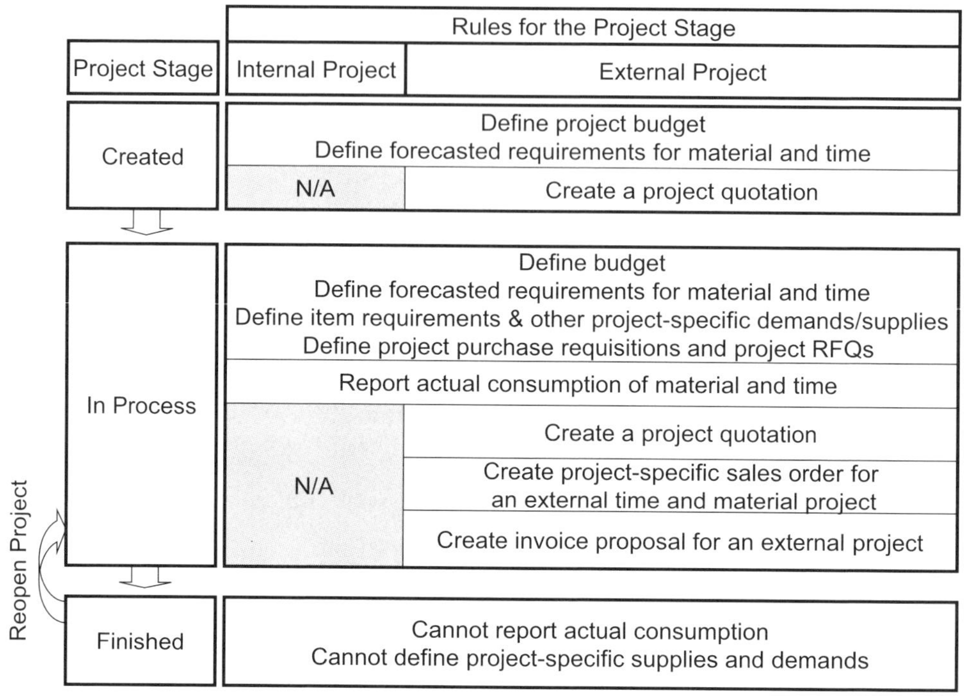

Figure 20.3 Significance of Project Stages

a linear progression through the project stages, and you manually indicate progression to the next stage. A second basic rule is that a newly created project is automatically assigned the first project stage applicable to the project type, such as the created or in process stage. Several rules apply to each stage, as illustrated in Figure 20.3 and described below.

- *Created.* The created stage is optional. It allows definition of forecasted requirements for material and time, but not for item requirements or other types of project-specific demands and supplies. You can optionally create a project quotation for an external project. Actual consumption of material or time cannot be reported against the project until it reaches the *in process* stage.
- *In Process.* Actual consumption can be reported against the project. You can define forecasted requirements for material and time, as well as item requirements and other types of project-specific demands and supplies. You can also create invoice proposals for an external project.

- *Finished.* Actual consumption cannot be reported against the project, and project-specific demands and supplies cannot be defined. A finished project can be re-opened for reporting further transactions by changing the project stage back to in process, as illustrated in Figure 20.3 by the arrow labeled Reopen Project.

Subprojects for a Project Some projects require segmentation for costing or scheduling purposes, or to reflect project ownership within an organizational hierarchy. Subprojects provide one approach to segmentation. Each project can be a parent to one or more child subprojects, thereby supporting a multi-level parent-child hierarchy. A subproject can have a specified project type and its own work breakdown structure, much like a project. Hence, a given project may consist of both internal and external subprojects. Aggregate costs—both budgeted and actual—can be viewed for a project and all of its subprojects.

The project number for each child project reflects the parent project number and a numeric suffix, such as a parent project of "P100" and a child project of "P100-01." The naming convention for the suffix reflects a user-defined mask (such as "- ##") specified for the parent project.

Activities and the Work Breakdown Structure (WBS) for a Project Activities provide another approach for segmenting a project for costing or scheduling purposes, especially for larger complex projects. A work breakdown structure may consist of a simple list of activities, or a hierarchical activity tree that reflects child activities assigned to an activity (which then becomes a summary activity).[2] The project and an activity can then be specified for budgets, forecasts, actual consumption, and project-specific demands and supplies.

Many scenarios have projects with a similar work breakdown structure. In these scenarios, it is helpful to define one or more templates of a work breakdown structure, and then create a project-specific WBS by copying a selected template. You can also copy the work breakdown structure from another project.

Project Categories for Project-Related Transactions Project-related transactions such as forecasts, item requirements, and consumption

[2]The activities defining a work breakdown structure are not the same things as the activities for a production flow for lean manufacturing (described in Section 15.4).

of actual material/time must identify a project and a project category. A project category provides segmentation for reporting purposes, and helps enforce several project accounting policies such as controlling the categories available to one project versus another. At least one user-defined project category must be defined for each type of project transaction (material, time and expense). General guidelines for project categories include the following.

- *Project Categories for Material (Items).* The project categories typically reflect the nature of material, and often parallel the item groups assigned to items. For example, the project categories for material could be electrical parts and mechanical parts.
- *Project Categories for Time (Hours).* The project categories for time typically reflect the nature of project activities, such as two categories of engineering design and testing for a new product development project. You can also define an hourly cost and sales price for each project category that will be used in forecasting hours and actual time reporting. Hence, different project categories may be defined to reflect differences in hourly costs and prices.

  When time reporting or forecasted hours apply to production resources, the project categories for time must also be applicable to the cost categories assigned to the production resource. The definition of cost categories was previously described for production resources (Section 6.2) and for resource costing (Section 8.5), where a cost category primarily defines the hourly rate for setup and run time at a resource. In summary, the definition of a cost category requires two steps. The first step defines whether a shared cost category can be applicable to production resources and projects. The second step defines the cost category information for production (such as the hourly rate within a costing version) and for projects (such the category group defining the relevant set of G/L accounts).
- *Project Categories for Expenses.* The project categories typically reflect the nature of expenses, such as hire of equipment, airfare, lodging, and photocopying.

Several additional considerations apply to each project category. These considerations include the concept of a default line property and a category group, as described below.

- *Default Line Property.* The line property determines whether a transaction will be chargeable to the project, and whether the cost or sales price should be used as the basis for charging the project. It also determines whether the charged costs will be available for capitalization. The default line property assigned to a project category can be overridden at the transaction level.
- *Category Group.* The category group assigned to each project category provides the basis for aggregate reporting, and for assignment of G/L accounts to project-related transactions.
- *Requirement for Worker ID.* This policy determines whether a worker ID must be entered when reporting transactions for the project category, such as reporting actual time or expenses.

20.3 Project Budget Based on Forecasted Requirements

A project budget can be directly entered, but it is typically calculated based on forecasted requirements for time, material and expenses. Within AX, these forecasted requirements must be for specified with a forecast identifier (aka forecast model) that typically represents a project-specific forecast. A different project budget requires a different forecast model. For example, a given project (say "Project XYZ") will have a user-defined forecast model corresponding to the original budget, such as a forecast model labeled "Project XYZ – Original Budget." A different forecast model would be used for a revised budget, such as a forecast model labeled "Project XYZ – 1st Revision of Budget." To simplify the revision process, you can copy a set of forecasted requirements from one forecast model to another, and then revise the requirements to calculate a revised project budget.

Forecasted requirements also apply to project quotations for external projects, since they provide the basis for calculating the costs and sales price for the project quotation. In addition, when a confirmed quote has been accepted by the customer, the forecasted requirements can be transferred to an actual project. A subsequent section provides further explanation of project quotations for external projects.

A project's forecasted requirements for material and time can optionally serve a second purpose for supporting a project-specific S&OP approach, as described in a subsequent section.

This section summarizes the various types of forecasted requirements—for items, hours and expenses—and how to enter them for projects.

Forecasted Items The forecasted requirement identifies an item, quantity, date, site/warehouse, a project category, an activity (if applicable) and a forecast identifier.

Forecasted Hours The forecasted requirements for time (termed *hour forecasts*) can be defined for a worker or for a production resource.

- *Forecasted hours for a worker.* Each forecasted requirement indicates the forecast identifier, a date, the number of processing hours, a project category and an activity (if applicable). It may optionally specify the desired worker, or a worker can be subsequently assigned.
- *Forecasted hours for a production resource.* Each forecasted requirement also specifies a production resource requirement, such as a specified resource or a resource capability.

Forecasted Expenses The project's forecasted expenses represent an estimate of direct charges, segmented by project categories for direct charges. The system also supports several approaches to allocating direct costs, such as allocating a percentage over several categories or several time periods.

20.4 Significance of an Item Requirement for a Project

An item requirement indicates a demand for a material item that should be satisfied by issuing inventory to the project. As implemented within AX, an item requirement is actually identified as a sales order with an order type of *item requirements* (rather than *sales order*), and you issue material to a project by posting the packing slip for the sales order. This approach means that the software capabilities associated with an item requirement are very similar to those for sales order processing described in Chapter 13. This approach also creates some difficulty in terminology, since the term "posting the packing slip for a sales order with an order type of item requirements" becomes cumbersome. For simplicity's sake, the book employs the interchangeable terms "issue material to a project-specific item requirement" and "post the packing slip for an item requirement."

Item requirements provide a key tool for supporting several S&OP approaches for project-oriented operations, as described in a subsequent section. An item requirement can be defined for any project type (except a project for time reporting purposes), but the project must have a specified customer in order to support creation of the corresponding sales order. The specified customer may represent an internal customer for internal projects. In addition, an item requirement can only be defined when the project stage has reached in process.

The two different order types of a sales order (termed item requirements and sales order, as previously noted) share many similarities and a few key differences. The similarities can be illustrated by the following list of capabilities.

- Calculate the earliest availability date
- Analyze supply options and reserve material
- Define the configuration for a configurable item
- Calculate the cost (and suggested sales price) via an order-specific cost calculation
- Anticipate picking activities and generate a picking list for item requirements
- Report actual shipment, and indicate the customer address for sending items
- Generate planned orders to satisfy the item requirement
- Create a project purchase order to satisfy the item requirement
- Create a project production order to satisfy the item requirement

The key differences between the two order types are summarized below.

- An item requirement does not involve invoicing
- Constraints on performing some transactions from the relevant form, where some transactions can only be performed on the Item Requirements form (such as posting the packing list), and others can only be performed on the Sales Order form (such as generating a sales event kanban order)

20.5 Typical Business Process for an Internal Project

A typical business process for an internal project is summarized in Figure 20.4 and described below. In this example, the project manager initially creates an internal project, and assigns an associated customer (representing an internal customer) in order to support S&OP game plans using item requirements. Additional steps involve the definition of subprojects and the activities representing the work breakdown structure (if applicable). As a short-cut to defining the work breakdown structure, the project manager can copy a predefined WBS template or copy the WBS from another project.

The project manager calculates the project budget based on entries of forecasted requirements for items, hours and expenses. If applicable, these requirements are specified for the associated subproject and WBS activity. Each forecasted requirement specifies a forecast model that represents a unique identifier for a version of the project budget. After actual project transactions have been reported, the project manager can analyze actual project costs versus a project budget (that reflects a specified forecast model).

The project manager may use the forecasted requirements for hours and items as the basis for a project-specific S&OP game plan. As an alternative S&OP approach, the project manager defines item requirements for a project. The simplified example in Figure 20.4 displays the use of forecasted hours and item requirements as the basis for the S&OP approach. You can optionally create project production orders for item requirements related to manufactured items, and issue completed items to the project. The engineers and other workers report their actual time against the project.

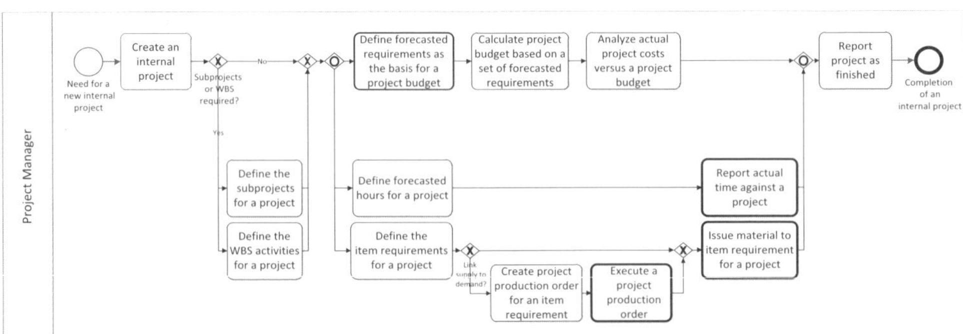

Figure 20.4 Typical Business Process for an Internal Project

As each project (or subproject) is finished, the project manager updates the project stage to a finished status, thereby preventing further transactions.

20.6 Typical Business Process for an External T&M Project

The typical business process for an external time-and-material (T&M) project has two key differences compared to one for an internal project. First, a T&M project involves generating an invoice based on incurred costs. Second, it may optionally involve an initial step of a project quotation, and a subsequent section provides further explanation of project quotations.

The key steps in generating an invoice for an external T&M project are illustrated in Figure 20.5 and explained below. The accounts receivable clerk creates a preliminary invoice (termed an invoice proposal) that reflects selected transactions for a project, and optionally edits the information, and then submits the invoice proposal for approval. Upon completion of the approval process, the accounts receivable clerk posts the approved invoice proposal, and sends the invoice to the customer. Alternatively, the invoice proposal may be automatically posted as part of the approval process.

A similar process applies to generation of credit note proposals and on-account proposals. In some cases, the accounts receivable clerk will create separate invoice proposals reflecting different transactions, such as specifying hours on one customer invoice and items on another.

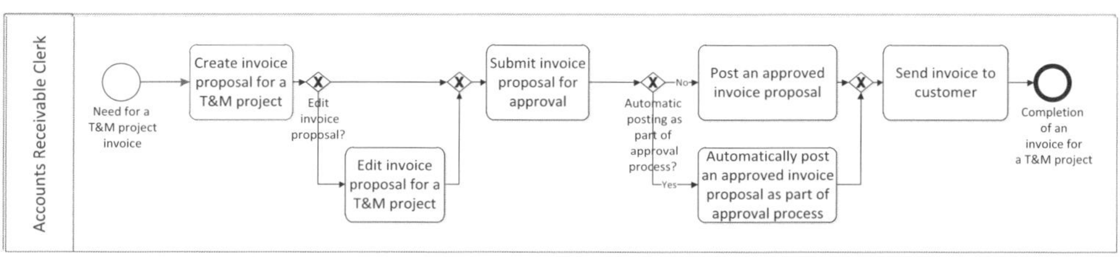

Figure 20.5 Typical Process to Generate an Invoice for an External T&M Project

20.7 S&OP Approaches for Project-Oriented Operations

Project-specific S&OP game plans can help ensure that material and resources are available to meet project requirements. They also provide the basis for assigning realistic due dates. They represent good business practices in comparison to unrealistic dates and simply issuing material and reporting resource time for a project. The S&OP game plans for project-oriented operations can be expressed through several different approaches, so that the relevant approach depends on the scenario. The item requirements approach represents the dominant business practice in most scenarios. This section summarizes the S&OP approaches for projects with item requirements, and also covers several other S&OP approaches.

S&OP Approaches for Projects with Item Requirements Item requirements act as the starting point for three different S&OP approaches in project-oriented scenarios, as summarized in Figure 20.6 and described below. These S&OP approaches for stocked items, make-to-order items and configure-to-order items have been previously described for general manufacturing scenarios (Section 11.1) and for lean manufacturing scenarios (Figure 15.5).

	Scenario	S&OP Approach	Comments	Basis of Delivery Promises
No Link	Stocked Item	Item Requirement	Planning calculations suggest planned orders	CTP
Link to Order	Buy-to-Order Item	Item Requirement with Project Purchase Order	Create project purchase order from item requirement	
	Make-to-Order or Configure-to-Order Item	Item Requirement with Project Production Order	Create project production order from item requirement	

Figure 20.6 Common S&OP Approaches for Projects with Item Requirements

An item requirement specifies the relevant item, quantity, due date and site/warehouse, and a realistic due date can be assigned based on capable to promise logic. Depending on the scenario, the item requirement may represent purchased material, or a manufactured end-item or component, so that a purchase order or production order can act as the supply. As shown in the left side of Figure 20.6, there may be "no link" or a "link to order" relationship between the project and the supply order. This linkage impacts planning calculations and treatment of actual costs for production orders.

- *Item Requirement.* The planning calculations will consider on hand inventory and generate planned orders (based on the item's planning data) to meet the demand. There is no link between the supply order and the project. When available, you issue the item's inventory to satisfy the item requirement.
- *Item Requirement with Project Purchase Order.* You create a project purchase order from the item requirement, which reserves the ordered material for the project. There is a direct link between the purchase order and the project, where the purchase order header indicates the project number and a line item indicates the project category. You can issue the item's inventory after receiving the order, or as part of recording the product receipt when prompted by the infolog question "Consume items for project immediately?"

  One alternative to this approach involves the direct creation of a purchase order from the project (rather than from the item requirement). This approach also provides a direct link between the purchase order and the project. After posting the vendor invoice, the system automatically issues the material to the project. As a general guideline, the direct creation of project purchase orders should not be used for material items; it should only be used for non-tangible items or services.
- *Item Requirement with Project Production Order.* You can create a single project production order from the item requirement, which reserves the ordered material for the project. There is a direct link between the production order and the project (and project category). You can issue the item's inventory after reporting finished quantities for the production the order. Issuing the inventory to the item requirement (via packing slip posting) will also post actual costs to the project (when using a posting method of finished item).

  The manufactured item may have buy-to-order or make-to-order components (designated by the BOM line type), which means that the associated reference orders will be automatically created and synchronized.

One alternative to this approach involves the direct creation of a production order from the project (rather than from the item requirement), or directly entering the order on the Project Production Order form. This approach also provides a direct link between the production order and the project, but does not require the additional step of issuing the material to the item requirement. Simply reporting the finished quantity for the project production order will post actual costs to the project (when using a posting method of finished item).

Other S&OP Approaches for Projects Several other S&OP approaches may be used in some project-oriented operations. These approaches included project-specific forecasts for items or hours, where the planning calculations must include the relevant forecast identifiers for each project. Other approaches include project sales orders, and a pipeline of project quotations.

❖ *Project-specific forecasts for items* The concept of a project-specific forecast for an item shares some similarity to a demand forecast for an item (see Section 11.3). Both approaches employ a forecast identifier, and it is critical that the planning calculations include demand forecasts for the relevant forecasts. Each project typically has a unique forecast identifier (representing its current budget), and these identifiers can be defined as sub-models of the forecast model used in planning calculations.

A project-specific forecast consists of a specified item, quantity, due date and the ship-from site/warehouse. This forecast is consumed by a project sales order or by an item requirement for the item, much like demand forecasts are consumed by sales orders. As noted earlier, an item requirement actually consists of a sales order with an order type of item requirements. The forecast consumption logic typically applies to a project, although it can be more granular.[3]

A project-specific forecast for items can be used on project quotations, especially when a detailed quote has been developed as the basis

[3]The forecast consumption logic can reflect the project and other factors such as the WBS activity and project category, as defined by the company-wide policies concerning forecast consumption on the Project Management and Accounting Parameters form.

for quoted costs. After winning a project quote, you typically transfer the detailed quote information to a project by converting the line items into item requirements. This approach reflects the dominant business practice of using item requirements as the basis for S&OP game plans.

- *Project-specific forecasts for hours related to production resources* This approach requires a separate scheduling task for the forecasted hours so that the time requirements will be recognized by planning calculations. You specify the scheduling direction (forward or backward) and date, and the scheduling method (job or operation scheduling). The scheduling task assigns time requirements to a resource, and may change the due date for the forecasted hours. This approach also requires a company-wide policy for including project-specific forecasts in the calculation of capacity requirements.[4] A project-specific forecast for hours is consumed by reporting actual time (via hours journal transactions for the project).[5]
- *Project sales order for a time-and-material project.* A project sales order can only be created for a project type of time and material. You can also define a project-specific sales agreement for assigning prices (or discounts) to these sales orders.
- *Pipeline of Project Quotations.* Some scenarios have a pipeline of project quotations with details about forecasted items, where the pipeline could be used to estimate demand. That is, a high win probability (say > 90%) assigned to a project quote (actually its associated opportunity) enables master scheduling logic to treat its item forecasts as demand.

20.8 Report Actual Material and Time Against a Project

Actual consumption can be reported using several types of project-related transactions when the project stage has reached in process. Some of these transactions have been described in the previous section about S&OP approaches, such as issuing material to satisfy an item requirement, the use of project production orders and project purchase orders, and the use of

[4]The company-wide policy to include project-specific forecasts for hours in capacity planning is specified on the Master Planning Parameters form.

[5]The forecast consumption logic can reflect the project and other factors such as the WBS activity and project category, as defined by the company-wide policies concerning forecast consumption on the Project Management and Accounting Parameters form.

project sales orders. This section describes several other transactions that employ journals for reporting actual material, time, and expenses against a project. It also describes the variations of production posting to a project.

Items Journal for a Project This journal records the material issued to a project from inventory. Each journal line indicates the quantity and stocking location of the item, and the associated project, project category and activity if applicable).

Hours Journal for a Project This journal records the hours expended on a project. Each journal line indicates the hours and the associated project, project category, activity (if applicable) and the relevant employee. You can use the Hours Journal form, a timesheet or a web journal for reporting actual time. Web journals are typically used for employees who are remote or seldom use the system. Information entered on a web journal must be transferred to an hours journal.

Expense Journal for a Project This journal records costs charged to a project. Each journal line indicates the nature of the costs—such as a ledger entry or A/P invoice—using the field termed the *offset account type*. For example, a journal line for a ledger entry indicates the G/L account. Additional line item information includes the cost and currency, the associated project and project category (such as travel expense), the relevant employee (if applicable), and transaction text.

Variations of Production Posting to a Project The posting of actual production costs to a project can differ based on two key factors: the linkage between a production order and the project, and the posting method assigned to a production order. A previous section about S&OP approaches explained how an item requirement for a project can have "no link" or a "link to order" with a production order. This section introduces the additional factor of the *posting method* for the production order, where the options include *consumed item* and *finished item.*[6] The posting method of consumed item means that costs can be immediately posted to the project based on the picking list and route card transactions for the production order. In contrast,

[6] *The posting method assigned to a production order can be initially defaulted from a company-wide policy defined on the Project Management and Accounting Parameters form. The posting method of consumed item represents a new capability within AX 2012.*

a posting method of finished item means that costs cannot be posted until the finished quantity has been reported and then issued to the item requirement.

The dominant business model employs a posting method of consumed item and production orders directly linked to the item requirements for a project. In this way, the actual project costs will be immediately updated as you report material and labor transactions against the production order. As an additional option, the same transactions for related reference orders can also update the actual project costs.[7]

Several guidelines apply to a posting method of consumed item with link to order. First, you should have completely defined the product structure prior to scheduling the project production order so that reference orders (for make-to-order components) can also be generated and linked. This becomes difficult when engineering has not been completed. Because of this problem, the second guideline is to flatten the product structure in terms of the BOM or subprojects

20.9 Considerations about Using Projects

Several considerations apply to project-oriented operations, such as changing the project type for a project, planning calculations, and the use of project MRP and project costing.

Changing a Project Type from Internal to External A project sometimes starts as an internal project and then changes to an external project, or vice versa. Use the Change Project Group function to change the project type for the project.

Using a Template to Create a New Project A given project can be designated as a template, and then used by the Project Wizard when creating a new project. The wizard walks you through several steps, such as specifying the new project number, the project contract, the start/end dates, and what information should be inherited from the template.

Project-Related Purchase Requisitions A project-related purchase requisition and workflow are almost exactly the same as a general-purpose

[7]This approach requires a company-wide policy for production (termed *Set subproduction to consumed*) that is defined on the Project Management and Accounting parameters form.

requisition. The same basic steps and setup information apply to both types of requisitions. The major differences include a unique workflow and the creation of a project-related purchase order rather than a normal purchase order.

Project-Related Requests for Quote (RFQ) A request for quote (RFQ) provides a structured approach for soliciting and using purchase quotations, and the business process for a project-related RFQ is almost as exactly the same as a normal RFQ. A project-related RFQ must be initiated from a project, and it involves the same basic steps. The basic steps include creating an RFQ, sending the vendor-specific RFQs to obtain reply information, receiving a reply for a vendor-specific RFQ, accepting or rejecting a reply, and automatic generation of a project-specific purchase order for an accepted reply. In addition, you can update purchase trade agreements with information that reflects a vendor reply.

Project MRP and Project Costing Some manufacturing environments require project MRP and project costing capabilities. Generating a project production order from an item requirement provides the first step for project MRP since it establishes direct linkage between a production order and the project. The system automatically generates linked production orders for make-to-order components and linked purchase orders for buy-to-order components. These linked orders provide visibility of project-specific requirements, and project costing throughout the product structure.

A material item that can be shared between projects should be identified as a normal component, and with a period reordering policy. This approach enables planning calculations to generate one supply order for shared material to cover multiple project-specific demands. If needed, you can use the marking capabilities for the supply order (to link receipt transactions to issue transactions) thereby tracking actual costs for the shared material and supporting project cost considerations.

20.10 Typical Business Process for a Project Quotation

A project quotation often represents an initial step for defining an external project for a customer or a prospect. The typical business process for a pro-

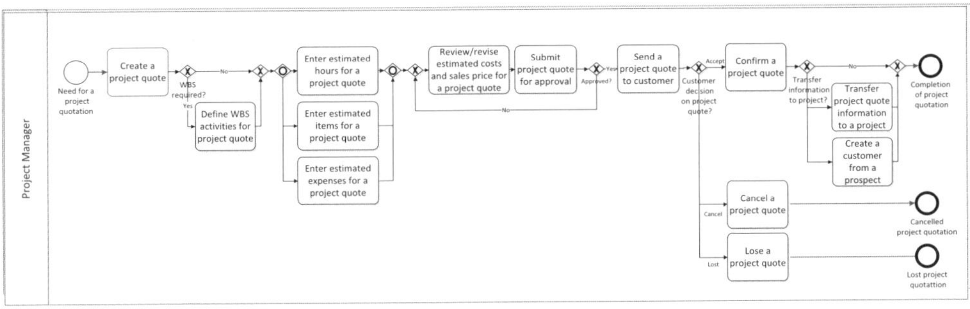

Figure 20.7 Typical Business Process for a Project Quotation

ject quotation consists of several steps illustrated in Figure 20.7 and summarized below. This typical business process provides the context for more detailed explanations in the next section.

The project manager initially creates a project quotation, and typically defines activities within a work breakdown structure for more complex quotations. A detailed quote for each activity can be defined in terms of the forecasted requirements for material, labor and expenses. The project manager submits a completed project quotation for internal approval, and an approved quote can be sent to the customer. The customer response indicates whether the project quote has been won, lost or cancelled, and the project manager updates the quote accordingly. For a winning quote, the project manager can optionally transfer the project quote information to a project, such as creating item requirements based on the forecasted items within the quote. The business relation for a project quotation must be converted to a customer.

20.11 Project Quotations for External Projects

A project quotation often represents an initial step for defining an external project. The line items on a quote define the project's forecasted requirements for material, labor, and expenses. These requirements are expressed for a forecast identifier (aka forecast model) that typically represents a unique forecast model for the quotation, just like a unique forecast model for a project budget (described in Section 20.3). The structure and life cycle of a project quotation provide a foundation for covering variations in using project quotations.

Structure and Life Cycle of a Project Quotation A project quotation is uniquely identified by a project quotation number, which can be manually or automatically assigned. The basic structure consists of a header and line item information. The header identifies the sold-to contact and related customer (if applicable). The line items can identify different types of forecasted requirements—for material items, hours, expenses and fees—that will be involved in the project.

The life cycle of a sales quotation consists of three basic steps (create, send, and disposition) and three possible dispositions (confirmed, lost or cancelled) that are represented by the following five statuses.

- *Created.* The quotation has been created. It can be sent but it cannot be updated to a disposition such as confirmed, lost or cancelled.
- *Sent.* The quotation has been sent to the business account. Changes are allowed but the specified business relation cannot be changed. The quotation can be updated to a disposition of confirmed, lost or cancelled.
- *Confirmed.* The quotation has been confirmed as won (via the Confirmation update). The quote information can now be transferred to a project.
- *Lost.* The quotation has been identified as lost (via the Quotation Lost update).
- *Cancelled.* The quotation has been identified as cancelled (via the Quotation Cancelled update).

When updating the disposition of a quotation, you can optionally record a reason code. Changes cannot be made to a quotation after it has been updated with a disposition.

Similarities and Differences with a Sales Quotation A project quotation shares many similarities to a sales quotation, as described below.

- A quotation can be created for a business relation that does not have to be a customer, and the business relation can be converted into a customer
- You can specify material items in a quotation line item, and the sales trade agreement information applies to these items
- You can define a configuration for a configurable item
- You can perform an order-specific cost calculation and transfer the calculated sales price to the quotation
- You can optionally employ delivery date control capabilities to the requested ship and delivery dates

- A promised delivery date cannot be calculated via capable to promise logic (aka the Explosion inquiry)

A project quotation is different than a sales quotation in several ways, as described below.

- A project quotation can specify line items for items, hours, expenses and fees, whereas a sales order can only specify items
- The price simulation capabilities only apply to sales quotations
- Sales quotations can be converted to sales orders, whereas project quotations can be converted to projects

Converting a Business Relation into a Customer A customer can be created from the business relation specified on a quotation (via the *Convert to Customer* function). After creating the customer, the system displays the customer master form so that additional information can be entered.

Transferring Information about a Project Quotation to a Project There are several variations of transferring information about a project quotation. One variation involves the creation of a new project from the project quotation. A second variation involves transferring the quotation line items to an existing project. These two variations have slightly different approaches for transferring line items from the quotation to a project. It is generally easier to start from an existing project, and then selectively transfer the quotation line items into the project.

With quotation line items representing forecasted requirements for items, for example, you have two separate options for using them to (a) create item forecasts and (b) create item requirements. Previous sections described the significance of item requirements, especially as an S&OP approach.

Versions of a Project Quotation A project quotation may be changed and then resent to the business relation in order to communicate the changes. The system automatically tracks each time a quotation is sent, and assigns a numeric suffix to the quotation identifier (such as -1 and -2) for each version. These historical versions can be viewed on the quotation inquiry and the Quotation Journal Inquiry. The system uses the latest version as the basis for confirming a quotation.

Relationship between Multiple Project Quotations Multiple project quotations may be required in certain situations, such as quotes for different quantity breakpoints. Other examples would be quotes for multiple phases or for different groups of items such as basic versus optional. You establish the relationship by starting with a parent quotation, and then assigning the child quotation(s) using the *Alternative Quotations* function. The same function displays alternative quotations that have already been defined.

Project Quotation Follow-Up Date and Expiration Date Each project quotation has a follow-up date and an expiration date. The dates provide reference information and the basis for selectively viewing project quotations.

Mass Creation of Project Quotations Using a Template Certain situations may require the mass creation of project quotations, such as providing the same quote to several different contacts or customers. An initial quote must be created and then designated as an active template (with a user-defined template name).[8] The *Mass Create Quotations* task can then be used with the specified template and a user-defined selection of business relations. The system creates a project quotation for each business relation.

Deleting Project Quotations Quotations are not automatically deleted by the system since win/loss analysis requires historical data. Periodic deletion of quotations should reflect the desired data retention policies. Use the Delete Quotations task to select quotations to be deleted based on criteria such as the status, creation date, and/or expiration date.

Additional Case Studies

Case 105: Visual Project Planning Project managers needed an advanced planning tool to visualize and efficiently manage their project plans.[9] Previous tools were the usual assortment of individually maintained spreadsheets and hard-copy documents. Using activity-based Gantt chart visualization tools, the project managers gained instant visual access to

[8]The planning calculations always ignore demands related to template quotations.

[9]See **www.columbusglobal.com** for further information about their Visual Project Planning module.

current planning, capacity, and logistic details of individual project tasks, as well as the relationships between multiple parent- and sub-projects. This approach employed a single system with all project planning data, and significantly reduced clerical errors and the time required to create and maintain accurate planning.

Case 106: Engineering Design Services A division of a manufacturing company provided several types of engineering design services. Each project involved customer billing for the design services, and many projects required a detailed project quotation beforehand. Their requirements included seamless integration with Microsoft Project, approval procedures for purchase requisitions, web access for customers to report support issues, and time and expense reporting with web-based applications.

Case 107: Projects for ETO Equipment An equipment company manufactured engineer-to-order (ETO) custom products, and wanted to manage the engineering design time as well as the production of each large piece of equipment. Every custom product consisted of several basic subassemblies (such as a base, a tower, and a table) that were unique to each order, and engineering time was required to design the product structure of each subassembly. For each custom product, the company used a product configurator to automatically generate new items for the end-item and subassemblies, and assign routing data (based on templates) for production time. This approach (termed a skeleton BOM) enabled the firm to calculate an availability date (several months into the future) based on existing factory loads and current engineering commitments. Additional bill of material data was entered as the engineers designed the parts, subassemblies and end-item. Most components reflected existing item numbers, but the custom design often required new items to be designed and defined. The long lead time components were entered first to coordinate critical-path supply chain activities.

Case 108: External Projects for Service Orders External projects provide the foundation for service orders and service agreements. In particular, each service order typically requires a separate project that defines the sold-to customer. Additional project-related information includes project categories and the costs and prices for technician time. Each external project requires a project contract that defines the bill-to customer. Project accounting handles the generation of invoice proposals and invoices after posting a service order as completed.

Case 109: Advanced Project Management Project managers and logistics planners at a discrete manufacturer required better tracking and analytical tools to efficiently manage projects and project quotations, and also manage the project-related inventory and costing.[10] For project quotations, they used multi-level work breakdown structures for faster and more accurate planning and costing. Margin control was maintained on individual nodes and the entire project. Inventory reservations and graphical logistics views greatly reduced the time to look up and manage inventory transactions by project. They used graphical and table KPIs in their respective Role Center pages to gain full insight into all project-related transactions and costs.

Executive Summary

A wide range of project-oriented operations may apply to a manufacturing or distribution business. This chapter focused on several typical scenarios and business processes, and highlighted some of the dominant business practices. For example, the dominant practices for defining S&OP game plans included the use of item requirements to define project-related demands, and to support generation of project-specific purchase orders and production orders. The S&OP approach impacts the approaches to reporting actual time and material. Some scenarios involve a project quotation with detailed information about forecasted requirements, where quote details can be transferred to a project after winning the quote. The case studies highlighted different project-oriented operations such as product R&D, engineering design services and an engineer-to-order equipment manufacturer.

[10]See **www.columbusglobal.com** for further information about their Advanced Project Management module.

Chapter 21

Service Order Processing

Many manufacturers and distributors provide value-added services such as installation, repair and periodic maintenance, where services are performed by field service personnel or internal service facilities. The most common examples reflect firms that sell and service equipment, such as computer products, home appliances and industrial equipment. Illustrations within this chapter focus on equipment, with services performed by field service or internal personnel. These personnel will be referred to as service technicians; other titles include field service engineers, account managers, and service specialists.

A service order provides the basic tool for defining requirements and reporting actual consumption of material and technician time. Common synonyms include a service work order or service call. Different examples of service orders reflect the differences between field service and internal service facilities.

- *Field service.* Examples include equipment installation, upgrades, and preventive maintenance, which typically reflect scheduled activities with predefined requirements for material and labor. Ad hoc activities such as equipment repairs or other emergency situations cannot be scheduled in advance, and the material and labor requirements can be difficult to anticipate. They often require response times in hours and minutes, and actual labor and material usage get reported after the fact. Field service technicians travel to the equipment location to perform the service.
- *Internal service facilities.* Examples include equipment repairs on a customer return or service work on a customer-supplied piece of equipment. These services are commonly performed by technicians within a repair department, or within a separate repair depot facility.

The materials required for performing service orders often represent a constraining factor. Too many service orders are not completed the first time because the right parts were not available. Service parts can be a large inventory investment. They tend to be slow moving, have short life cycles and highly variable demand, and high carrying and obsolescence costs. The same parts may also be needed for production or selling directly to customers.

The people resources required for performing service orders can also be a constraining factor. These personnel often require advanced skill sets and experience. They cannot be easily hired and trained to meet overloaded situations, and extended periods of underutilization represent significant expense.

Effective management of service orders can help minimize the constraining factors associated with service parts and people resources, while supporting technicians with their day-to-day tasks. This chapter starts with an explanation of service orders, and covers the following major topics.

1. Typical Business Process for a Service Order
2. Service Orders
3. Service Order Considerations
4. Supporting Repair Activity as Part of a Service Order
5. Service Agreements
6. S&OP Considerations for Service Parts

Service orders can optionally involve supplemental capabilities for handling repairs. Service orders may also reflect the use of service agreements for defining periodic service activities. Several case studies describe the use of service orders for equipment installation and repair, and the use of service agreements for periodic maintenance. The chapter concludes with suggestions about the S&OP game plans for equipment-related services.

21.1 Typical Business Process for a Service Order

The typical business process for a service order has several variations that reflect different starting points for creating the order, but the ensuing steps remain the same. The simplest starting point involves the direct creation of the service order and its related project to satisfy a customer request for service. Other starting points involve the creation of a service order from a sales order (such as the service order to install the sold equipment), or the generation of multiple service orders based on service agreements (such as periodic maintenance of equipment at a customer site). Using the simplest starting point, the typical business process for a service order is summarized in Figure 21.1 and described below.

The project manager initially creates a service order and its related project, such as an external time-and-materials project to support invoicing to the customer. Optional information includes the assignment of service tasks to the project (to provide segmentation for larger complex service efforts), as well as the service object (representing the equipment to be serviced) and a service BOM (representing the common replacement parts for the equipment).

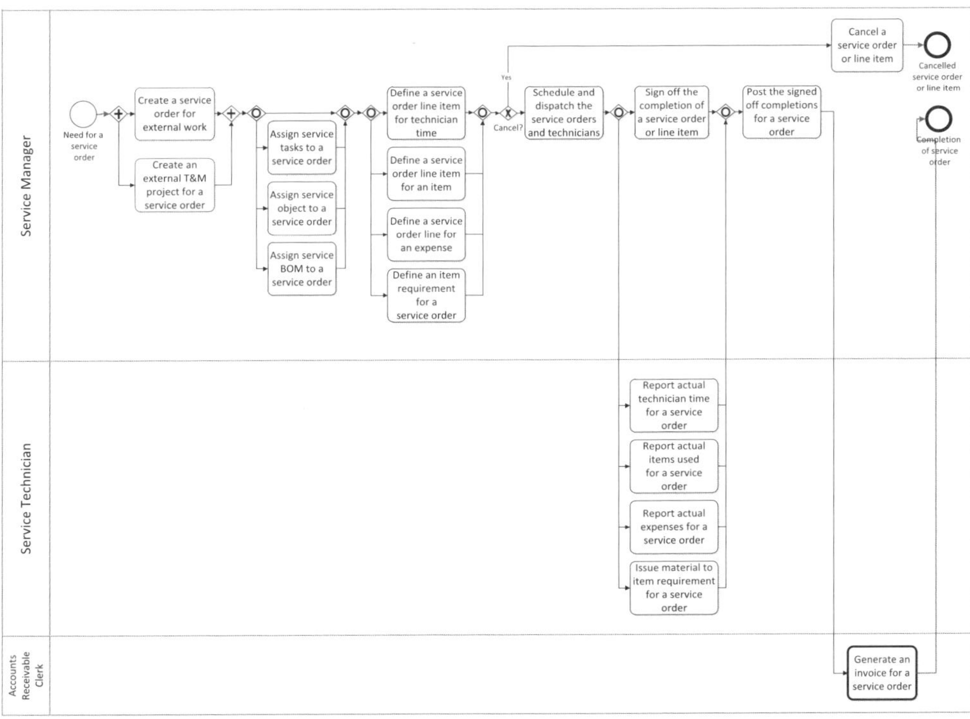

Figure 21.1 Typical Business Process for a Service Order

The project manager defines the anticipated work as separate line items on a service order. A line item can define the expected technician time and preferred technician, along the delivery date considerations. A line item can also define an expected expense or a material item. As an alternative approach for material, the expected material items are defined as an item requirement rather than a line item. After defining the anticipated work, the project manager schedules the service order and technicians to meet the delivery date considerations.

The service technicians report their actual time, expenses and material usage, which get recorded against the line items on the service order. The actual material usage can also be recorded by issuing material to satisfy an item requirement.

The project manager or technician must sign off the completion of each line item (or the entire service order) before you can post the transactions that will act as the basis for invoicing.

The accounts receivable clerk generates an invoice for the service order and its related T&M project. This involves several steps described in the previous chapter about projects (Section 20.6).

21.2 Service Orders

Service orders can be characterized by their structure and life cycle, and by the types of line items on a service order. Service orders build on the foundation of project information, where you typically create and assign a unique project to each service order. This can reflect an external time-and-material (T&M) project or an internal project, but further explanation focuses on the use of external T&M projects that support invoicing to the customer.

Structure and Life Cycle of a Service Order The basic structure of a service order consists of header and line item information. The header identifies the project and related sold-to customer, a delivery date, a brief description, and some optional information about the service to be performed. The optional information includes:

- *Address for delivering the service.* The address can guide field service calls, but is probably unnecessary for an internal repair depot.
- *Segmentation of service tasks.* Service tasks provide segmentation for larger complex services so that information can be specified for the ser-

vice task rather than for the entire service order. Each service task can have an extended description.

- *Service object(s) being serviced.* This provides guidance for performing the work on a specified piece of equipment, and the starting point for tracking repair history by service object. A subsequent subsection provides further explanation of service objects and an associated service BOM.
- *Service BOM for the service object.* This provides the basis for tracking changes to the service object, such as component replacement.

The life cycle of a service order consists of three steps represented by an order status (termed *progress status*) automatically updated by the system.

- *In Process.* The order has been created. The system also assigns this status after a cancelled order has been revoked, or when the user reopens an order by adding a line to a cancelled or posted order.
- *Cancelled.* This indicates the user has cancelled the order.
- *Posted.* This indicates the service order has been posted to the project accounting journal for subsequent invoicing. At least one line item must be signed off as complete in order to allow posting. The system prevents changes to the service order, but additional line items can be entered (thereby reopening the order to an in process status).

Situations requiring more detailed tracking of order progress (from in-process to posting) employ a second status termed *service stage*. For example, the user-defined service stages may indicate steps in the process, or convey situations such as waiting for parts. At least one service stage must be defined, which may be sufficient for simple situations.

Service order line items define the anticipated requirements for performing the service order, where a line item can specify either the anticipated technician time, material or expense. The same line items are used to report actual consumption, and line items can be added after the fact to report actual consumption. A line item's life cycle consists of the following three statuses.

- *Created.* The line item has been created. The system also assigns this status after a cancelled order has been revoked.
- *Cancelled.* This indicates the user has cancelled the line or order.
- *Posted.* This indicates the line item has been posted. The line item must be signed off as complete in order to allow posting. The system prevents changes to the line item after it has been posted.

Types of Line Items on a Service Order Service order line items define anticipated requirements for performing the service. The line item information varies by the designated *transaction type* of hours, items and expense. Similar types of line items were previously described for projects (Section 20.3).

- *Hours (Labor).* The line item specifies the technician's employee ID, the project category for hours, and the number of hours. Optional information includes descriptive text about the technician's work, the assignment to a service task and service object, and delivery date considerations.[1] The line item also indicates the labor rates for cost and sales price.
- *Expense.* The line item specifies the quantity, the project category for expenses, descriptive information, and the associated cost and price per unit. Optional information includes the assignment to a service task and service object.
- *Item (Material).* The line item specifies the item number, quantity, the issue-from location, and the project category for material. Optional information includes an extended description of the item, the assignment to a service task and service object, and delivery date considerations.

  An alternative approach employs item requirements (rather than line items) to define expected material, as described in the next subsection.

Item Requirements for a Service Order An item requirement indicates a demand for a material item that should be satisfied by issuing the material to the project associated with the service order. As implemented within AX, an item requirement is actually identified as a sales order with an order type of *item requirements* (rather than sales order), and you issue material by posting the packing slip for the sales order. The previous chapter (Section 20.4) explained the significance of an item requirement, and the capabilities for supporting supply chain coordination.

With respect to service orders, for example, using the item requirements approach can support a picking list for the bringing (or shipping) the material to the customer site; the definition and production of a custom part (via a configurable item); and the purchase of a special order part.

[1] The delivery date considerations include a specified delivery date, along with a time window (expressed as a range of dates) and time constraints (expressed as times for start after and/or end before) for performing the service. The time window provides the basis for grouping together service work that can be performed on the same date.

Example of a Service Order for Equipment Installation An example of equipment installation at a customer site illustrates the nature of a service order. The same example was previously used as case study (Case 9). The service order was typically created as part of sales order processing, since the sales line identified the equipment to be installed. The key information for an example service order is summarized in Figure 21.2 and described below. In this example, the service manager assigned a service object (identified as Equipment XYZ in the figure) to the service order, and attached a template BOM (reflecting the bill of material for Equipment XYZ) to create a Service BOM. The Service BOM enables a technician to easily review product structure information should the installation require replacement parts. The service manager also assigned three service tasks (labeled Prep, Install and Test) to the service order, and prepared detailed notes about each task. Finally, the service manager created service order line items that identified the anticipated requirements for materials and the technician's time, and the line items were assigned to the relevant service task. The installation required two types of technicians (mechanical and electrical), and the line items for technician time were assigned to employees Joe and Sue. The technicians reported actual consumption of materials and time against the service order line items, and also signed off on the completion of each line item.

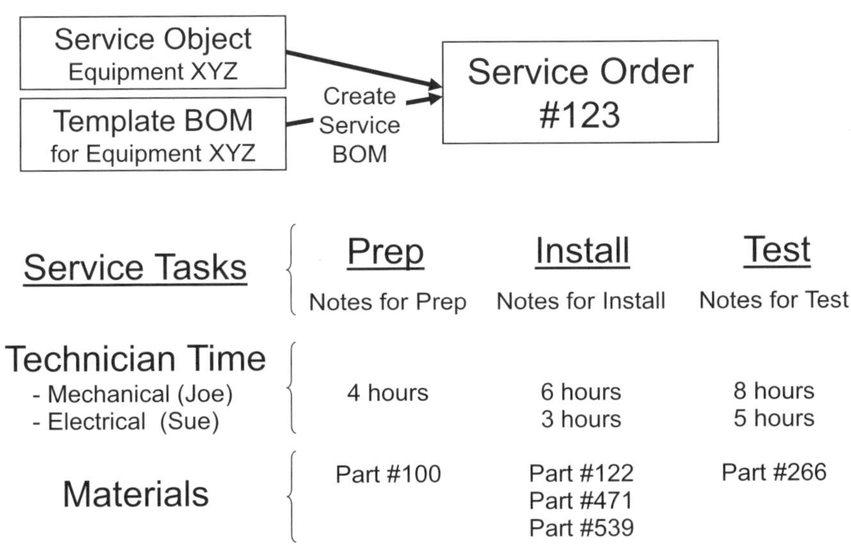

Figure 21.2 Example Service Order for Equipment Installation

21.3 Service Order Considerations

Variations to the basic service order process reflect different ways of doing business with customers and different internal procedures. These variations include identifying the service object(s) and service tasks, progress tracking of service orders, defining response time requirements, and coordinating service orders via the dispatch board.

Service Objects on a Service Order A service object identifies an item that will serviced. With equipment, for example, it could represent an item, a specific serial number of an item, a custom product configuration, a group of equipment, or a type of equipment. It can optionally refer to an item number. One or more service objects can be specified on a service order. Individual line items can optionally refer to a specified service object, thereby providing direction for the technician about what to work on. A service object must be specified in order to support repair functionality. The system automatically tracks all service orders performed on a service object.

Service BOM on a Service Order Bill of material information about a service object is defined separately; first as a *template BOM*, which can then be attached to a service object specified on a service order. This is termed the *service BOM* after it has been attached to a service order. A template BOM (and resulting service BOM) typically represents a list of common replacement parts for a given piece or type of equipment, so that a different template BOM is defined for each piece or type of equipment. The template BOM sometimes represents the entire bill of a material for a piece of equipment, so that the template BOM can be created by copying the item's bill of material. A service BOM must be used to support tracking of repair history against a service object, as described in a subsequent about repair activity (Section 21.4).

Using Service Tasks on a Service Order Service tasks provide descriptive information about the work that needs to be performed. They also provide a method for segmenting work, especially with more complex service work.

- *Using Service Tasks for Descriptive Information.* Each service task has two sets of extended text for describing the work to be performed; one set for internal purposes and one for external purposes. The internal notes can provide comprehensive work instructions, whereas external notes can assist customer understanding. Many situations can employ just one set of notes.

- *Using Service Tasks for Segmentation of Complex Services.* An additional purpose of user-defined service tasks is to segment more complex service work into major phases. For example, the tasks for repairing an item could be inspection, teardown, and rebuild. A simple service order may employ a single service task or none at all.

Communicating Service Requirements via Printed Paperwork

A primary method for communicating service requirements consists of the printed paperwork for a service order. The standard paperwork is termed the *work description* for internal purposes, and the *work receipt* for external purposes. Effective internal paperwork helps deliver the service; it also acts as a turnaround document for reporting actual resource consumption. Effective external paperwork clarifies the expected services (beforehand) and the actual services delivered (afterward). Most firms will customize their paperwork, and the following suggestions can help increase the effectiveness of the paperwork.

- *Standard Information.* The standard information consists of the service order line items in three groups—technicians, materials, and expenses. The materials group includes item requirements. Each line item indicates the assigned service object (thereby directing work to the right object) and service task (thereby grouping the line items into relevant phases). Extended text can be entered for the technician and material line items, but this typically reflects supplemental topics not covered in the descriptive information for service tasks.
- *Service Tasks.* Each service task has two sets of extended text for describing the work to be performed, as described earlier. Many situations can employ just one set, or just the extended text associated with technician and material line items. Service tasks also provide segmentation for complex service work.
- *Documents.* Documents can be attached to the service order header and line items, and incorporated into customized paperwork. For example, the documents could include schematics, installation guides or user manuals.

- *Turnaround Document for Reporting Actuals.* The printed paperwork often provides the basis for hand-written notes about actual hours and materials, which the technician (or some other person) uses for computer data entry.

Create Service Order Lines via the Copy Function Copying provides a short-cut approach to creating service order line items. Line items can be copied from another service order (or service agreement), with an option to copy the information about service objects and service tasks. They can also be copied from a template service agreement, with the additional capability to copy selected line items from the template. The copy function adds line items to existing line items.

Detailed Progress Tracking of Service Orders Some situations require more detailed tracking of order progress between service order creation and completion. A separate status (termed *service stage*) can help track progress through user-defined stages. The stages may represent steps in the process, or situations such as waiting for parts. The user manually initiates an update to the next (or previous) stage, and the system prompts the user to select the desired stage (and optionally indicate a reason code).

You can tailor the policies for each service stage about permissible actions. For a given stage, these policies determine whether service order information can be modified or deleted, whether the user can cancel or post the order, and whether a reason code must be entered for changing the stage. For example, the reason code could indicate the reason for a cancelled service order. The companywide stages and their policies are defined as part of parameters for service management. At least one service stage must be defined, which may be sufficient for simple situations.

Reporting Actual Labor and Materials for a Service Order Consumption of actual labor and on-site materials is reported by posting the service order. The user must sign-off completion of one or more line items, or the entire service order, before it can be posted. The sign-off consists of a checkbox. The line items and quantities represent actual usage, so you may need to update previously entered information prior to posting. Posting updates the project associated with the service order, and provides the basis for invoice proposals and invoices. The actual material consumption for an item requirement is reported by issuing the material to the project (aka via packing slip posting).

Handling Service Orders through the Enterprise Portal The Enterprise Portal provides access to service order information for service technicians. With this portal (termed the technician portal), service technicians can view and maintain their service orders and the related service object(s), tasks and repair lines. They can also create new service orders, report actual labor, material and expenses, and sign off a completed service order linc item.

The Enterprise Portal provides 24/7 customer access to service order and service agreement information. With this portal (termed the customer portal), the customer can view information about their planned and requested service orders, and initiate a request for a new service order. The customer's requested service order must then be transferred to a normal service order.

Defining Response Time Requirements via Service Level Agreements Service-oriented operations frequently have a response time requirement, such as responding within 4 hours after creation of a service order. A service level agreement defines the response time requirement, which can be expressed in hours, minutes or days. A user-defined service level agreement is required for each response time requirement; it can then be assigned to a service agreement or a service order. Scheduling a service order beyond the required response time will result in a warning. Detailed reporting of actual time and task completion provides the basis for tracking performance against the response time requirement.

Coordinating Service Orders via the Dispatch Board A dispatch board provides the primary tool for coordinating technician time to perform service orders. The displayed information reflects in-process service orders with a line item defining labor requirements, an assigned technician, and an assigned service task.[2] The displayed information also reflects user-defined dispatch teams, with technicians assigned to a dispatch team in the employee master information.

The dispatch board provides a tabular format and a Gantt chart format for viewing service orders with labor requirements within a specified date interval. Service order information can be filtered and sorted in the tabular

[2]Service orders with a planned status are not displayed on the dispatch board; change the status to in-process to display the information. In addition, the dispatch board does not display time requirements unless the service order line item has an assigned task and technician.

format, such as sorting based on the service date/time, service task, customer, or priority level. The Gantt chart format displays dispatch teams (and associated technicians) on the Y-axis, the date interval on the X-axis, and the current assignment of service orders. It supports drag-and-drop assignment of the technician and date/time; it also supports drill-downs about the related service order and service task. Both formats support the concept of dispatching a service order, where a dispatched status indicates confirmation of the scheduled date/time and technician.

The dispatch board supports several functions for coordinating technician time to perform service orders, as illustrated below.

- Assign (or reassign) a preferred technician to a service order
- Assign (or reschedule) a preferred date/time for performing the service order
- Assign a dispatched status to indicate confirmation of the assigned technician and date/time to the service order
- View undispatched service orders, and assign a dispatched status
- View service level agreement information about required response time, and provide a warning when the assigned date/time is greater than the required response time
- View the priority of a service order, with color coding (such as red, yellow, green) for priorities of high, normal, and low
- Reverse changes to the dispatch board prior to saving the changes
- Save changes to the dispatch board, which automatically updates service orders with the assigned technician and service date/time

Management Reports about Service Orders The standard reports include a customer schedule, a progress report, a margin report, and summarized data about hours consumption and order count. For example, the customer schedule coordinates activity by identifying the service orders being performed at a customer, along with the progress status, delivery date and time constraints, and associated service agreement (if applicable). The service order progress report provides similar information about each service order, with additional information about the service stage and reason codes. A service order margin report provides a summary of the sales, costs and margin; it also provides a detailed breakout by line item.

21.4 Supporting Repair Activity as Part of a Service Order

Service orders are often used for coordinating and reporting repair activities. To support repair activities, you must add a repair line item (to the service order) to specify the service object being repaired. Additional information about the repair line item can help track repair progress, capture detailed information about the symptom/diagnosis/resolution, or track repair history against components.

Case 110: Service Order for Equipment Repair

An equipment manufacturer employed service orders to repair equipment at the customer site. The key information for an example service order is summarized in Figure 21.3 and described below. In this example, the service manager assigned a predefined service object (Equipment Type ABC) to the service order, and attached a copy of a predefined template BOM reflecting the commonly replaced components on this type of equipment. This copied information (termed the Service BOM) enables a technician to easily identify

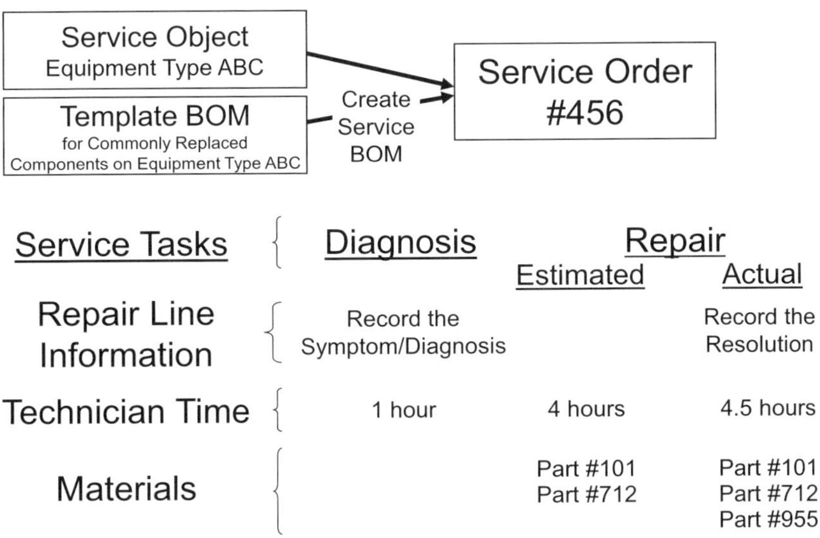

Figure 21.3 Example Service Order for Equipment Repair

component replacements, thereby creating repair history information. The service manager also assigned two service tasks (diagnosis and repair) to the service order.

The service manager initially created one line item for 1 hour of technician time to diagnose the problem, and several other line items represented the anticipated time and materials to repair the equipment. The technician could automatically add line items by using the service BOM to indicate the need for a replacement part. The technician also created a repair line for reporting information about the symptoms and diagnosis of the problem. After completing the repair, the technician reported the actual consumption of time and material, and the problem resolution. This example depicts actual consumption of a part (Part #955) that was not included in the estimated requirements.

The estimated requirements provided the basis for an estimated cost (which sometimes required customer approval before proceeding); actual consumption provided the basis for actual costs. The system automatically tracked repair history when the technician reported the replacement parts against the service BOM; it also tracked the information about the symptom/diagnosis/resolution.

Detailed Progress Tracking of Repair Activity Some situations require more detailed tracking of repair activity. A separate status (termed *repair stage*) can help track progress through predefined stages. The stages may represent steps in the process, or situations such as parts ordered for shipment to customer. The user manually assigns and updates a repair stage to each service object being repaired. Repair stages are not required, and a repair stage does not have to be entered. The companywide repair stages are defined as part of setup information.

Capturing Detailed Information about the Nature of Repairs Basic information about repair history includes the service orders performed on the service object and some descriptive text. A structured reporting approach can provide additional information about the nature of each repair, thereby assisting efforts to improve product design and customer service. Dynamics AX includes one structured reporting approach using predefined categories to describe a repair problem in terms of the symptom, diagnosis and resolution. The information reflects the two viewpoints of the customer and the technician.

- *Customer viewpoint of the problem.* This viewpoint consists of the general symptom (termed Symptom Area) and the specific problem (termed Symptom Code), along with information about when the problem occurs (termed the Condition) and descriptive text. As a simplistic example involving a car repair, the customer describes the general problem as the "engine will not start" and the specific problem as "it makes a clicking noise" under the conditions of "cold weather."
- *Technician viewpoint of the problem.* This viewpoint consists of the general diagnosis (termed Diagnosis Area) and specific diagnosis (termed Diagnosis Code), along with the suggested or actual resolution (termed Resolution). Continuing with the car example, the general diagnosis would the electrical system, the specific diagnosis is a dead battery, and the resolution would be to replace the battery. The technician can optionally enter a note with unlimited descriptive text about the repair.

A service object(s) must be assigned to the service order, and a repair line created, in order to report a problem. Information can be entered piecemeal or all at once. Definition of the predefined categories (for the symptom codes, resolutions, and so forth) typically requires expertise in the problem domain, thereby minimizing confusion when reporting a problem and when analyzing repair history.

Product Structure Data (Template BOMs) about Items to be Repaired The template BOMs represent a repository of product structure data about objects that might be repaired, and each template BOM has a unique identifier. For example, a template BOM could reflect the bill of material for an item or a specific serial number of an item. It typically represents a list of commonly repaired components. A template BOM identifier (and its initial bill of material) can be created four different ways.

- Copy an item's BOM version.
- Copy the order-dependent bill for a finished production order. Information about serial or batch numbers is not copied.
- Copy an existing template BOM.
- Manual. Nothing is copied.

After creating the Template BOM, the component information can be manually maintained. You can add components using drag-and-drop capabilities from item master information, much like the BOM designer capabilities. A distribution item, for example, would require manual maintenance to define the components in its template BOM. A standard manufactured product could use the copy of the item's BOM version as the basis for components. A custom manufactured product could use the production order as the basis for components.

A template BOM provides the baseline for creating a separate service BOM; this service BOM can then be used to record repair history against the components. The system does not automatically update the template BOM based on changes to the service BOM.

Tracking Repair History against Components using the Service BOM Once the Template BOMs have been defined, the definition of a Service BOM consists of two steps: assign the service object to the service order and attach a template BOM. This creates a separate bill of material that can be maintained to track repair history against components. The system automatically tracks the repair history based on several changes to the components.

- Replace component with same item (via the edit function), and optionally add the material usage as a service order line item.
- Change the component quantity (via edit), and optionally add the material usage as a service order line item due to an increase in quantity.
- Add a component (via drag-and-drop from the item master information), and optionally add the material usage as a service order line item.
- Delete a component.

When reporting a change to a component, the user can optionally generate service order line items to reflect material usage such as a replacement. Manual additions of service order line items do not update the repair history. The two steps—assign a service object and attach a template BOM—must be repeated for each service order that repairs the service object. Hence, the separate service BOM does not represent the cumulative changes caused by multiple service orders. For some situations, a suggested approach treats the Service BOM (and associated Template BOM) as a tickler list of commonly repaired components, thereby providing a prompt for technicians and a shortcut for reporting component changes. The repair history information gives a better idea about what components require replacement, and about potential design changes to reduce the amount of repairs.

Management Reports about Repair History The three aspects of supplemental functionality—repair progress, symptom/diagnosis/resolution information, and component changes in the service BOM—provide the basis for several management reports. These reports include repair history by service object, by service BOM and by technician (with details about each service order); and the frequency distribution of resolution by symptom and by diagnosis.

21.5 Service Agreements

A service agreement provides the basis for generating service orders, especially for periodic services. It specifies contractual details and a time period duration, along with the objects to be serviced and the tasks to be performed.[3] The information in a service agreement closely mirrors that in a service order, with additional information about how to generate service orders. We'll start with the structure of a service agreement, since this provides the basis for creating service orders.

Structure of a Service Agreement The basic structure of a service agreement consists of a header and line item information. The header identifies the project and a brief description, and five additional types of information about the service to be performed. The first three types of information (listed below) act as defaults for service orders created from the service agreement; the last two items provide constraints on creating service orders.

- Segmentation/description of service tasks to be performed.
- Service object(s) being serviced.
- Bill of material for a service object. The user can manually maintain this service BOM after attaching a template BOM to the service object.
- Start and end dates. These constrain the dates for service orders generated from the agreement, or attached to the agreement after the fact.
- Grouping basis. This policy determines how line items will be combined into service orders generated from an agreement. For example, grouping can be based on line items for the same service object, task or technician.

[3] A service agreement wizard can also be used to create a service agreement.

A service agreement has only two statuses: active and suspended. Service orders cannot be generated from or attached to a suspended agreement.

Service agreement line items define the technician time, material and expenses that are anticipated to be requirements for performing the service order. A previous section covered the types of line items and the required information. A service agreement specifies additional line item information about a service interval and time window. The system uses this information when automatically creating service orders for the service agreement.

- *Service interval.* The user-defined service intervals indicate when to perform the line item (daily, weekly, monthly, annually) and the frequency (such as once per month).
- *Time window.* This indicates the acceptable range of delivery dates, with predefined values for the possible range. For example, the range could be 1 day, 14 days, or within a month.

A service agreement line item has only two statuses: active and stopped. Service orders will not be generated for a stopped line item.

Automatically Creating Service Orders from a Service Agreement

Service orders can be created from a service agreement. When using the Create Service Orders function, the dialogue provides user options about the time period (expressed as from and to dates), the desired transaction types, and selection criteria. It is typically performed for the entire service agreement.[4] It generates service orders based on the time intervals for line items, and the agreement's grouping basis for line items. For example, let's say the line items represent requirements to perform monthly preventive maintenance on a piece of equipment. All line items have monthly time intervals and the same service object, and the service object acts as the grouping basis. If the user specifies a 6 month time period, the system will generate 6 service orders. The user must specify address information on the created orders when they reflect field service calls.

The Create Service Orders function can be performed multiple times for a service agreement, such as generating orders for different time periods. The system understands when service orders have been generated, so that it does not create additional orders (unless the orders have been deleted).

[4] The create service orders function can also be performed for a single line item on a service agreement. For example, this may represent sending a single technician to the site for a service call (per the service agreement).

Using a Template Service Agreement A template service agreement provides a short-cut approach for copying line items into a service agreement or service order. To create a template, start by creating a service agreement and its line items, and then designate it as a template.[5]

For example, let's say we have multiple pieces of equipment requiring monthly preventive maintenance, and we want a service agreement for each piece of equipment. A template would define the line items representing requirements to perform this preventive maintenance. We can then copy these line items into each service agreement, and add information about the service object.

Case 111: Service Agreements for Periodic Maintenance

An equipment manufacturer employed service agreements for periodic equipment maintenance at customer sites. A key aspect of each service agreement defined information about the service interval for each line item, so that service orders could be created automatically. Figure 21.4 illustrates the service agreement line items for technician time (3 line items) and material (5 line items). Each line item has a specified service interval of monthly, quarterly or annual. The service tasks (and related notes) reflect the names of the different intervals. Each line item is also associated with a service task and the service object.

Automatic creation of service orders for a one year time period would result in 12 monthly service orders. Using a grouping basis of service object, the monthly service orders would include relevant line items with quarterly and annual service intervals. The service tasks provide descriptive notes and segmentation about the monthly, quarterly and annual activities.

A technician may report repair activities during a preventive maintenance call. In this case, the technician should report the replacement parts against the service BOM to build a repair history. The technician could also create a repair line for reporting information about the symptoms/diagnosis/resolution of the problem.

[5] Assign a service template group to the service agreement in order to designate it as a template. The service template groups are user defined. They typically reflect categories of service, such types of installations or field service.

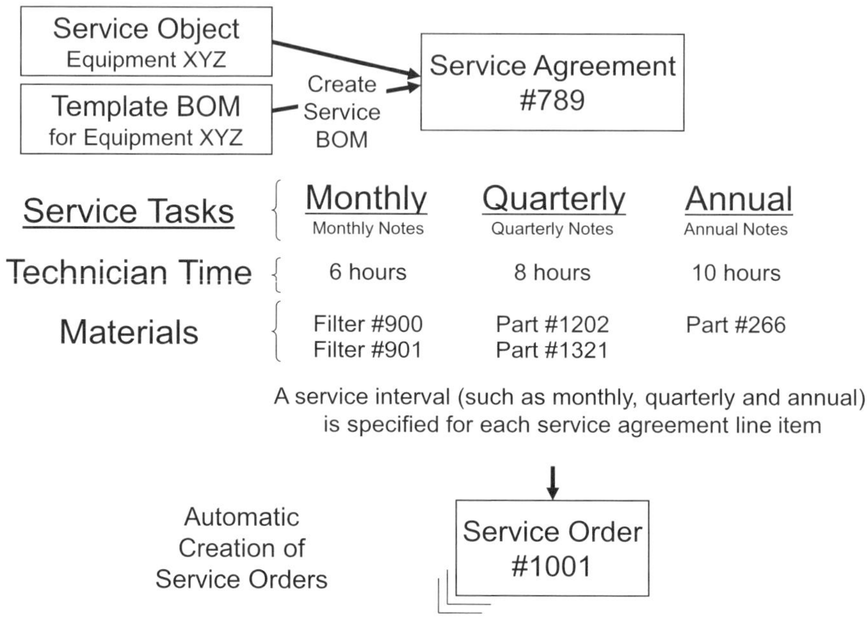

Figure 21.4 Example Service Agreement for Periodic Maintenance

21.6 S&OP Considerations for Service Parts

The basic coordination tools for performing service orders consist of a customer schedule and a technician schedule. Anticipating the material and labor requirements can help minimize constraints while supporting technicians in their day-to-day tasks of performing the service orders. Anticipated requirements reflect a key aspect of the S&OP game plans for service activities. The following suggestions can guide the development of S&OP game plans.

Separate Warehouse for Service Parts This approach supports replenishment based on site/warehouse-specific coverage data, and possible use of site/warehouse-specific sales price trade agreements. It supports warehouse management practices that pertain to services and service parts, such as handling customer returns to the repair department, communication of shipping requirements, and default bin locations. Other unique requirements may include differentiation of new/used/repaired parts and customer-supplied parts.

Service parts inventory is stocked in delivery vans in some situations. These vans could be viewed as separate bin locations or separate warehouses.

Visibility of Service Order Requirements for Material Planning calculations do not recognize the service order line items (for material) as demands, although they do recognize the demands associated with an item requirement. This represents one advantage of using the item requirements approach. In addition, planning calculations do not recognize the anticipated material requirements within service agreements. Case 112 describes a customization so that planning calculations recognize the anticipated demand.

Common S&OP Approaches for Service Parts The S&OP game plans for service parts can reflect different approaches, as summarized in Figure 21.5 and described below. Similar S&OP approaches were described for general manufacturing (Section 11.1) and project-oriented operations (Section 20.7).

	Scenario	S&OP Approach	Comments	Basis of Delivery Promises
No Link to Order	Stocked Item	Min-Max	Calculation of minimum quantity	CTP
		Supply Forecast	Forecast consumption policies	
		Item Requirement	Planning calculations suggest planned orders	
Link to Order	Buy-to-Order Item	Item Requirement with Project Purchase Order	Create project purchase order from item requirement	
	MTO/CTO Item	Item Requirement with Project Production Order	Create project production order from item requirement	

Figure 21.5 Common S&OP Approaches for Service Parts

- *Min-max for service parts.* A min-max approach works best when using a separate warehouse for service parts. The minimum quantity can be calculated (based on historical usage) to meet a desired customer service level such as 95%. Variable min-max quantities can support different demand patterns.
- *Supply forecast for service parts.* A supply forecast can reflect projected requirements for a service part. Some scenarios can benefit from a supply forecast for a group of service parts (aka item allocation key), since it can reflect the mix percentages of anticipated parts. With equipment repairs, for example, the forecasted quantity for the item allocation key could represent the number of units in the field that need to be repaired.
- *Item requirement.* The visibility of item requirements is limited to existing service orders. The approach can optionally provide linkage to orders, such as project purchase orders and production orders. The approach also supports delivery promises and CTO service parts.

Additional Case Studies

Case 112: Planning Calculations for Service Parts An equipment company wanted to improve planning for their service parts inventory. They currently use a separate warehouse for service parts inventory, with items replenished based on min/max quantities. Most of the service parts demand stemmed from scheduled service orders with predefined material requirements (and technician requirements). They wanted to customize the planning calculations so that anticipated service order requirements were recognized as demands for material. This would provide visibility for stocking needed parts.

Case 113: Repair Department A consumer products company had an internal repair department that charged customers on a time-and-material basis for repairing electrical products. Most products were received via returned item sales orders, and a repair technician established a service order (and a related project) for diagnosing and repairing each returned product. Repairs were undertaken after getting customer approval for the estimated repair costs, where the diagnosis defined the anticipated repair requirements (for material and technician time) as service order line items. Actual consumption was reported against the service order. Customers were billed through project invoicing for the diagnosis and repair costs.

Case 114: Installation Services An equipment distributor sold industrial equipment and provided field services for subsequent installations. Each installation required a service order (and a related external project) that defined the service object and anticipated requirements for material, technician time and expenses. Most installation requirements could be predefined via a template service agreement, and these were copied into the service order. The technician obtained the materials before going to the customer, and then reported actual consumption after making the field service call. Many calls identified a need for shipping additional materials to the customer, as defined in the item requirements for the service order.

Executive Summary

Many manufacturers and distributors provide field services and/or internal service facilities. A service order acts as the basic tool for defining requirements and reporting actual consumption of material and resources. A service agreement defines resource requirements with periodic service intervals (such as weekly or monthly), which can be used to automatically create service orders to perform the periodic activities. Scenarios illustrated the use of service orders for equipment installation by field service personnel, for equipment repair by an internal department, and for using service agreements to manage periodic equipment maintenance. Case studies included other illustrations, such as planning calculations for service parts.

Chapter 22

Summary

This book focused on how Microsoft Dynamics AX 2012 provides an integrated ERP system to support supply chain management in discrete manufacturing firms. These firms share many similarities in ERP system requirements, and Dynamics AX provides the foundation for addressing these requirements. The nature of discrete manufacturing applies to a broad spectrum of industries, ranging from industrial equipment and automotive components to aerospace and electronics.

The targeted reader included those individuals implementing or considering Dynamics AX as their ERP system, as well as those providing consulting assistance. The book contents provided a complete walk through of functionality related to operations and supply chain management, and numerous case studies highlighted system usage related to discrete manufacturing. This chapter summarizes the book contents for those new to AX, as well as those already familiar with previous AX versions.

22.1 Summarizing the Book Contents

The book contents provided a complete walk through of AX software functionality related to supply chain management in discrete manufacturing and distribution. Not all topics will apply to a given company or reader, so that you can selectively focus on topics. This section summarizes the selective reading of book contents.

Discrete Manufacturing and Distribution Firms The book contents were segmented to support targeted readers in discrete manufacturing and distribution firms, so that you can focus on just the relevant chapters or sections within a chapter. The suggested chapters (and chapter numbers) are summarized below.

- *Distribution firms.* The reader can focus on the definition of items (Chapter 3), product costing for purchased items (Chapter 8), batch and serial tracking considerations (Chapter 9), coverage planning data for purchases and transfers (Chapter 10), sales and operations planning for distribution scenarios (Chapter 11), sales order processing (Chapter 12), purchase order processing (Chapter 13), transfers in a multisite operation (Chapter 17), quality management for purchased items (Chapter 18), and inventory/warehouse management (Chapter 10). Some distribution scenarios also involve projects or service orders (Chapters 21 and 22).
- *Manufacturing firms.* In addition to the above-mentioned topics, the reader can focus on bill of material information (Chapter 4), resources and routings (Chapter 6), configuration technologies for defining custom products (Chapter 7), product costing for manufactured items (Chapter 8), coverage planning data for manufactured items (Chapter 10), sales and operations planning for manufacturing scenarios (Chapter 11), production orders for internal manufacturing and subcontracted production (Chapters 14 and 16), lean manufacturing (Chapter 15), and quallity management for manufactured items (Chapter 18). Some manufacturing scenarios also involve projects or service orders (Chapters 21 and 22).

  Many discrete manufacturers operate with a mixed mode environment, such as scenarios that also involve process manufacturing or lean manufacturing (described in Chapters 5 and 15). AX provides a single system for supporting these environments, and it also supports the various maturity stages of lean manufacturing.

Common Scenarios and Case Studies for Discrete Manufacturing
Common scenarios and case studies illustrated how the AX software functionality applies to many different industries that represent discrete manufacturers. These industries were summarized at the beginning of the book (Section 2.1). The 100+ case studies highlighted many instances of solving key business problems using standard AX functionality and add-on functionality. Links were provided for further information about these add-on modules, which represent a majority of the solution set for handling variations of discrete manufacturing requirements. Each chapter included case studies applicable to the topic, and a complete list of case studies is provided at the end of the book.

Prescriptive Business Processes Each chapter included typical business processes that summarized key tasks and the functional roles responsible for these tasks. These diagrams reflected best practices and dominant business models for using AX, and provided an organizing focus for more detailed explanations. The typical business processes can help the project team gain an overall understanding of system usage and each team member's roles. These roles reflected the standard roles within Dynamics AX, and they provide the foundation for role-centered pages and role-based security.

The typical business processes provided a foundation for explaining how to use Dynamics AX to manage the business, and for explaining variations in business practices. The book covered a subset of typical business processes; a comprehensive set of business processes is also available.[1] These prescriptive processes can help accelerate the implementation of Dynamics AX in an organization. The selective choice of business processes defines the scope for implementation, and they provide the starting point for defining "to be" business processes and a gap/fit analysis.

Accelerate the Learning Process for those New to Dynamics AX

The initial steps in a typical implementation process involve learning the embedded conceptual models within AX that represent a new business model. This book provided a linear progression for learning AX 2012 capabilities for supply chain management, where each chapter built on topics previously covered. A comprehensive explanation of given topic was only provided once—typically when it was first introduced—so that it could be easily referred to in other book sections.

Learning the AX software capabilities involves a combination of approaches, including hands-on experience, training materials with details about key-stroke navigation, and user documentation. These approaches can help you understand the embedded conceptual models. Until the project team has a basic understanding of the system capabilities, it is difficult to leverage AX for your business processes except for just asking that the system must do what the current system does today.

[1] A comprehensive set of prescriptive business processes for discrete manufacturing is available as part of the RapidValue tool from Columbus. See **www.ColumbusGlobal.com** for more information.

22.2 Suggestions for the Knowledgeable AX Reader

One purpose of the book is to assist readers with prior AX knowledge so they can focus on incremental learning of new topics applicable to discrete manufacturing. A knowledgeable AX person can build on what they already know about the functionality within the previous AX 2009 version. A helpful starting point involves a rough measure of the previous versus new functionality within AX 2012, which indicates the proportionate amount of change. One rough measure can be based on a page count analysis of this book, since each chapter provides a complete walkthrough of using AX 2012 for supply chain management in a discrete manufacturing/distribution firm. The heat map displayed in Figure 22.1 summarizes the book topics, and a bar chart portrayal of previous functionality (shown in light grey) and the incre-

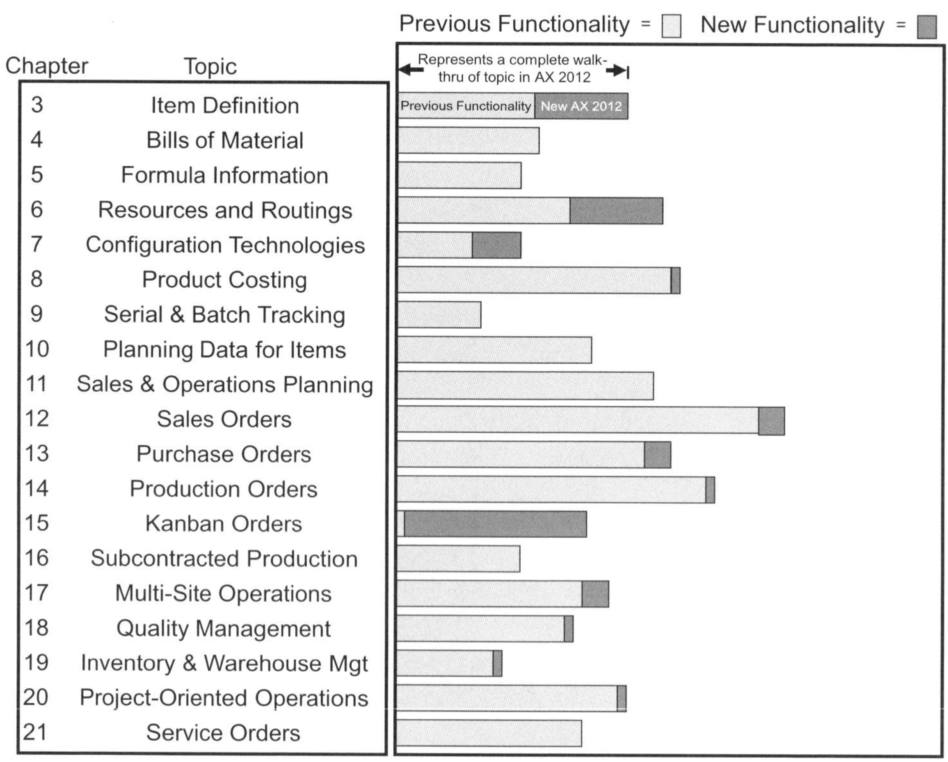

Figure 22.1 Heat Map for Incremental Learning of Dynamics AX

mentally new functionality within AX 2012 (shown in dark grey). The entire length of a bar represents a complete walkthrough of the topic using AX 2012, so you get a proportionate sense of magnitude.

As you can see by the yardsticks within Figure 22.1, the magnitude of previous versus new functionality varies by topic. For example, the largest degree of incremental change involves item definition, the definition of resources and routings, the options for configuration technologies, and kanban orders for lean manufacturing. In contrast, several topics have no change in functionality while other topics have small incremental changes.

Several caveats apply to this heat map. First, the topics reflect the context of supply chain management and do not include accounting/human resources and software development/system administration. Second, the topics reflect a discrete manufacturing environment. The heat map for another industry such as food or chemical manufacturing would be different, since it would involve a different focus and different topics. Third, it is difficult to quantify the significant amount of incremental learning associated with the new user interface. With these limitations in mind, the analysis can still provide rough yardsticks of incremental learning.

In summary, the rough yardsticks of incremental change suggest that the new capabilities within AX 2012 represent an approximate 15% change to the embedded conceptual models within the previous version of AX 2009. Stated differently, almost 85% of the embedded conceptual models have remained the same, so that you can build on what you already know.

The details about each topic's incremental changes are described below, along with the relevant book sections (in parentheses) providing extended explanations.

Item Definition The most significant changes involve the enterprise- versus company-level information for an item, and the different approaches to item identification. These and other changes impacting item definition are summarized below.

- Enterprise versus company information for an item (Sections 3.1 and 3.2)
- Different approaches to item identification (Section 3.3)
- Significance of the production type for a material item (Sections 3.7 and 5.2)
- Using templates to partially populate item information (Section 3.4)
- Approach to defining units of measure (Section 3.6)
- Assignment of a product category to an item, and the definition of a category hierarchy, for sales and purchasing purposes (Section 3.1)

Bills of Material Information A small change was introduced to support step-function requirements for a component quantity (Section 4.4).

Formula Information A small change was introduced for the definition of co-product information that affects its cost calculation via total cost allocation.

Resources and Routings The most significant changes involve new constructs for replacement of the functionality associated with work centers. These new constructs include the definition of resources and resource groups (Section 6.2), and the definition of resource capabilities (Section 6.3) and employee competencies (Section 6.4). These changes impact how you define the requirements within a routing operation (Section 6.8), and evaluate the feasibility of a route version (Section 6.9).

Configuration Technologies The most significant changes include the designation of a configured item and the associated options for a configuration technology (Section 7.1). AX 2012 includes a new option—termed a constraint-based configuration technology—which requires definition of product configuration models (Sections 7.4, 7.5 and 7.6) to support the configuration process. AX 2012 supports the two previously available options that are commonly termed the bill of options approach and the product builder approach.[2] However, the product builder approach will be discontinued in future releases because it has been replaced by the new constraint-based configuration technology.

Product Costing The changes include the definition of resource costs (Section 8.5), and the additional capabilities within the costing sheet and cost calculations to support new approaches to overhead calculations for manufactured items and the definition of purchased material overhead costs (Section 8.6).

Sales & Operations Planning An item's requirements can now be viewed in user-definable patterns of time periods (termed period templates), such as different combinations of daily, weekly, and monthly periods. As a

[2]The product builder approach – now termed a rules-based configuration technology – has also been referred to as using a modeling-enabled item and product models. The bill of options approach—now termed a dimension-based configuration technology— was previously termed the configurable item approach. This book uses the term "configurable item" as a generic term applicable to the three major variations of a configuration technology.

slight change, the terms for sales forecast and purchase forecast have been replaced by demand forecast and supply forecast.

Sales Order Processing The basic model of sales order processing has changed slightly with an optional delivery schedule for a line item (Section 12.2). Another change involves the introduction of sales agreements to replace the previous capability for blanket orders (Section 12.5). Other small changes include the approach to maintaining sales trade agreements (Section 12.4).

Purchase Order Processing The basic model of purchase order processing has changed slightly with an optional delivery schedule for a line item and an additional required step in its life cycle. The additional step involves confirming the purchase order when information has been completely entered, which changes its approval status from *approved* to *confirmed* (Section 13.2). Two prior steps may be involved when using an approval process for a manually entered purchase order, where the approval status starts with *draft* and *in review* until successful completion results in an *approved* status (Section 13.9). The changes also include the introduction of purchase agreements to replace the previous capability for blanket orders (Section 13.6), and the definition and enforcement of approved vendors (Section 13.3).

Production Order Processing The changes include the Manufacturing Execution System (as a replacement for the previous Shop Floor Control capabilities) to support production reporting and also time and attendance (Section 14.7).

Kanban Orders The conceptual models for supporting kanban orders significantly changed in AX 2012, and completely replaced the previous approaches within AX 2009. For example, the conceptual models involve a production flow and its activities, and variations of kanban rules, as the basis for coordinating production via kanban orders and graphical kanban boards. A separate chapter (Chapter 15) summarizes the lean manufacturing approaches. In particular, these approaches have multiple impacts on the conceptual models for traditional manufacturing, such as replacing the use of resources/routing information and the related changes to product costing for manufactured items (Section 15.6).

Multisite Operations The major changes include the simplification of setup information for handling intercompany orders (Section 17.5), and the communication of planned intercompany demand when master scheduling across a multicompany supply chain (Section 17.6).

Quality Management The changes include inventory blocking for quality purposes (Section 18.3), the use of cases to support quality management purposes (Section 18.6), and the approach to defining rules for automatic generation of quality orders, including quality orders for co-products (Section 18.4).

Project-Oriented Operations The changes include a new approach for reporting time via timesheets. The Enterprise Portal supports timesheet entries, and can also be used to create and maintain projects and project quotations. A new capability for production orders related to projects (termed the posting method) enables production order transactions for material and labor to immediately update the project costs (Section 20.8).

Summary The rough yardsticks of incremental learning suggest that the new capabilities within AX 2012 represent a cumulative 15% change to the embedded conceptual models within the previous version of AX 2009. Stated differently, almost 85% of the embedded conceptual models have remained the same, so that you can build on what you already know. The different user interface in AX 2012 often represents another aspect of incremental learning.

22.3 Concluding Remarks

When reviewing or learning any ERP software package, it is important to understand its underlying conceptual models and how it supports variations in business processes. It is easy to get bogged down in the navigational details. This chapter summarized the book contents to highlight how Microsoft Dynamics AX 2012 can support the supply chain management requirements of discrete manufacturers and distributors. It also addressed the learning approaches for those new to AX as well as those already familiar with AX.

List of Figures

List of Cases

Chapter 6: Resources and Routings

Chapter 7: Configuration Technologies for Custom Products Manufacturing

Chapter 8: Product Costing

Chapter 9: Serial and Batch Tracking

Chapter 10: Coverage Planning Data for Item Replenishment

Chapter 11: Sales and Operations Planning

Chapter 12: Sales Order Processing

Chapter 13: Purchase Order Processing

Chapter 14: Production Order Processing

Chapter 15: Transitioning from Traditional to Lean Manufacturing

About the Author

Scott Hamilton has specialized in ERP/SCM information systems for manufacturing and distribution for three decades as a consultant, developer, user, and researcher. He has consulted worldwide with over a thousand firms, conducted several hundred executive seminars, helped design several influential ERP packages, and taught ERP/SCM as an MBA professor at universities in North America, Europe and the Pacific Rim. Scott earned a doctorate in information systems specializing in manufacturing, and has won the rarely given Microsoft MVP Award for Dynamics AX. His regular column, "The AX Solution Architect," is published in MSDynamicsWorld.com. He lives in Minnesota, a place where people still build ice castles.